Personally, I really like Ruri.

In the beginning, I never would've anticipated featuring her

as the centerpiece of the cover illustration. For the next volume

Ruri will probably be in the drawing on this page.

Naoshi Komi

NAOSHI KOMI was born in Kochi Prefecture, Japan, on March 28, 1986. His first serialized work in *Weekly Shonen Jump* was the series *Double Arts*. His current series, *Nisekoi*, is serialized in *Weekly Shonen Jump*.

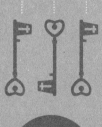

NISEKOI: False Love

VOLUME 7

SHONEN JUMP Manga Edition

Story and Art by
NAOSHI KOMI

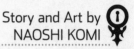

Translation — Camellia Nieh
Touch-Up Art & Lettering — Stephen Dutro
Design — Fawn Lau
Shonen Jump Series Editor — John Bae
Graphic Novel Editor — Amy Yu

Printed in the U.S.A.

Published by VIZ Media, LLC
P.O. Box 77010
San Francisco, CA 94107

10 9 8 7 6 5 4 3 2
First printing, January 2015
Second printing, February 2016

RATED T FOR TEEN

PARENTAL ADVISORY
NISEKOI: FALSE LOVE is rated T for Teen and is recommended for ages 13 and up. This volume contains realistic and fantasy violence.

ratings.viz.com

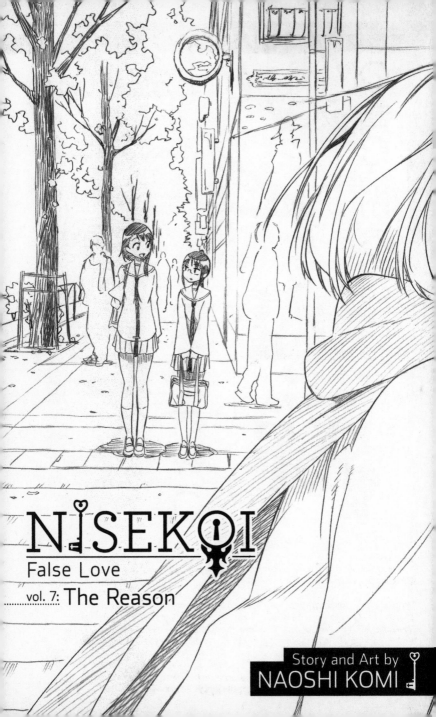

NISEKOI
False Love
vol. 7: The Reason

Story and Art by
NAOSHI KOMI

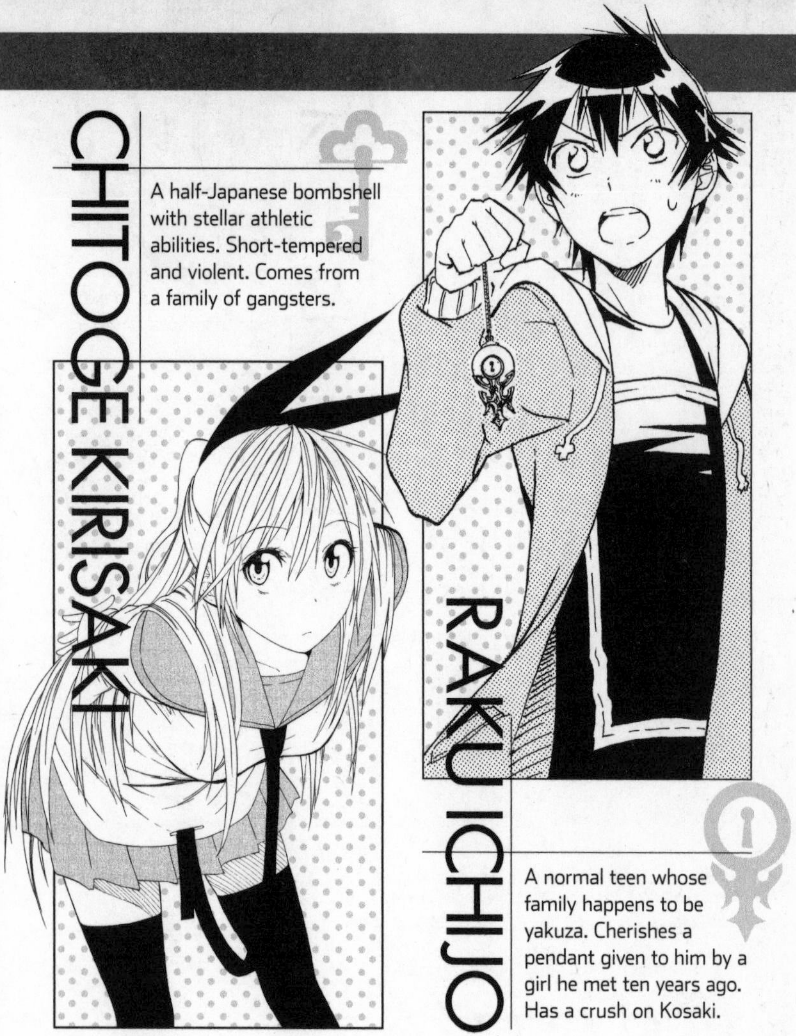

CHITOGE KIRISAKI

A half-Japanese bombshell with stellar athletic abilities. Short-tempered and violent. Comes from a family of gangsters.

RAKU ICHIJO

A normal teen whose family happens to be yakuza. Cherishes a pendant given to him by a girl he met ten years ago. Has a crush on Kosaki.

Raku Ichijo is an ordinary teen...who just happens to come from a family of yakuza! His most treasured item is a pendant he was given ten years ago by a girl whom he promised to meet again one day and marry.

Thanks to family circumstances, Raku is forced into a false relationship with Chitoge, the daughter of a rival gangster, to keep their families from shedding blood. Despite their constant spats, Raku and Chitoge somehow manage to fool everyone. One day, Chitoge discovers an old key, jogging memories of her own first love ten years earlier. Meanwhile, Raku's crush, Kosaki, confesses that she also has a key and made a promise with a boy ten years ago. To complicate matters, Marika Tachibana, a girl who claims to be Raku's fiancée, has a key as well and remembers a promise ten years ago. Plus, Chitoge's acting weird ever since their trip to the beach. Could it be that she has feelings for Raku?!

THE STORY THUS FAR

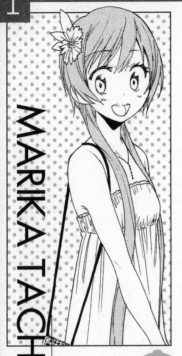

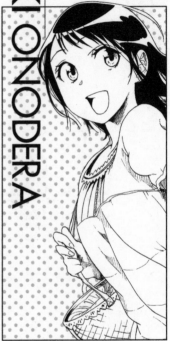

KOSAKI ONODERA

A girl Raku has a crush on. Beautiful and sweet, Kosaki has no shortage of admirers. She's a terrible cook but makes food that *looks* amazing.

MARIKA TACHIBANA

Daughter of the chief of police, Marika is Raku's fiancée, according to an agreement made by their fathers—an agreement Marika takes very seriously! Also has a key and remembers making a promise with Raku ten years ago.

SEISHIRO TSUGUMI

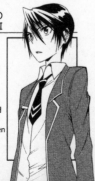

Adopted by Claude as a young child and raised as a top-notch assassin, Seishiro is 100% devoted to Chitoge. Often mistaken for a boy, Tsugumi's really a girl.

SHU MAIKO

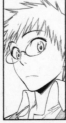

Raku's best friend. Outgoing and girl-crazy. Always tuned in to the latest gossip at school.

RURI MIYAMOTO

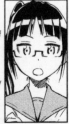

Kosaki's best gal pal. Comes off as aloof, but is actually a devoted and highly intuitive friend.

Hrm...

NISEKOI
False Love
vol. 7: The Reason

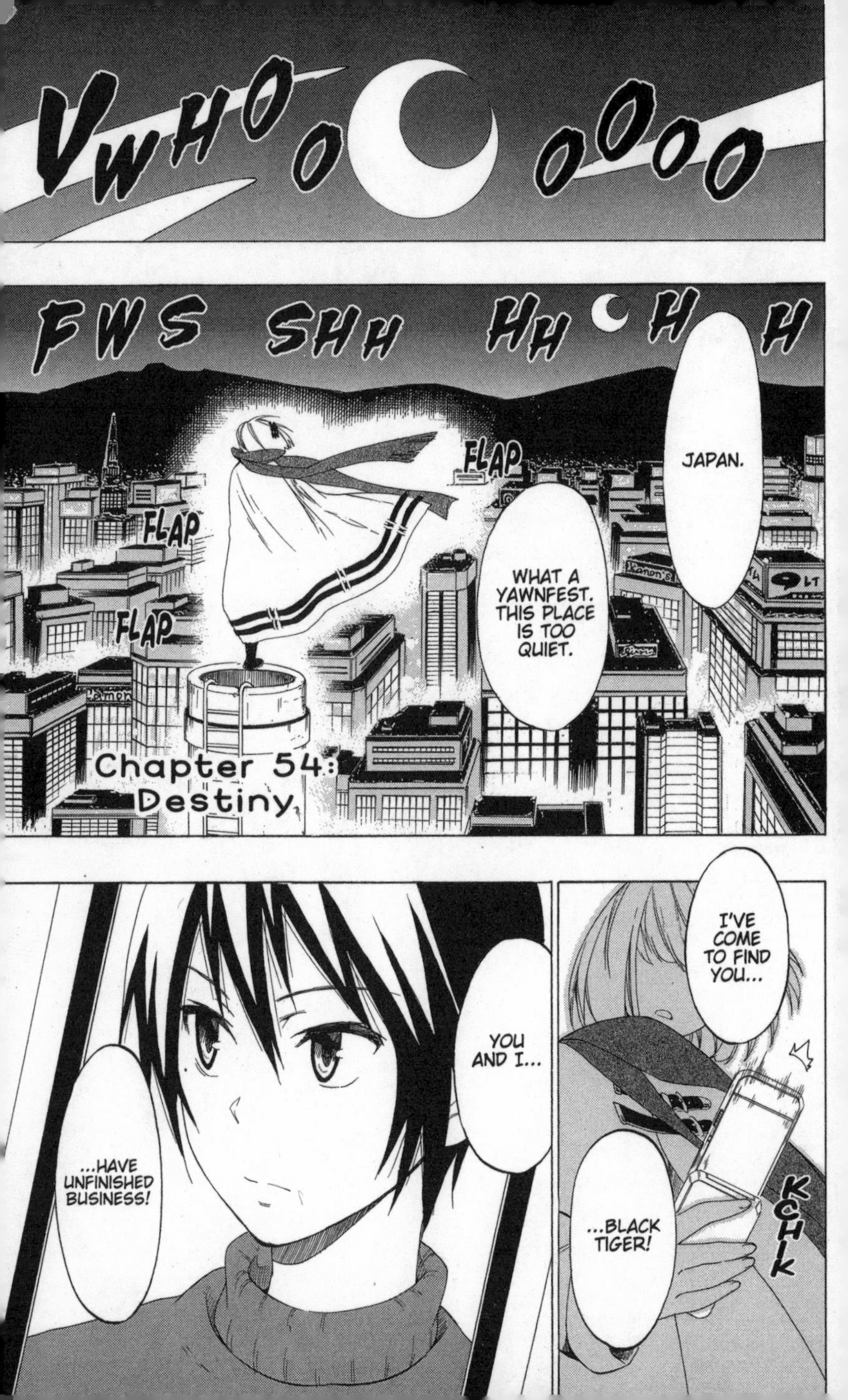
VWHOOOOOOOO
FWS SHH HH H H
JAPAN.
WHAT A YAWNFEST. THIS PLACE IS TOO QUIET.
FLAP
FLAP
FLAP
Chapter 54: Destiny
I'VE COME TO FIND YOU...
...BLACK TIGER!
KCHK
YOU AND I...
...HAVE UNFINISHED BUSINESS!

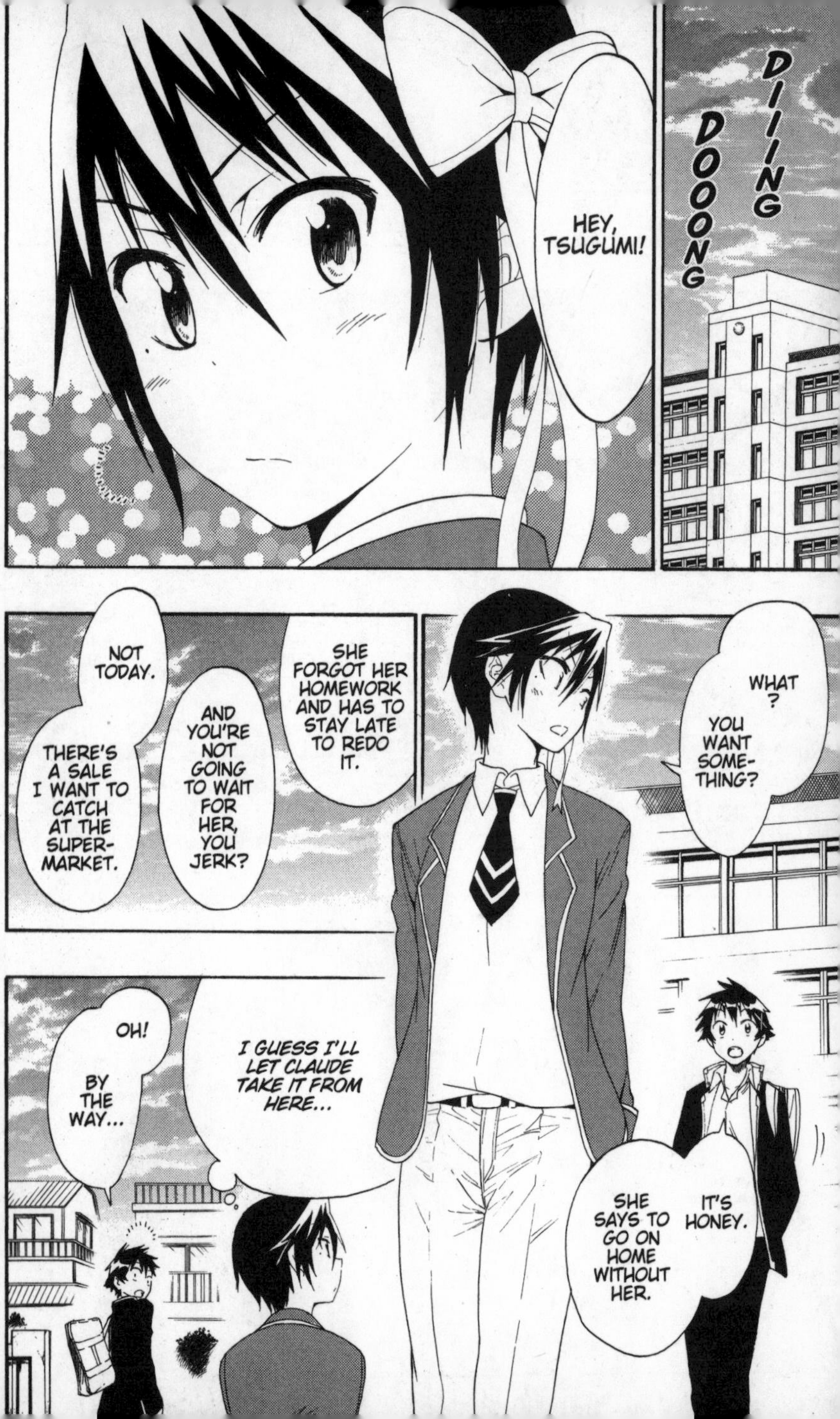

DIIING
DOOONG
HEY, TSUGUMI!
WHAT? YOU WANT SOMETHING?
IT'S HONEY.
SHE SAYS TO GO ON HOME WITHOUT HER.
SHE FORGOT HER HOMEWORK AND HAS TO STAY LATE TO REDO IT.
AND YOU'RE NOT GOING TO WAIT FOR HER, YOU JERK?
NOT TODAY.
THERE'S A SALE I WANT TO CATCH AT THE SUPER-MARKET.
I GUESS I'LL LET CLAUDE TAKE IT FROM HERE...
OH!
BY THE WAY...

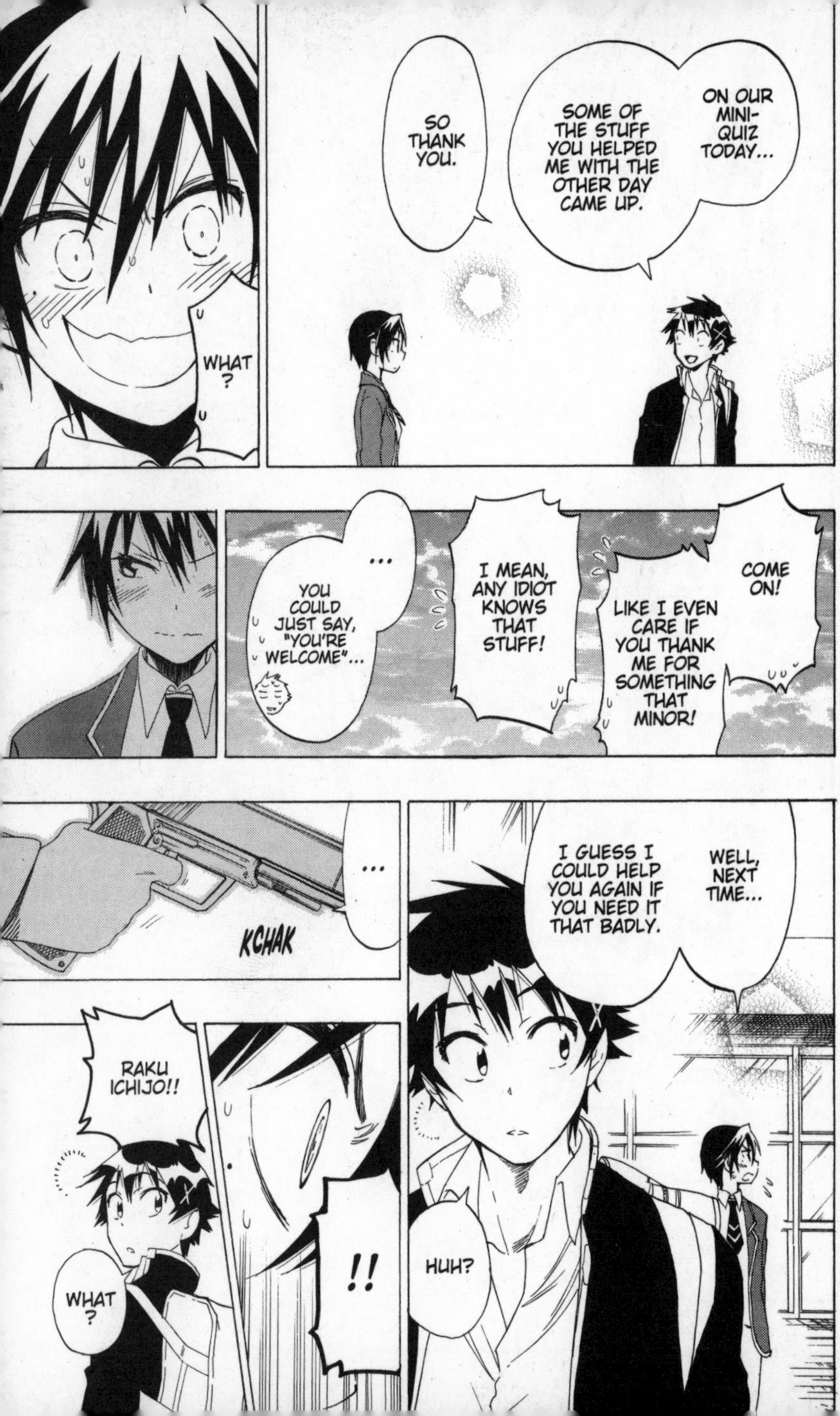

ON OUR MINI-QUIZ TODAY...
SOME OF THE STUFF YOU HELPED ME WITH THE OTHER DAY CAME UP.
SO THANK YOU.
WHAT?
COME ON!
LIKE I EVEN CARE IF YOU THANK ME FOR SOMETHING THAT MINOR!
I MEAN, ANY IDIOT KNOWS THAT STUFF!
...
YOU COULD JUST SAY, "YOU'RE WELCOME"...
WELL, NEXT TIME...
I GUESS I COULD HELP YOU AGAIN IF YOU NEED IT THAT BADLY.
HUH?
...
KCHAK
!!
RAKU ICHIJO!!
WHAT?

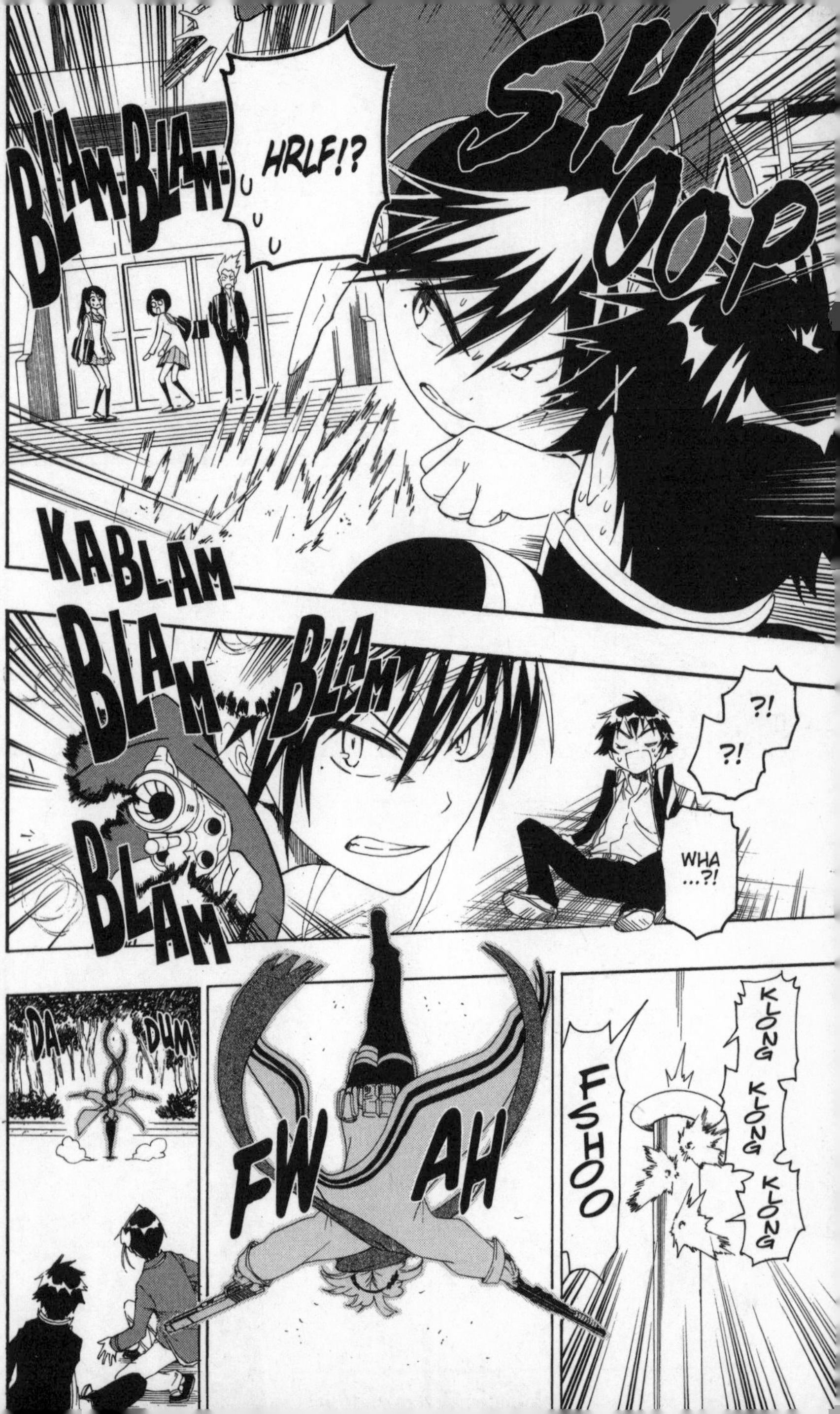
SHOOOP
HRLF!?
BLAM BLAM
KABLAM
?!
?!
WHA ...?!
BLAM
BLAM
BLAM
KLONG KLONG KLONG KLONG
FSHOO
FWAH
DA DUM

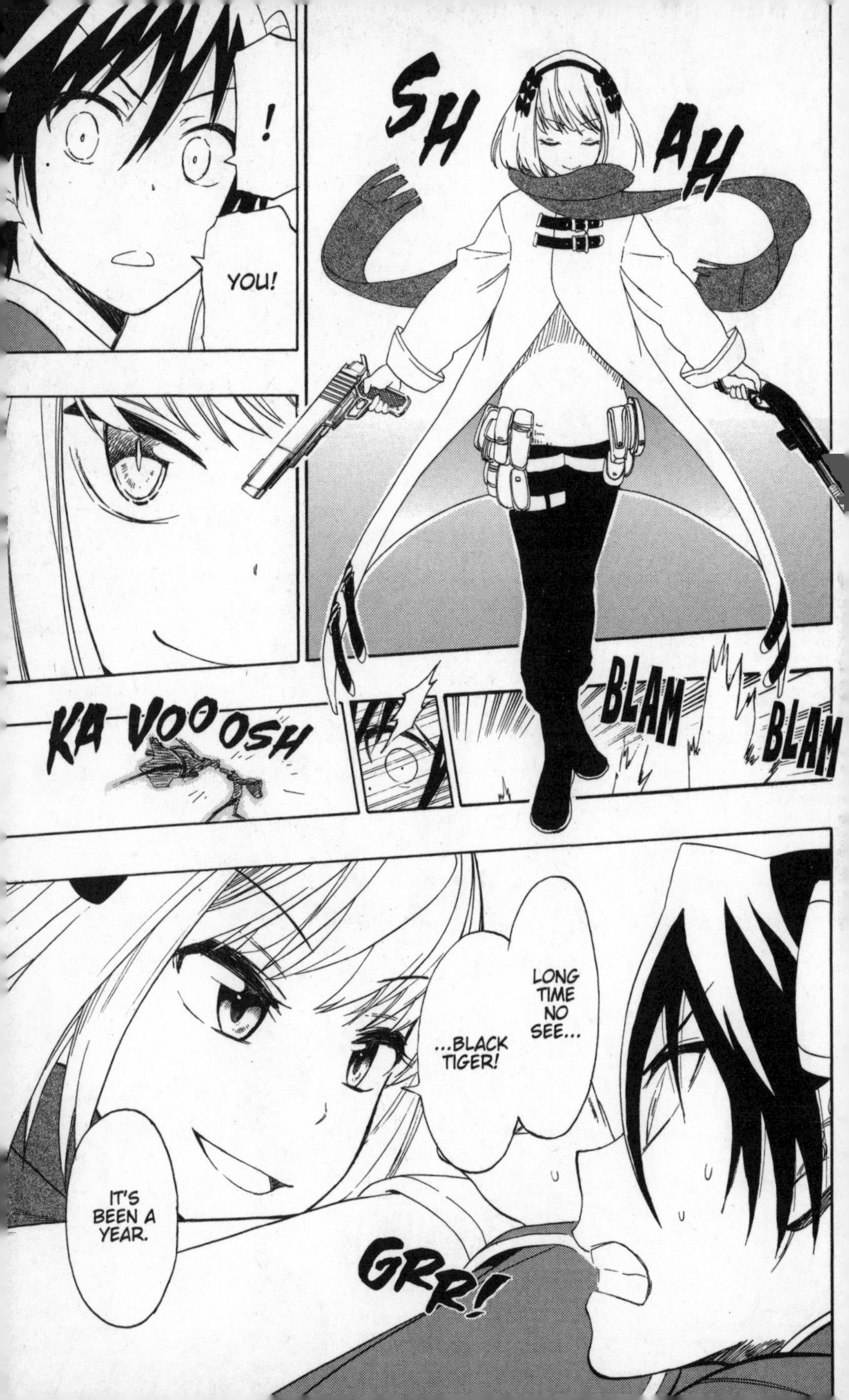
SH AH
!
YOU!
BLAM
BLAM
KA VOOOSH
LONG TIME NO SEE... ...BLACK TIGER!
IT'S BEEN A YEAR.
GRR!

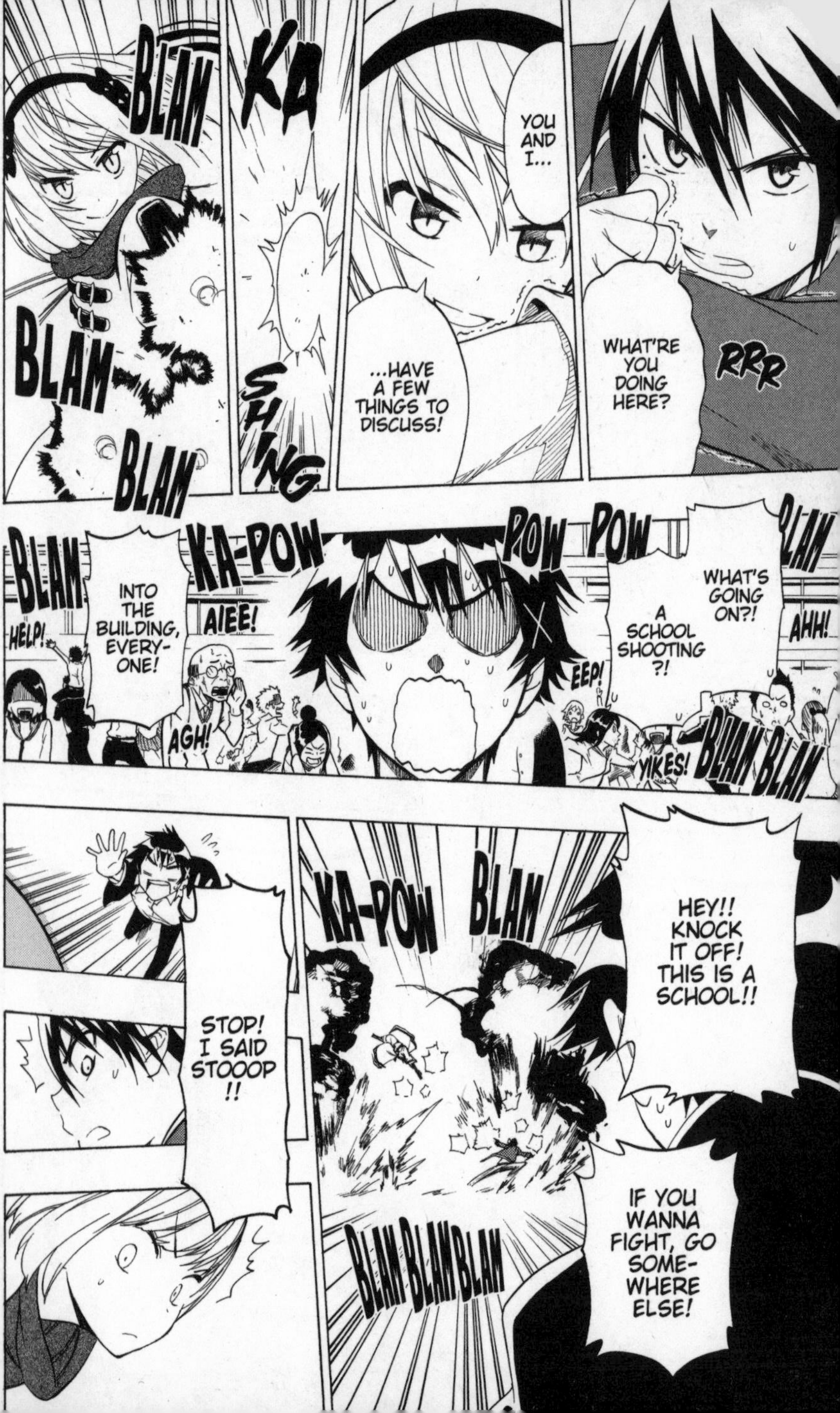
WHAT'RE YOU DOING HERE?
RRR
YOU AND I...
...HAVE A FEW THINGS TO DISCUSS!
KA
SHING
BLAM
BLAM-
BLAM
BLAM
WHAT'S GOING ON?!
AHH!
A SCHOOL SHOOTING?!
BLAM BLAM
YIKES!
EEP!
POW POW
KA-POW
AIEE!
AGH!
INTO THE BUILDING, EVERY-ONE!
BLAM
HELP!
HEY!! KNOCK IT OFF! THIS IS A SCHOOL!!
BLAM
KA-POW
IF YOU WANNA FIGHT, GO SOME-WHERE ELSE!
BLAM BLAM BLAM
STOP! I SAID STOOOP!!

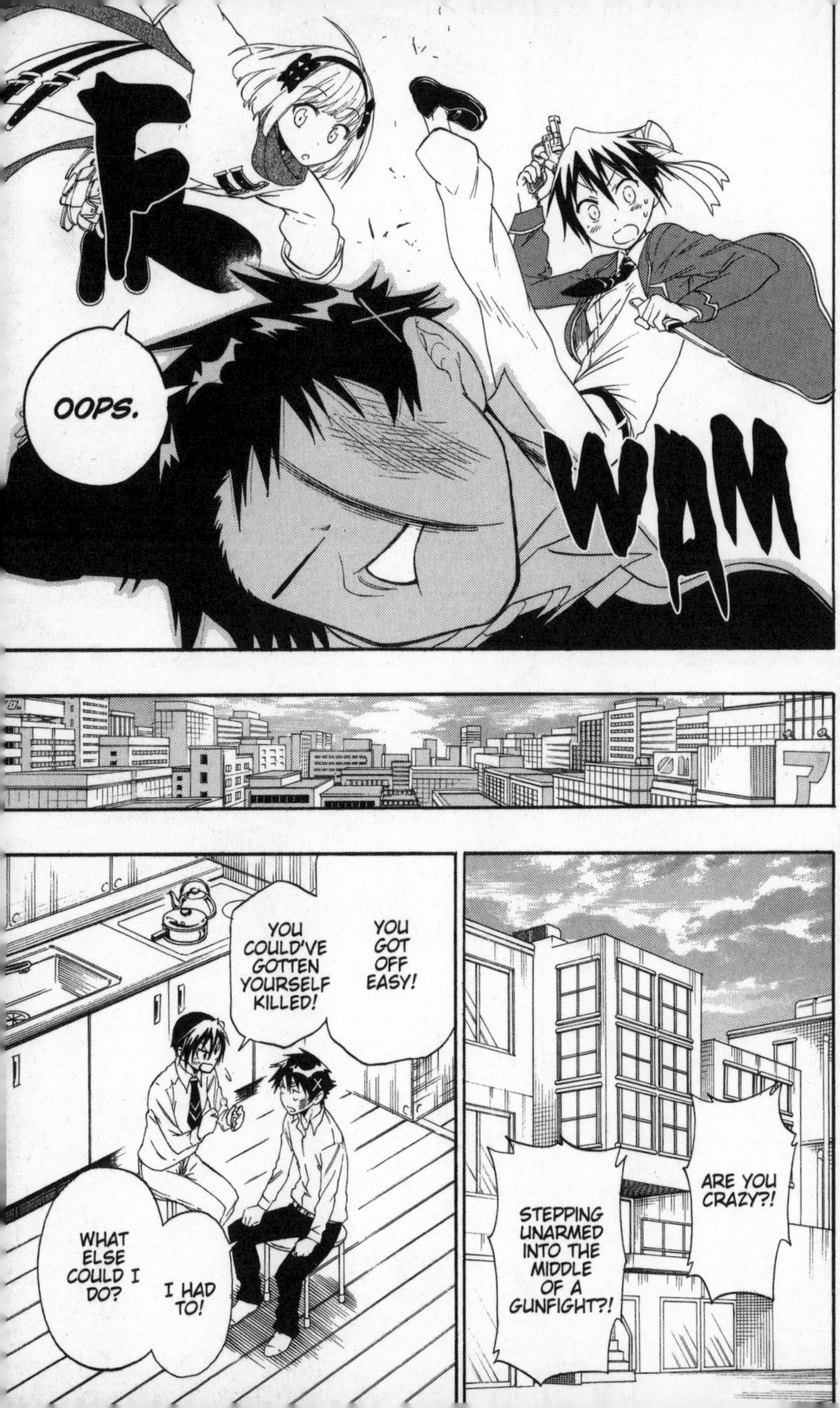
WAM
OOPS.
ARE YOU CRAZY?!
STEPPING UNARMED INTO THE MIDDLE OF A GUNFIGHT?!
YOU GOT OFF EASY!
YOU COULD'VE GOTTEN YOURSELF KILLED!
I HAD TO!
WHAT ELSE COULD I DO?

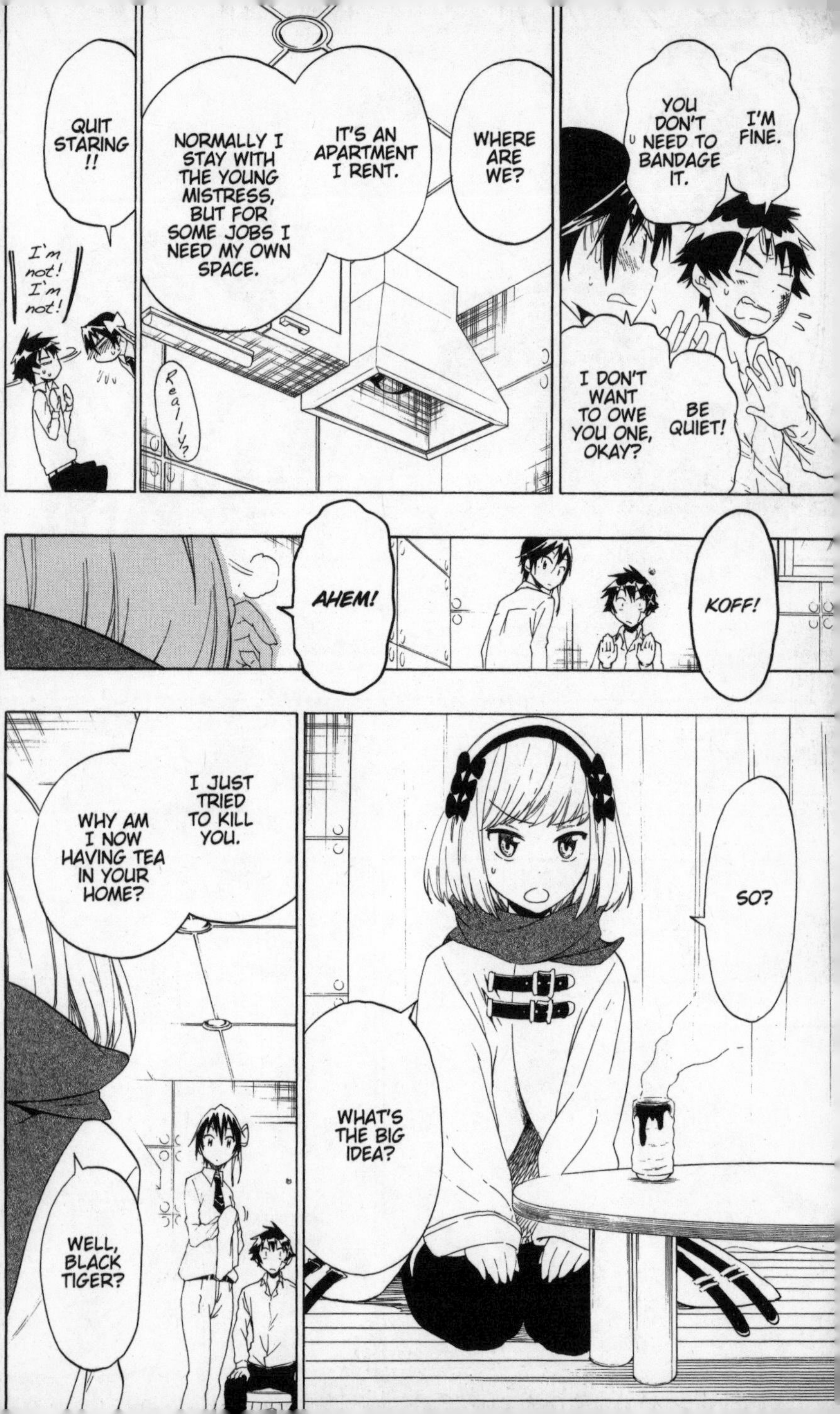
I'M FINE.
YOU DON'T NEED TO BANDAGE IT.
BE QUIET!
I DON'T WANT TO OWE YOU ONE, OKAY?
WHERE ARE WE?
IT'S AN APARTMENT I RENT.
NORMALLY I STAY WITH THE YOUNG MISTRESS, BUT FOR SOME JOBS I NEED MY OWN SPACE.
Really?
QUIT STARING!!
I'm not! I'm not!
KOFF!
AHEM!
SO?
WHAT'S THE BIG IDEA?
I JUST TRIED TO KILL YOU.
WHY AM I NOW HAVING TEA IN YOUR HOME?
WELL, BLACK TIGER?

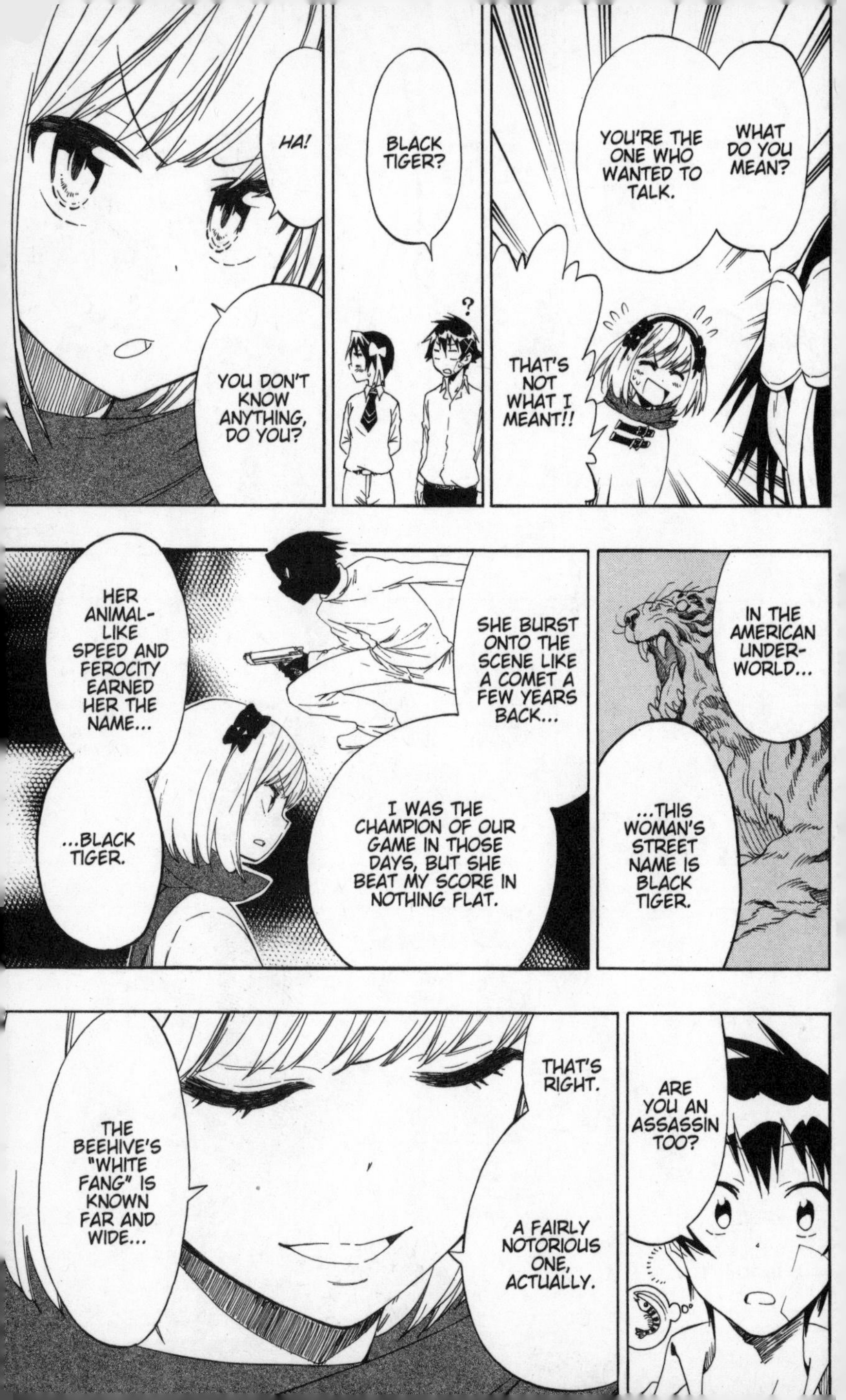
WHAT DO YOU MEAN?
YOU'RE THE ONE WHO WANTED TO TALK.
THAT'S NOT WHAT I MEANT!!
BLACK TIGER?
HA!
YOU DON'T KNOW ANYTHING, DO YOU?
IN THE AMERICAN UNDER-WORLD...
...THIS WOMAN'S STREET NAME IS BLACK TIGER.
SHE BURST ONTO THE SCENE LIKE A COMET A FEW YEARS BACK...
I WAS THE CHAMPION OF OUR GAME IN THOSE DAYS, BUT SHE BEAT MY SCORE IN NOTHING FLAT.
HER ANIMAL-LIKE SPEED AND FEROCITY EARNED HER THE NAME...
...BLACK TIGER.
ARE YOU AN ASSASSIN TOO?
THAT'S RIGHT.
A FAIRLY NOTORIOUS ONE, ACTUALLY.
THE BEEHIVE'S "WHITE FANG" IS KNOWN FAR AND WIDE...

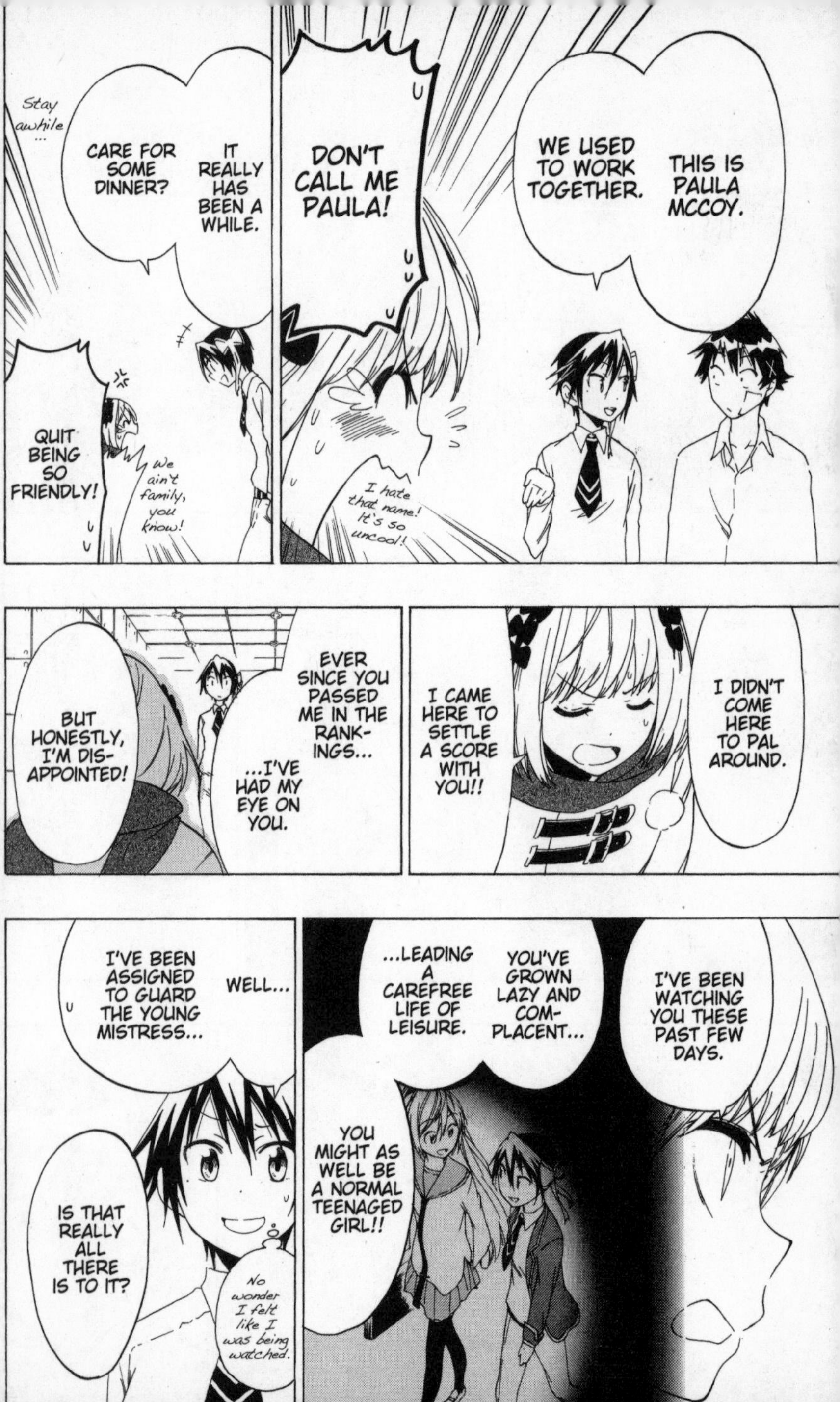
THIS IS PAULA MCCOY.
WE USED TO WORK TOGETHER.
DON'T CALL ME PAULA!
I hate that name! It's so uncool!
IT REALLY HAS BEEN A WHILE.
CARE FOR SOME DINNER?
Stay awhile...
QUIT BEING SO FRIENDLY!
We ain't family, you know!
I DIDN'T COME HERE TO PAL AROUND.
I CAME HERE TO SETTLE A SCORE WITH YOU!!
EVER SINCE YOU PASSED ME IN THE RANK-INGS...
...I'VE HAD MY EYE ON YOU.
BUT HONESTLY, I'M DIS-APPOINTED!
I'VE BEEN WATCHING YOU THESE PAST FEW DAYS.
YOU'VE GROWN LAZY AND COM-PLACENT...
...LEADING A CAREFREE LIFE OF LEISURE.
YOU MIGHT AS WELL BE A NORMAL TEENAGED GIRL!!
WELL...
I'VE BEEN ASSIGNED TO GUARD THE YOUNG MISTRESS...
IS THAT REALLY ALL THERE IS TO IT?
No wonder I felt like I was being watched.

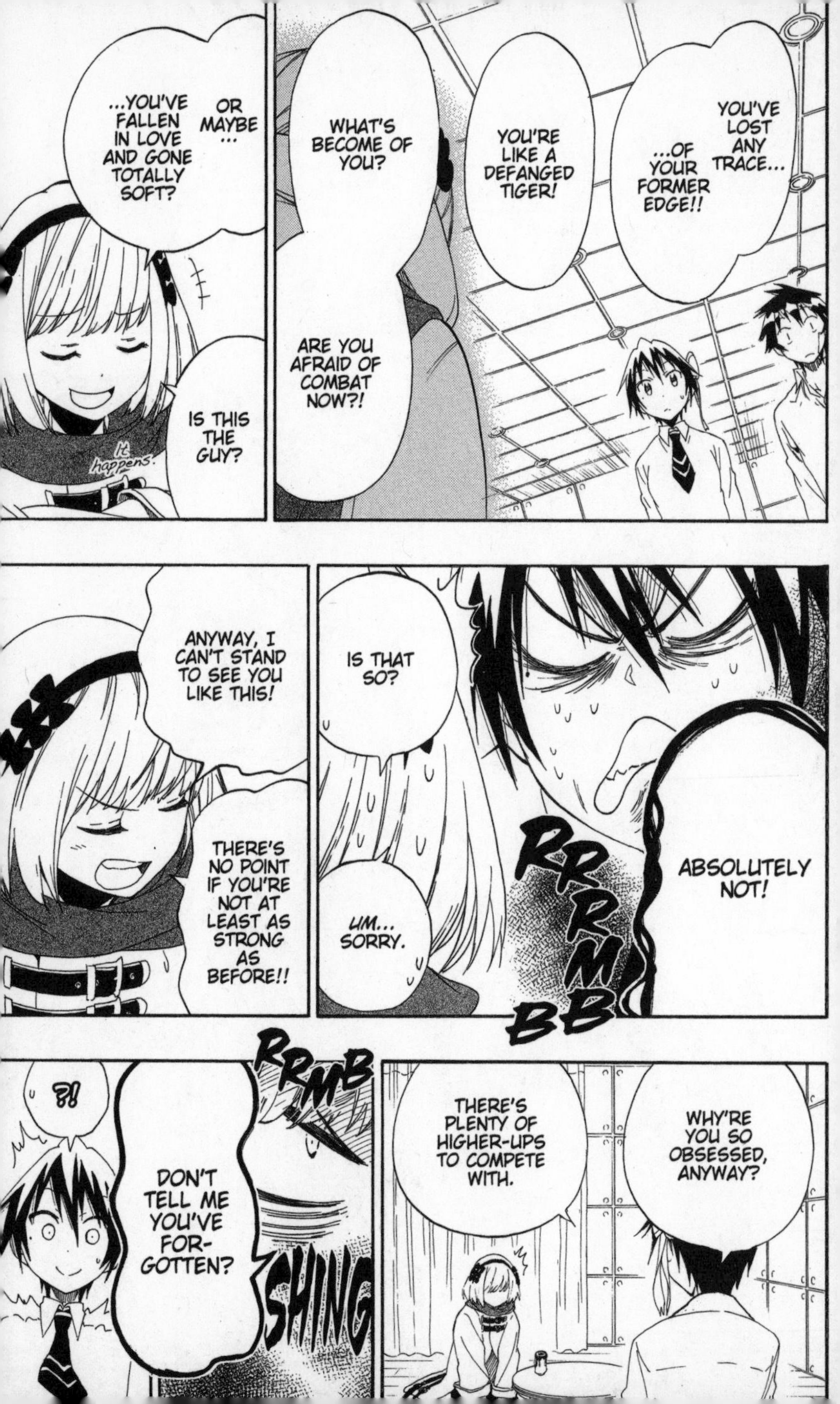
YOU'VE LOST ANY TRACE...
...OF YOUR FORMER EDGE!!
YOU'RE LIKE A DEFANGED TIGER!
WHAT'S BECOME OF YOU?
ARE YOU AFRAID OF COMBAT NOW?!
OR MAYBE...
...YOU'VE FALLEN IN LOVE AND GONE TOTALLY SOFT?
IS THIS THE GUY?
It happens.
ABSOLUTELY NOT!
RRRMBB
IS THAT SO?
UM... SORRY.
ANYWAY, I CAN'T STAND TO SEE YOU LIKE THIS!
THERE'S NO POINT IF YOU'RE NOT AT LEAST AS STRONG AS BEFORE!!
WHY'RE YOU SO OBSESSED, ANYWAY?
THERE'S PLENTY OF HIGHER-UPS TO COMPETE WITH.
RRMB
DON'T TELL ME YOU'VE FOR-GOTTEN?
SHING
?!

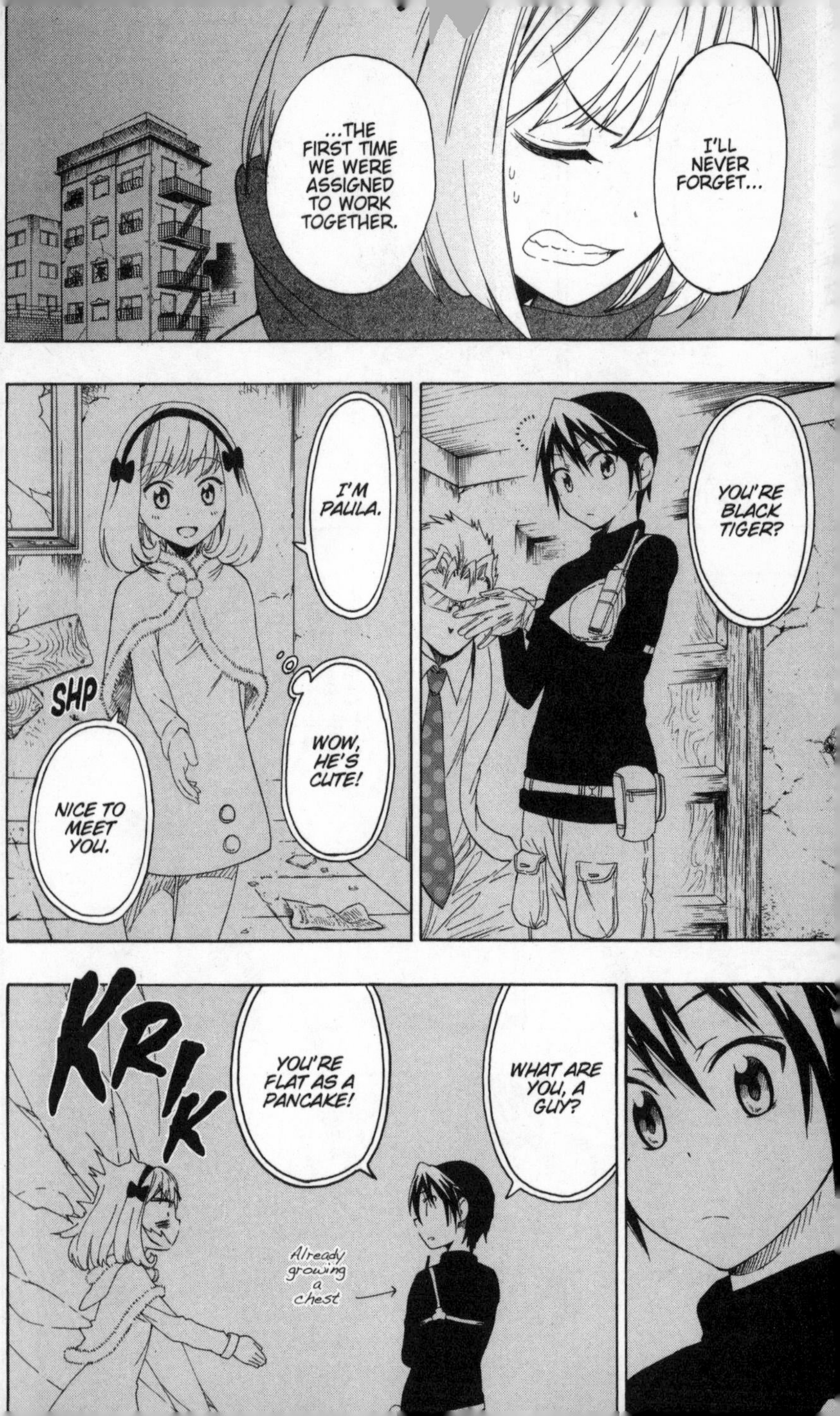
I'LL NEVER FORGET...
...THE FIRST TIME WE WERE ASSIGNED TO WORK TOGETHER.
YOU'RE BLACK TIGER?
I'M PAULA.
WOW, HE'S CUTE!
SHP
NICE TO MEET YOU.
WHAT ARE YOU, A GUY?
YOU'RE FLAT AS A PANCAKE!
KRIK
Already growing a chest

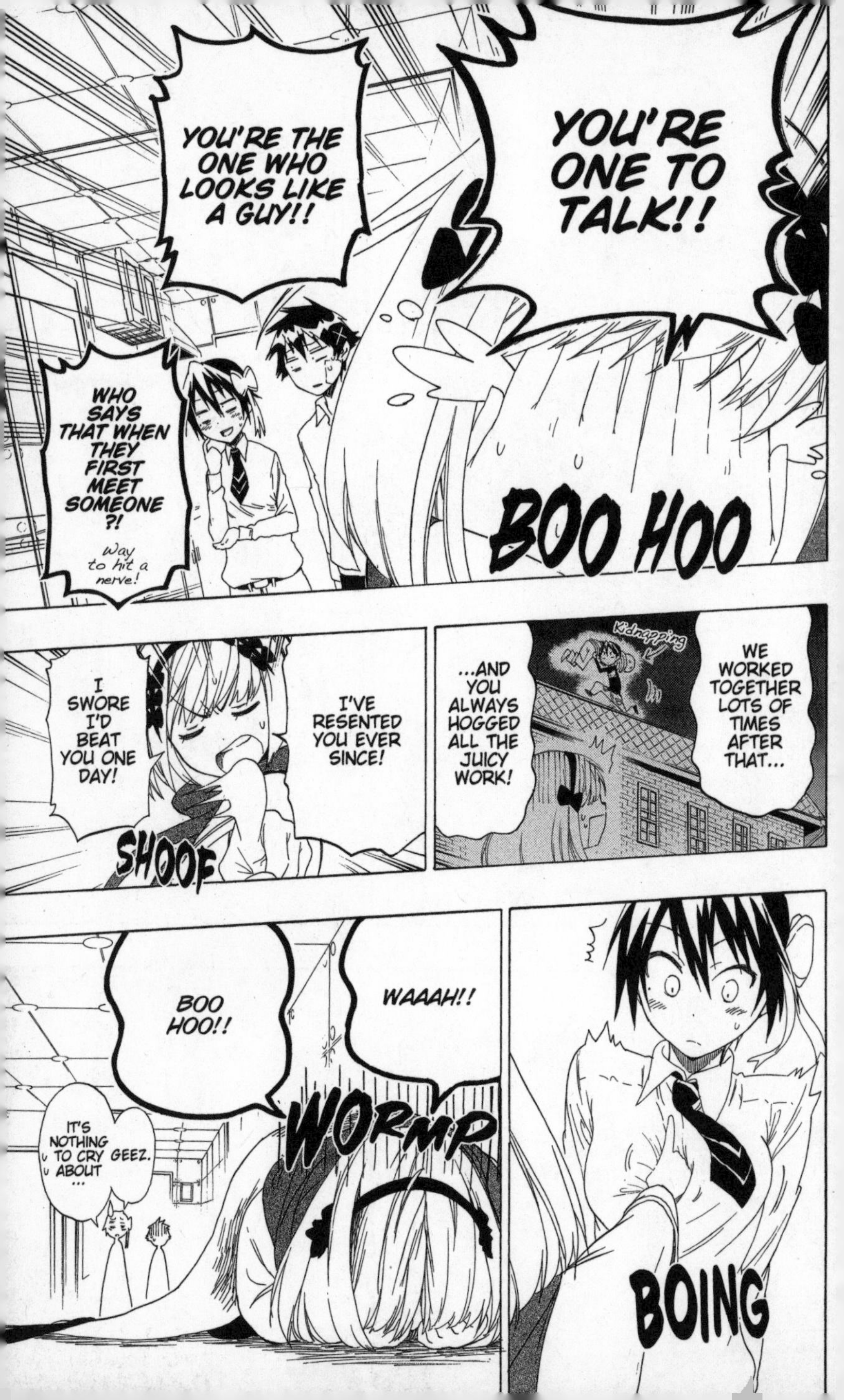
YOU'RE ONE TO TALK!!
YOU'RE THE ONE WHO LOOKS LIKE A GUY!!
BOO HOO
WHO SAYS THAT WHEN THEY FIRST MEET SOMEONE?!
Way to hit a nerve!
Kidnapping
WE WORKED TOGETHER LOTS OF TIMES AFTER THAT...
...AND YOU ALWAYS HOGGED ALL THE JUICY WORK!
I'VE RESENTED YOU EVER SINCE!
I SWORE I'D BEAT YOU ONE DAY!
SHOOF
BOING
WAAAH!!
BOO HOO!!
WORMP
GEEZ.
IT'S NOTHING TO CRY ABOUT...

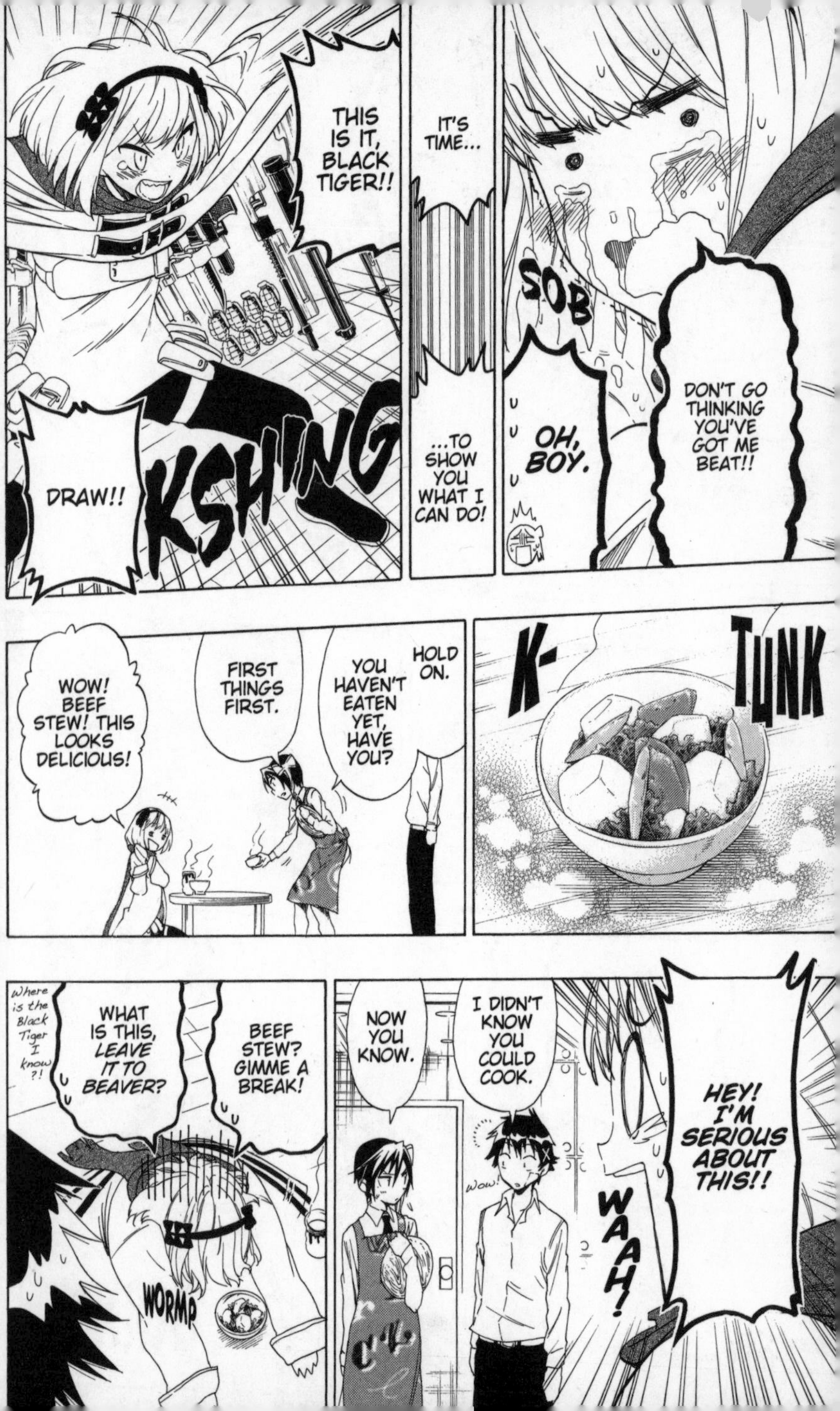
DON'T GO THINKING YOU'VE GOT ME BEAT!!
SOB
OH, BOY.
IT'S TIME...
...TO SHOW YOU WHAT I CAN DO!
THIS IS IT, BLACK TIGER!!
KSHING
DRAW!!
K-
TUNK
HOLD ON.
YOU HAVEN'T EATEN YET, HAVE YOU?
FIRST THINGS FIRST.
WOW! BEEF STEW! THIS LOOKS DELICIOUS!
HEY! I'M SERIOUS ABOUT THIS!!
WAAH!
I DIDN'T KNOW YOU COULD COOK.
NOW YOU KNOW.
Wow!
BEEF STEW? GIMME A BREAK!
WHAT IS THIS, LEAVE IT TO BEAVER?
Where is the Black Tiger I know?!
WORMP

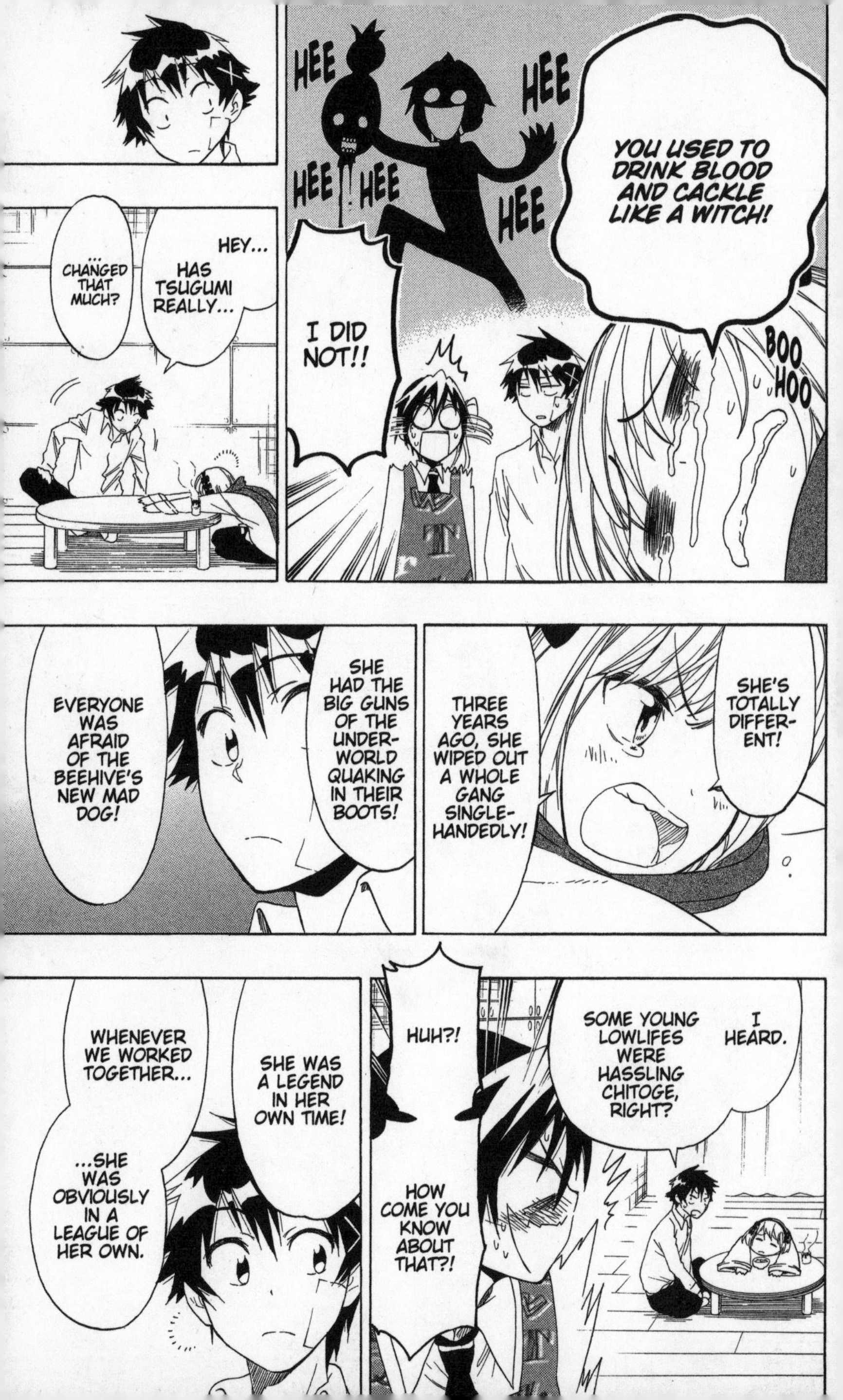
YOU USED TO DRINK BLOOD AND CACKLE LIKE A WITCH!
BOO HOO
HEE
HEE
HEE
HEE
HEE
I DID NOT!!
HEY... HAS TSUGUMI REALLY...
...CHANGED THAT MUCH?
SHE'S TOTALLY DIFFER-ENT!
THREE YEARS AGO, SHE WIPED OUT A WHOLE GANG SINGLE-HANDEDLY!
SHE HAD THE BIG GUNS OF THE UNDER-WORLD QUAKING IN THEIR BOOTS!
EVERYONE WAS AFRAID OF THE BEEHIVE'S NEW MAD DOG!
I HEARD.
SOME YOUNG LOWLIFES WERE HASSLING CHITOGE, RIGHT?
HUH?!
HOW COME YOU KNOW ABOUT THAT?!
SHE WAS A LEGEND IN HER OWN TIME!
WHENEVER WE WORKED TOGETHER...
...SHE WAS OBVIOUSLY IN A LEAGUE OF HER OWN.

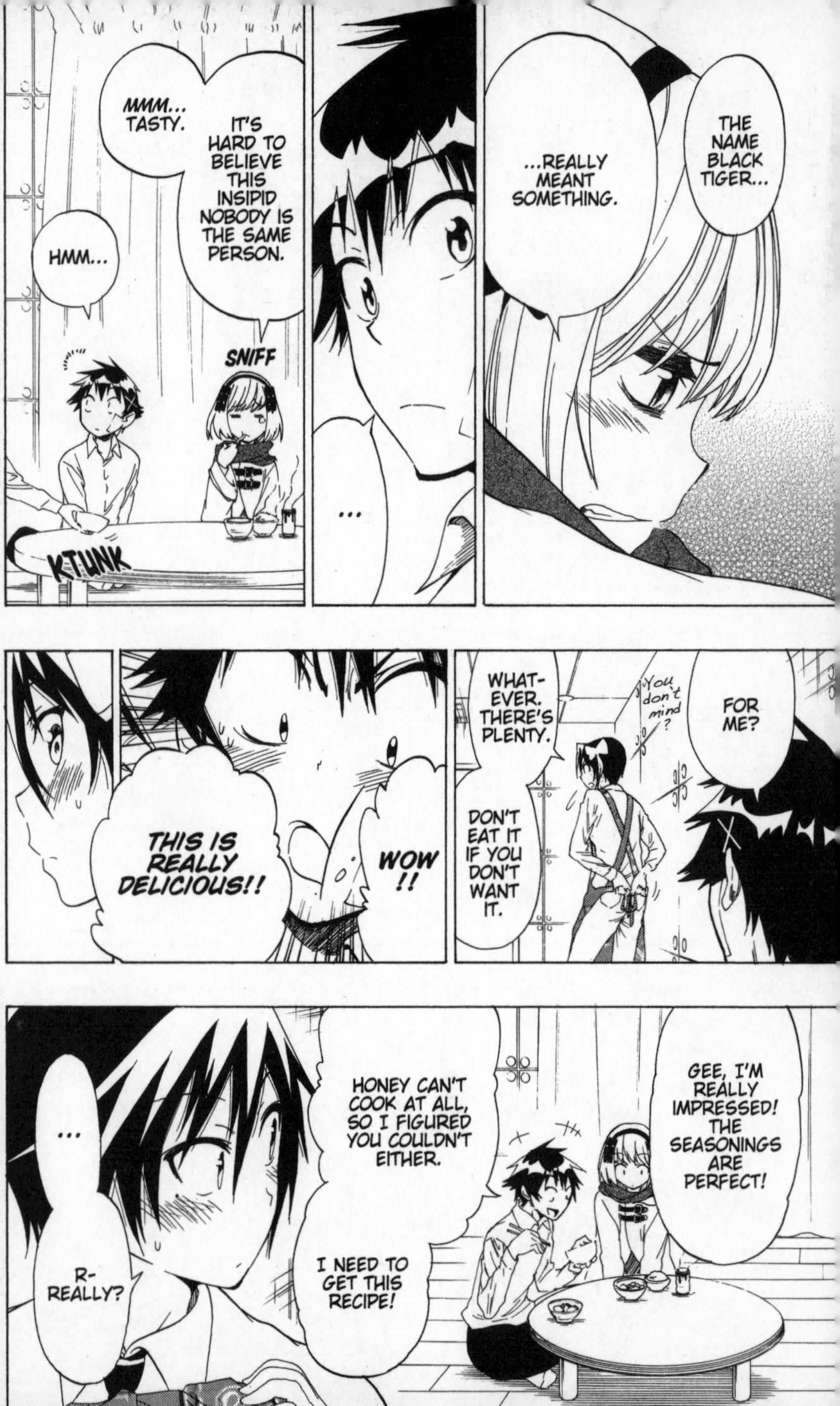
THE NAME BLACK TIGER...
...REALLY MEANT SOMETHING.
...
MMM... TASTY.
IT'S HARD TO BELIEVE THIS INSIPID NOBODY IS THE SAME PERSON.
SNIFF
HMM...
KTUNK
FOR ME?
You don't mind?
WHAT-EVER. THERE'S PLENTY.
DON'T EAT IT IF YOU DON'T WANT IT.
WOW!!
THIS IS REALLY DELICIOUS!!
GEE, I'M REALLY IMPRESSED! THE SEASONINGS ARE PERFECT!
HONEY CAN'T COOK AT ALL, SO I FIGURED YOU COULDN'T EITHER.
I NEED TO GET THIS RECIPE!
...
R-REALLY?

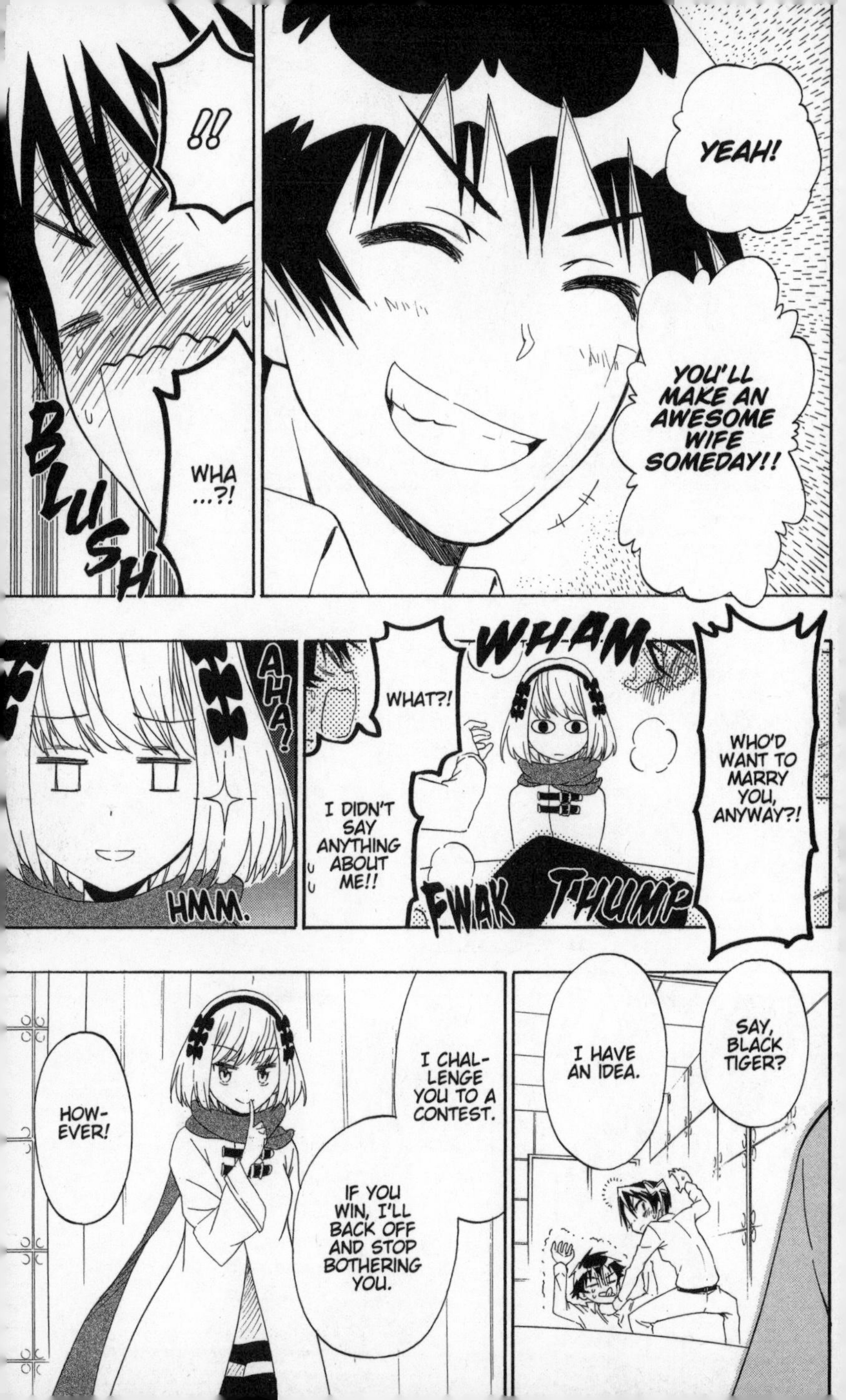
YEAH!
YOU'LL MAKE AN AWESOME WIFE SOMEDAY!!
!!
WHA ...?!
BLUSH
WHO'D WANT TO MARRY YOU, ANYWAY?!
WHAM
WHAT?!
FWAK THUMP
I DIDN'T SAY ANYTHING ABOUT ME!!
AHA!
HMM.
SAY, BLACK TIGER?
I HAVE AN IDEA.
I CHAL-LENGE YOU TO A CONTEST.
IF YOU WIN, I'LL BACK OFF AND STOP BOTHERING YOU.
HOW-EVER!

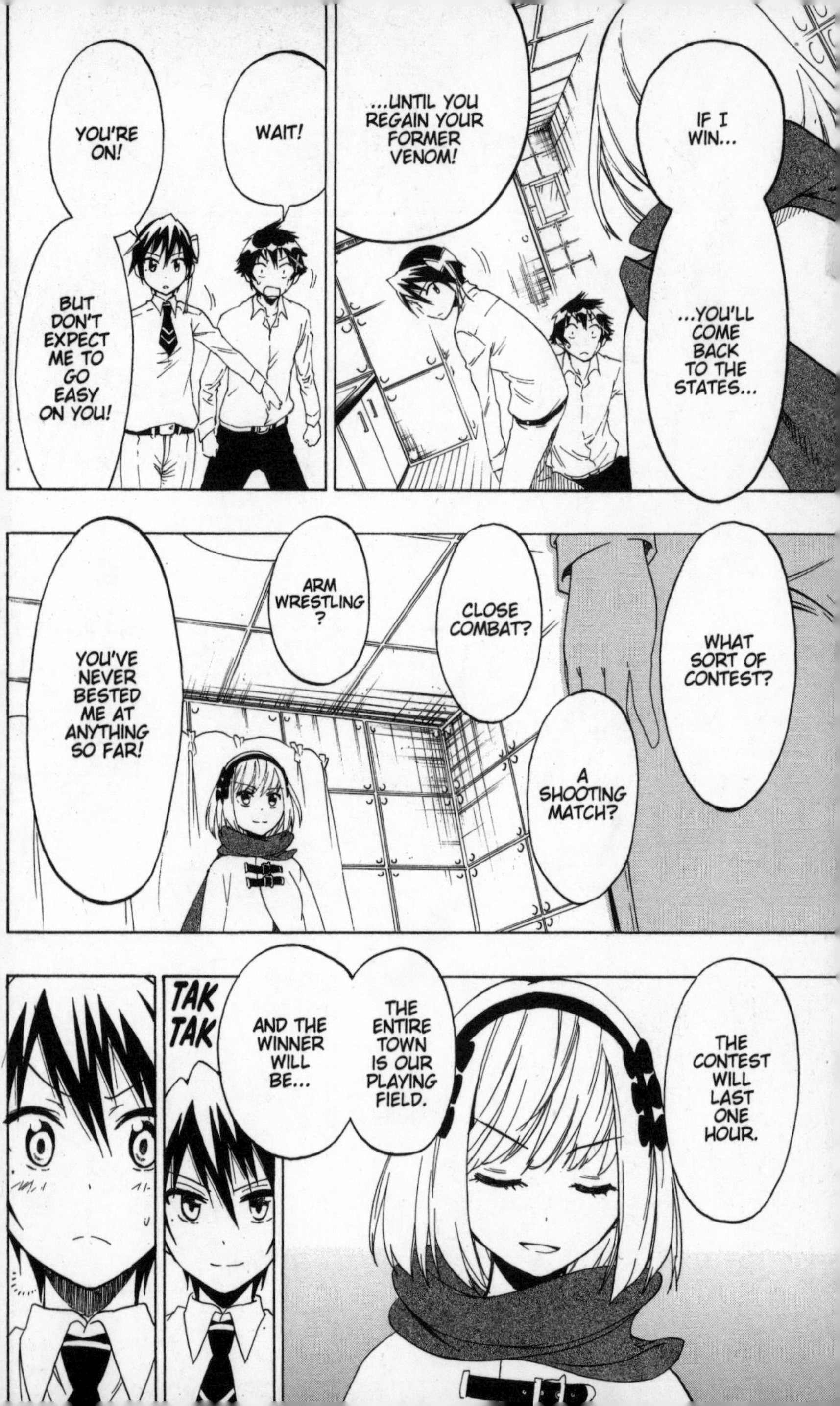
IF I WIN...
...YOU'LL COME BACK TO THE STATES...
...UNTIL YOU REGAIN YOUR FORMER VENOM!
WAIT!
YOU'RE ON!
BUT DON'T EXPECT ME TO GO EASY ON YOU!
WHAT SORT OF CONTEST?
A SHOOTING MATCH?
CLOSE COMBAT?
ARM WRESTLING?
YOU'VE NEVER BESTED ME AT ANYTHING SO FAR!
THE CONTEST WILL LAST ONE HOUR.
THE ENTIRE TOWN IS OUR PLAYING FIELD.
AND THE WINNER WILL BE...
TAK TAK

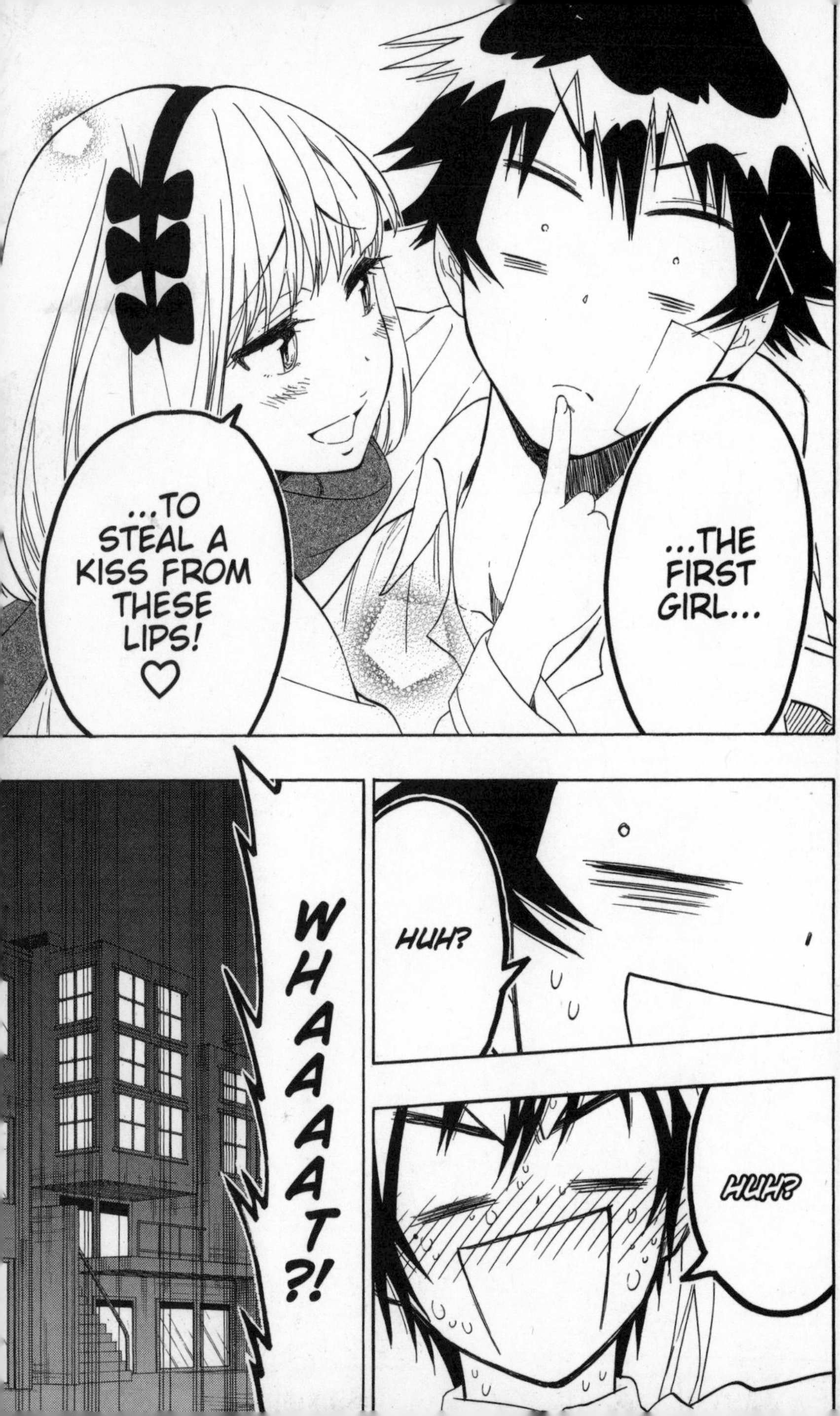
...THE FIRST GIRL...
...TO STEAL A KISS FROM THESE LIPS! ♡
HUH?
HUH?
WHAAAAAT?!

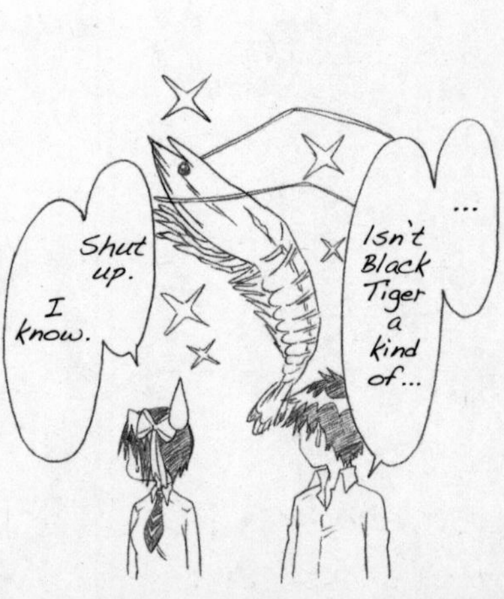
... Isn't Black Tiger a kind of...
Shut up. I know.

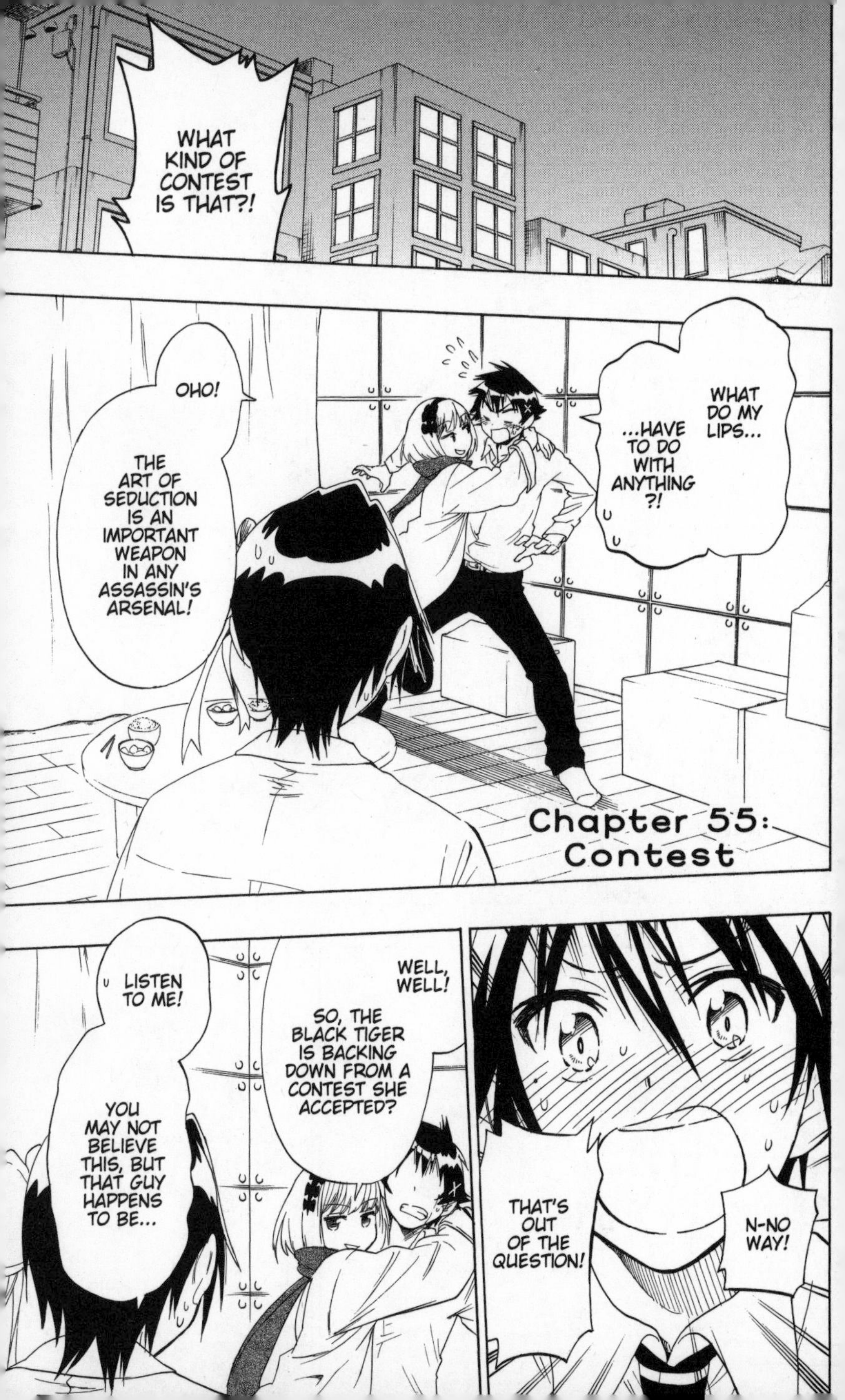
WHAT KIND OF CONTEST IS THAT?!
WHAT DO MY LIPS...
...HAVE TO DO WITH ANYTHING?!
OHO!
THE ART OF SEDUCTION IS AN IMPORTANT WEAPON IN ANY ASSASSIN'S ARSENAL!
Chapter 55: Contest
N-NO WAY!
THAT'S OUT OF THE QUESTION!
WELL, WELL!
SO, THE BLACK TIGER IS BACKING DOWN FROM A CONTEST SHE ACCEPTED?
LISTEN TO ME!
YOU MAY NOT BELIEVE THIS, BUT THAT GUY HAPPENS TO BE...

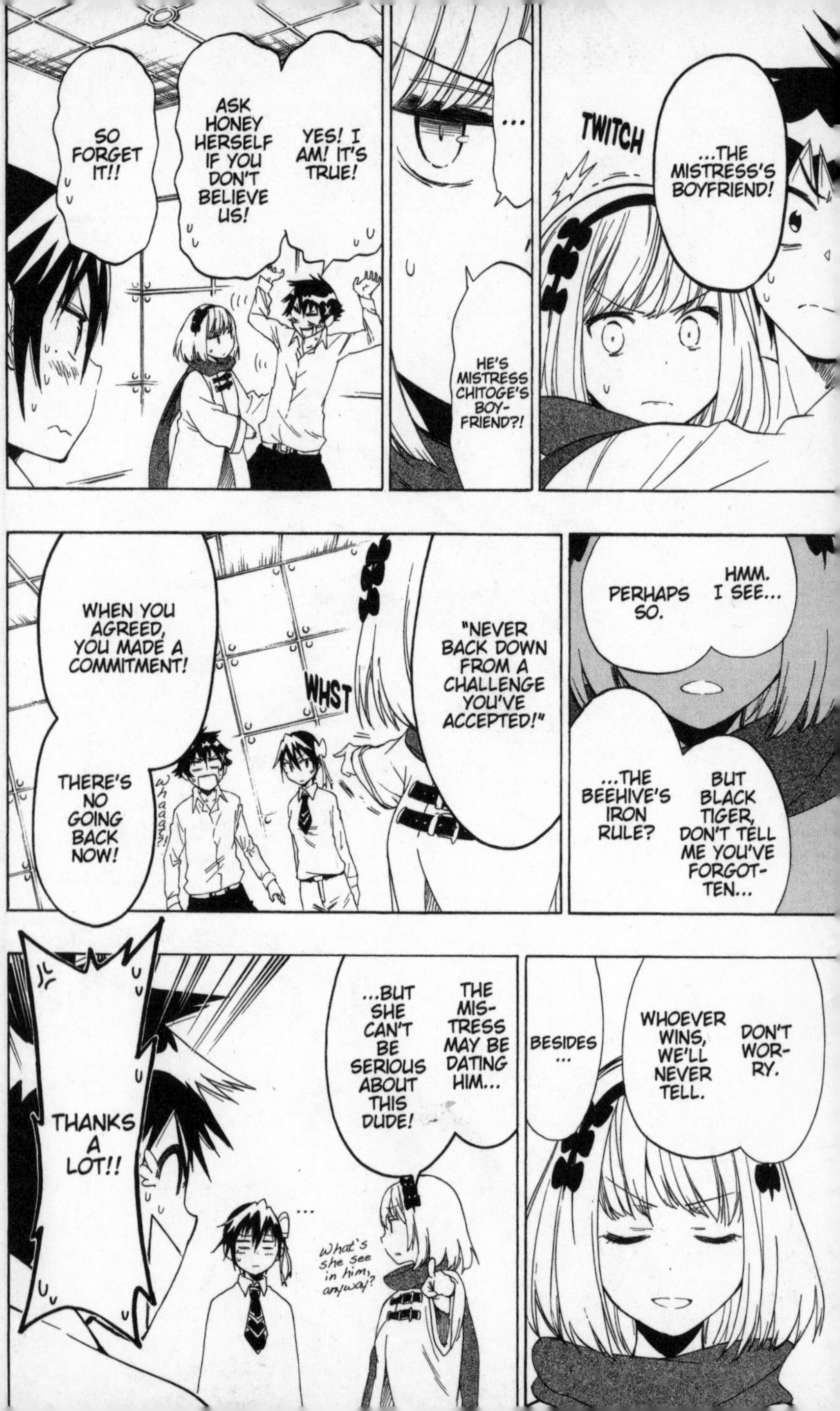
TWITCH
...THE MISTRESS'S BOYFRIEND!
...
HE'S MISTRESS CHITOGE'S BOY-FRIEND?!
YES! I AM! IT'S TRUE!
ASK HONEY HERSELF IF YOU DON'T BELIEVE US!
SO FORGET IT!!
HMM. I SEE...
PERHAPS SO.
BUT BLACK TIGER, DON'T TELL ME YOU'VE FORGOT-TEN...
...THE BEEHIVE'S IRON RULE?
"NEVER BACK DOWN FROM A CHALLENGE YOU'VE ACCEPTED!"
WHST
WHEN YOU AGREED, YOU MADE A COMMITMENT!
THERE'S NO GOING BACK NOW!
Whaaaa?!
DON'T WOR-RY.
WHOEVER WINS, WE'LL NEVER TELL.
BESIDES...
THE MIS-TRESS MAY BE DATING HIM...
...BUT SHE CAN'T BE SERIOUS ABOUT THIS DUDE!
What's she see in him, anyway?
...
THANKS A LOT!!

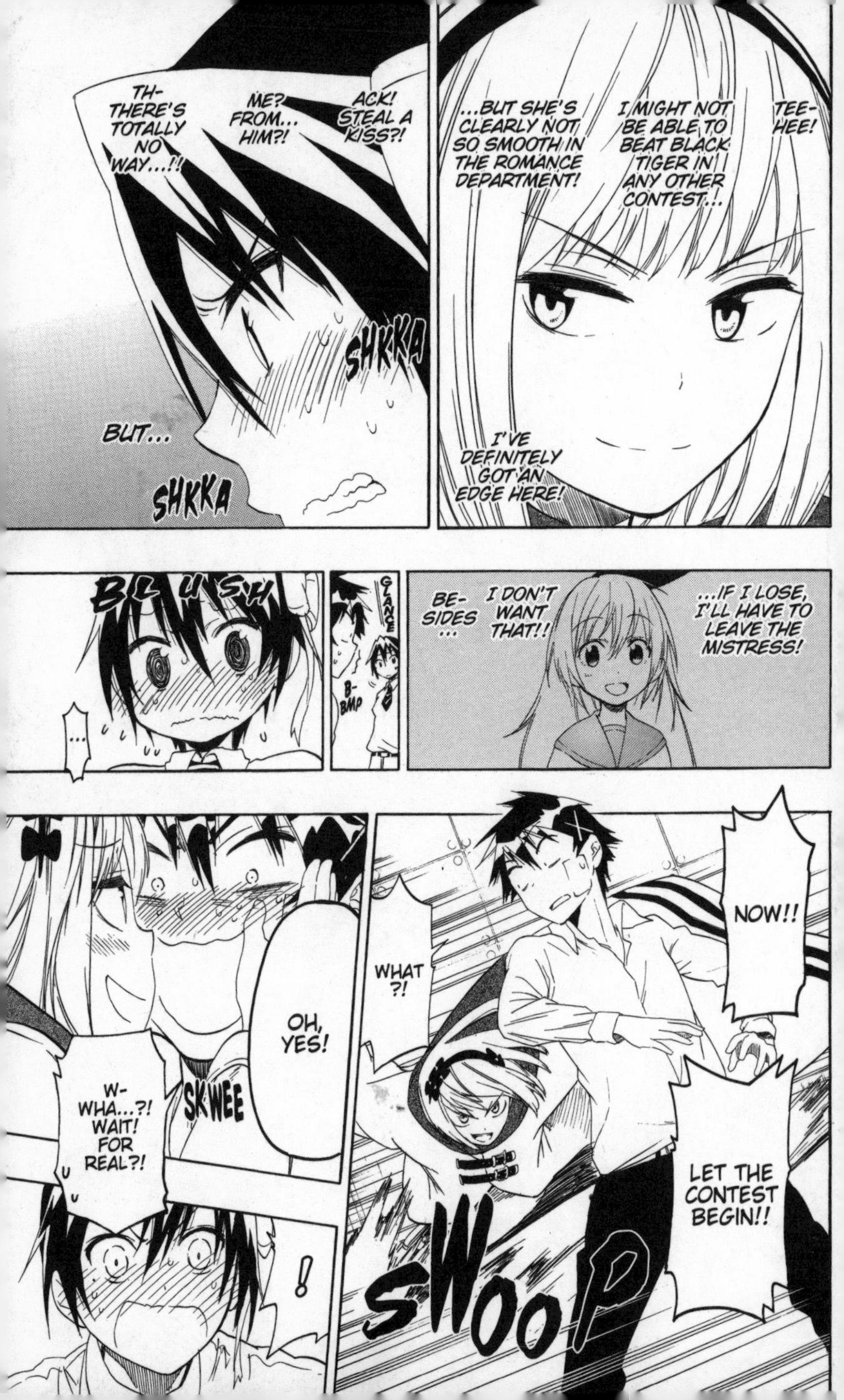
TEE-HEE!
I MIGHT NOT BE ABLE TO BEAT BLACK TIGER IN ANY OTHER CONTEST...
...BUT SHE'S CLEARLY NOT SO SMOOTH IN THE ROMANCE DEPARTMENT!
I'VE DEFINITELY GOT AN EDGE HERE!
ACK! STEAL A KISS?!
ME? FROM... HIM?!
TH- THERE'S TOTALLY NO WAY...!!
SHKKA
BUT...
SHKKA
...IF I LOSE, I'LL HAVE TO LEAVE THE MISTRESS!
I DON'T WANT THAT!!
BE-SIDES...
GLANCE
B-BMP
BLUSH
...
NOW!!
WHAT?!
LET THE CONTEST BEGIN!!
SWOOP
OH, YES!
SKWEE
W-WHA...?! WAIT! FOR REAL?!
!

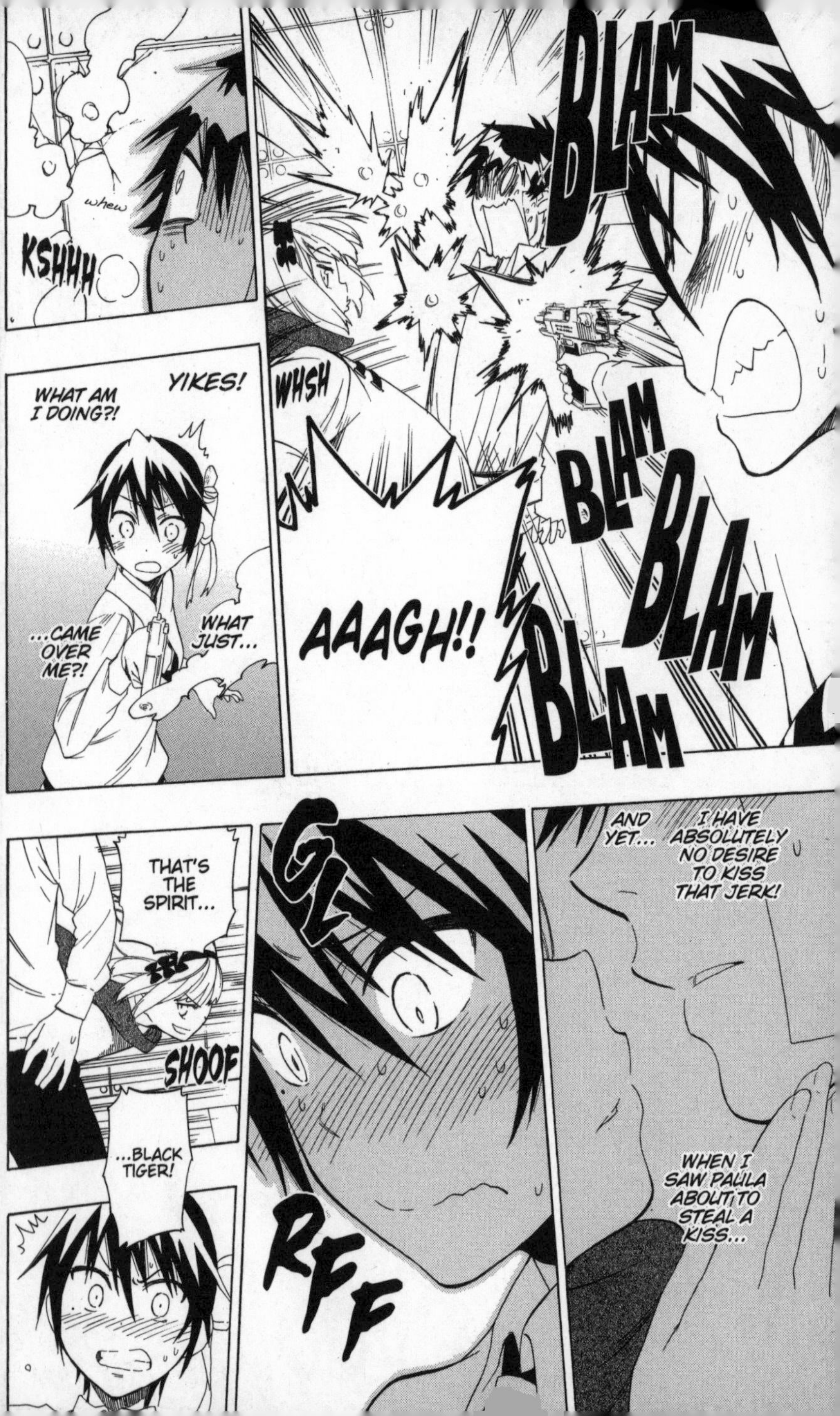
BLAM
WHSH
BLAM
BLAM
BLAM
BLAM
AAAGH!!
whew
KSHHH
YIKES!
WHAT AM I DOING?!
WHAT JUST...
...CAME OVER ME?!
I HAVE ABSOLUTELY NO DESIRE TO KISS THAT JERK!
AND YET...
WHEN I SAW PAULA ABOUT TO STEAL A KISS...
RFF
THAT'S THE SPIRIT...
SHOOF
...BLACK TIGER!

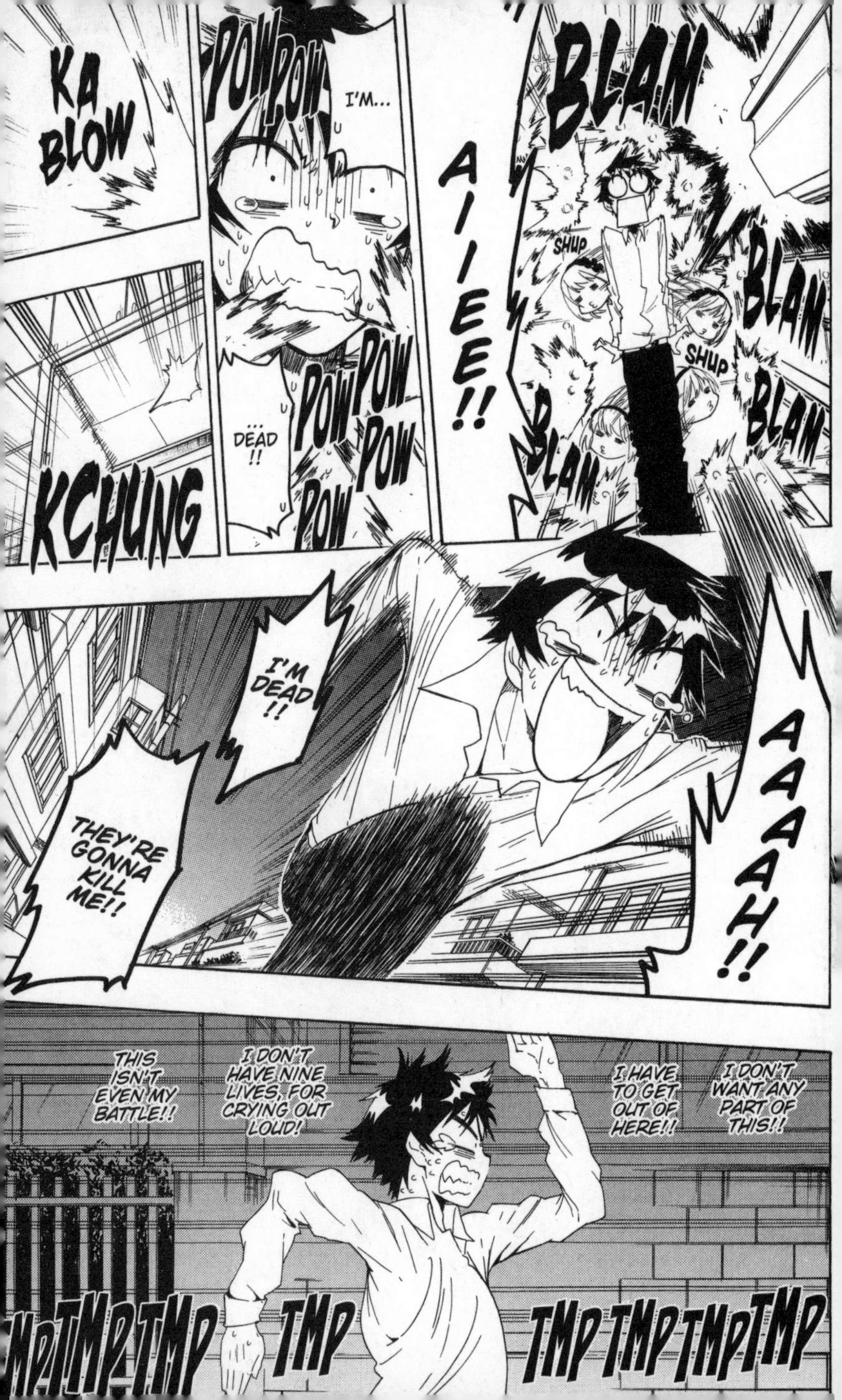
BLAM
BLAM
BLAM
SHUP
SHUP
AIIEE!!
BLAM
BLAM
POW POW
I'M...
POW POW
POW POW
...DEAD!!
POW
KA BLOW
KCHUNG
AAAAAH!!
I'M DEAD!!
THEY'RE GONNA KILL ME!!
I DON'T WANT ANY PART OF THIS!!
I HAVE TO GET OUT OF HERE!!
I DON'T HAVE NINE LIVES, FOR CRYING OUT LOUD!
THIS ISN'T EVEN MY BATTLE!!
TMP TMP TMP TMP
TMP
TMP TMP TMP TMP

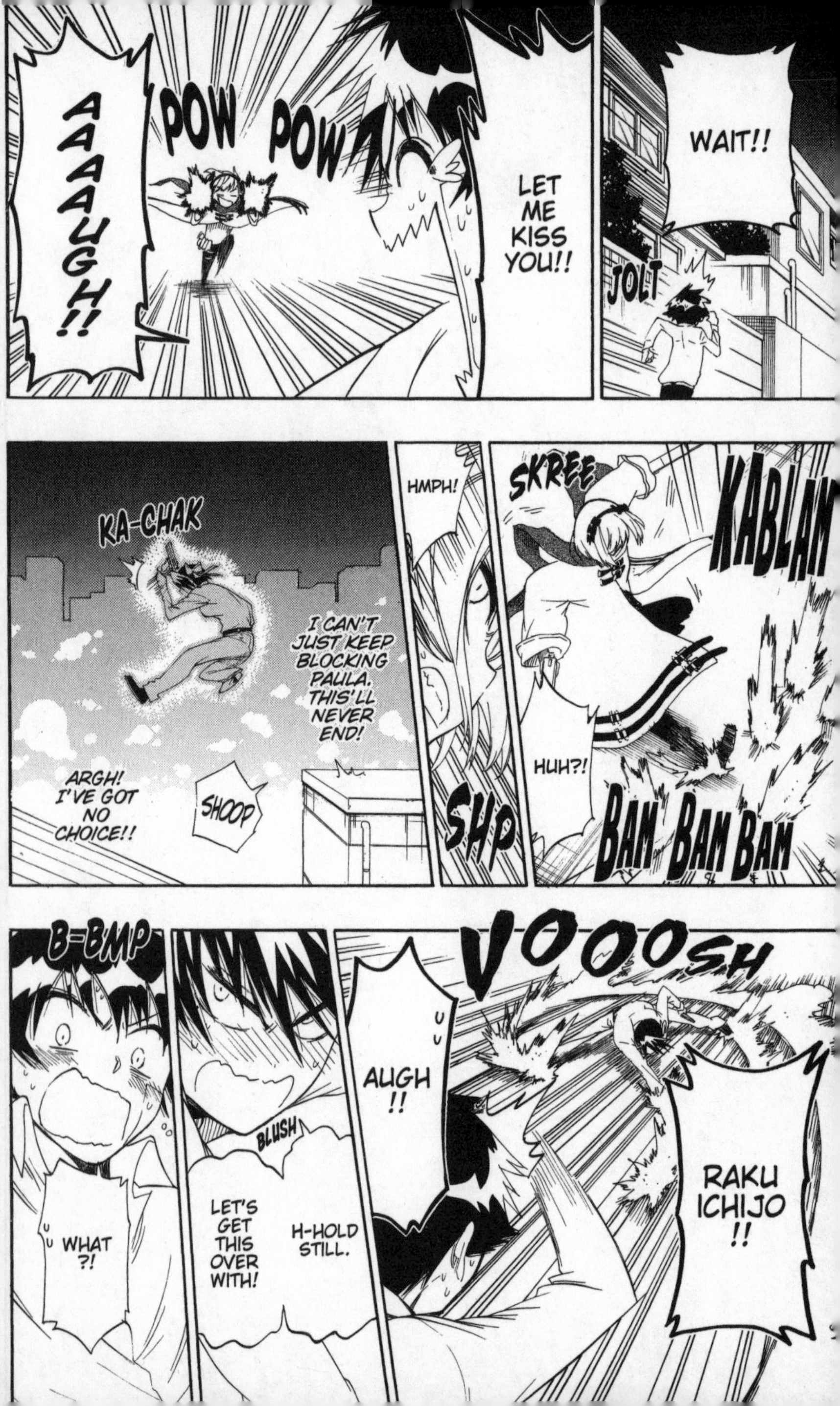
WAIT!!
JOLT
LET ME KISS YOU!!
POW POW
AAAAUGH!!
SKREE
KABLAM
HUH?!
BAM BAM BAM
HMPH!
SHP
KA-CHAK
I CAN'T JUST KEEP BLOCKING PAULA. THIS'LL NEVER END!
ARGH! I'VE GOT NO CHOICE!!
SHOOP
VOOOSH
RAKU ICHIJO!!
AUGH!!
BLUSH
H-HOLD STILL.
LET'S GET THIS OVER WITH!
B-BMP
WHAT?!

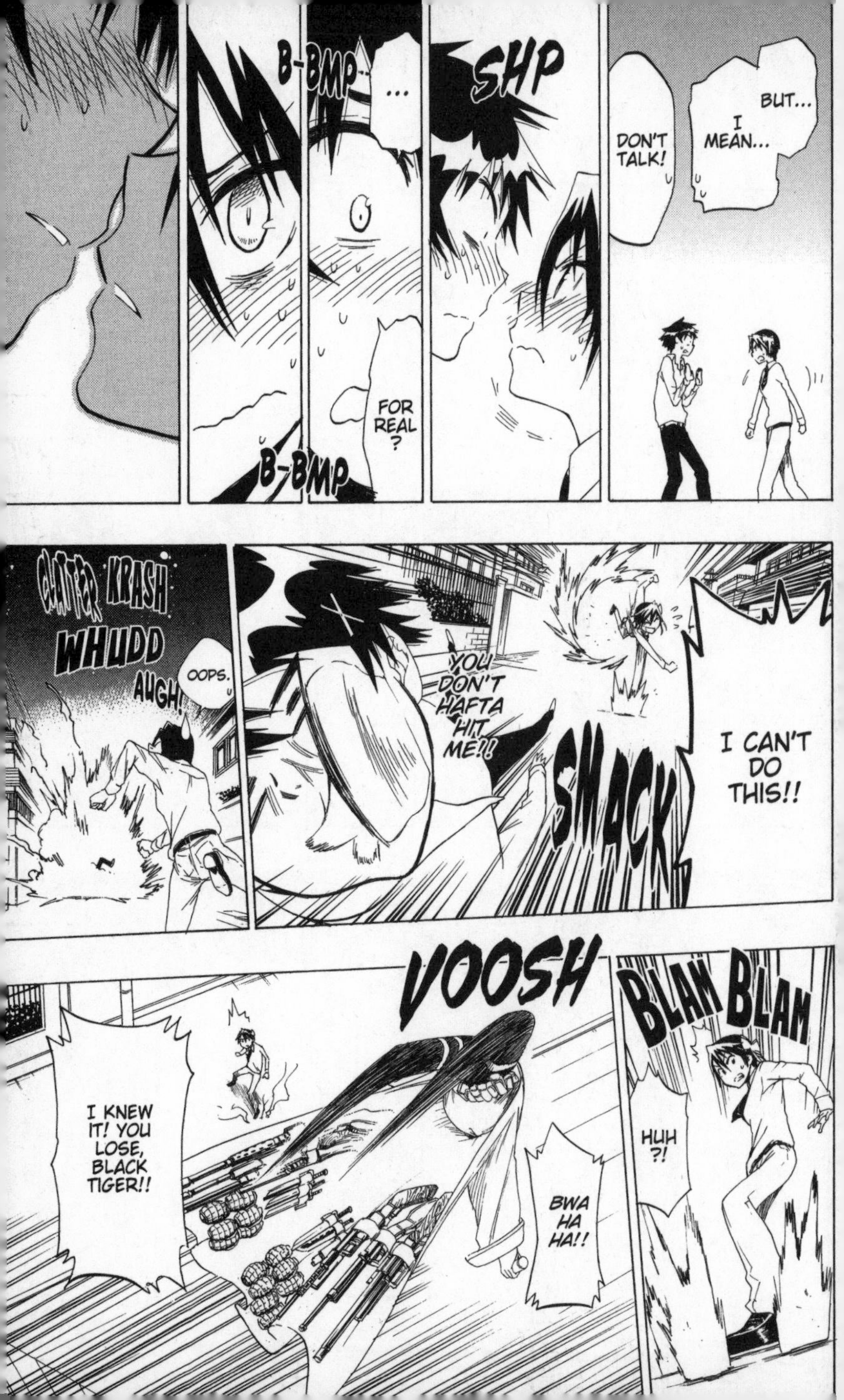
BUT... I MEAN...
DON'T TALK!
SHP
B-BMP...
...
FOR REAL?
B-BMP
I CAN'T DO THIS!!
SMACK
YOU DON'T HAFTA HIT ME!!
OOPS.
CLATTER KRASH
WHUDD
AUGH!
BLAM BLAM
HUH?!
VOOSH
BWA HA HA!!
I KNEW IT! YOU LOSE, BLACK TIGER!!

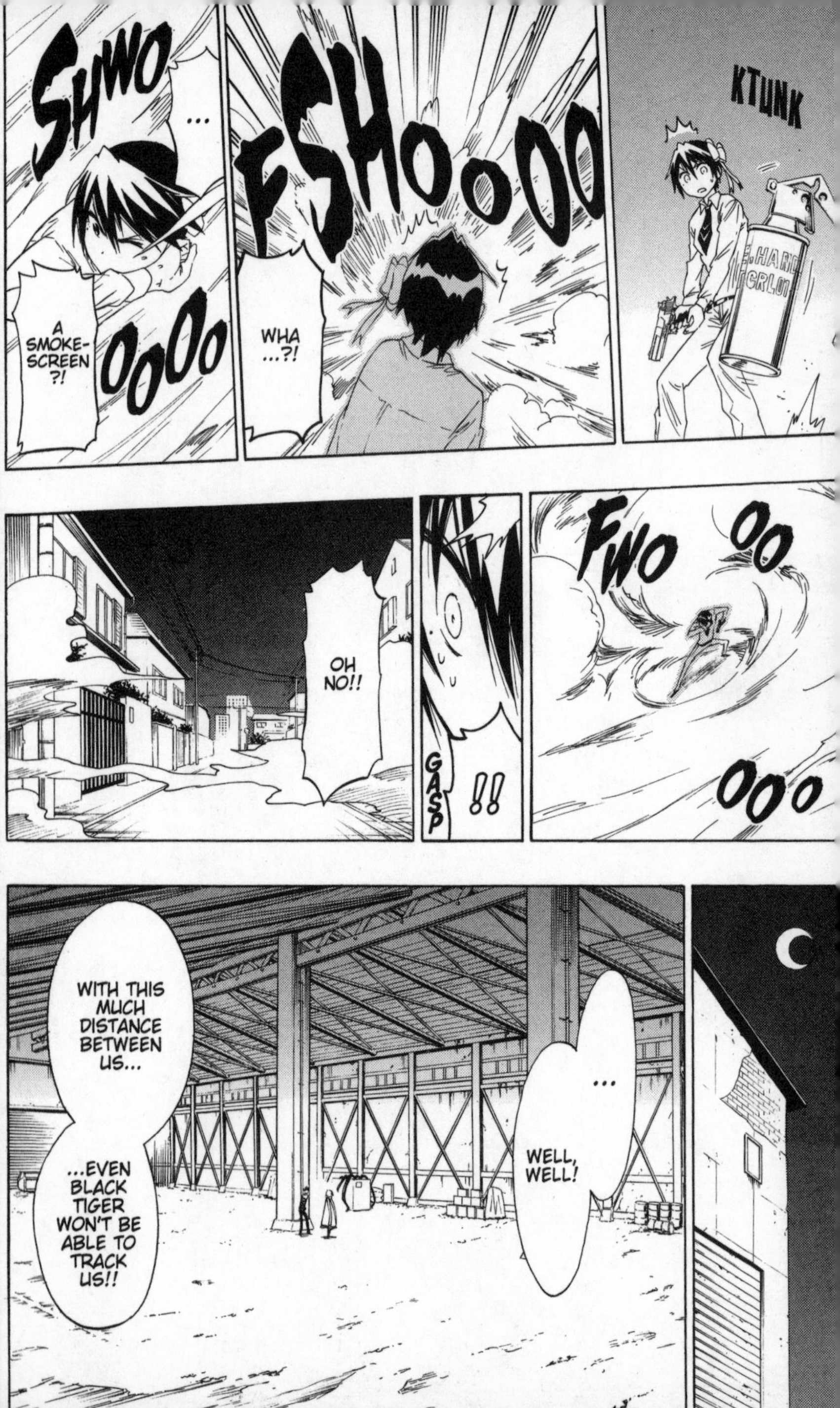
KTUNK
FSHOOOO
WHA ...?!
SHWO
...
A SMOKE-SCREEN ?!
OOOO
FWO OO
OOO
GASP
!!
OH NO!!
WITH THIS MUCH DISTANCE BETWEEN US...
...EVEN BLACK TIGER WON'T BE ABLE TO TRACK US!!
...
WELL, WELL!

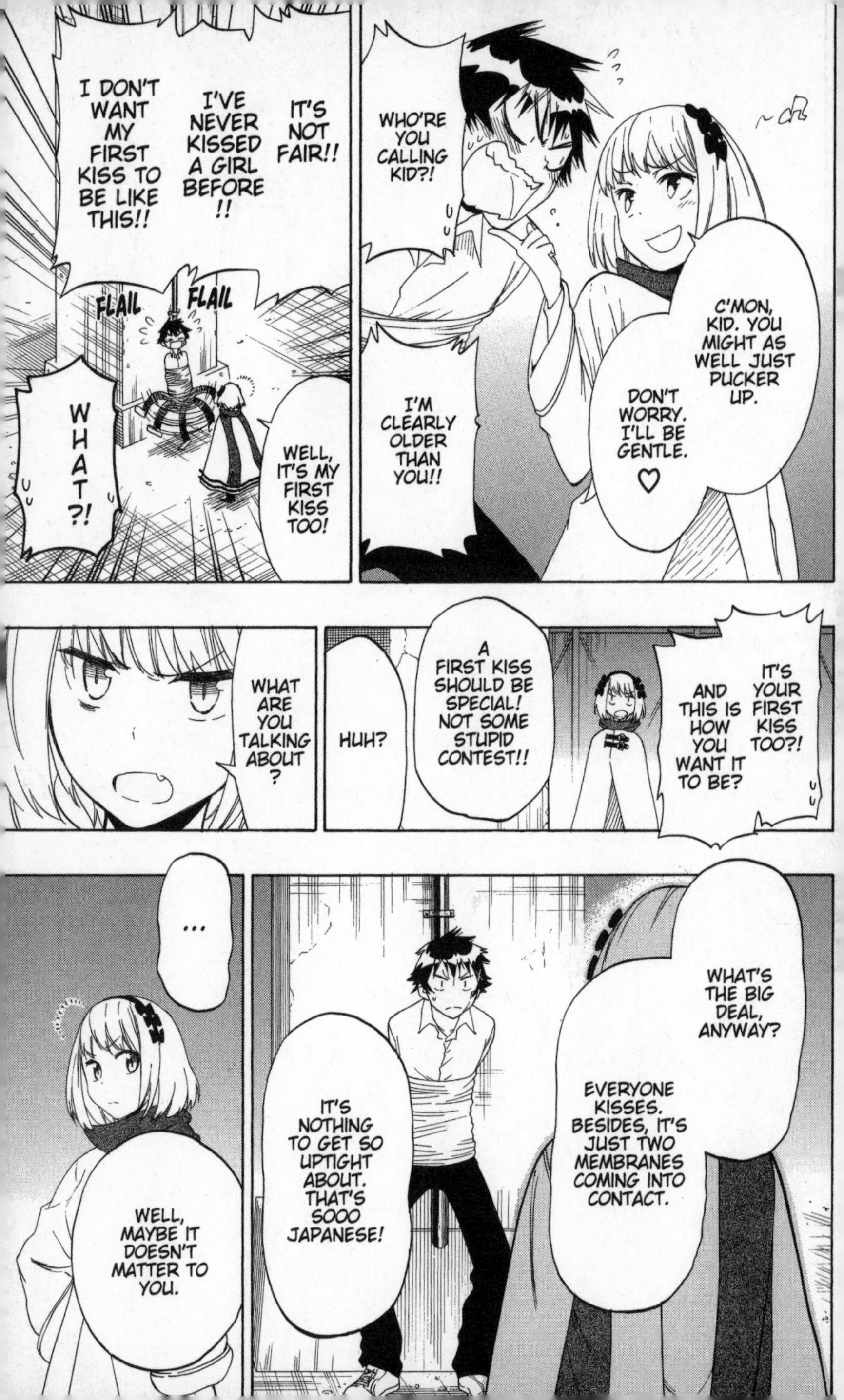
C'MON, KID. YOU MIGHT AS WELL JUST PUCKER UP.
DON'T WORRY. I'LL BE GENTLE. ♡
WHO'RE YOU CALLING KID?!
I'M CLEARLY OLDER THAN YOU!!
IT'S NOT FAIR!!
I'VE NEVER KISSED A GIRL BEFORE!!
I DON'T WANT MY FIRST KISS TO BE LIKE THIS!!
FLAIL
FLAIL
WELL, IT'S MY FIRST KISS TOO!
WHAT?!
IT'S YOUR FIRST KISS TOO?!
AND THIS IS HOW YOU WANT IT TO BE?
A FIRST KISS SHOULD BE SPECIAL! NOT SOME STUPID CONTEST!!
HUH?
WHAT ARE YOU TALKING ABOUT?
WHAT'S THE BIG DEAL, ANYWAY?
EVERYONE KISSES. BESIDES, IT'S JUST TWO MEMBRANES COMING INTO CONTACT.
IT'S NOTHING TO GET SO UPTIGHT ABOUT. THAT'S SOOO JAPANESE!
...
WELL, MAYBE IT DOESN'T MATTER TO YOU.

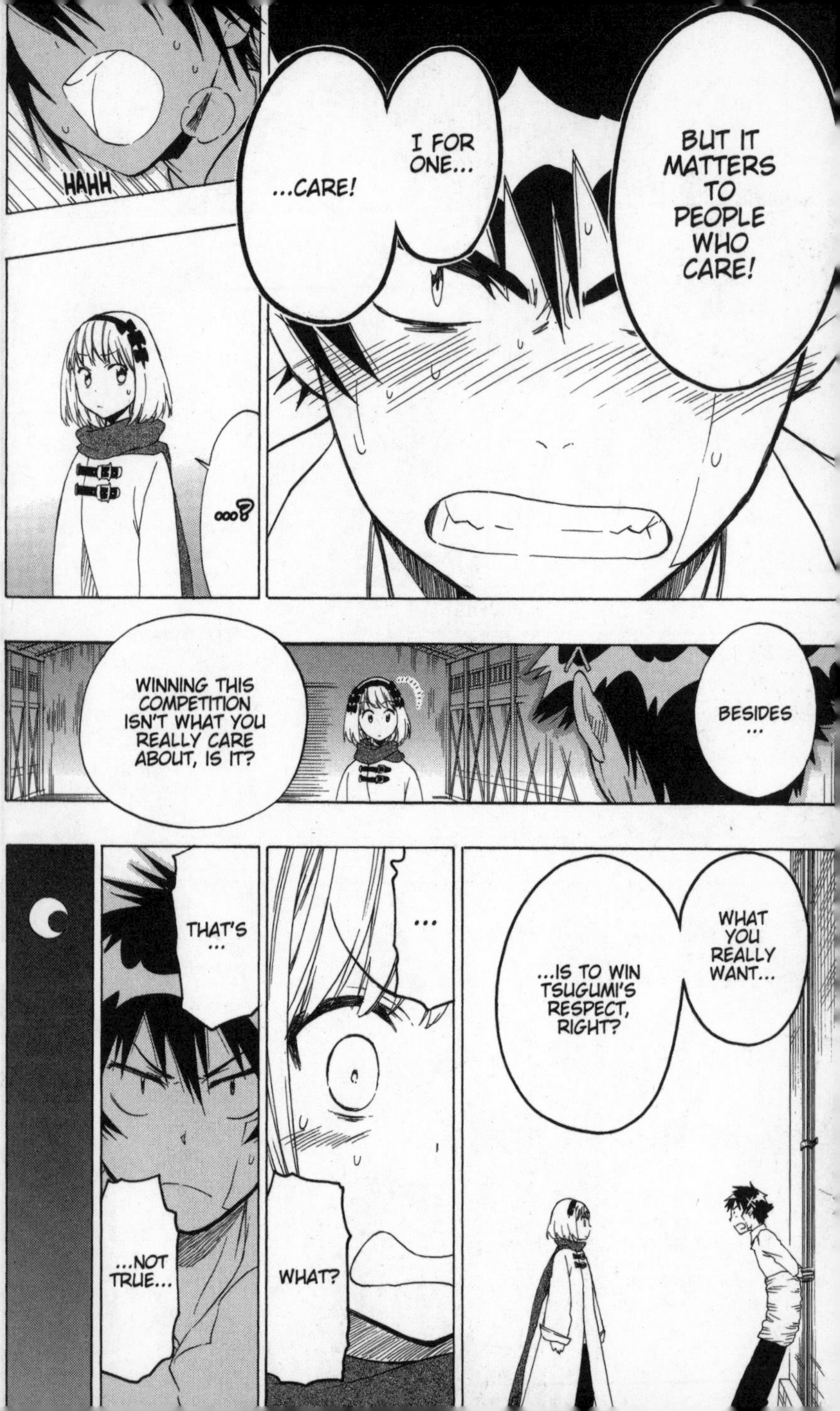
BUT IT MATTERS TO PEOPLE WHO CARE!
I FOR ONE...
...CARE!
HAHH
...?
BESIDES...
WINNING THIS COMPETITION ISN'T WHAT YOU REALLY CARE ABOUT, IS IT?
WHAT YOU REALLY WANT...
...IS TO WIN TSUGUMI'S RESPECT, RIGHT?
...
WHAT?
THAT'S...
...NOT TRUE...

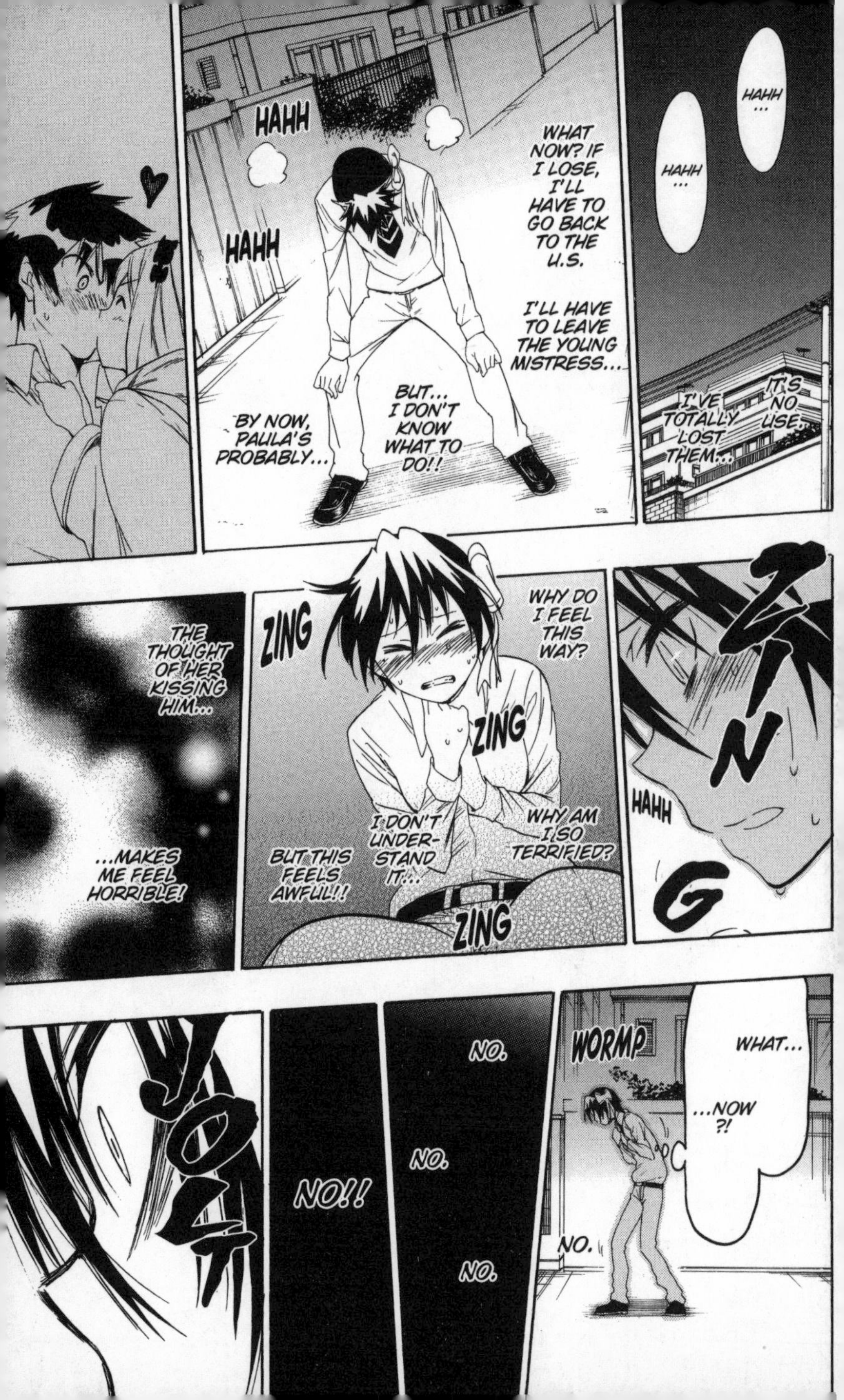
HAHH...
HAHH...
IT'S NO USE.
I'VE TOTALLY LOST THEM...
HAHH
HAHH
WHAT NOW? IF I LOSE, I'LL HAVE TO GO BACK TO THE U.S.
I'LL HAVE TO LEAVE THE YOUNG MISTRESS...
BUT... I DON'T KNOW WHAT TO DO!!
BY NOW, PAULA'S PROBABLY...
ZING
HAHH
ZING
WHY DO I FEEL THIS WAY?
ZING
WHY AM I SO TERRIFIED?
I DON'T UNDER-STAND IT...
BUT THIS FEELS AWFUL!!
ZING
THE THOUGHT OF HER KISSING HIM...
...MAKES ME FEEL HORRIBLE!
WORMP
WHAT...
...NOW?!
NO.
NO.
NO.
NO.
NO!!
JOLT

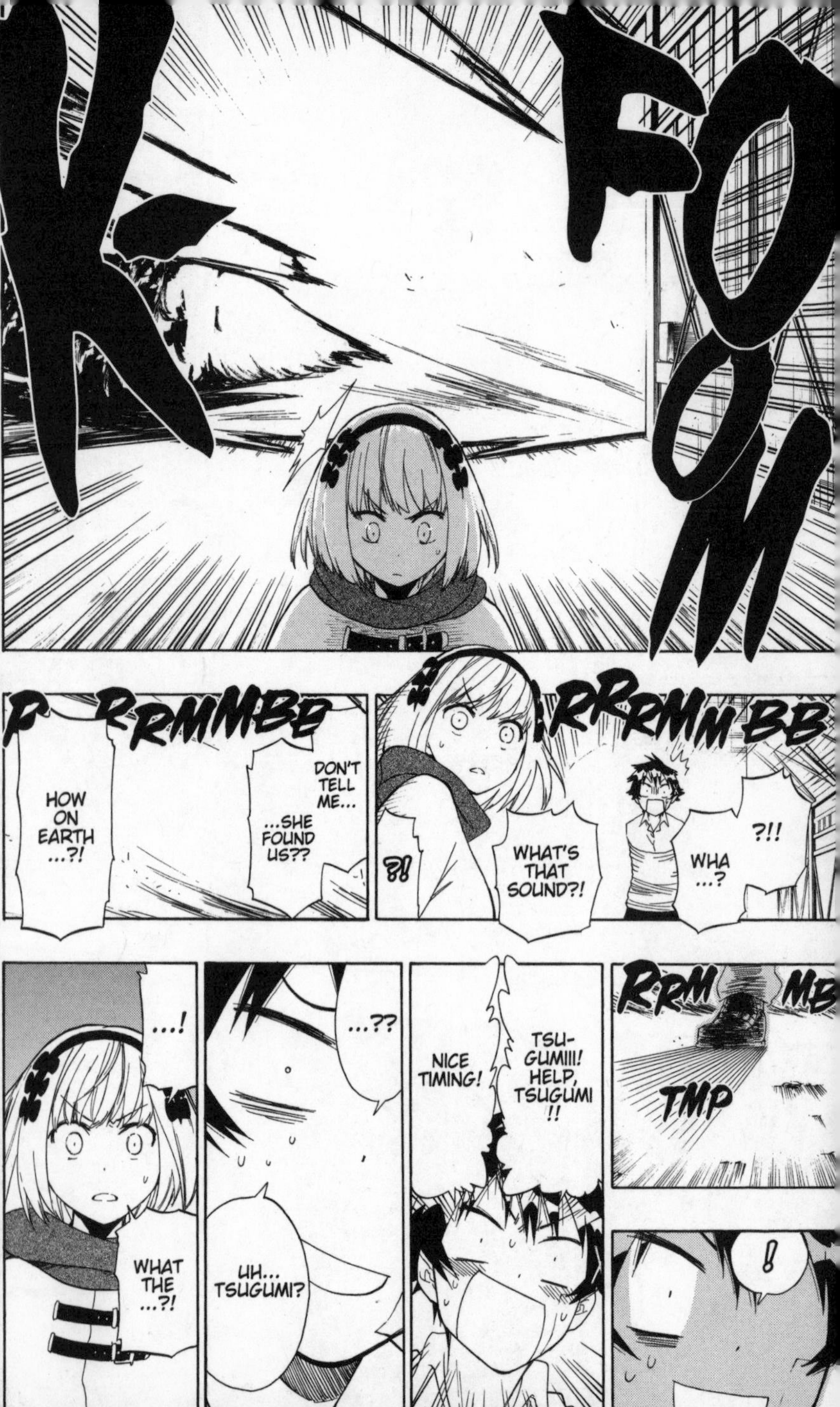
FOOM
RRRMMBB
?!!
WHA ...?
WHAT'S THAT SOUND?!
?!
DON'T TELL ME...
...SHE FOUND US??
HOW ON EARTH ...?!
RRM MB
TMP
!
TSU-GUMIII! HELP, TSUGUMI!!
NICE TIMING!
...??
UH... TSUGUMI?
...!
WHAT THE ...?!

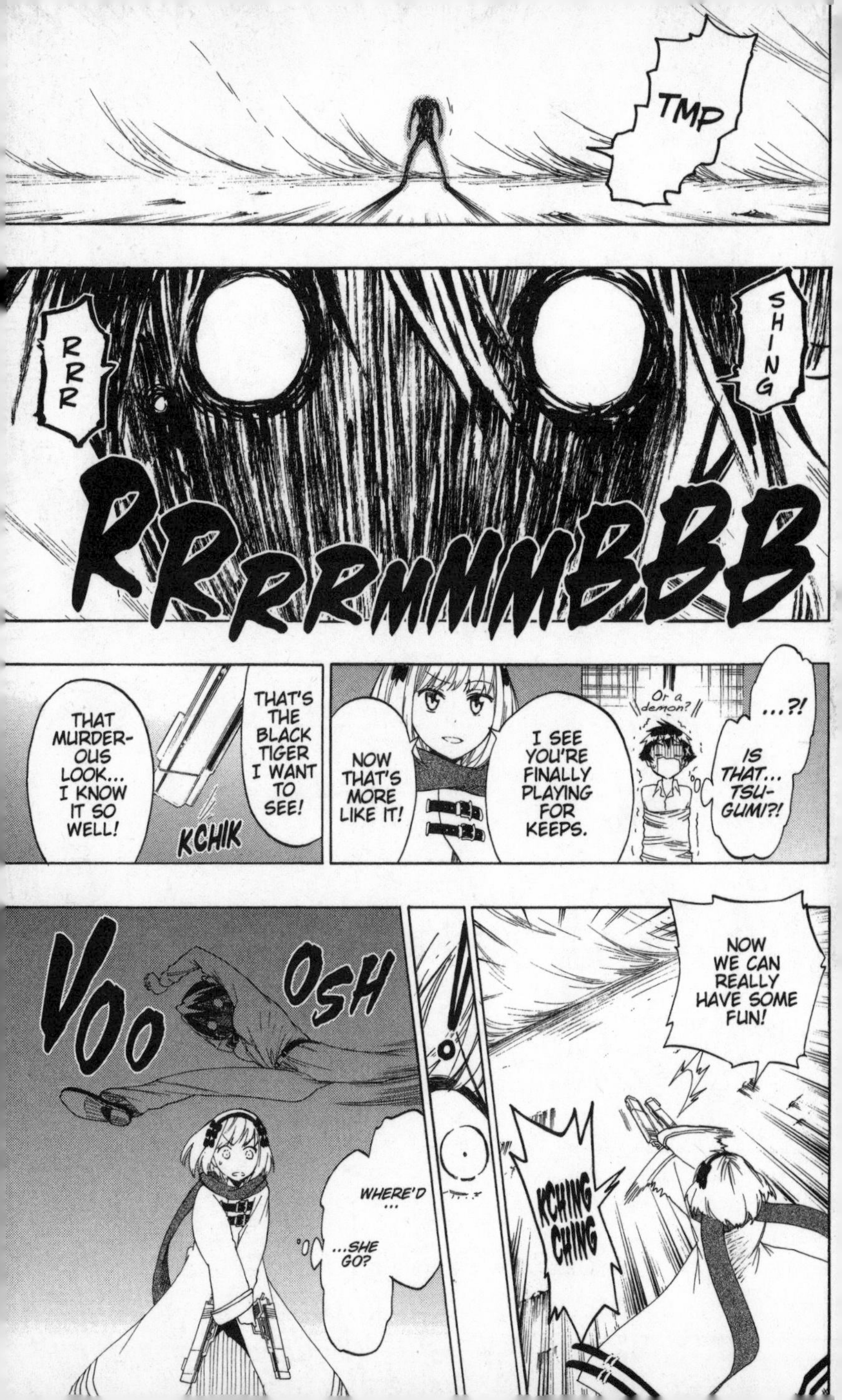
TMP
SHING
RRR
RRRRMMMMBBB
...?!
IS THAT... TSUGUMI?!
Or a demon?
I SEE YOU'RE FINALLY PLAYING FOR KEEPS.
NOW THAT'S MORE LIKE IT!
THAT'S THE BLACK TIGER I WANT TO SEE!
THAT MURDEROUS LOOK... I KNOW IT SO WELL!
KCHIK
NOW WE CAN REALLY HAVE SOME FUN!
KCHING CHING
!
WHERE'D ...
...SHE GO?
VOOOSH

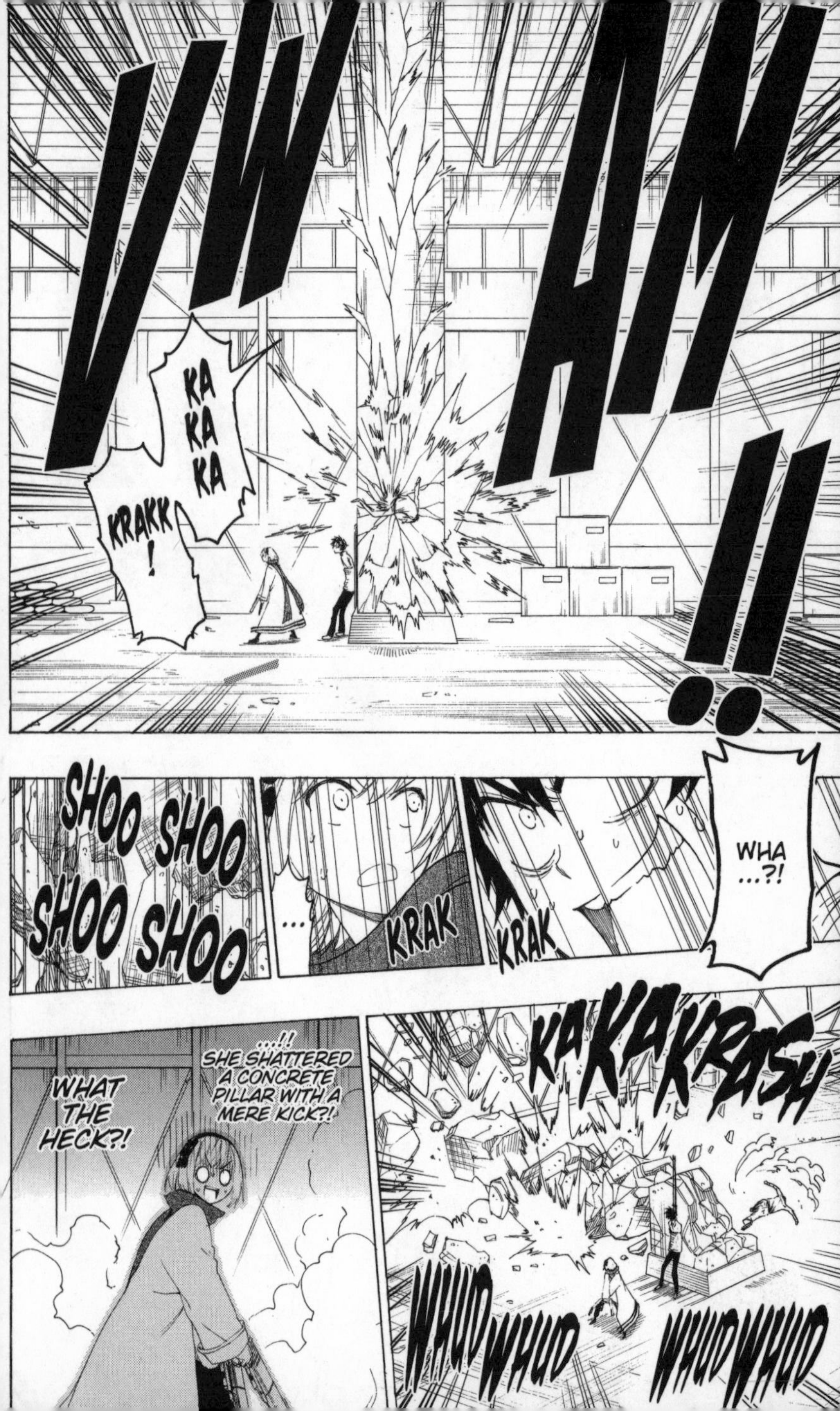
VWHAM!!
KA KA KA KRAKK!
WHA...?!
KRAK
KRAK
...
SHOO SHOO SHOO SHOO
KA KA KRASH
WHUD WHUD
WHUD WHUD
...!! SHE SHATTERED A CONCRETE PILLAR WITH A MERE KICK?!
WHAT THE HECK?!

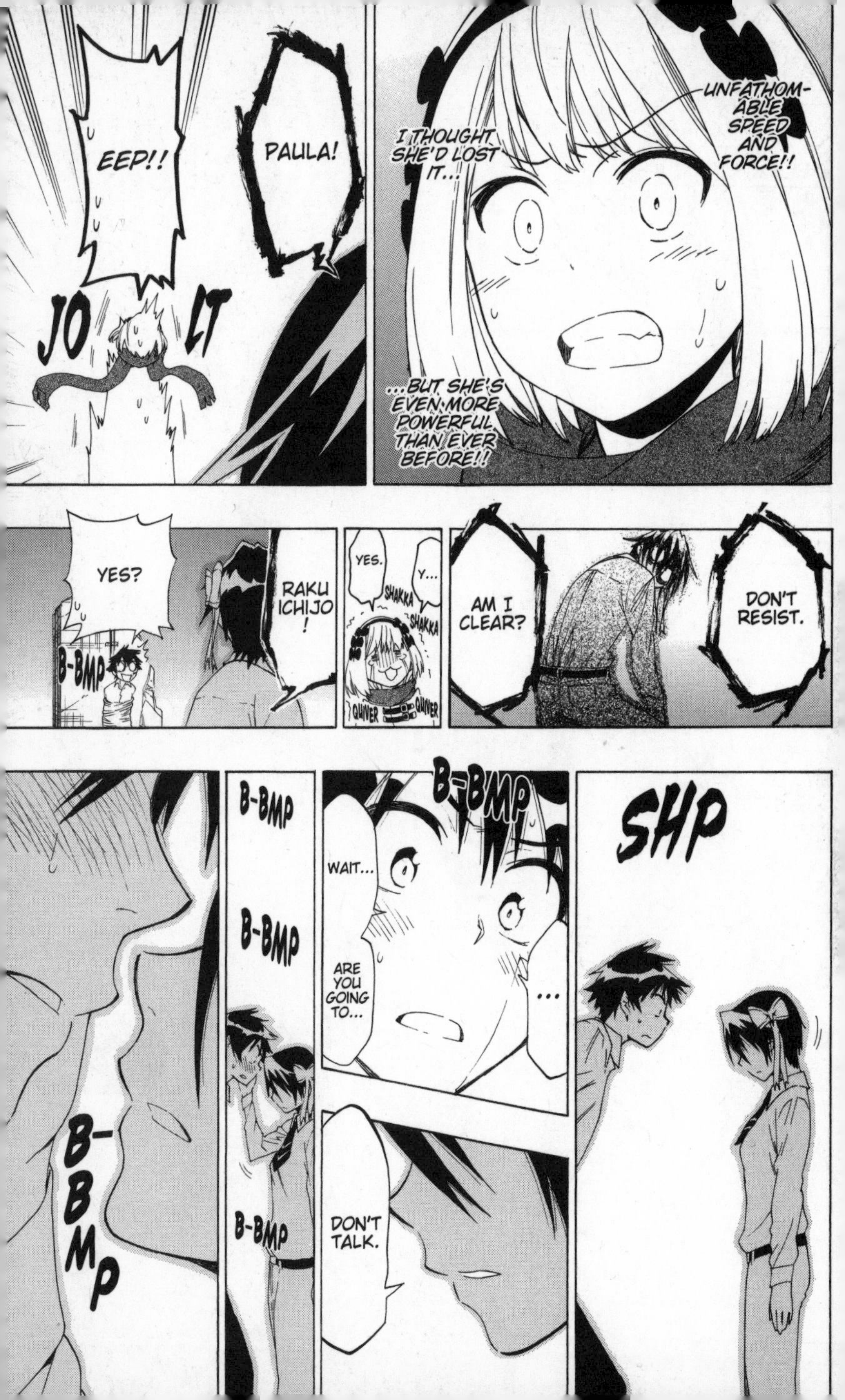
UNFATHOMABLE SPEED AND FORCE!!
I THOUGHT SHE'D LOST IT...
...BUT SHE'S EVEN MORE POWERFUL THAN EVER BEFORE!!
PAULA!
EEP!!
JOLT
DON'T RESIST.
AM I CLEAR?
Y...
YES.
SHAKKA
SHAKKA
QUIVER
QUIVER
RAKU ICHIJO!
YES?
B-BMP
SHP
B-BMP
...
WAIT...
ARE YOU GOING TO...
DON'T TALK.
B-BMP
B-BMP
B-BMP
B-BBMP

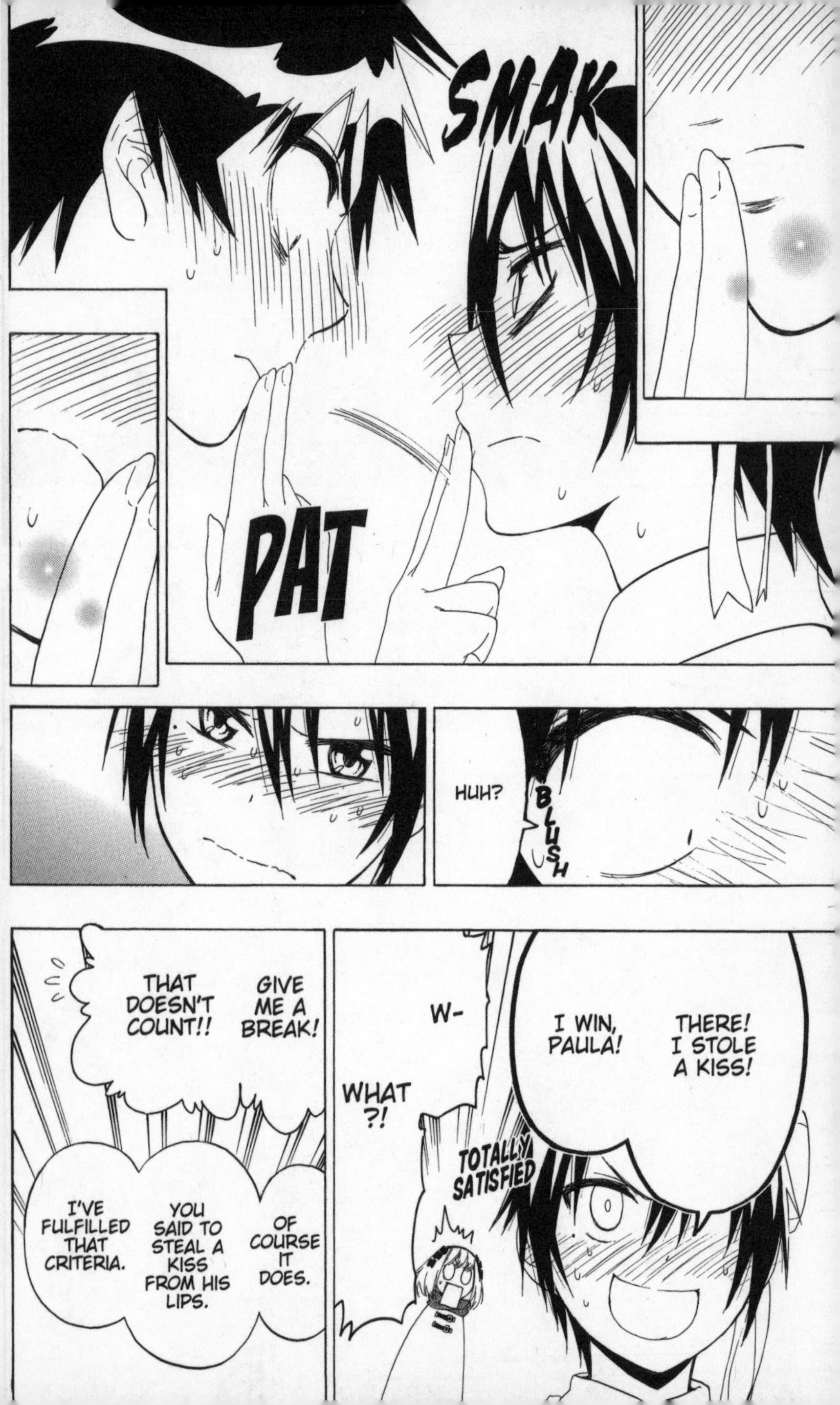
SMAK
PAT
HUH?
BLUSH
THERE! I STOLE A KISS!
I WIN, PAULA!
W-
WHAT?!
TOTALLY SATISFIED
GIVE ME A BREAK!
THAT DOESN'T COUNT!!
OF COURSE IT DOES.
YOU SAID TO STEAL A KISS FROM HIS LIPS.
I'VE FULFILLED THAT CRITERIA.

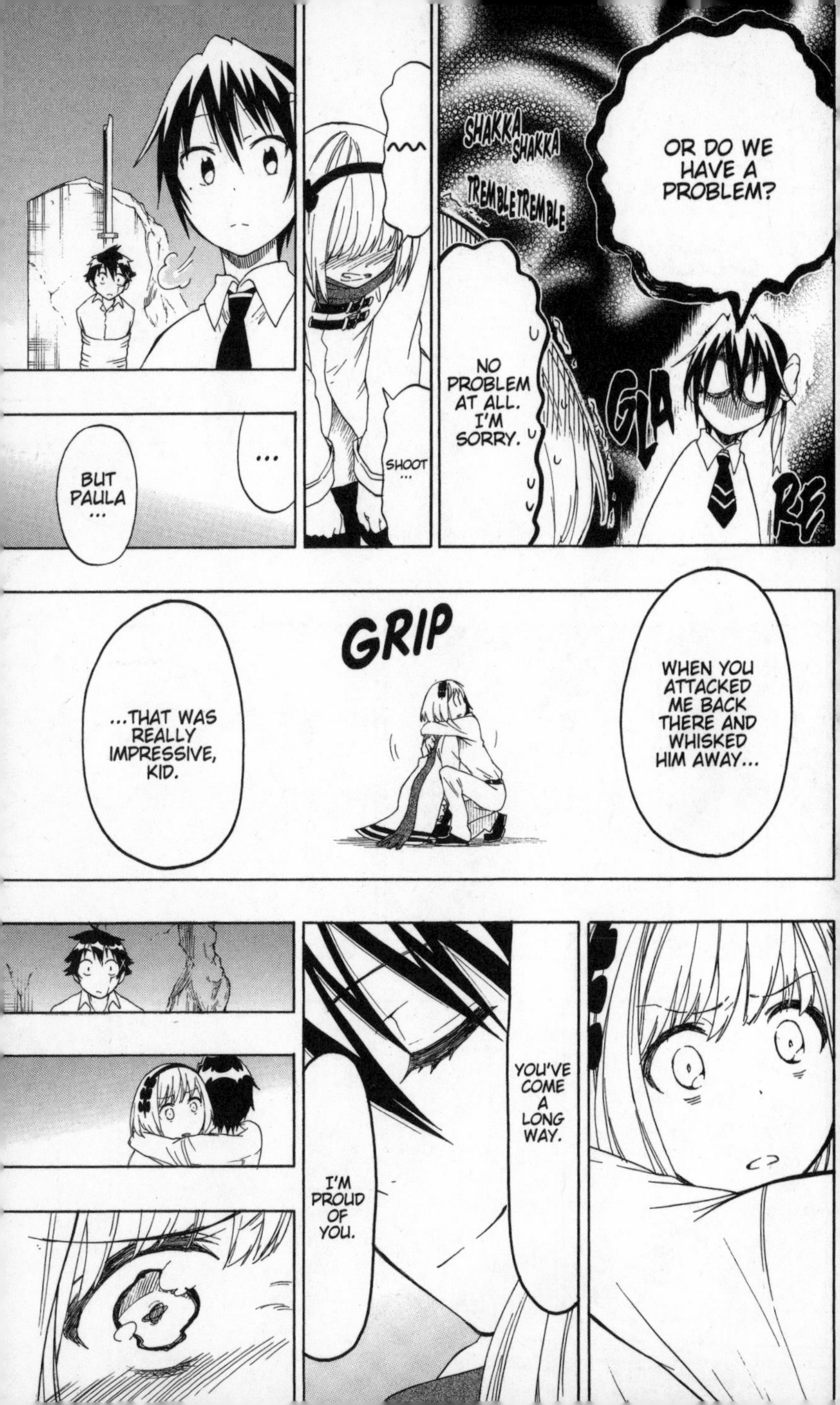
OR DO WE HAVE A PROBLEM?
GLARE
SHAKKA SHAKKA
TREMBLETREMBLE
NO PROBLEM AT ALL. I'M SORRY.
SHOOT...
...
BUT PAULA...
WHEN YOU ATTACKED ME BACK THERE AND WHISKED HIM AWAY...
GRIP
...THAT WAS REALLY IMPRESSIVE, KID.
YOU'VE COME A LONG WAY.
I'M PROUD OF YOU.

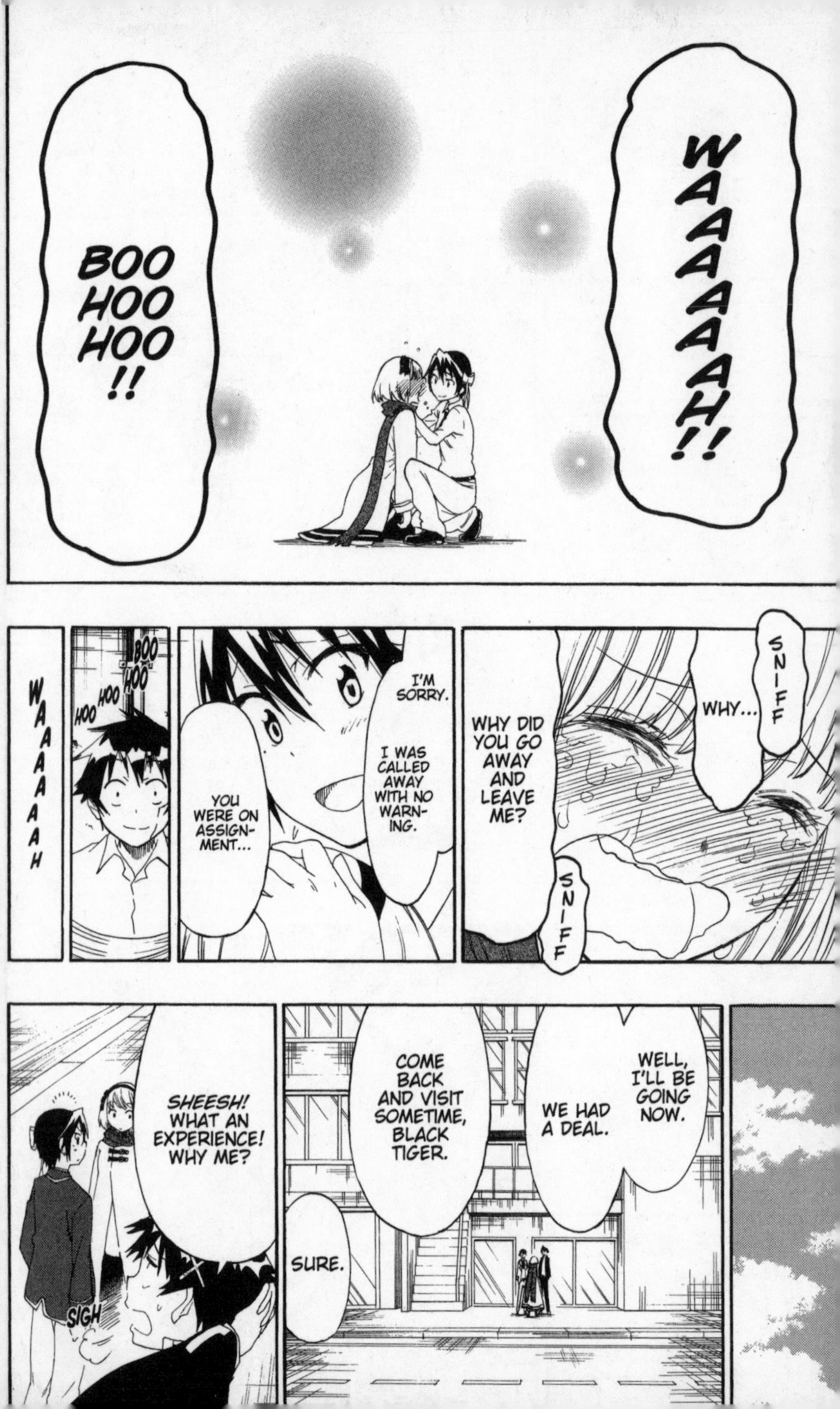
WAAAAAAH!!
BOO HOO HOO!!
SNIFF
WHY...
WHY DID YOU GO AWAY AND LEAVE ME?
SNIFF
I'M SORRY.
I WAS CALLED AWAY WITH NO WARN-ING.
YOU WERE ON ASSIGN-MENT...
BOO HOO
HOO
HOO
WAAAAAAH
WELL, I'LL BE GOING NOW.
WE HAD A DEAL.
COME BACK AND VISIT SOMETIME, BLACK TIGER.
SURE.
SHEESH! WHAT AN EXPERIENCE! WHY ME?
SIGH

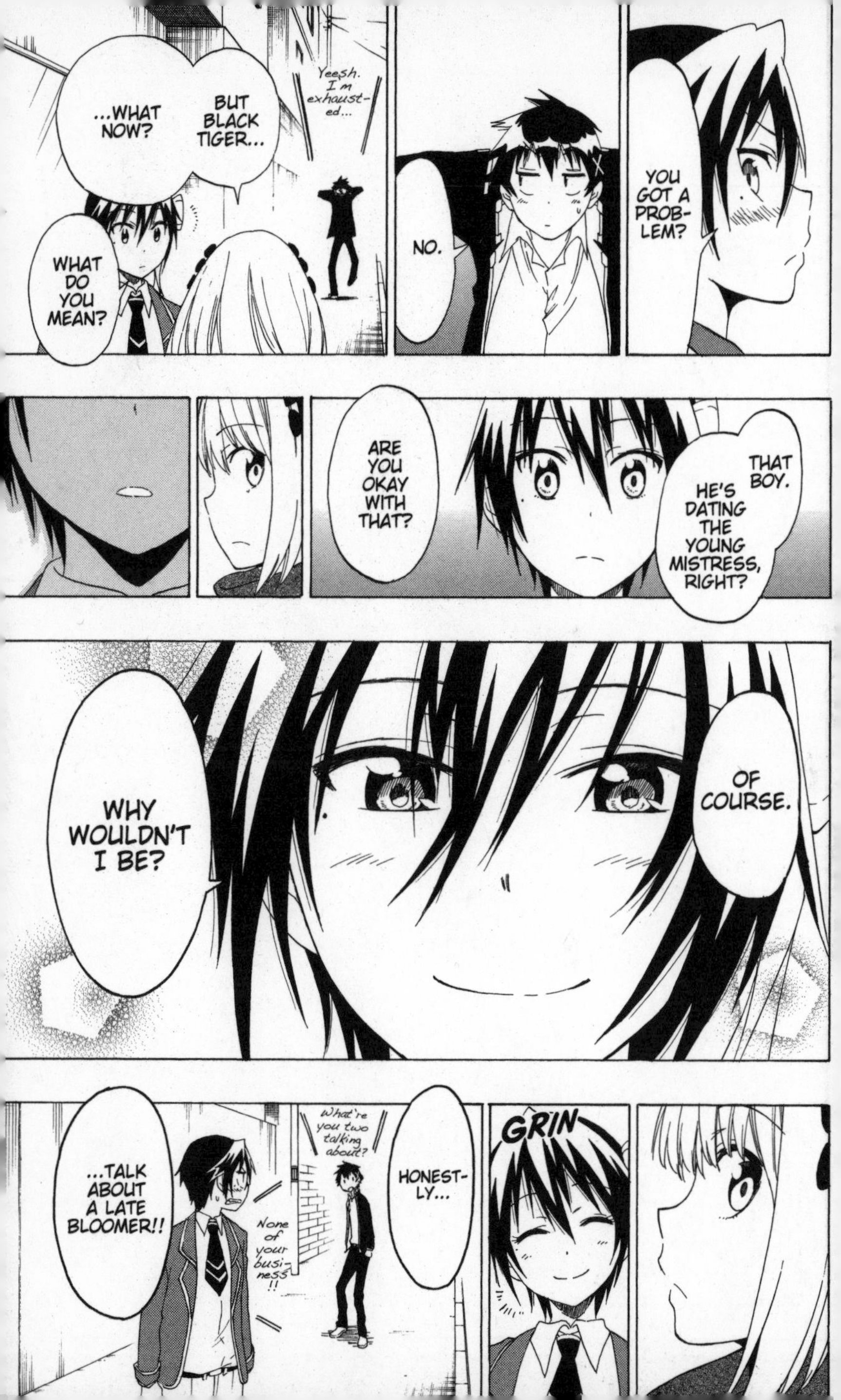
YOU GOT A PROB-LEM?
NO.
Yeesh. I'm exhaust-ed...
BUT BLACK TIGER...
...WHAT NOW?
WHAT DO YOU MEAN?
THAT BOY. HE'S DATING THE YOUNG MISTRESS, RIGHT?
ARE YOU OKAY WITH THAT?
OF COURSE.
WHY WOULDN'T I BE?
GRIN
HONEST-LY...
What're you two talking about?
...TALK ABOUT A LATE BLOOMER!!
None of your busi-ness!!

Sniffle...

When will I see her again?

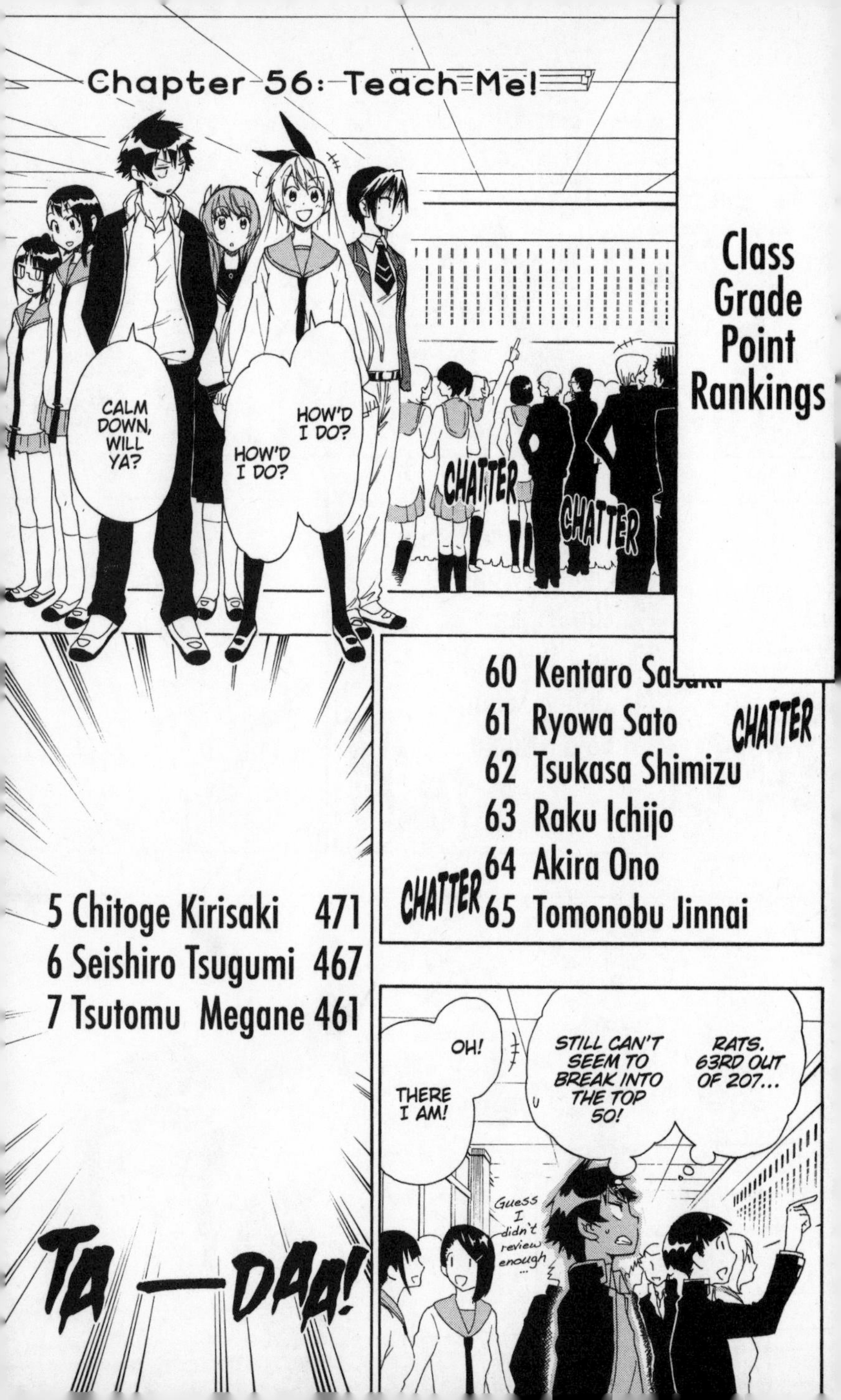
Chapter 56: Teach Me!
Class Grade Point Rankings
CHATTER
CHATTER
HOW'D I DO?
HOW'D I DO?
CALM DOWN, WILL YA?
60 Kentaro Sasaki
61 Ryowa Sato
62 Tsukasa Shimizu
63 Raku Ichijo
64 Akira Ono
65 Tomonobu Jinnai
CHATTER
CHATTER
RATS. 63RD OUT OF 207...
STILL CAN'T SEEM TO BREAK INTO THE TOP 50!
OH!
THERE I AM!
Guess I didn't review enough...
5 Chitoge Kirisaki 471
6 Seishiro Tsugumi 467
7 Tsutomu Megane 461
TA—DAA!

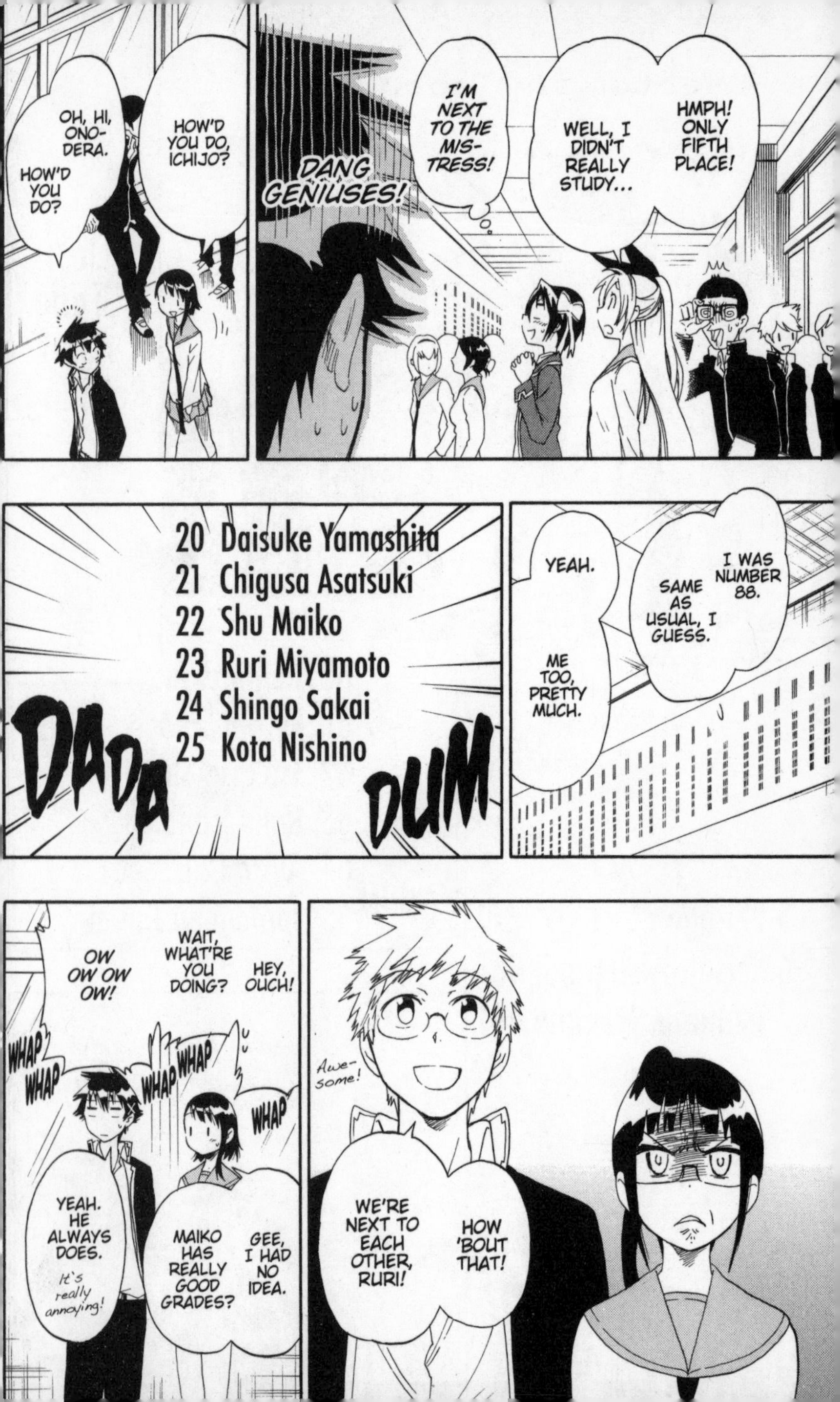
HMPH! ONLY FIFTH PLACE!
WELL, I DIDN'T REALLY STUDY...
I'M NEXT TO THE MIS-TRESS!
DANG GENIUSES!
HOW'D YOU DO, ICHIJO?
OH, HI, ONO-DERA.
HOW'D YOU DO?
I WAS NUMBER 88.
SAME AS USUAL, I GUESS.
YEAH.
ME TOO, PRETTY MUCH.
20 Daisuke Yamashita
21 Chigusa Asatsuki
22 Shu Maiko
23 Ruri Miyamoto
24 Shingo Sakai
25 Kota Nishino
DADA DUM
HOW 'BOUT THAT!
WE'RE NEXT TO EACH OTHER, RURI!
Awe-some!
HEY, OUCH!
WAIT, WHAT'RE YOU DOING?
OW OW OW OW!
WHAP WHAP WHAP WHAP WHAP
GEE, I HAD NO IDEA.
MAIKO HAS REALLY GOOD GRADES?
YEAH. HE ALWAYS DOES.
It's really annoying!

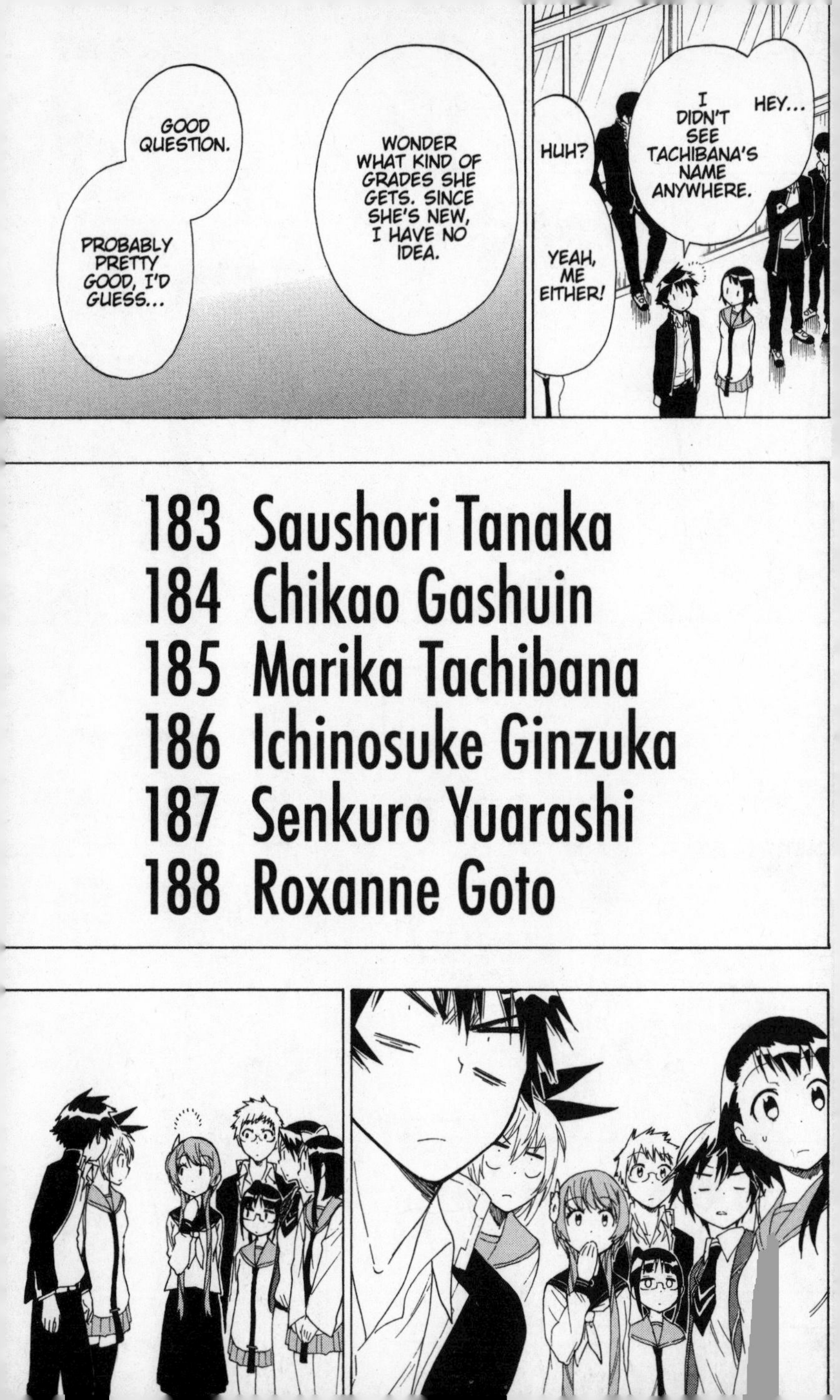
HEY...
I DIDN'T SEE TACHIBANA'S NAME ANYWHERE.
HUH?
YEAH, ME EITHER!
WONDER WHAT KIND OF GRADES SHE GETS. SINCE SHE'S NEW, I HAVE NO IDEA.
GOOD QUESTION.
PROBABLY PRETTY GOOD, I'D GUESS...
183 Saushori Tanaka
184 Chikao Gashuin
185 Marika Tachibana
186 Ichinosuke Ginzuka
187 Senkuro Yuarashi
188 Roxanne Goto

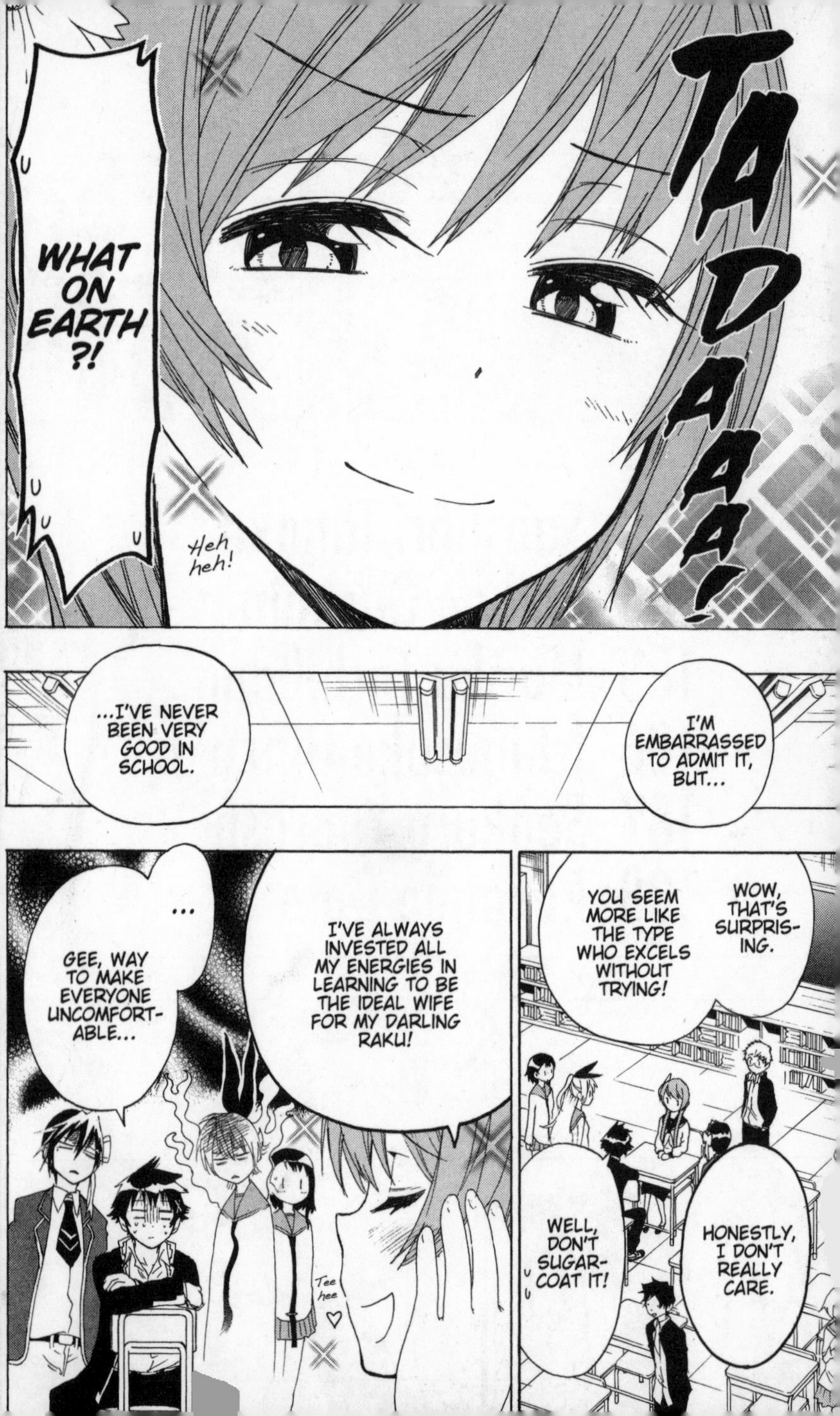
TADAAAA!
Heh heh!
WHAT ON EARTH?!
I'M EMBARRASSED TO ADMIT IT, BUT...
...I'VE NEVER BEEN VERY GOOD IN SCHOOL.
WOW, THAT'S SURPRISING.
YOU SEEM MORE LIKE THE TYPE WHO EXCELS WITHOUT TRYING!
HONESTLY, I DON'T REALLY CARE.
WELL, DON'T SUGAR-COAT IT!
I'VE ALWAYS INVESTED ALL MY ENERGIES IN LEARNING TO BE THE IDEAL WIFE FOR MY DARLING RAKU!
Tee hee
...
GEE, WAY TO MAKE EVERYONE UNCOMFORT-ABLE...

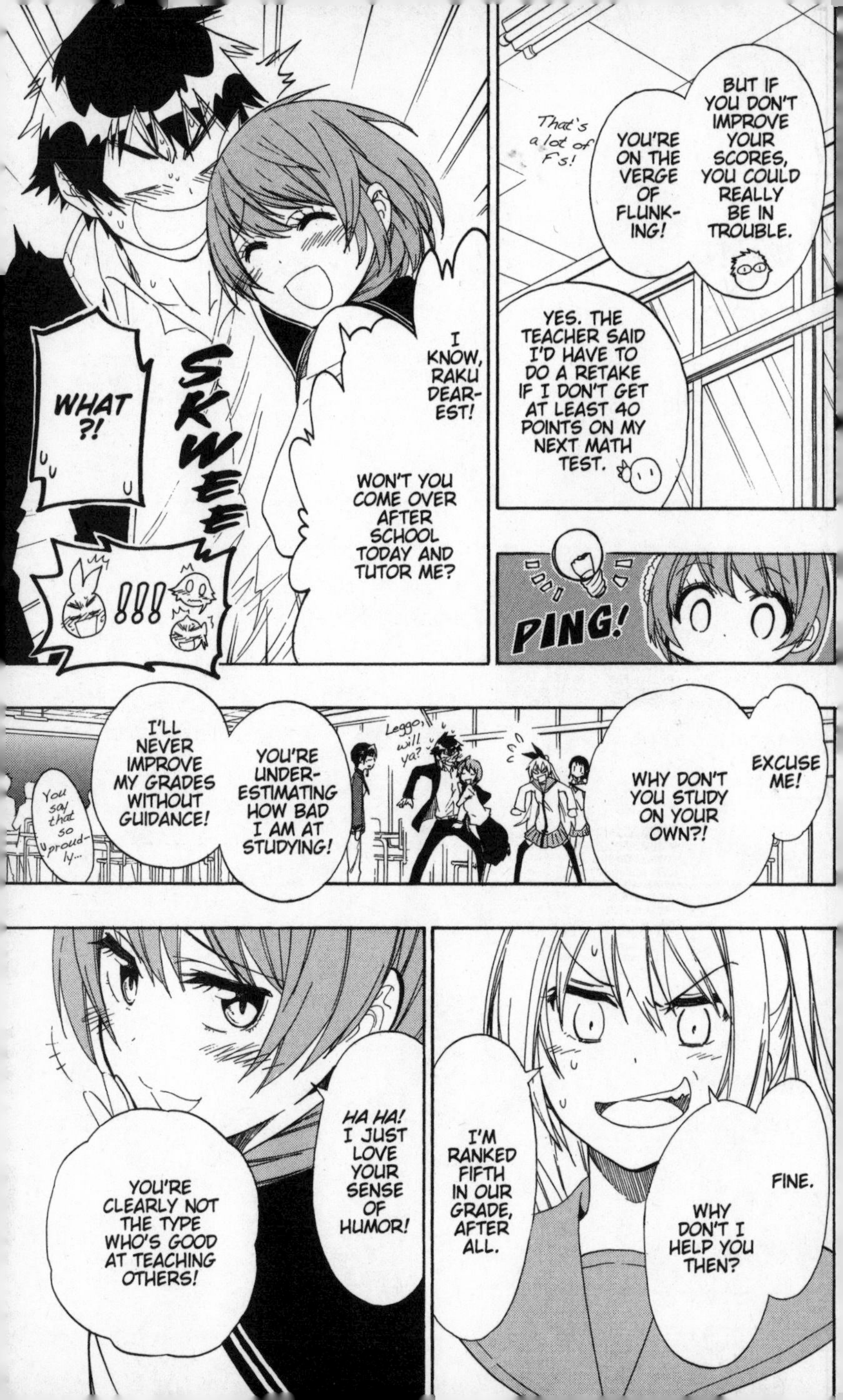
BUT IF YOU DON'T IMPROVE YOUR SCORES, YOU COULD REALLY BE IN TROUBLE.
YOU'RE ON THE VERGE OF FLUNK-ING!
That's a lot of F's!
YES. THE TEACHER SAID I'D HAVE TO DO A RETAKE IF I DON'T GET AT LEAST 40 POINTS ON MY NEXT MATH TEST.
PING!
I KNOW, RAKU DEAR-EST!
WON'T YOU COME OVER AFTER SCHOOL TODAY AND TUTOR ME?
SKWEE
WHAT?!
!!!
EXCUSE ME!
WHY DON'T YOU STUDY ON YOUR OWN?!
Leggo, will ya?
YOU'RE UNDER-ESTIMATING HOW BAD I AM AT STUDYING!
I'LL NEVER IMPROVE MY GRADES WITHOUT GUIDANCE!
You say that so proud-ly...
FINE.
WHY DON'T I HELP YOU THEN?
I'M RANKED FIFTH IN OUR GRADE, AFTER ALL.
HA HA! I JUST LOVE YOUR SENSE OF HUMOR!
YOU'RE CLEARLY NOT THE TYPE WHO'S GOOD AT TEACHING OTHERS!

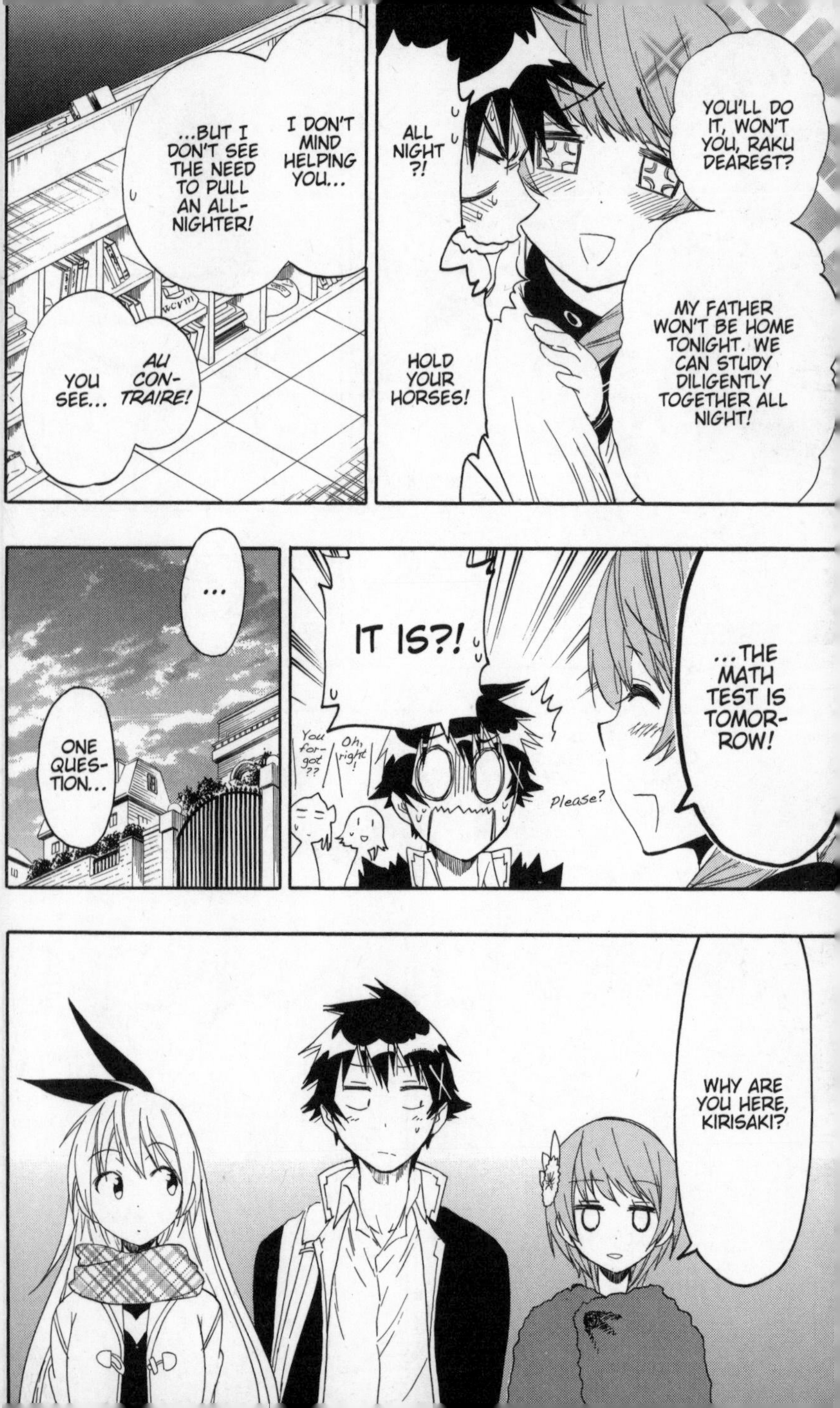
YOU'LL DO IT, WON'T YOU, RAKU DEAREST?
MY FATHER WON'T BE HOME TONIGHT. WE CAN STUDY DILIGENTLY TOGETHER ALL NIGHT!
ALL NIGHT ?!
HOLD YOUR HORSES!
I DON'T MIND HELPING YOU...
...BUT I DON'T SEE THE NEED TO PULL AN ALL-NIGHTER!
AU CONTRAIRE!
YOU SEE...
...THE MATH TEST IS TOMORROW!
Please?
IT IS?!
Oh, right!
You forgot??
...
ONE QUESTION...
WHY ARE YOU HERE, KIRISAKI?

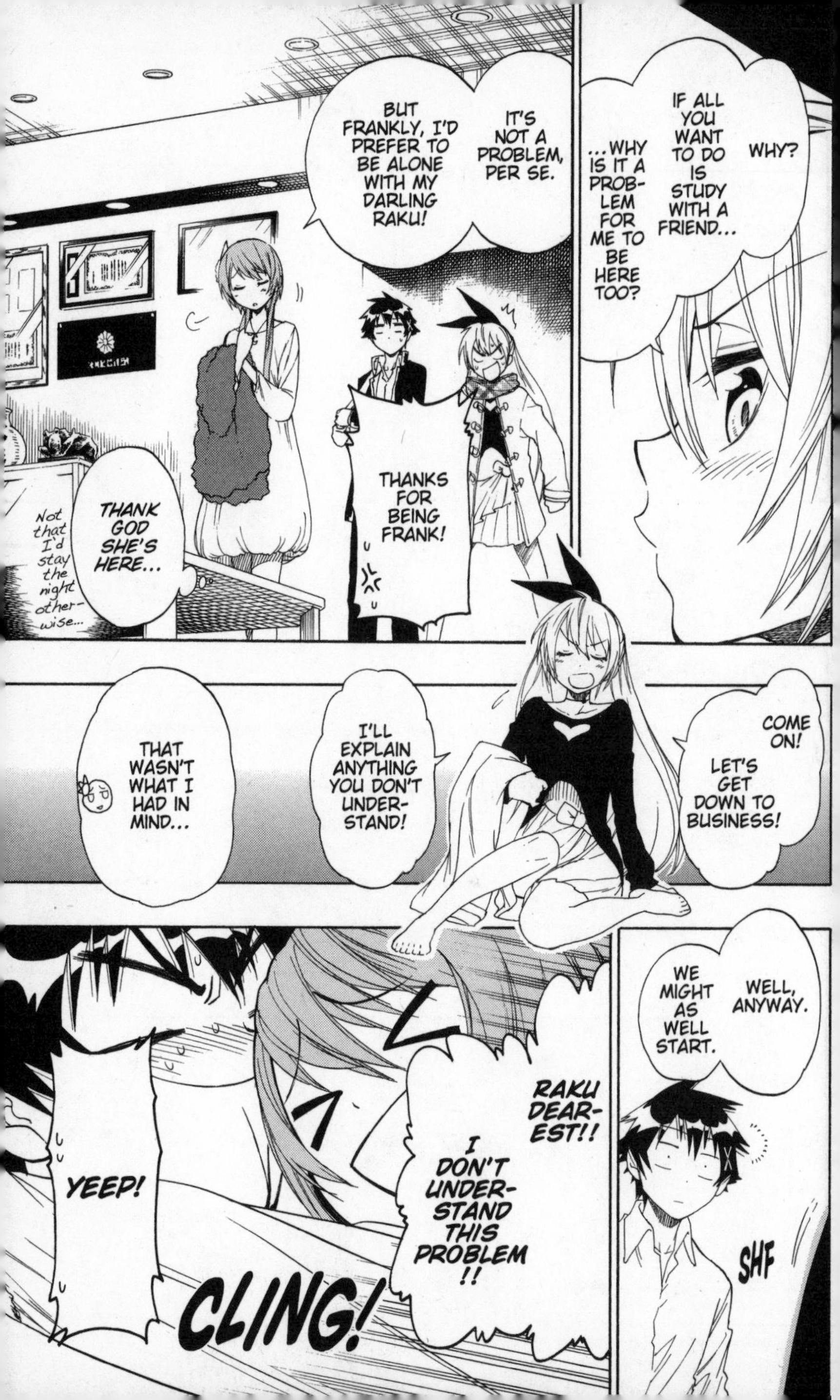
WHY?
IF ALL YOU WANT TO DO IS STUDY WITH A FRIEND...
...WHY IS IT A PROBLEM FOR ME TO BE HERE TOO?
IT'S NOT A PROBLEM, PER SE.
BUT FRANKLY, I'D PREFER TO BE ALONE WITH MY DARLING RAKU!
THANKS FOR BEING FRANK!
THANK GOD SHE'S HERE...
Not that I'd stay the night otherwise...
COME ON!
LET'S GET DOWN TO BUSINESS!
I'LL EXPLAIN ANYTHING YOU DON'T UNDERSTAND!
THAT WASN'T WHAT I HAD IN MIND...
WELL, ANYWAY.
WE MIGHT AS WELL START.
SHF
RAKU DEAREST!!
I DON'T UNDERSTAND THIS PROBLEM!!
CLING!
YEEP!

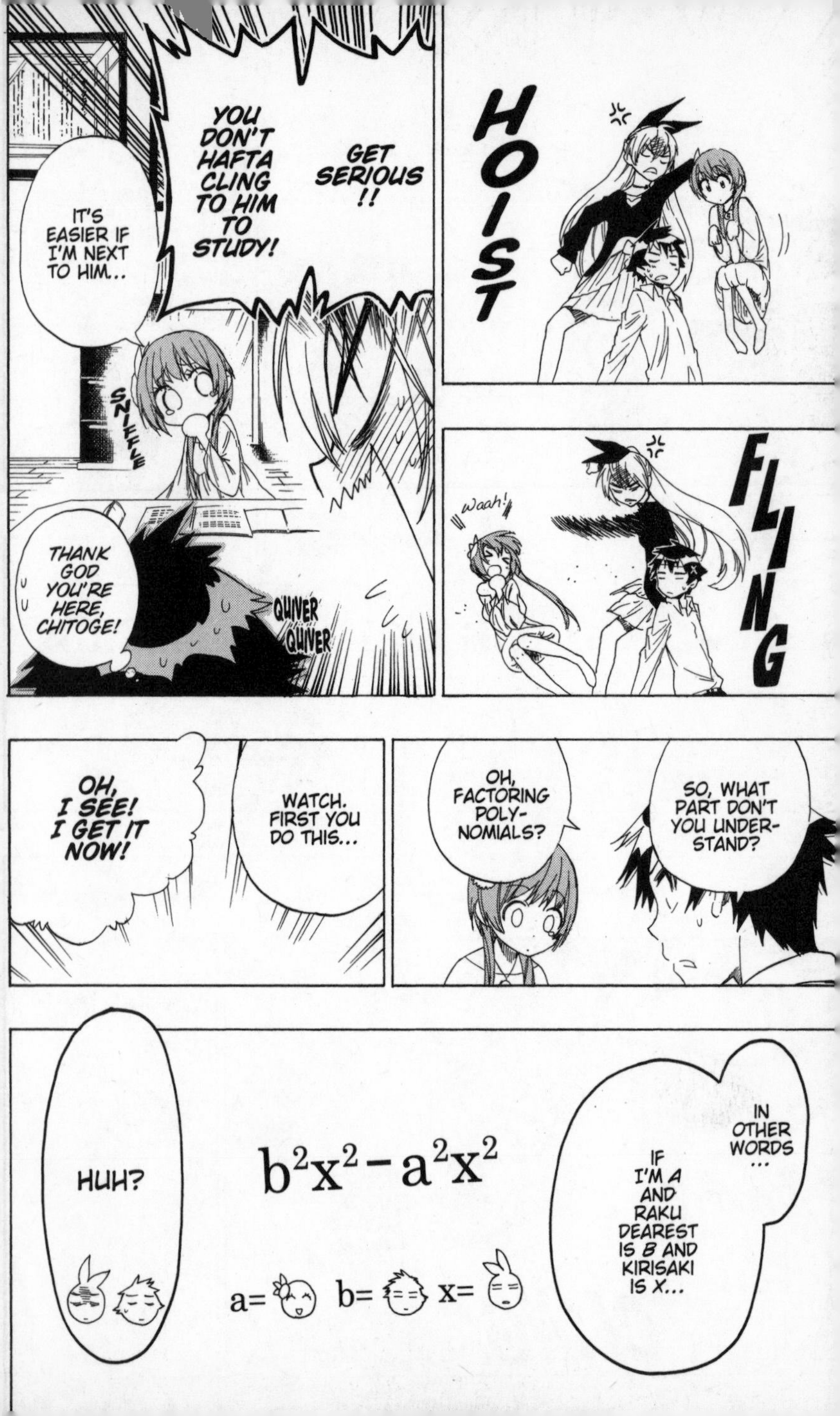
HOIST
FLING
Waah!
GET SERIOUS!!
YOU DON'T HAFTA CLING TO HIM TO STUDY!
IT'S EASIER IF I'M NEXT TO HIM...
SNIFFLE
THANK GOD YOU'RE HERE, CHITOGE!
QUIVER QUIVER
SO, WHAT PART DON'T YOU UNDER-STAND?
OH, FACTORING POLY-NOMIALS?
WATCH. FIRST YOU DO THIS...
OH, I SEE! I GET IT NOW!
IN OTHER WORDS...
IF I'M A AND RAKU DEAREST IS B AND KIRISAKI IS X...
$b^2x^2-a^2x^2$
a= b= x=
HUH?

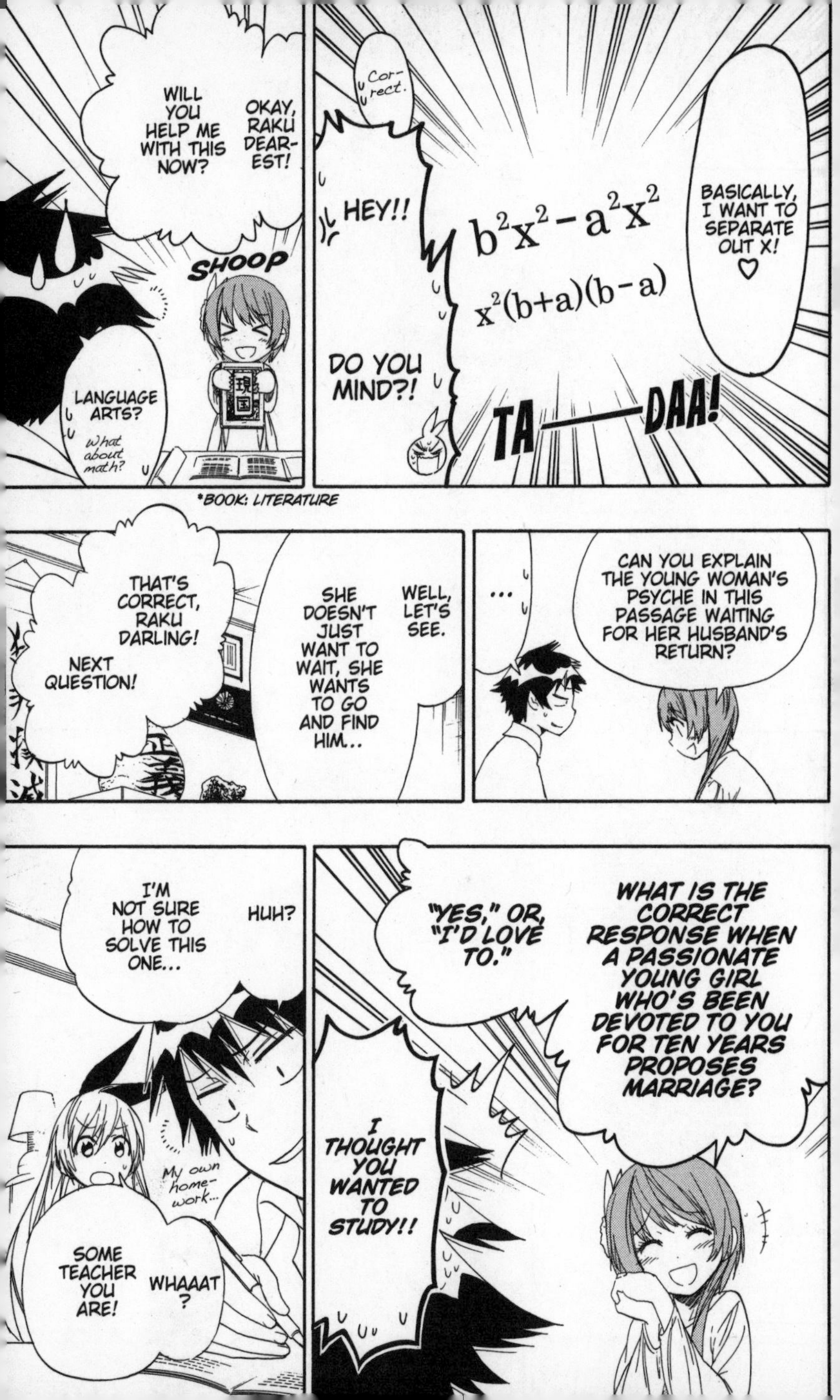
BASICALLY, I WANT TO SEPARATE OUT X! ♡
$b^2x^2 - a^2x^2$
$x^2(b+a)(b-a)$
Cor-rect.
HEY!!
DO YOU MIND?!
TA——DAA!
OKAY, RAKU DEAREST!
WILL YOU HELP ME WITH THIS NOW?
SHOOP
現国
LANGUAGE ARTS?
What about math?
*BOOK: LITERATURE
CAN YOU EXPLAIN THE YOUNG WOMAN'S PSYCHE IN THIS PASSAGE WAITING FOR HER HUSBAND'S RETURN?
...
WELL, LET'S SEE.
SHE DOESN'T JUST WANT TO WAIT, SHE WANTS TO GO AND FIND HIM...
THAT'S CORRECT, RAKU DARLING!
NEXT QUESTION!
WHAT IS THE CORRECT RESPONSE WHEN A PASSIONATE YOUNG GIRL WHO'S BEEN DEVOTED TO YOU FOR TEN YEARS PROPOSES MARRIAGE?
"YES," OR, "I'D LOVE TO."
I THOUGHT YOU WANTED TO STUDY!!
HUH?
I'M NOT SURE HOW TO SOLVE THIS ONE...
My own home-work...
WHAAAT?
SOME TEACHER YOU ARE!

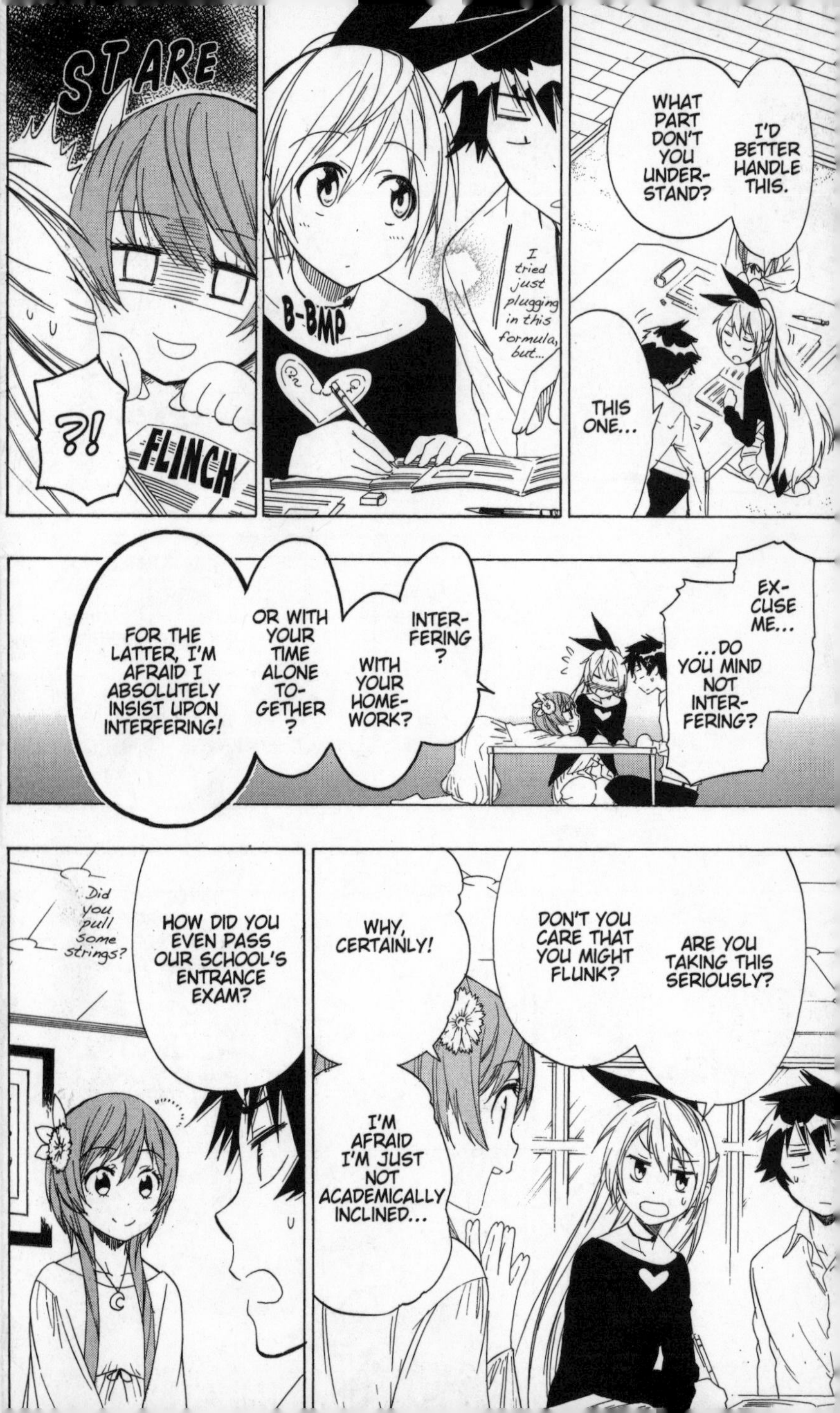
I'D BETTER HANDLE THIS.
WHAT PART DON'T YOU UNDERSTAND?
THIS ONE...
I tried just plugging in this formula, but...
B-BMP
STARE
?!
FLINCH
EXCUSE ME...
...DO YOU MIND NOT INTERFERING?
INTERFERING?
WITH YOUR HOMEWORK?
OR WITH YOUR TIME ALONE TOGETHER?
FOR THE LATTER, I'M AFRAID I ABSOLUTELY INSIST UPON INTERFERING!
ARE YOU TAKING THIS SERIOUSLY?
DON'T YOU CARE THAT YOU MIGHT FLUNK?
WHY, CERTAINLY!
I'M AFRAID I'M JUST NOT ACADEMICALLY INCLINED...
HOW DID YOU EVEN PASS OUR SCHOOL'S ENTRANCE EXAM?
Did you pull some strings?

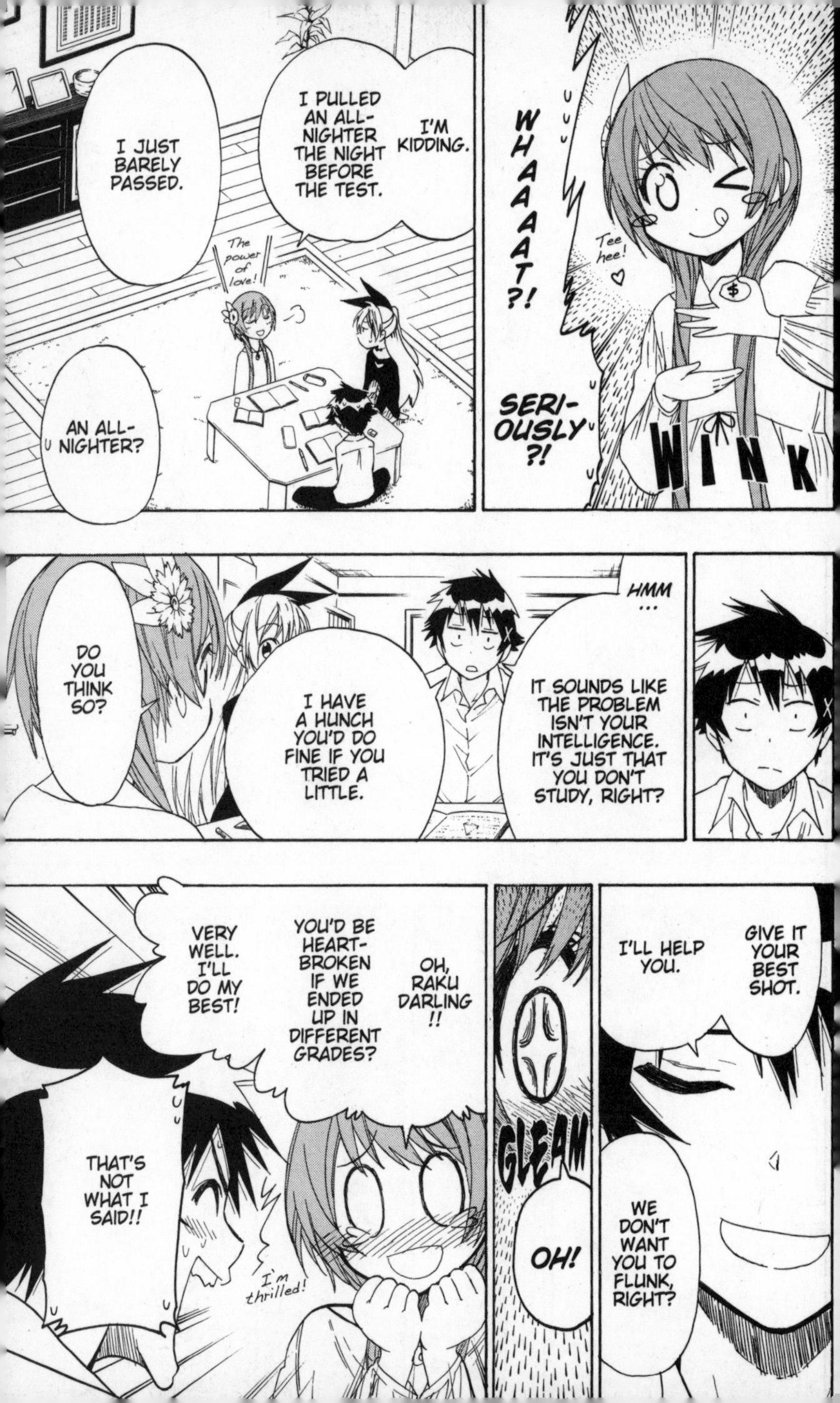
WHAAAAAT?!
SERIOUSLY?!
Tee hee!
WINK
I'M KIDDING.
I PULLED AN ALL-NIGHTER THE NIGHT BEFORE THE TEST.
I JUST BARELY PASSED.
The power of love!
AN ALL-NIGHTER?
HMM...
IT SOUNDS LIKE THE PROBLEM ISN'T YOUR INTELLIGENCE. IT'S JUST THAT YOU DON'T STUDY, RIGHT?
I HAVE A HUNCH YOU'D DO FINE IF YOU TRIED A LITTLE.
DO YOU THINK SO?
GIVE IT YOUR BEST SHOT.
I'LL HELP YOU.
WE DON'T WANT YOU TO FLUNK, RIGHT?
GLEAM
OH!
OH, RAKU DARLING!!
YOU'D BE HEARTBROKEN IF WE ENDED UP IN DIFFERENT GRADES?
VERY WELL. I'LL DO MY BEST!
I'm thrilled!
THAT'S NOT WHAT I SAID!!

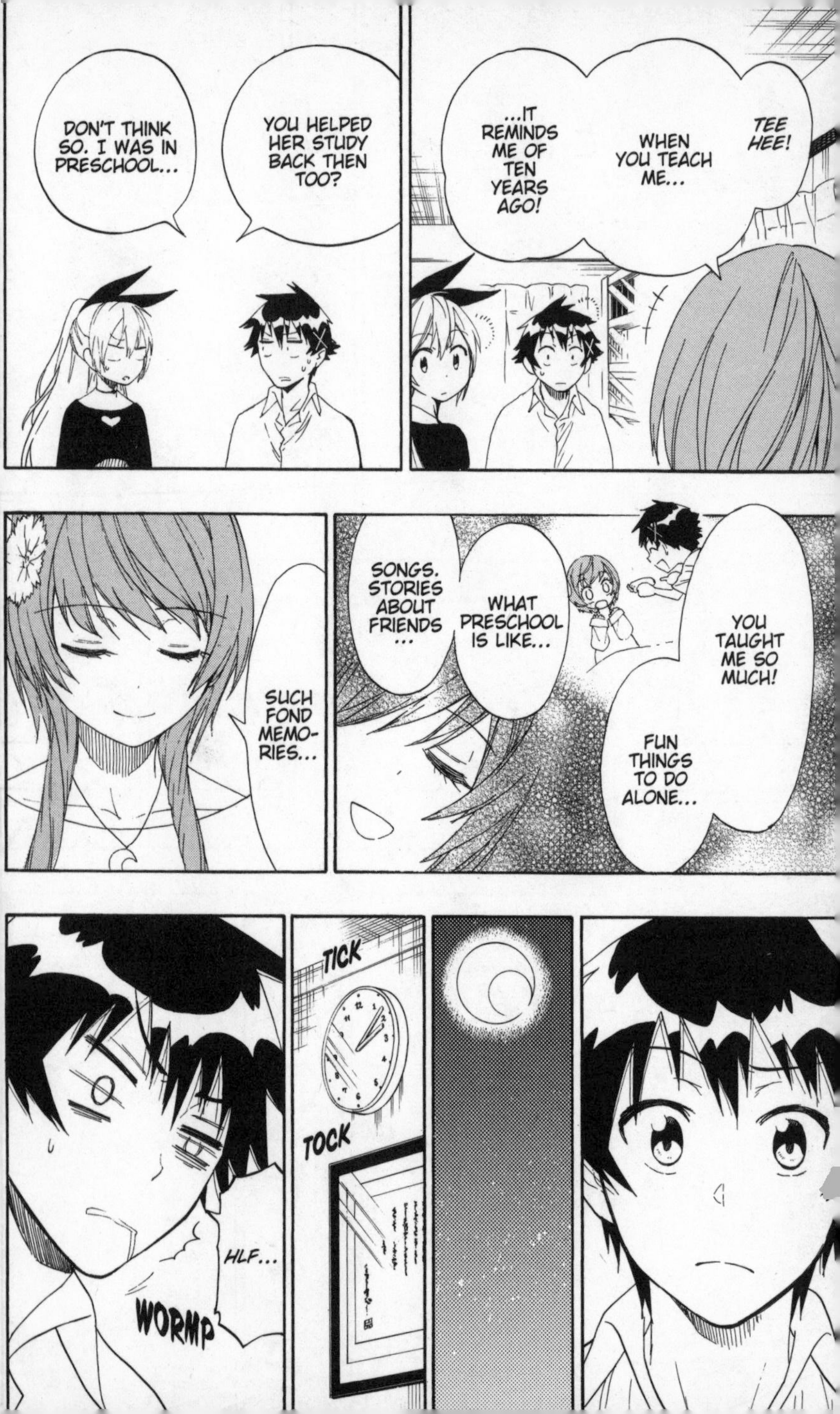
TEE HEE!
WHEN YOU TEACH ME...
...IT REMINDS ME OF TEN YEARS AGO!
YOU HELPED HER STUDY BACK THEN TOO?
DON'T THINK SO. I WAS IN PRESCHOOL...
YOU TAUGHT ME SO MUCH!
FUN THINGS TO DO ALONE...
WHAT PRESCHOOL IS LIKE...
SONGS. STORIES ABOUT FRIENDS...
SUCH FOND MEMORIES...
TICK
TOCK
HLF...
WORMP

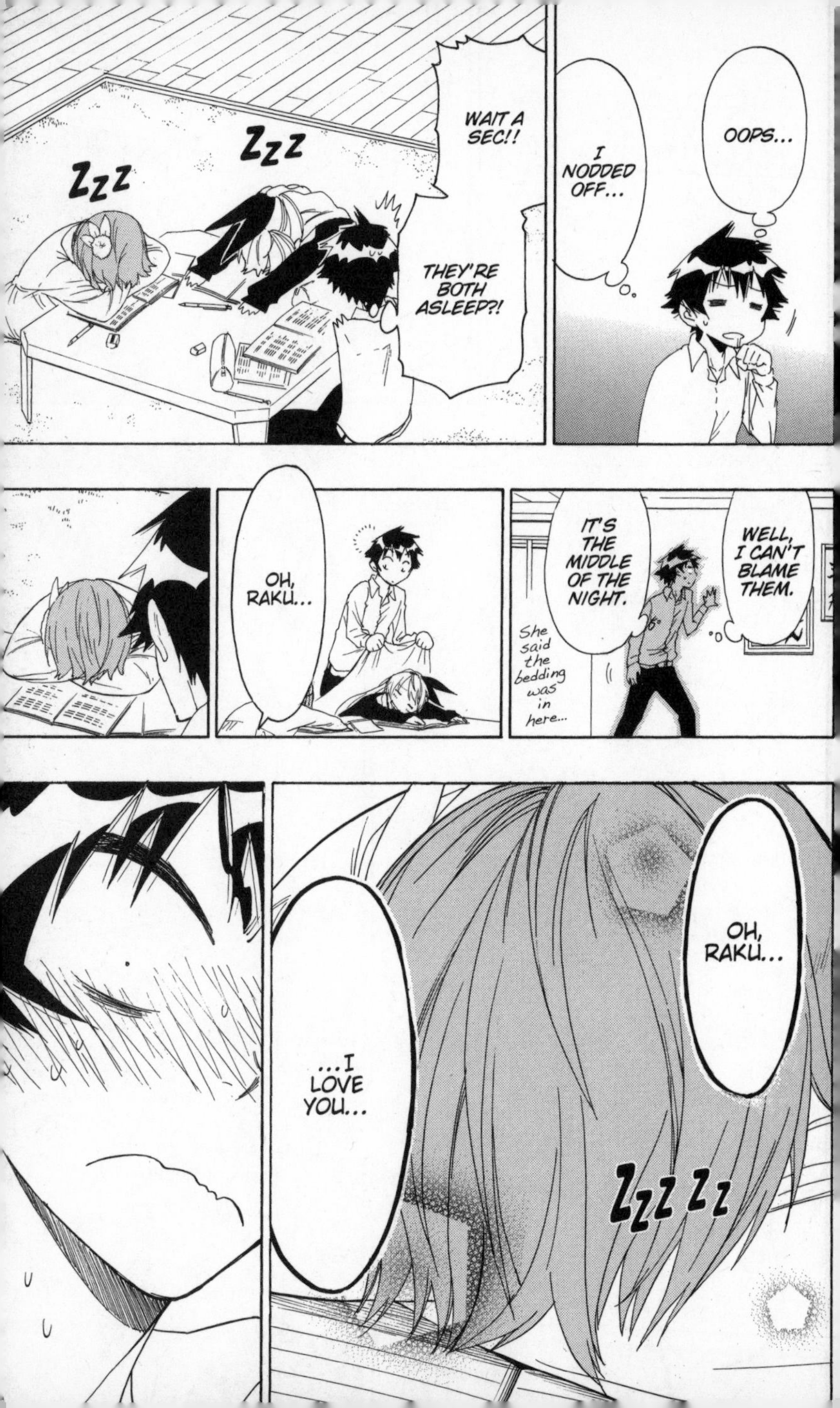
OOPS...
I NODDED OFF...
WAIT A SEC!!
THEY'RE BOTH ASLEEP?!
ZZZ
ZZZ
WELL, I CAN'T BLAME THEM.
IT'S THE MIDDLE OF THE NIGHT.
She said the bedding was in here...
OH, RAKU...
OH, RAKU...
...I LOVE YOU...
ZZZ ZZ

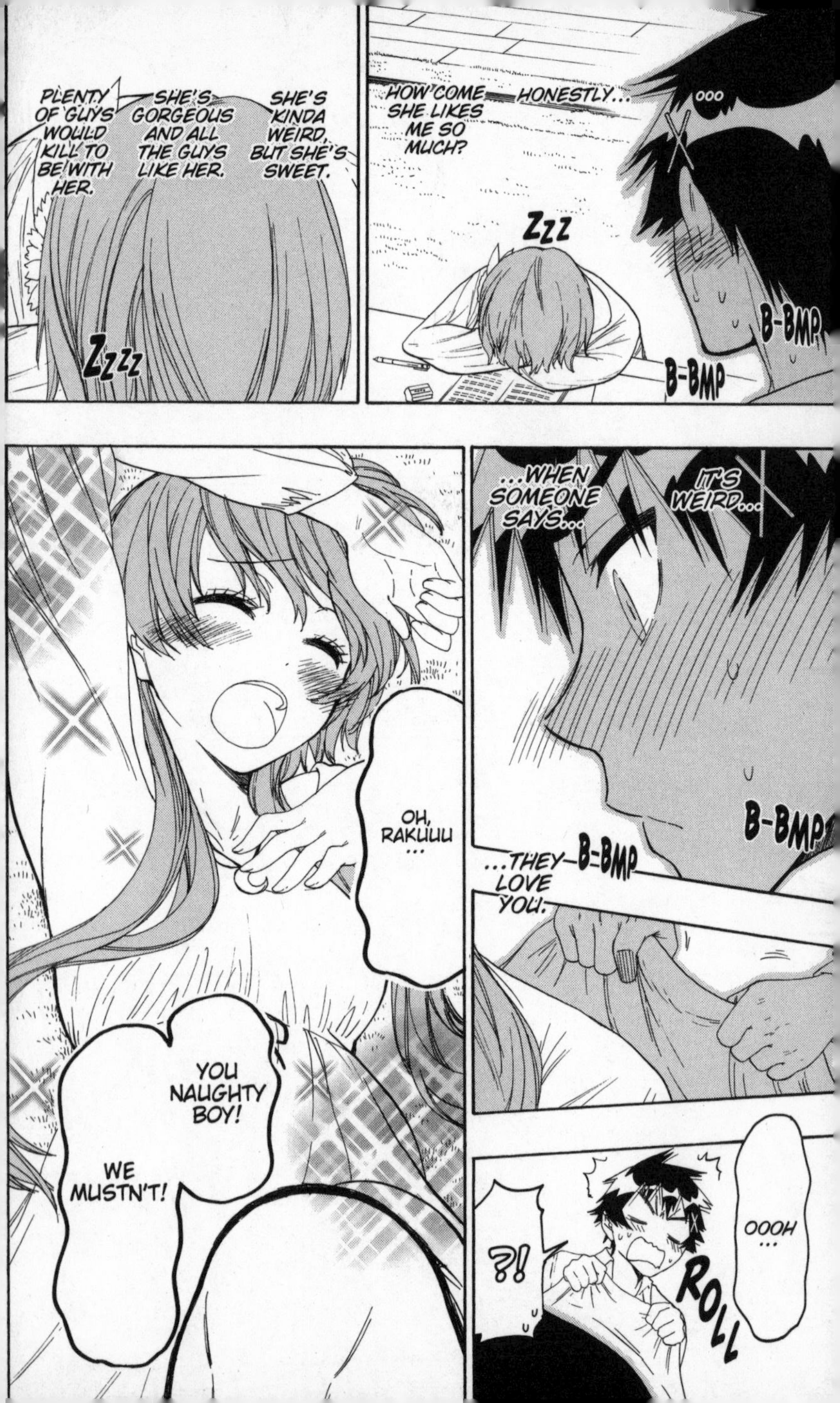
ooo
HONESTLY...
HOW COME SHE LIKES ME SO MUCH?
ZZZ
B-BMP
B-BMP
SHE'S KINDA WEIRD, BUT SHE'S SWEET.
SHE'S GORGEOUS AND ALL THE GUYS LIKE HER.
PLENTY OF GUYS WOULD KILL TO BE WITH HER.
ZZZZ
IT'S WEIRD...
...WHEN SOMEONE SAYS...
B-BMP
B-BMP
...THEY LOVE YOU.
OOOH...
ROLL
?!
OH, RAKUUU...
YOU NAUGHTY BOY!
WE MUSTN'T!

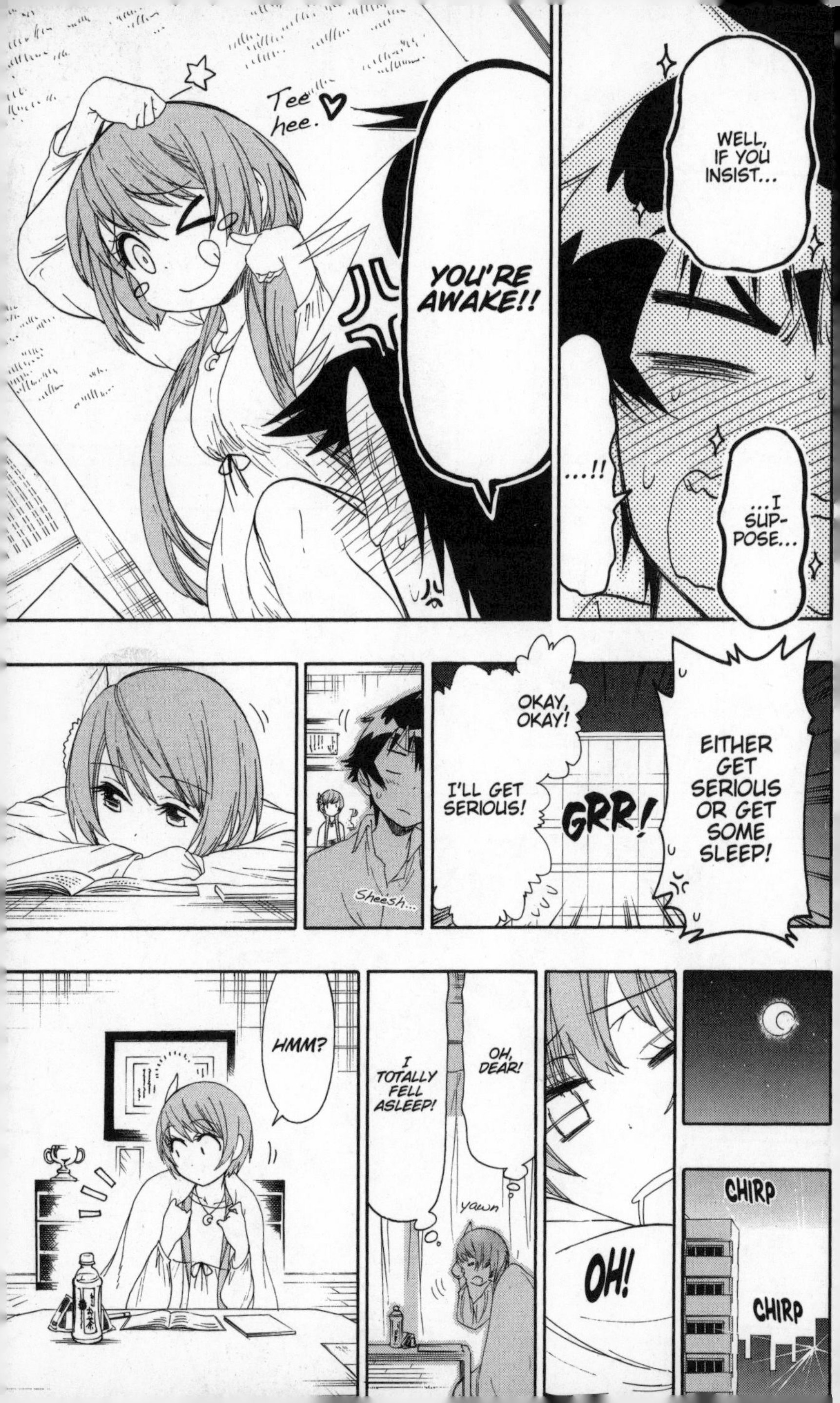
WELL, IF YOU INSIST...
...!!
...I SUP-POSE...
YOU'RE AWAKE!!
Tee hee.
EITHER GET SERIOUS OR GET SOME SLEEP!
GRR!
OKAY, OKAY!
I'LL GET SERIOUS!
Sheesh...
CHIRP
CHIRP
OH!
OH, DEAR!
I TOTALLY FELL ASLEEP!
yawn
HMM?

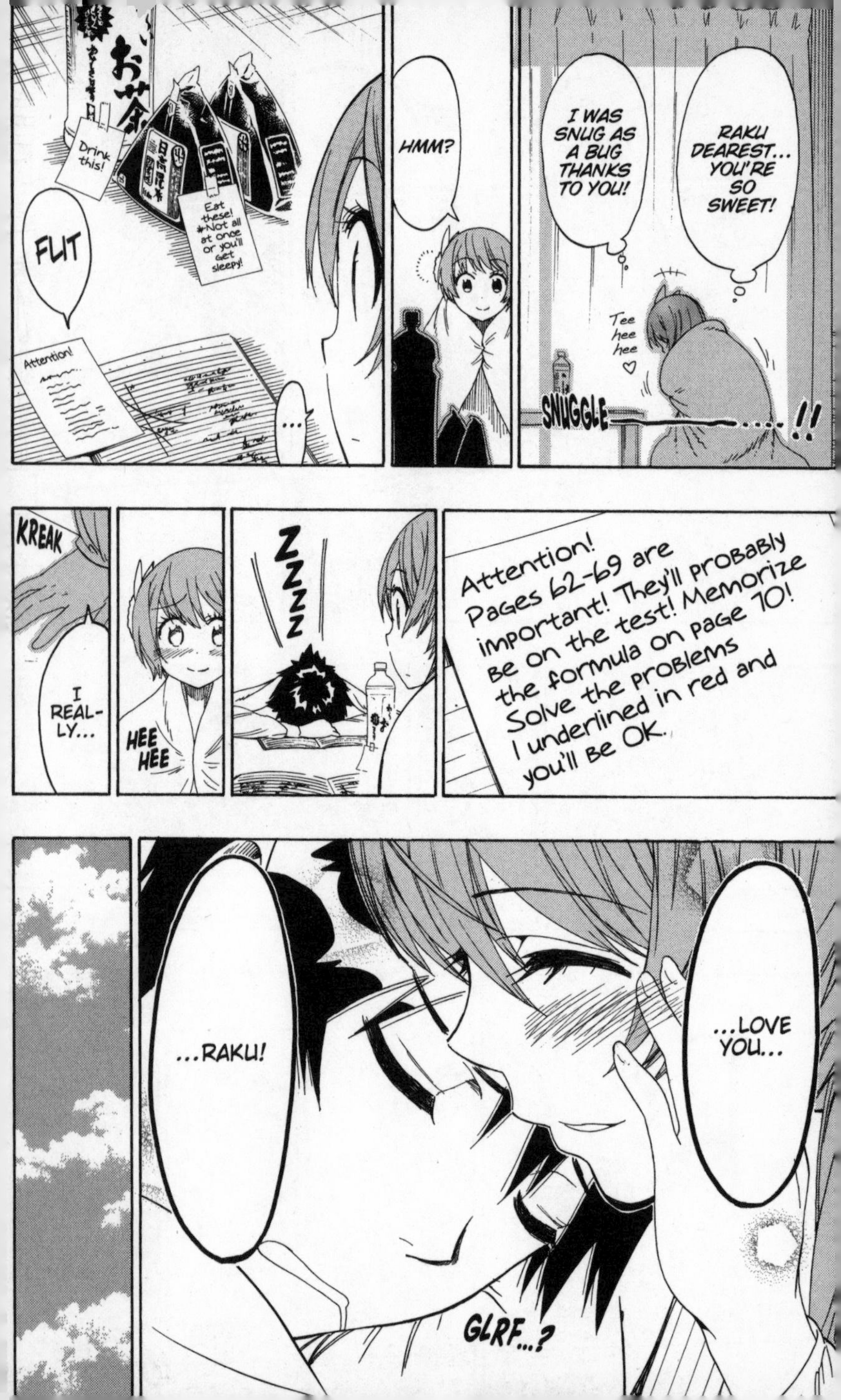
RAKU DEAREST... YOU'RE SO SWEET!
I WAS SNUG AS A BUG THANKS TO YOU!
Tee hee hee ♥
SNUGGLE.....!!
HMM?
お茶
Drink this!
Eat these! *Not all at once or you'll get sleepy!
FLIT
Attention!
...
Attention! Pages 62-69 are important! They'll probably be on the test! Memorize the formula on page 70! Solve the problems I underlined in red and you'll be OK.
ZZZZ
HEE HEE
KREAK
I REALLY...
...LOVE YOU...
...RAKU!
GLRF...?

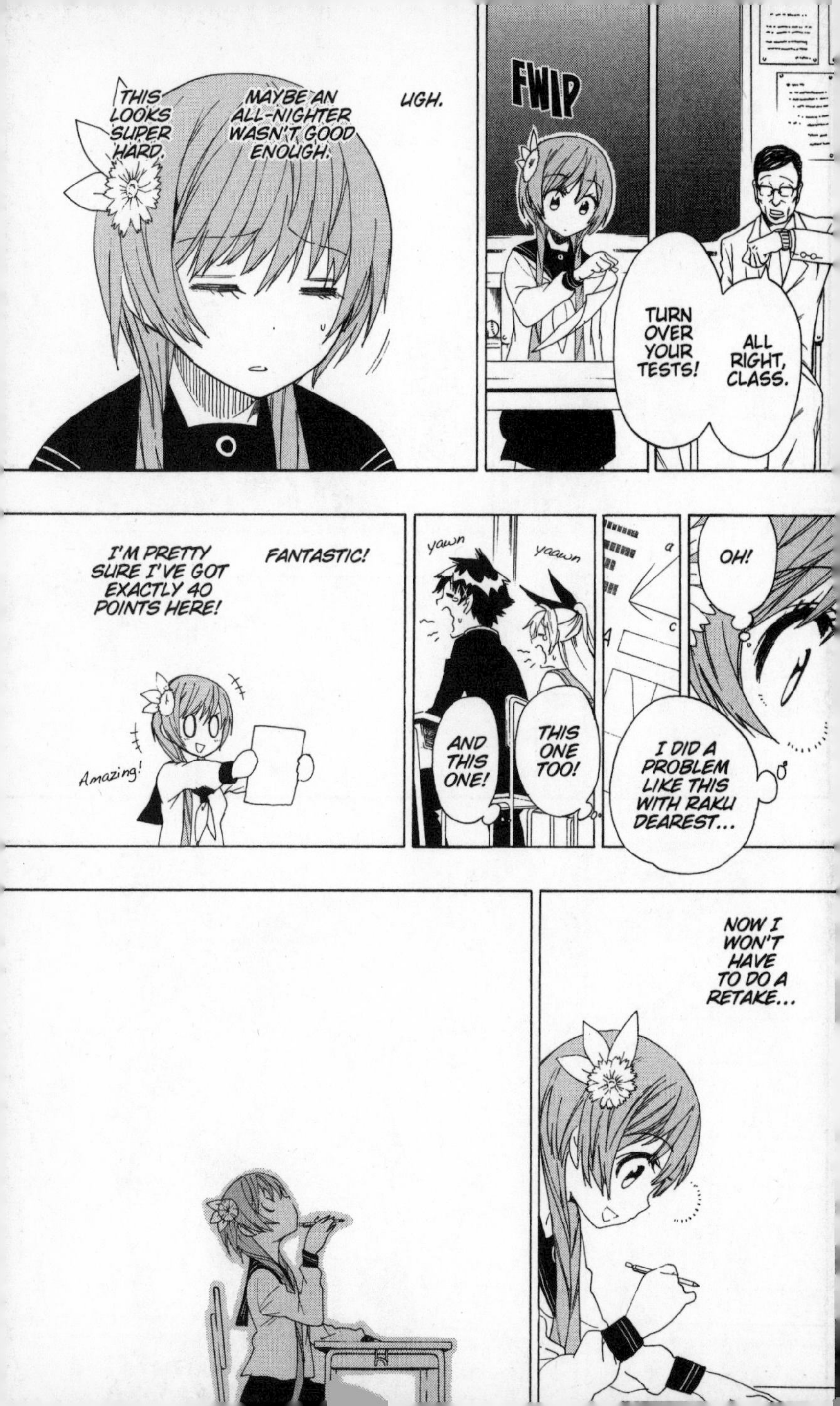
ALL RIGHT, CLASS.
TURN OVER YOUR TESTS!
FWIP
UGH.
MAYBE AN ALL-NIGHTER WASN'T GOOD ENOUGH.
THIS LOOKS SUPER HARD.
OH!
I DID A PROBLEM LIKE THIS WITH RAKU DEAREST...
yaawn
yawn
THIS ONE TOO!
AND THIS ONE!
FANTASTIC!
I'M PRETTY SURE I'VE GOT EXACTLY 40 POINTS HERE!
Amazing!
NOW I WON'T HAVE TO DO A RETAKE...

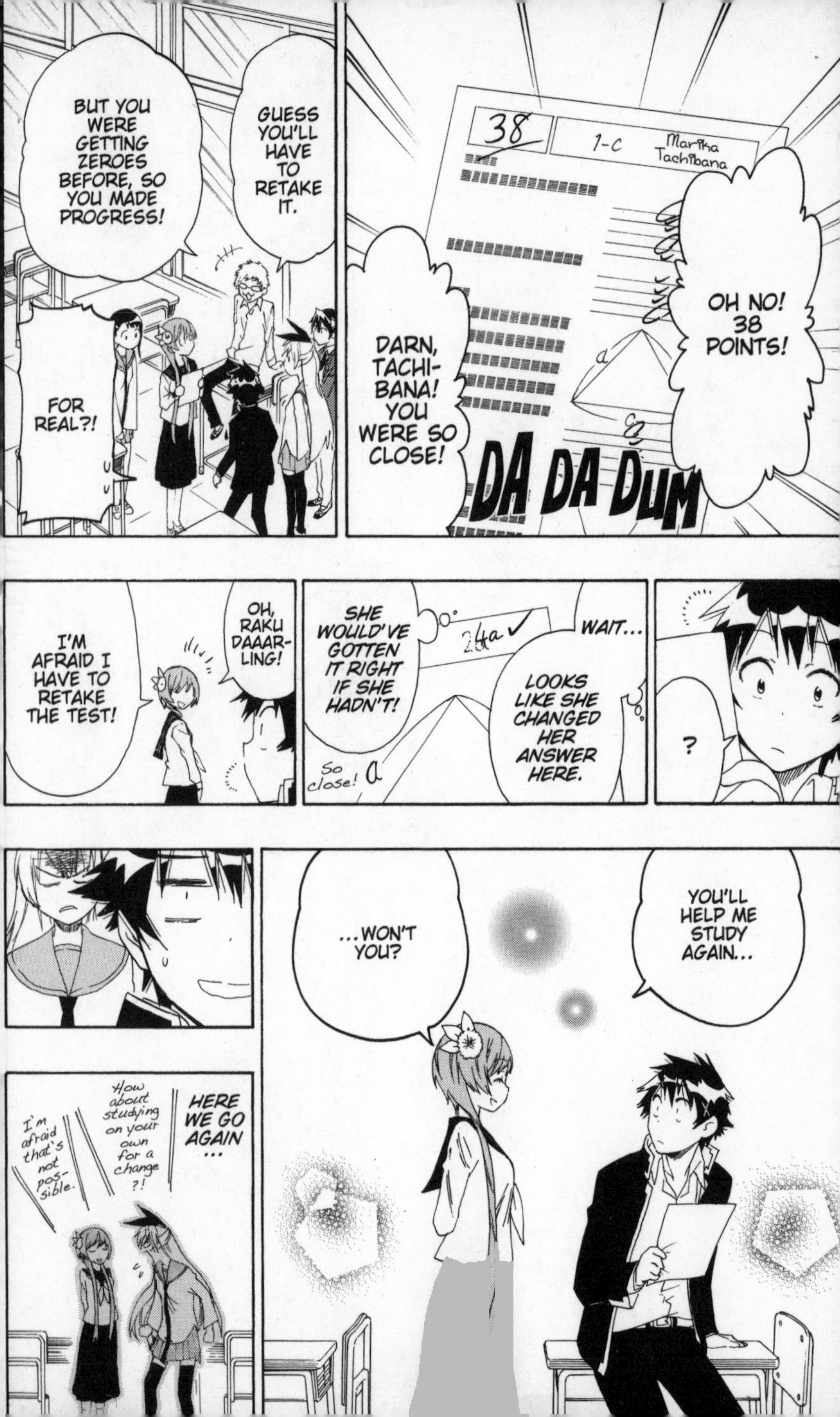
38
1-C
Marika Tachibana
OH NO! 38 POINTS!
DARN, TACHIBANA! YOU WERE SO CLOSE!
DA DA DUM
GUESS YOU'LL HAVE TO RETAKE IT.
BUT YOU WERE GETTING ZEROES BEFORE, SO YOU MADE PROGRESS!
FOR REAL?!
?
WAIT...
LOOKS LIKE SHE CHANGED HER ANSWER HERE.
SHE WOULD'VE GOTTEN IT RIGHT IF SHE HADN'T!
So close!
OH, RAKU DAAARLING!
I'M AFRAID I HAVE TO RETAKE THE TEST!
YOU'LL HELP ME STUDY AGAIN...
...WON'T YOU?
HERE WE GO AGAIN...
How about studying on your own for a change?!
I'm afraid that's not possible.

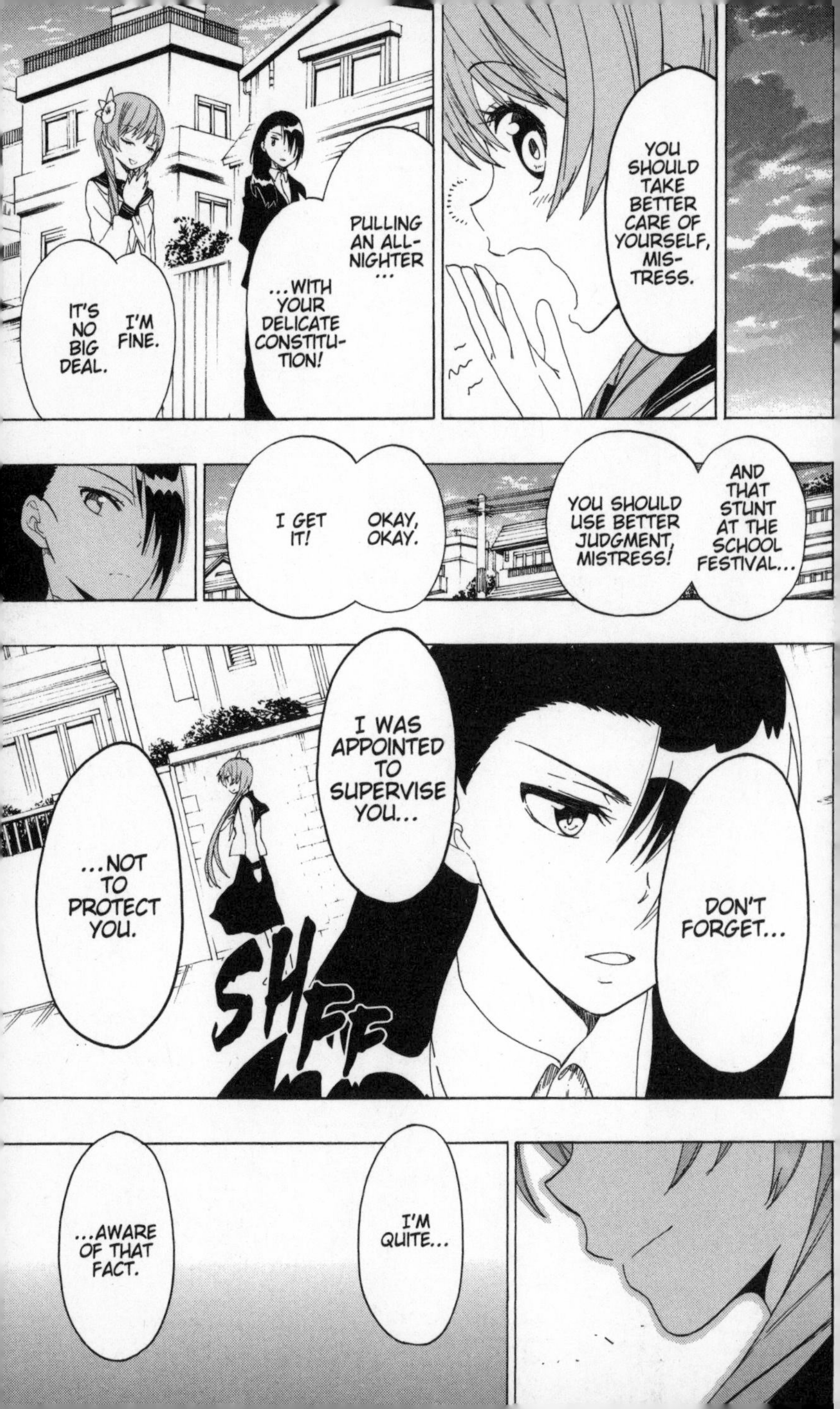
YOU SHOULD TAKE BETTER CARE OF YOURSELF, MISTRESS.
PULLING AN ALL-NIGHTER...
...WITH YOUR DELICATE CONSTITUTION!
I'M FINE.
IT'S NO BIG DEAL.
AND THAT STUNT AT THE SCHOOL FESTIVAL...
YOU SHOULD USE BETTER JUDGMENT, MISTRESS!
OKAY, OKAY.
I GET IT!
DON'T FORGET...
I WAS APPOINTED TO SUPERVISE YOU...
...NOT TO PROTECT YOU.
SHFF
I'M QUITE...
...AWARE OF THAT FACT.

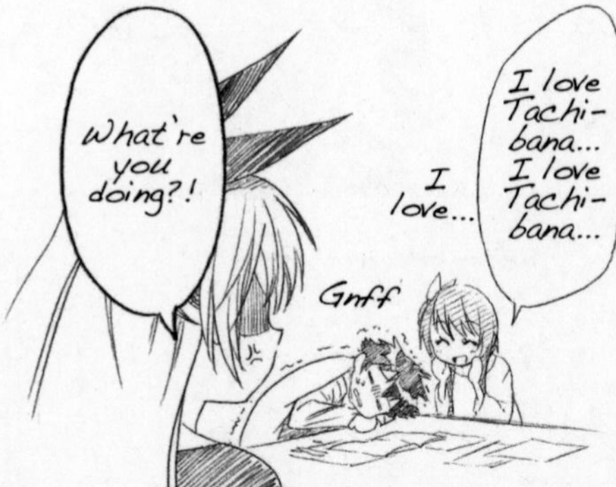
I love Tachi-bana... I love Tachi-bana...
I love...
What're you doing?!
Gnff

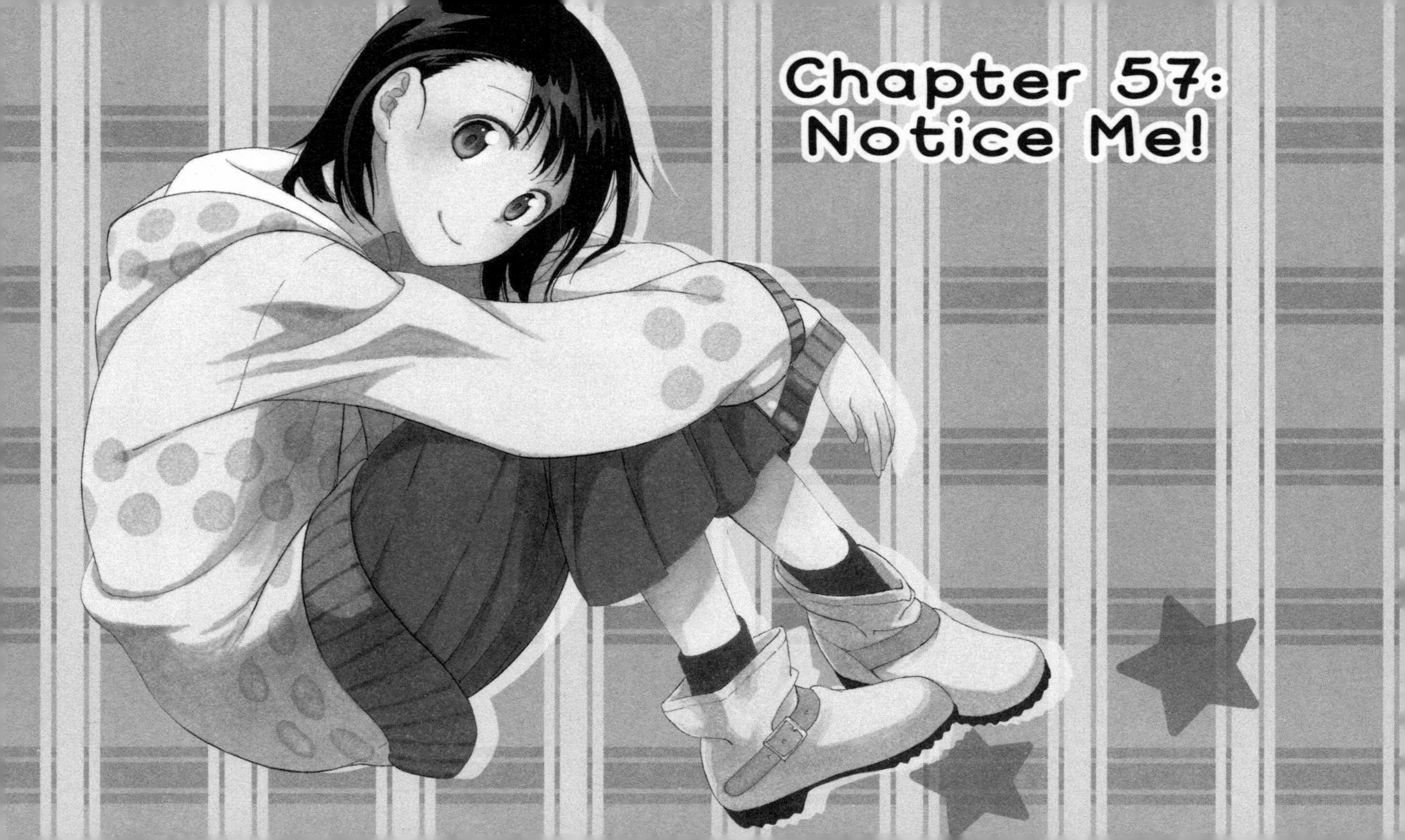
Chapter 57:
Notice Me!

Onodera?!

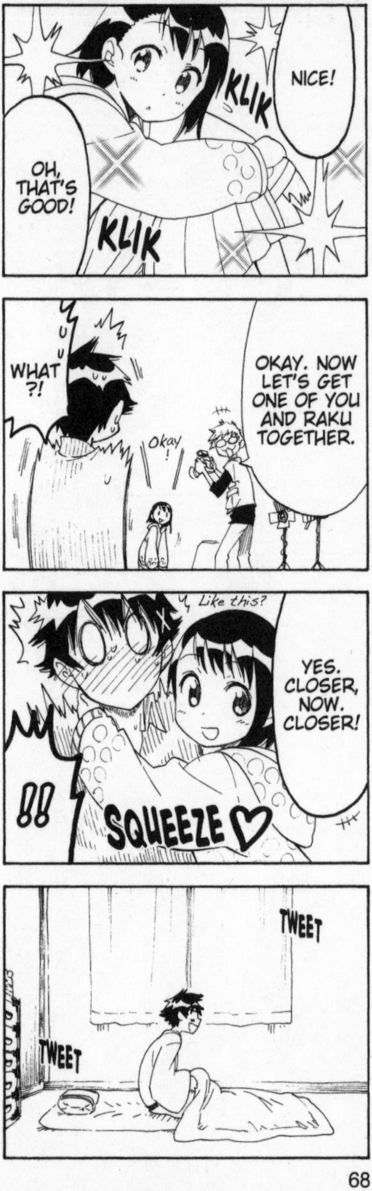
NICE!
KLIK
OH, THAT'S GOOD!
KLIK
OKAY. NOW LET'S GET ONE OF YOU AND RAKU TOGETHER.
Okay!
WHAT?!
Like this?
YES. CLOSER, NOW. CLOSER!
SQUEEZE ♡
!!
TWEET
TWEET

Onodera?!!

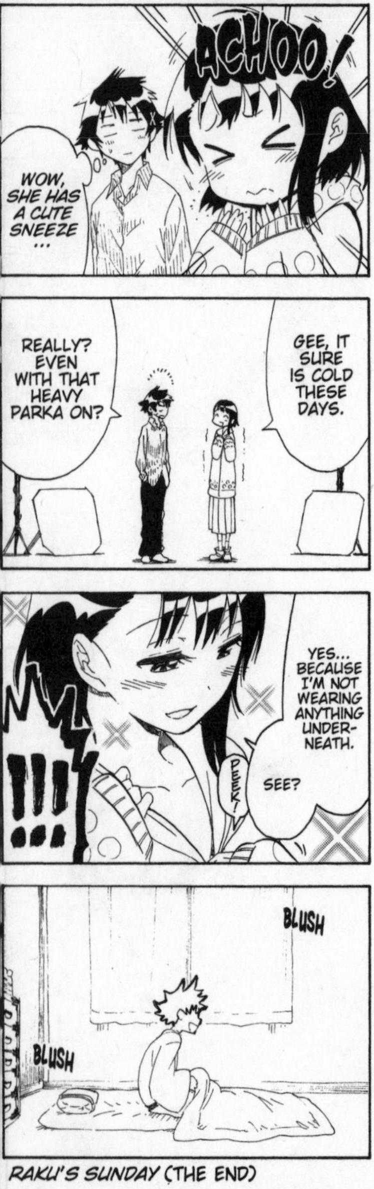
ACHOO!
WOW, SHE HAS A CUTE SNEEZE...
GEE, IT SURE IS COLD THESE DAYS.
REALLY? EVEN WITH THAT HEAVY PARKA ON?
YES... BECAUSE I'M NOT WEARING ANYTHING UNDER-NEATH.
PEEK!
SEE?
!!!
BLUSH
BLUSH

RAKU'S SUNDAY (THE END)

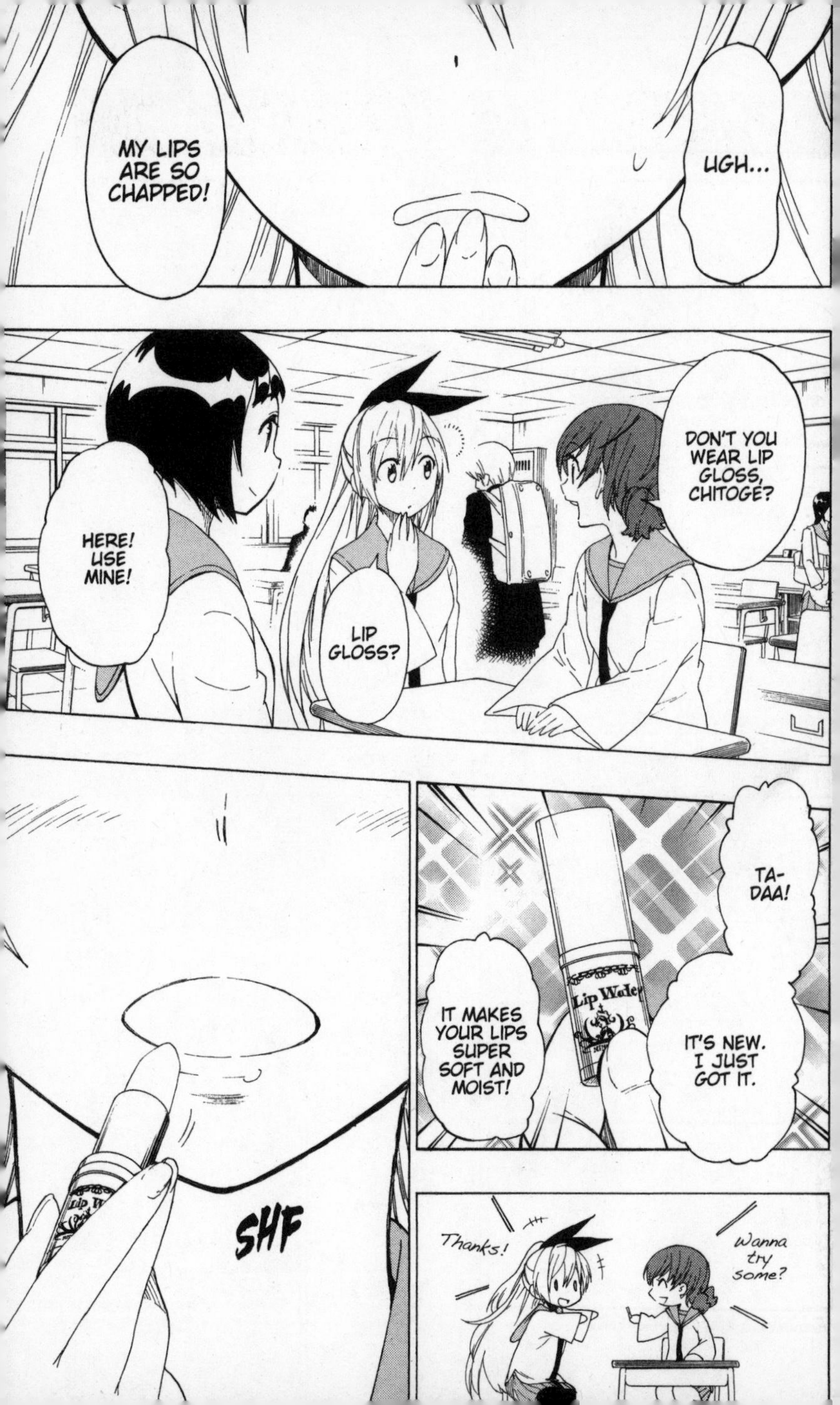
UGH...
MY LIPS ARE SO CHAPPED!
DON'T YOU WEAR LIP GLOSS, CHITOGE?
LIP GLOSS?
HERE! USE MINE!
TA-DAA!
IT'S NEW. I JUST GOT IT.
IT MAKES YOUR LIPS SUPER SOFT AND MOIST!
Wanna try some?
Thanks!
SHF

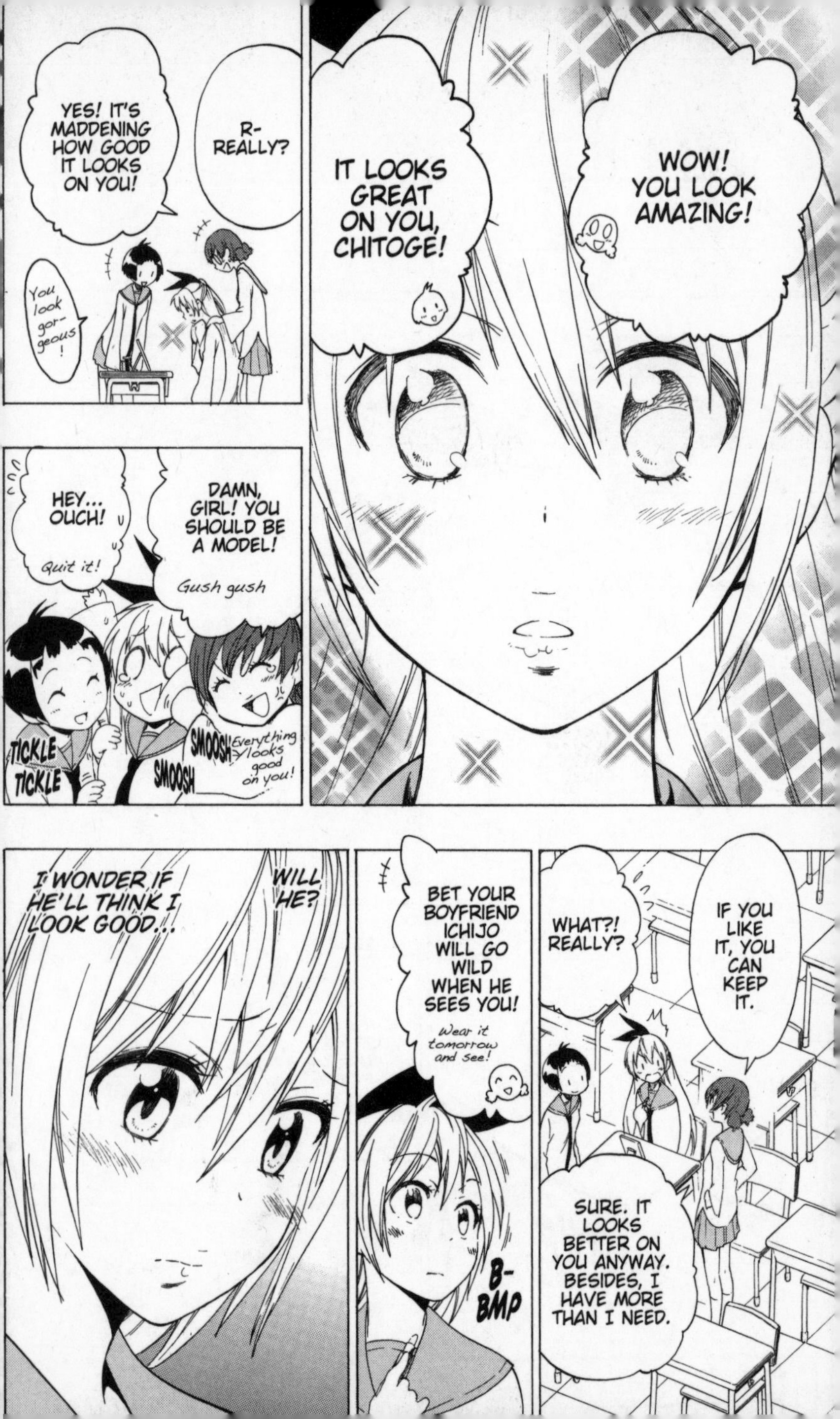
WOW! YOU LOOK AMAZING!
IT LOOKS GREAT ON YOU, CHITOGE!
R- REALLY?
YES! IT'S MADDENING HOW GOOD IT LOOKS ON YOU!
You look gorgeous!
DAMN, GIRL! YOU SHOULD BE A MODEL!
Gush gush
HEY... OUCH!
Quit it!
SMOOSH
SMOOSH
Everything looks good on you!
TICKLE
TICKLE
IF YOU LIKE IT, YOU CAN KEEP IT.
WHAT?! REALLY?
SURE. IT LOOKS BETTER ON YOU ANYWAY. BESIDES, I HAVE MORE THAN I NEED.
BET YOUR BOYFRIEND ICHIJO WILL GO WILD WHEN HE SEES YOU!
Wear it tomorrow and see!
B-BMP
WILL HE?
I WONDER IF HE'LL THINK I LOOK GOOD...

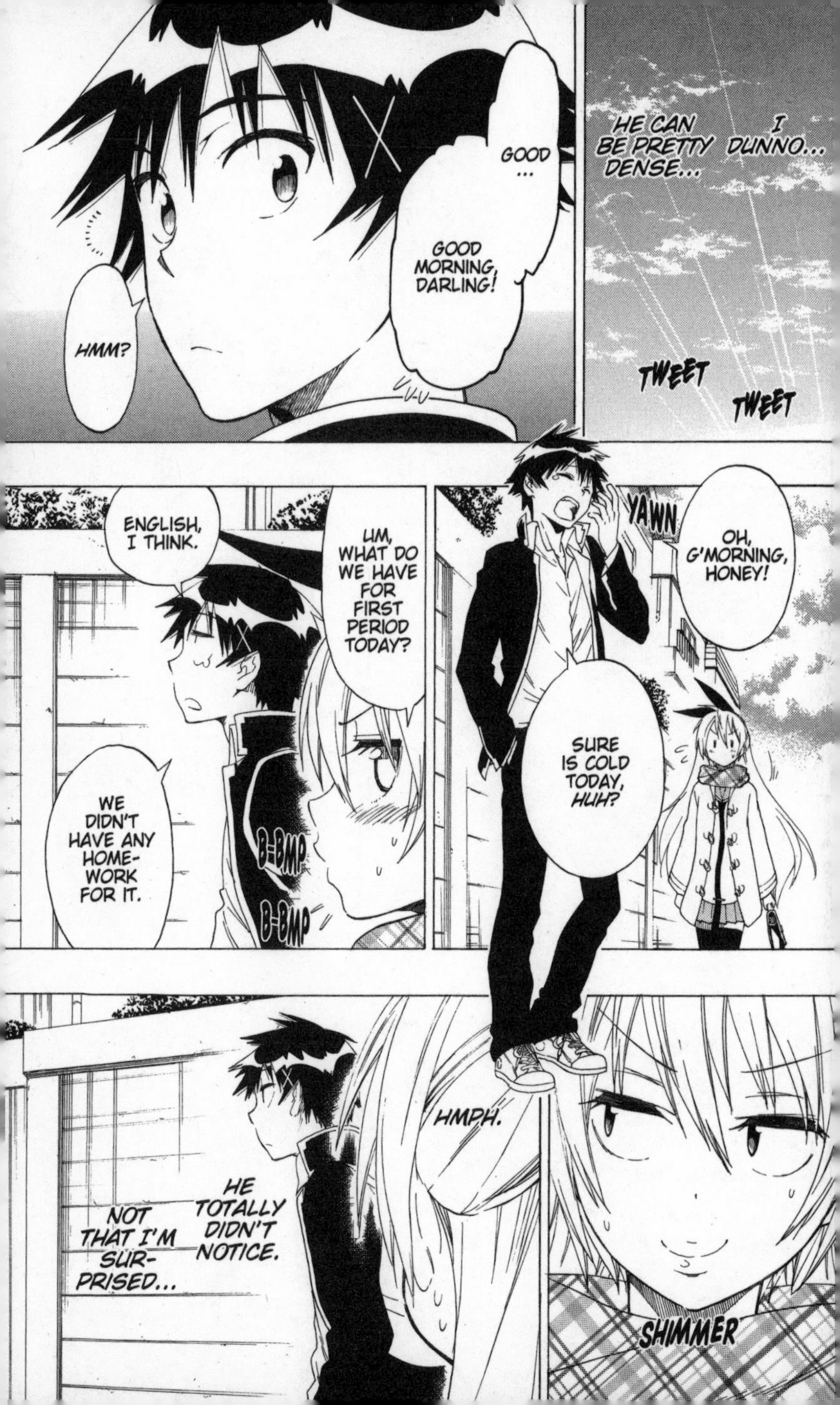
I DUNNO...
HE CAN BE PRETTY DENSE...
TWEET
TWEET
GOOD...
GOOD MORNING, DARLING!
HMM?
YAWN
OH, G'MORNING, HONEY!
SURE IS COLD TODAY, HUH?
UM, WHAT DO WE HAVE FOR FIRST PERIOD TODAY?
ENGLISH, I THINK.
WE DIDN'T HAVE ANY HOME-WORK FOR IT.
B-BMP
B-BMP
HMPH.
HE TOTALLY DIDN'T NOTICE.
NOT THAT I'M SUR-PRISED...
SHIMMER

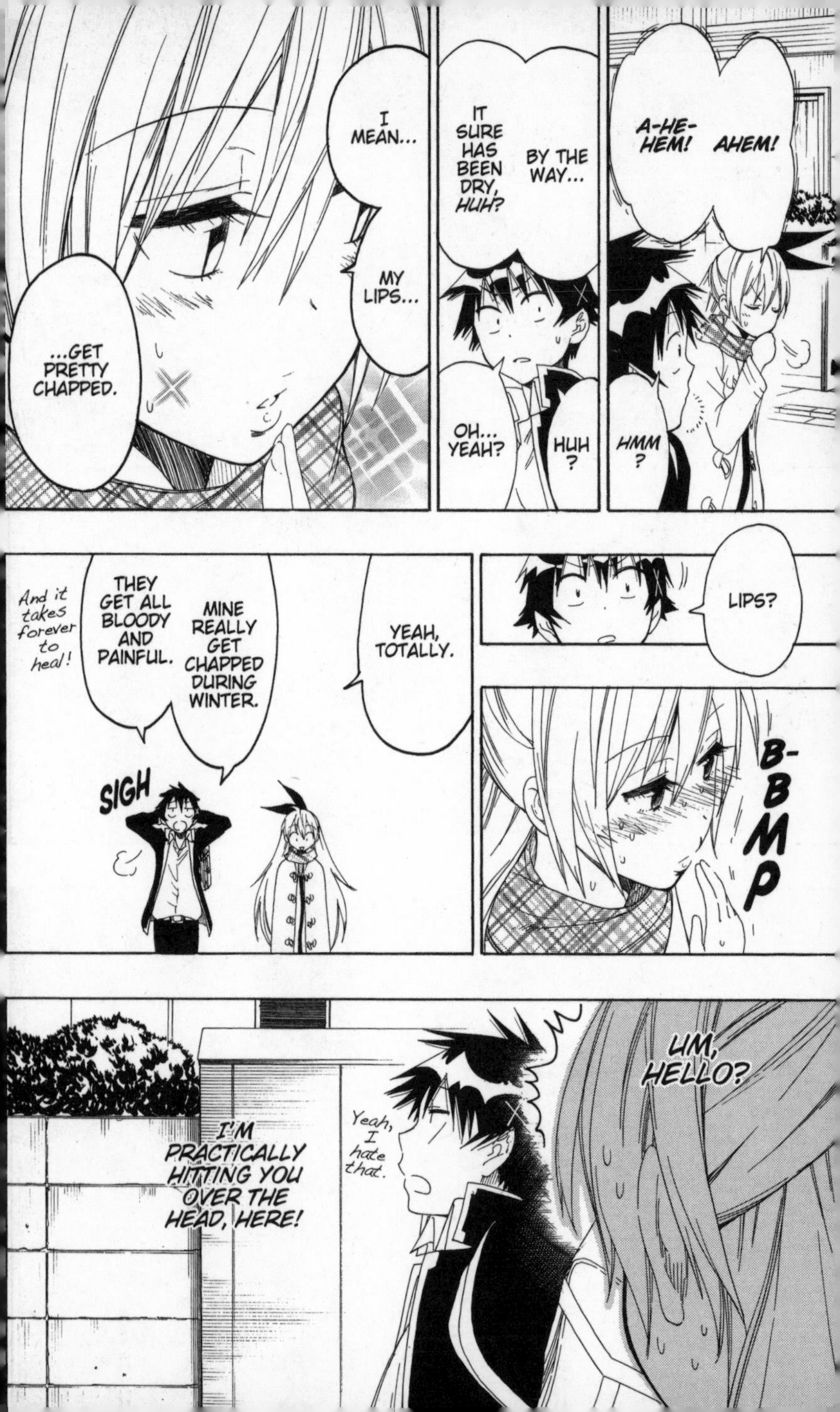
AHEM!
A-HE-HEM!
HMM?
BY THE WAY...
IT SURE HAS BEEN DRY, HUH?
HUH?
OH... YEAH?
I MEAN...
MY LIPS...
...GET PRETTY CHAPPED.
LIPS?
B-BBMP
YEAH, TOTALLY.
MINE REALLY GET CHAPPED DURING WINTER.
THEY GET ALL BLOODY AND PAINFUL.
And it takes forever to heal!
SIGH
UM, HELLO?
Yeah, I hate that.
I'M PRACTICALLY HITTING YOU OVER THE HEAD, HERE!

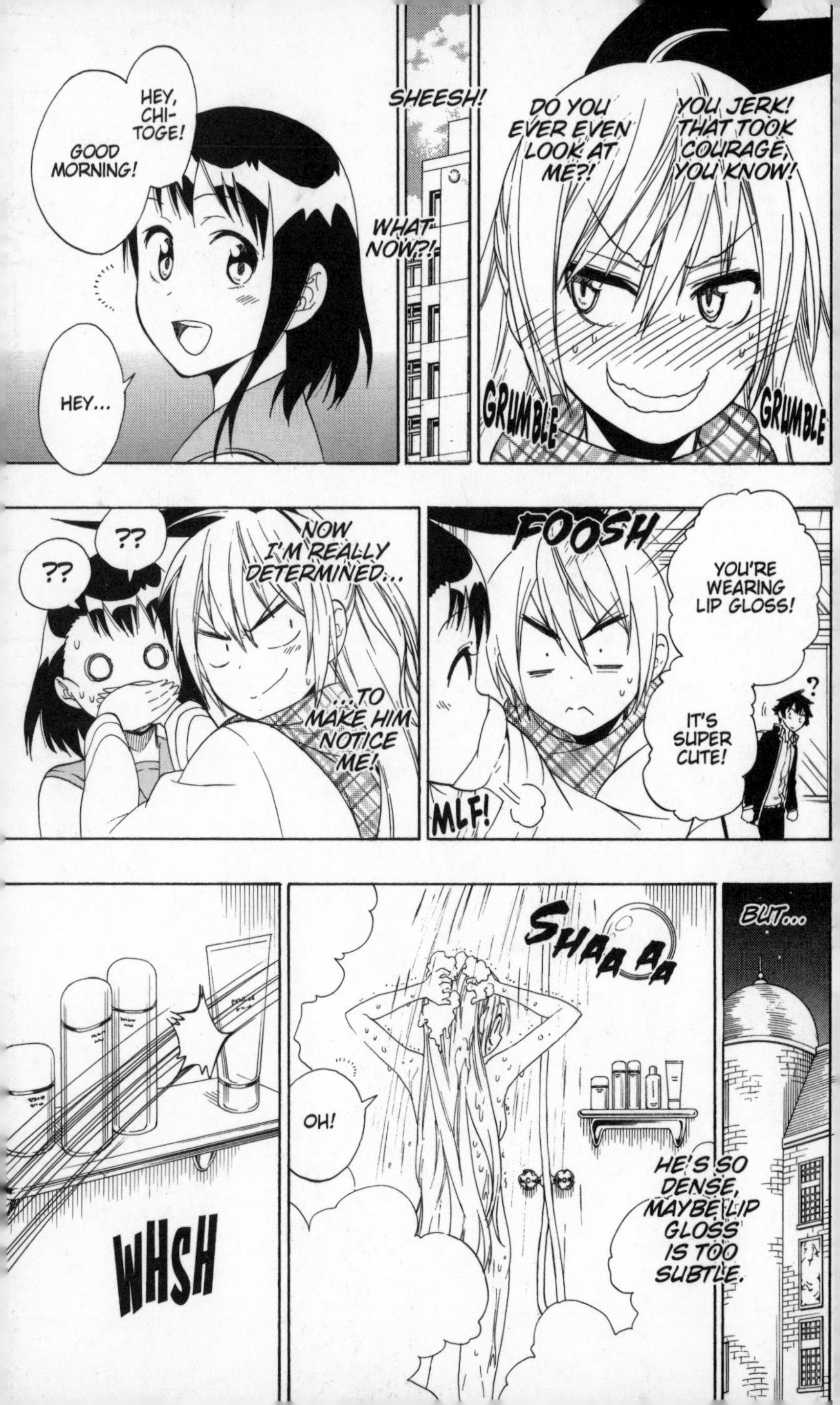
YOU JERK! THAT TOOK COURAGE, YOU KNOW!
DO YOU EVER EVEN LOOK AT ME?!
GRUMBLE
GRUMBLE
SHEESH!
WHAT NOW?!
HEY, CHI-TOGE!
GOOD MORNING!
HEY...
FOOSH
YOU'RE WEARING LIP GLOSS!
IT'S SUPER CUTE!
MLF!
??
??
NOW I'M REALLY DETERMINED...
...TO MAKE HIM NOTICE ME!
BUT...
HE'S SO DENSE, MAYBE LIP GLOSS IS TOO SUBTLE.
SHAAAA
OH!
WHSH

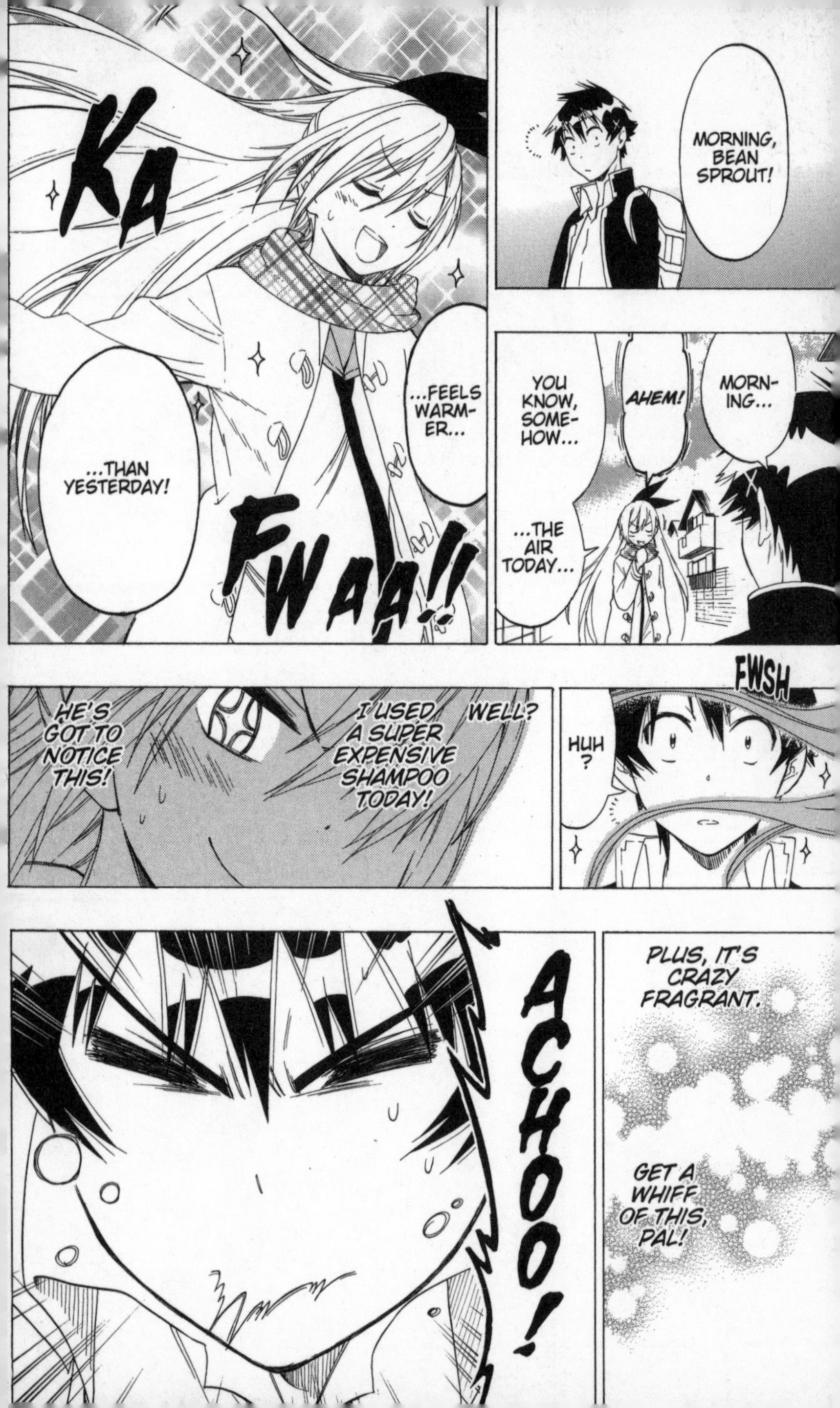
MORNING, BEAN SPROUT!
MORNING...
AHEM!
YOU KNOW, SOMEHOW...
...THE AIR TODAY...
KA
...FEELS WARMER...
...THAN YESTERDAY!
FWAA!!
FWSH
HUH?
WELL?
I USED A SUPER EXPENSIVE SHAMPOO TODAY!
HE'S GOT TO NOTICE THIS!
PLUS, IT'S CRAZY FRAGRANT.
GET A WHIFF OF THIS, PAL!
ACHOO!

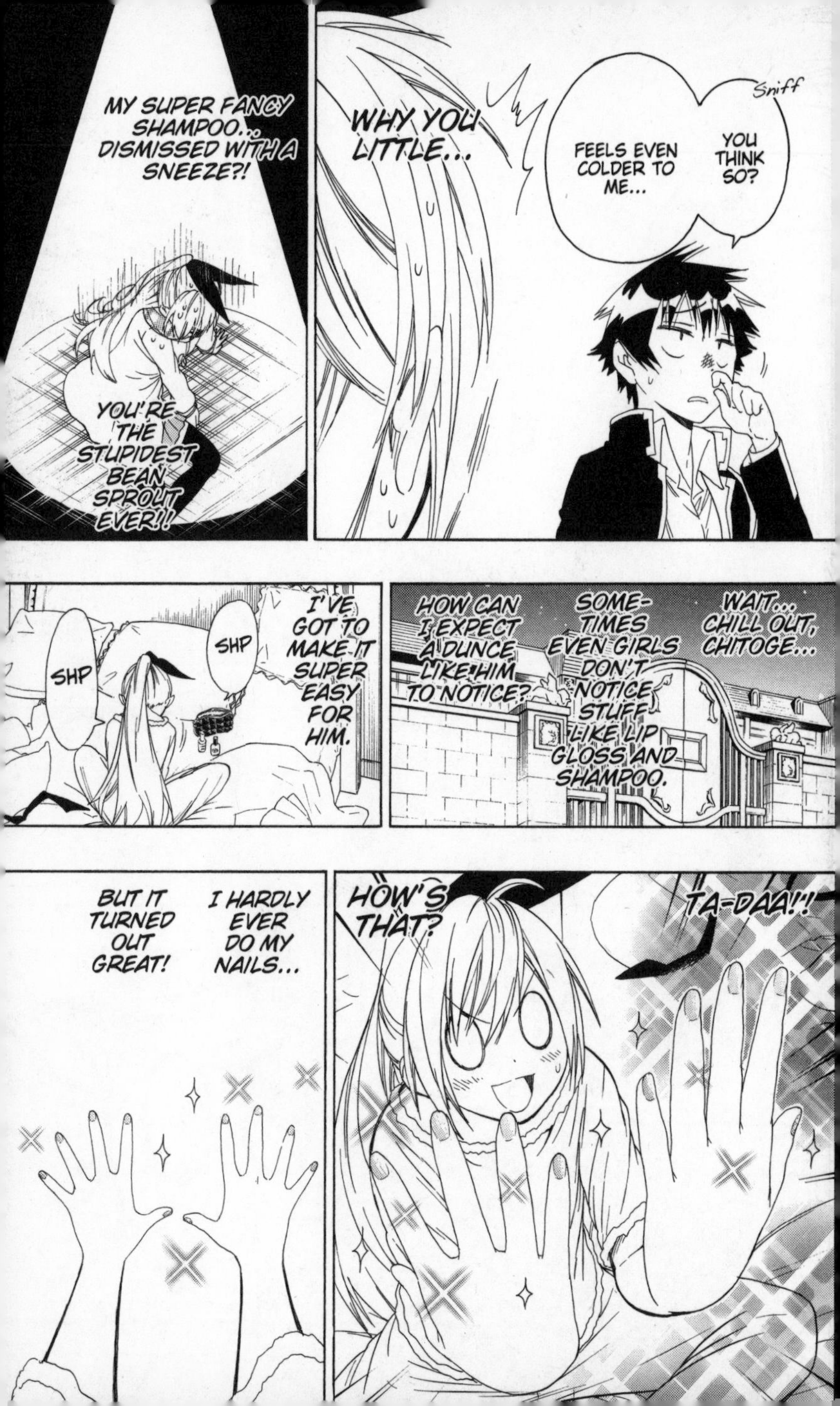
Sniff
YOU THINK SO?
FEELS EVEN COLDER TO ME...
WHY YOU LITTLE...
MY SUPER FANCY SHAMPOO... DISMISSED WITH A SNEEZE?!
YOU'RE THE STUPIDEST BEAN SPROUT EVER!!
WAIT... CHILL OUT, CHITOGE...
SOME-TIMES EVEN GIRLS DON'T NOTICE STUFF LIKE LIP GLOSS AND SHAMPOO.
HOW CAN I EXPECT A DUNCE LIKE HIM TO NOTICE?
I'VE GOT TO MAKE IT SUPER EASY FOR HIM.
SHP
SHP
TA-DAA!!
HOW'S THAT?
I HARDLY EVER DO MY NAILS...
BUT IT TURNED OUT GREAT!

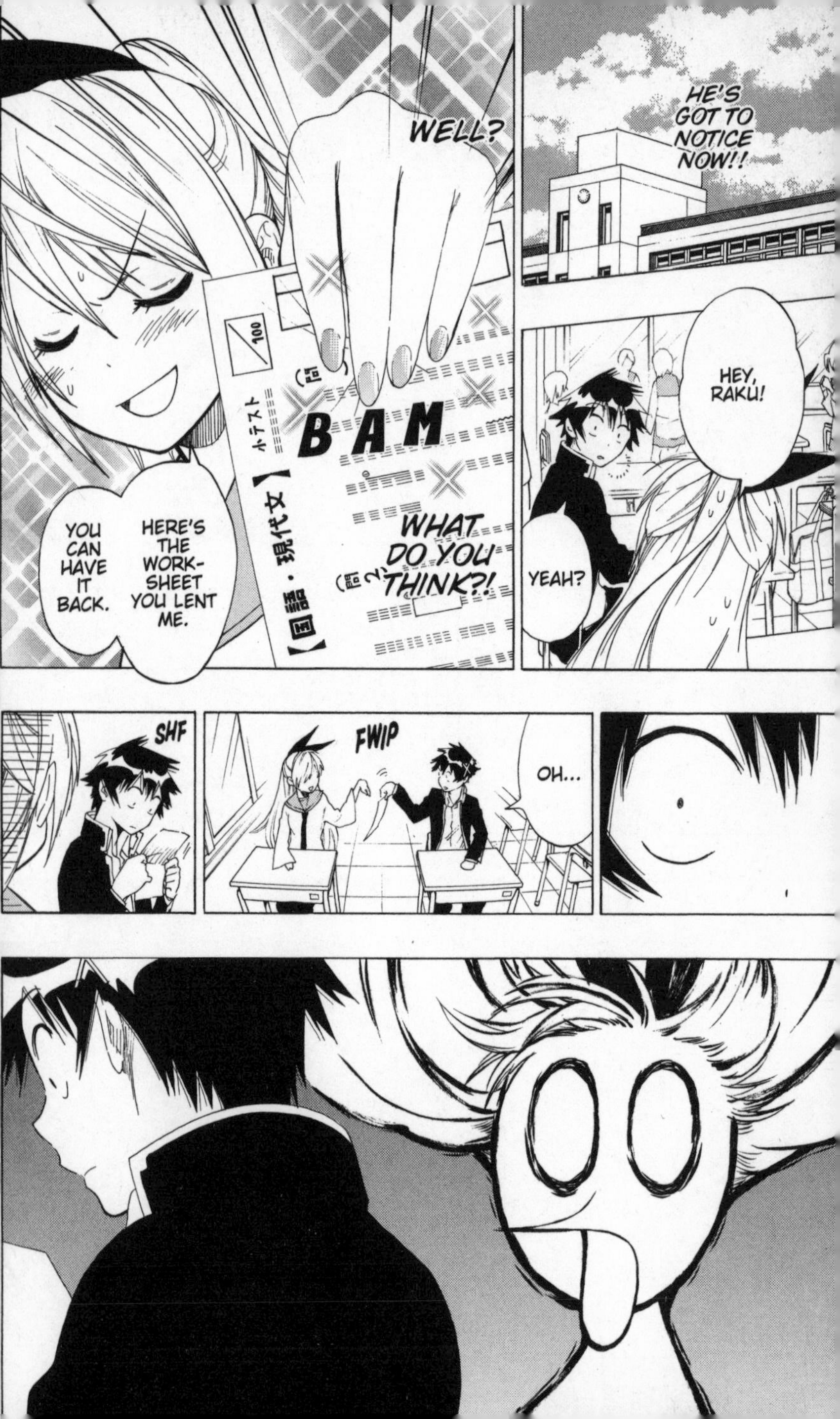
HE'S GOT TO NOTICE NOW!!
HEY, RAKU!
YEAH?
WELL?
BAM
WHAT DO YOU THINK?!
【国語・現代文】小テスト
HERE'S THE WORK-SHEET YOU LENT ME.
YOU CAN HAVE IT BACK.
OH...
FWIP
SHF

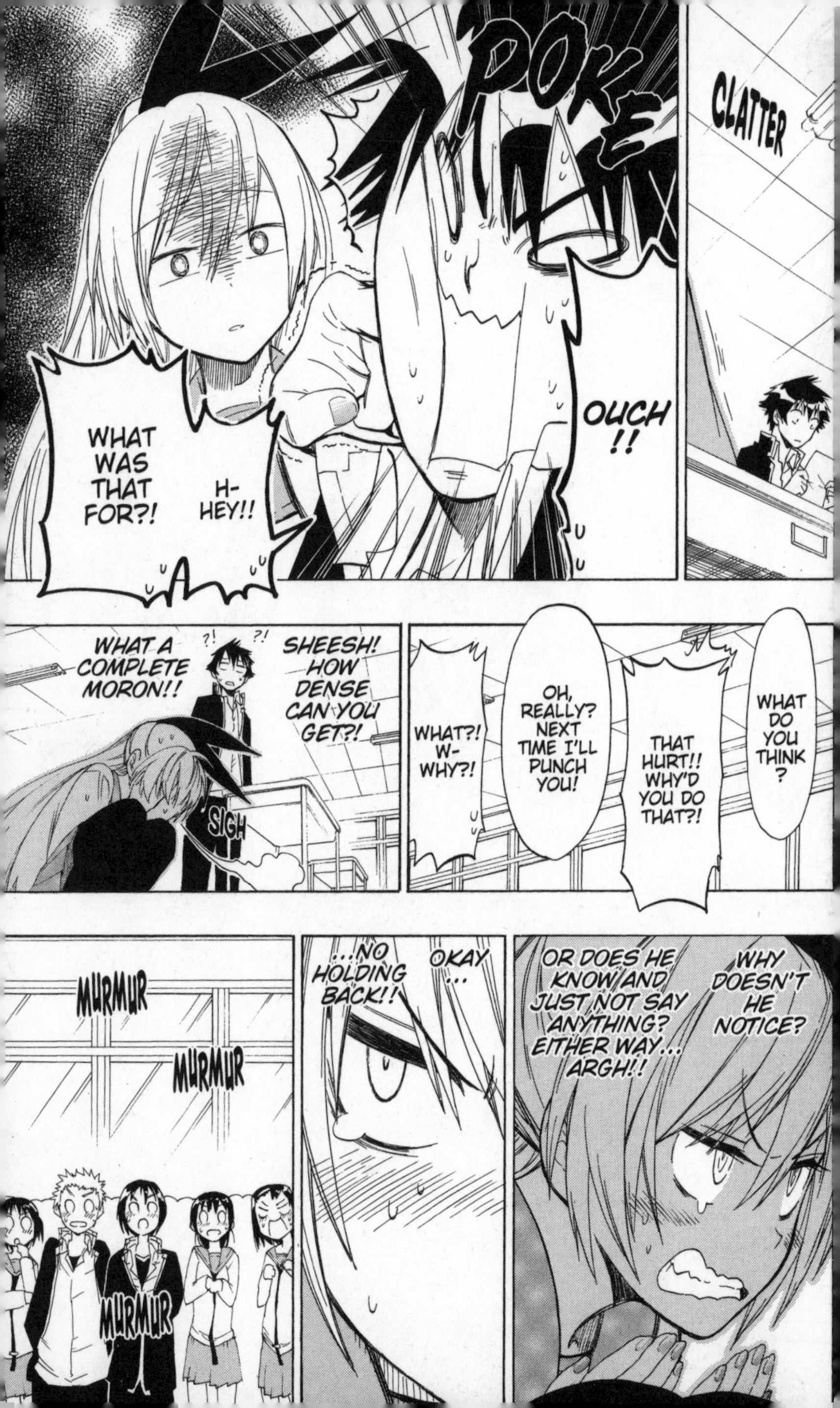

CLATTER
POKE
OUCH!!
H-HEY!!
WHAT WAS THAT FOR?!
WHAT DO YOU THINK?
THAT HURT!! WHY'D YOU DO THAT?!
OH, REALLY? NEXT TIME I'LL PUNCH YOU!
WHAT?! W-WHY?!
SHEESH! HOW DENSE CAN YOU GET?!
?!
?!
WHAT A COMPLETE MORON!!
SIGH
WHY DOESN'T HE NOTICE?
OR DOES HE KNOW AND JUST NOT SAY ANYTHING? EITHER WAY... ARGH!!
OKAY...
...NO HOLDING BACK!!
MURMUR
MURMUR
MURMUR

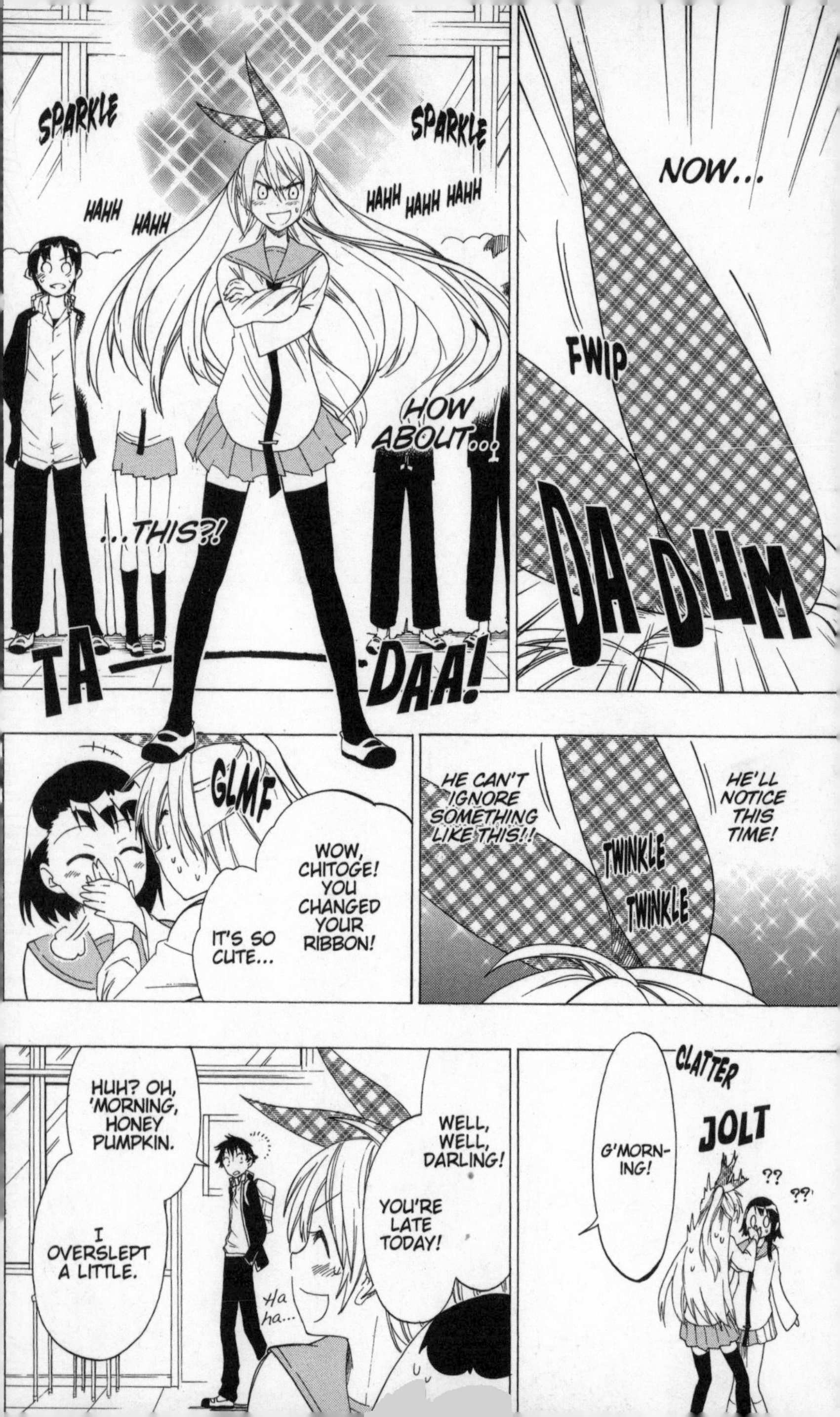
NOW...
FWIP
DA DUM
SPARKLE
SPARKLE
HAHH HAHH HAHH
HAHH HAHH
HOW ABOUT...
...THIS?!
TA-DAA!
HE'LL NOTICE THIS TIME!
HE CAN'T IGNORE SOMETHING LIKE THIS!!
TWINKLE
TWINKLE
WOW, CHITOGE! YOU CHANGED YOUR RIBBON!
IT'S SO CUTE...
GLMF
CLATTER
G'MORN-ING!
JOLT
??
??
WELL, WELL, DARLING!
YOU'RE LATE TODAY!
HUH? OH, 'MORNING, HONEY PUMPKIN.
I OVERSLEPT A LITTLE.
Ha ha...

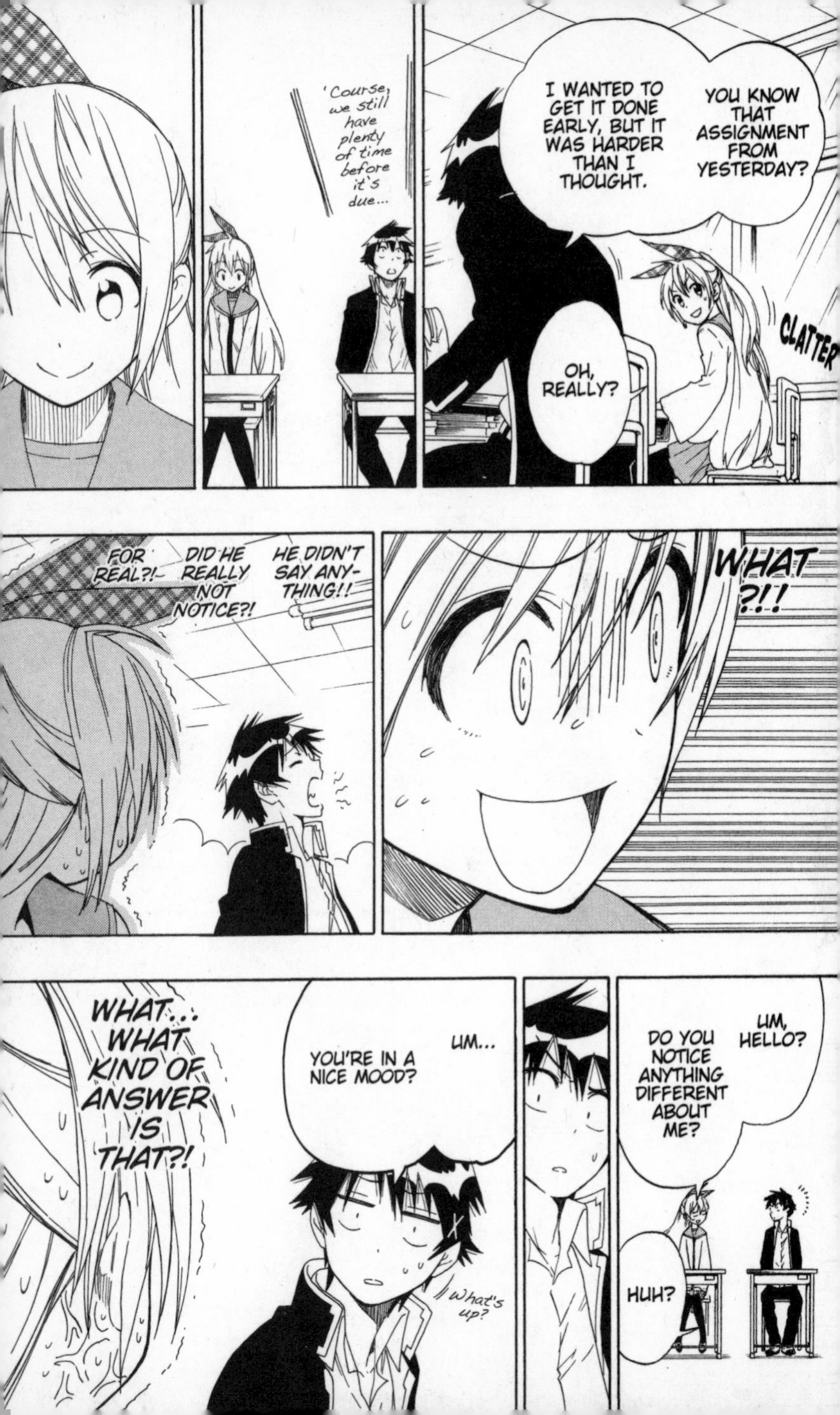
YOU KNOW THAT ASSIGNMENT FROM YESTERDAY?
I WANTED TO GET IT DONE EARLY, BUT IT WAS HARDER THAN I THOUGHT.
CLATTER
OH, REALLY?
'Course, we still have plenty of time before it's due...
WHAT?!!
HE DIDN'T SAY ANY-THING!!
DID HE REALLY NOT NOTICE?!
FOR REAL?!
UM, HELLO?
DO YOU NOTICE ANYTHING DIFFERENT ABOUT ME?
HUH?
UM...
YOU'RE IN A NICE MOOD?
What's up?
WHAT... WHAT KIND OF ANSWER IS THAT?!

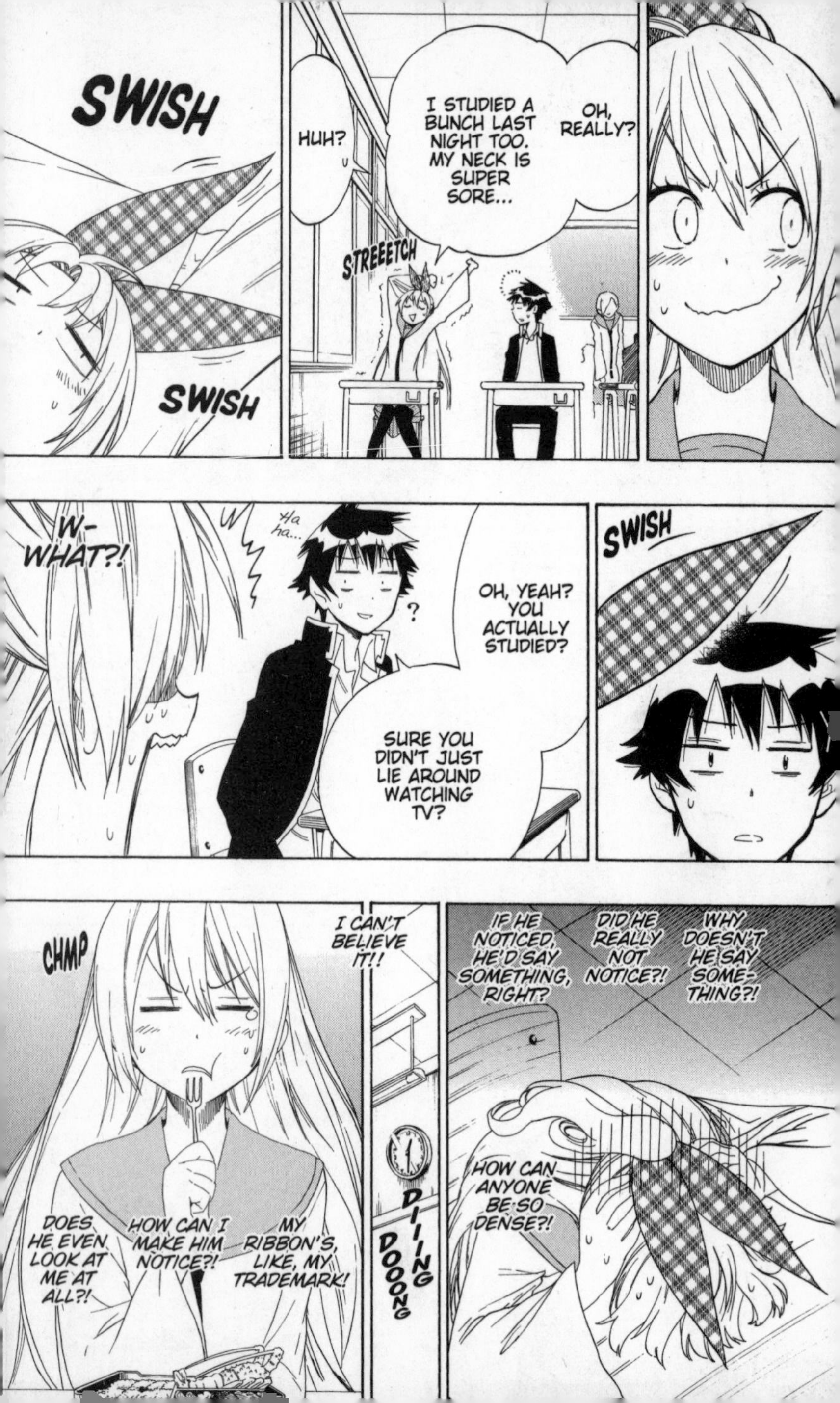
OH, REALLY?
I STUDIED A BUNCH LAST NIGHT TOO. MY NECK IS SUPER SORE...
HUH?
STREEETCH
SWISH
SWISH
SWISH
OH, YEAH? YOU ACTUALLY STUDIED?
SURE YOU DIDN'T JUST LIE AROUND WATCHING TV?
Ha ha...
?
W-WHAT?!
WHY DOESN'T HE SAY SOME-THING?!
DID HE REALLY NOT NOTICE?!
IF HE NOTICED, HE'D SAY SOMETHING, RIGHT?
HOW CAN ANYONE BE SO DENSE?!
I CAN'T BELIEVE IT!!
DIIING DOOONG
CHMP
MY RIBBON'S, LIKE, MY TRADEMARK!
HOW CAN I MAKE HIM NOTICE?!
DOES HE EVEN LOOK AT ME AT ALL?!

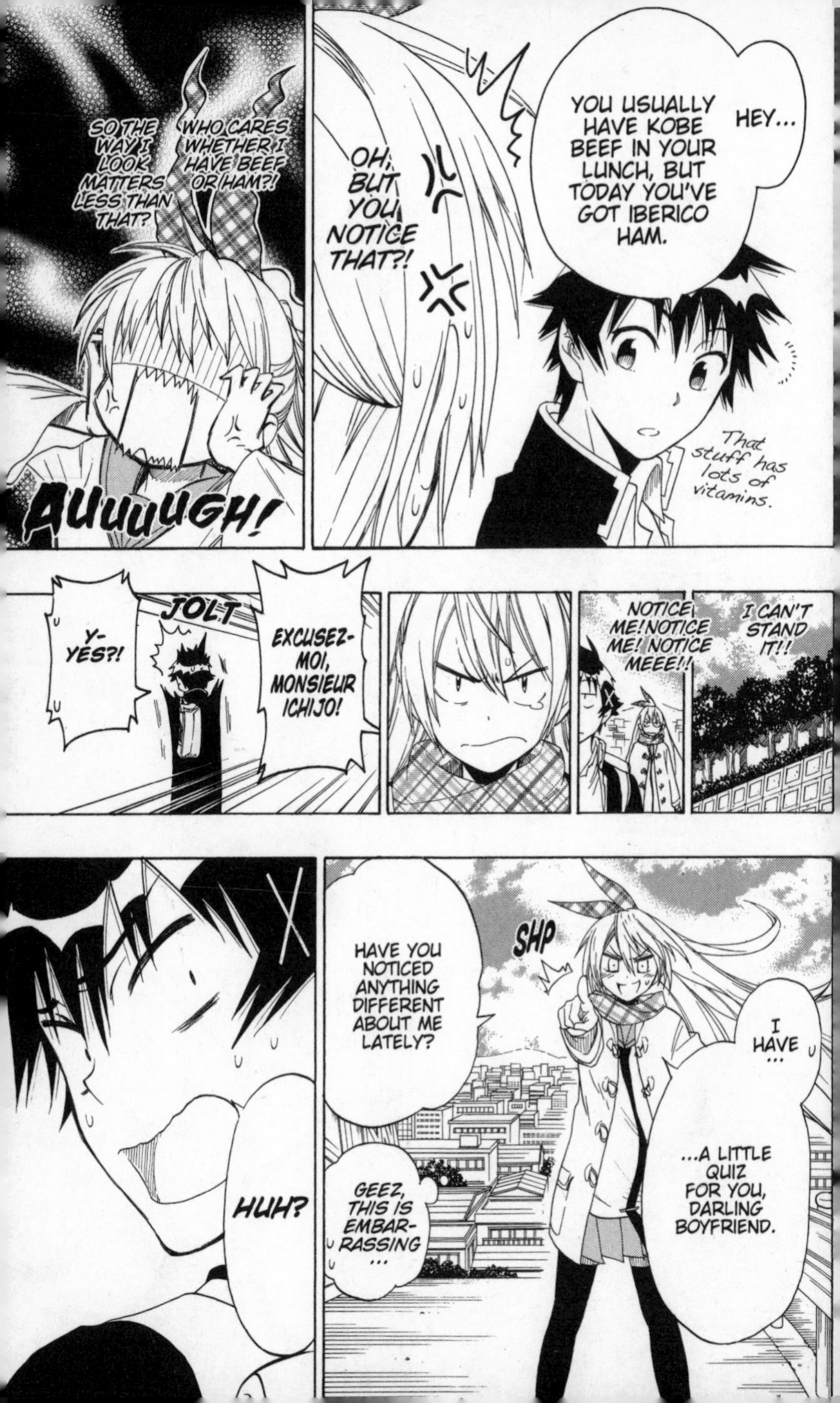
HEY...
YOU USUALLY HAVE KOBE BEEF IN YOUR LUNCH, BUT TODAY YOU'VE GOT IBERICO HAM.
That stuff has lots of vitamins.
OH, BUT YOU NOTICE THAT?!
WHO CARES WHETHER I HAVE BEEF OR HAM?!
SO THE WAY I LOOK MATTERS LESS THAN THAT?
AUUUUGH!
I CAN'T STAND IT!!
NOTICE ME! NOTICE ME! NOTICE MEEE!!
EXCUSEZ-MOI, MONSIEUR ICHIJO!
JOLT
Y-YES?!
I HAVE...
...A LITTLE QUIZ FOR YOU, DARLING BOYFRIEND.
SHP
HAVE YOU NOTICED ANYTHING DIFFERENT ABOUT ME LATELY?
GEEZ, THIS IS EMBARRASSING...
HUH?

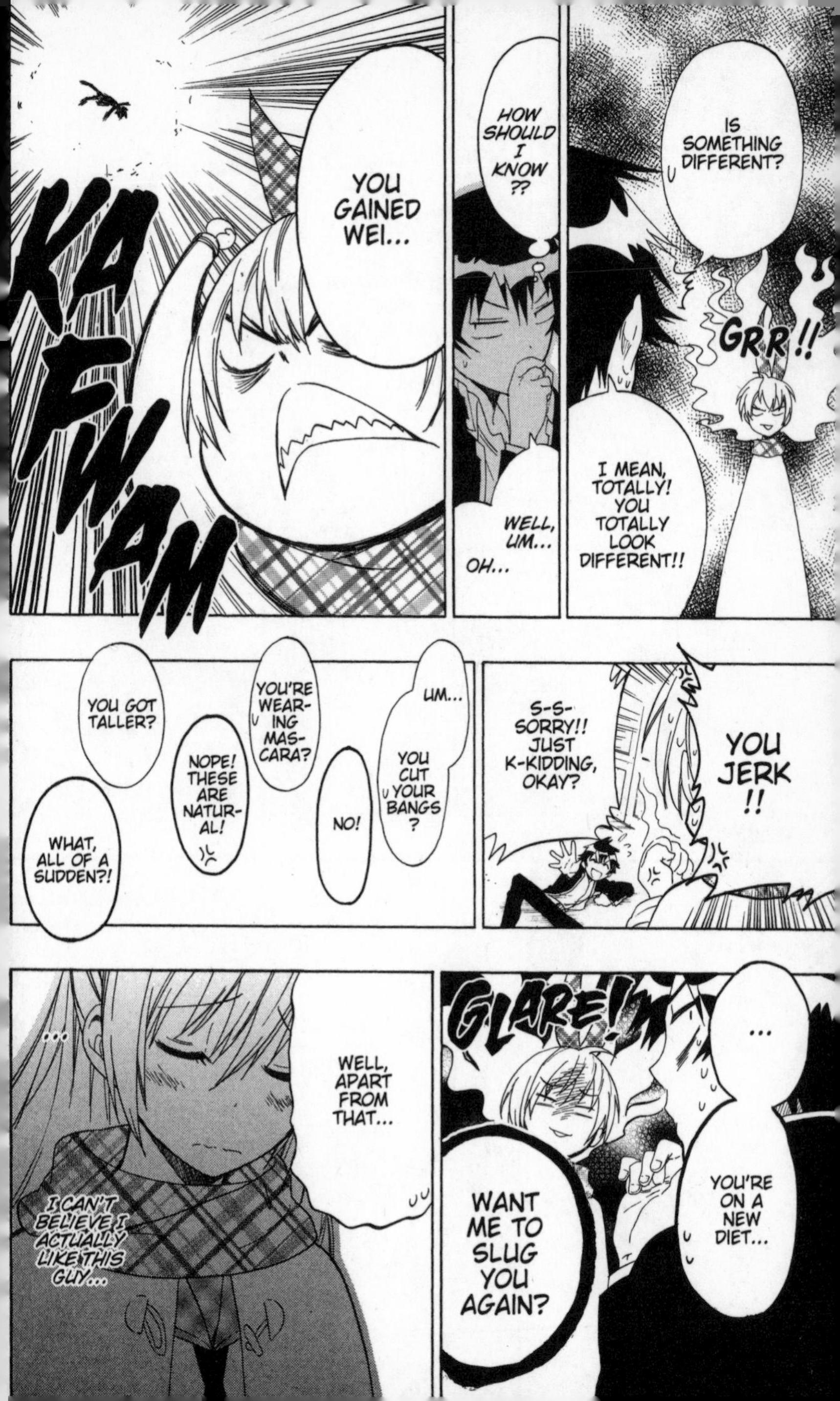
IS SOMETHING DIFFERENT?
GRR!!
I MEAN, TOTALLY! YOU TOTALLY LOOK DIFFERENT!!
HOW SHOULD I KNOW??
WELL, UM...
OH...
YOU GAINED WEI...
KA FWAM
YOU JERK!!
S-S-SORRY!! JUST K-KIDDING, OKAY?
UM...
YOU CUT YOUR BANGS?
NO!
YOU'RE WEARING MASCARA?
NOPE! THESE ARE NATURAL!
YOU GOT TALLER?
WHAT, ALL OF A SUDDEN?!
...
YOU'RE ON A NEW DIET...
GLARE!
WANT ME TO SLUG YOU AGAIN?
WELL, APART FROM THAT...
...
I CAN'T BELIEVE I ACTUALLY LIKE THIS GUY...

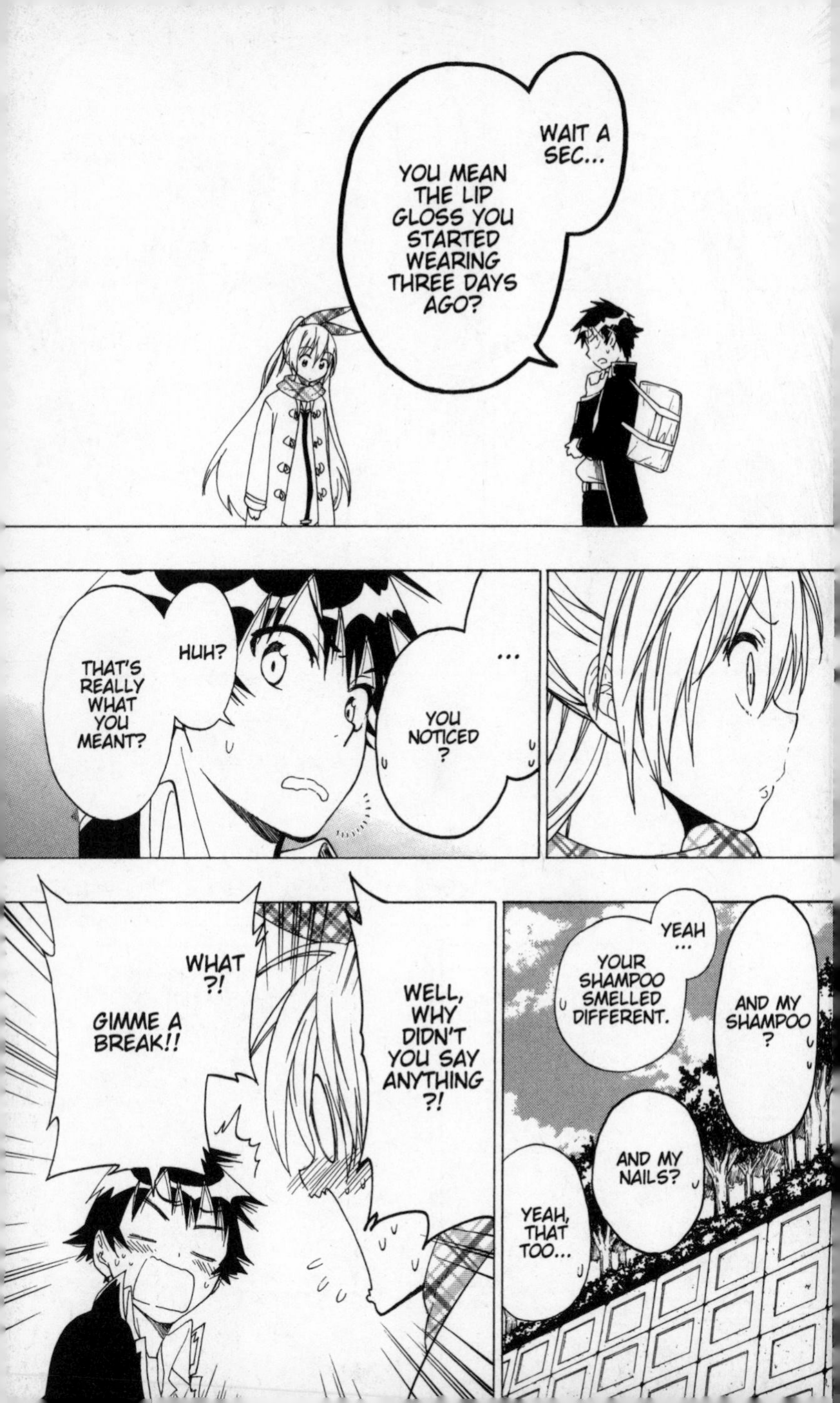
WAIT A SEC... YOU MEAN THE LIP GLOSS YOU STARTED WEARING THREE DAYS AGO?
... YOU NOTICED?
HUH? THAT'S REALLY WHAT YOU MEANT?
AND MY SHAMPOO?
YEAH... YOUR SHAMPOO SMELLED DIFFERENT.
AND MY NAILS?
YEAH, THAT TOO...
WELL, WHY DIDN'T YOU SAY ANYTHING?!
WHAT?! GIMME A BREAK!!

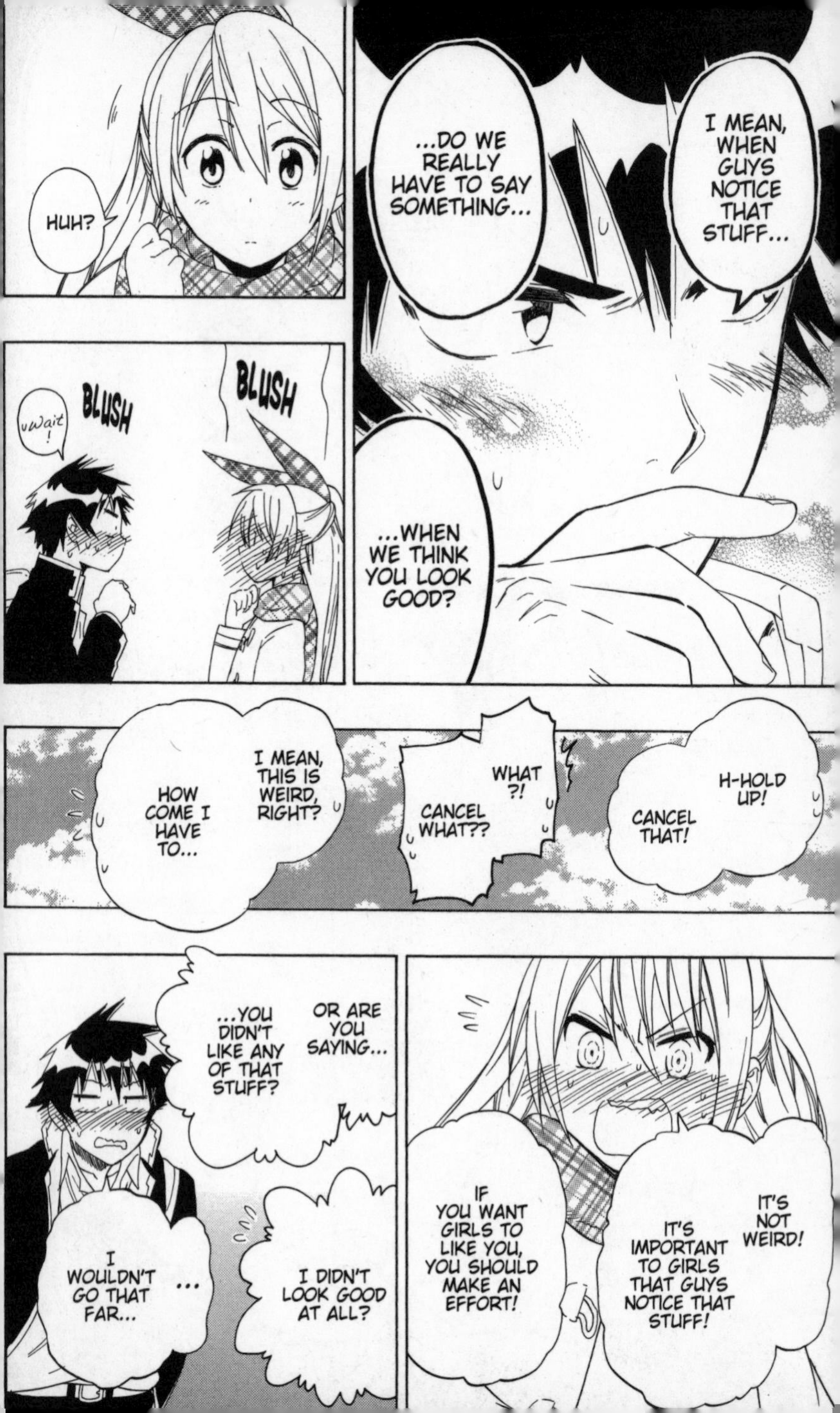
I MEAN, WHEN GUYS NOTICE THAT STUFF...
...DO WE REALLY HAVE TO SAY SOMETHING...
...WHEN WE THINK YOU LOOK GOOD?
HUH?
BLUSH
BLUSH
Wait!
H-HOLD UP!
CANCEL THAT!
WHAT?!
CANCEL WHAT??
I MEAN, THIS IS WEIRD, RIGHT?
HOW COME I HAVE TO...
IT'S NOT WEIRD!
IT'S IMPORTANT TO GIRLS THAT GUYS NOTICE THAT STUFF!
IF YOU WANT GIRLS TO LIKE YOU, YOU SHOULD MAKE AN EFFORT!
OR ARE YOU SAYING...
...YOU DIDN'T LIKE ANY OF THAT STUFF?
I DIDN'T LOOK GOOD AT ALL?
...
I WOULDN'T GO THAT FAR...

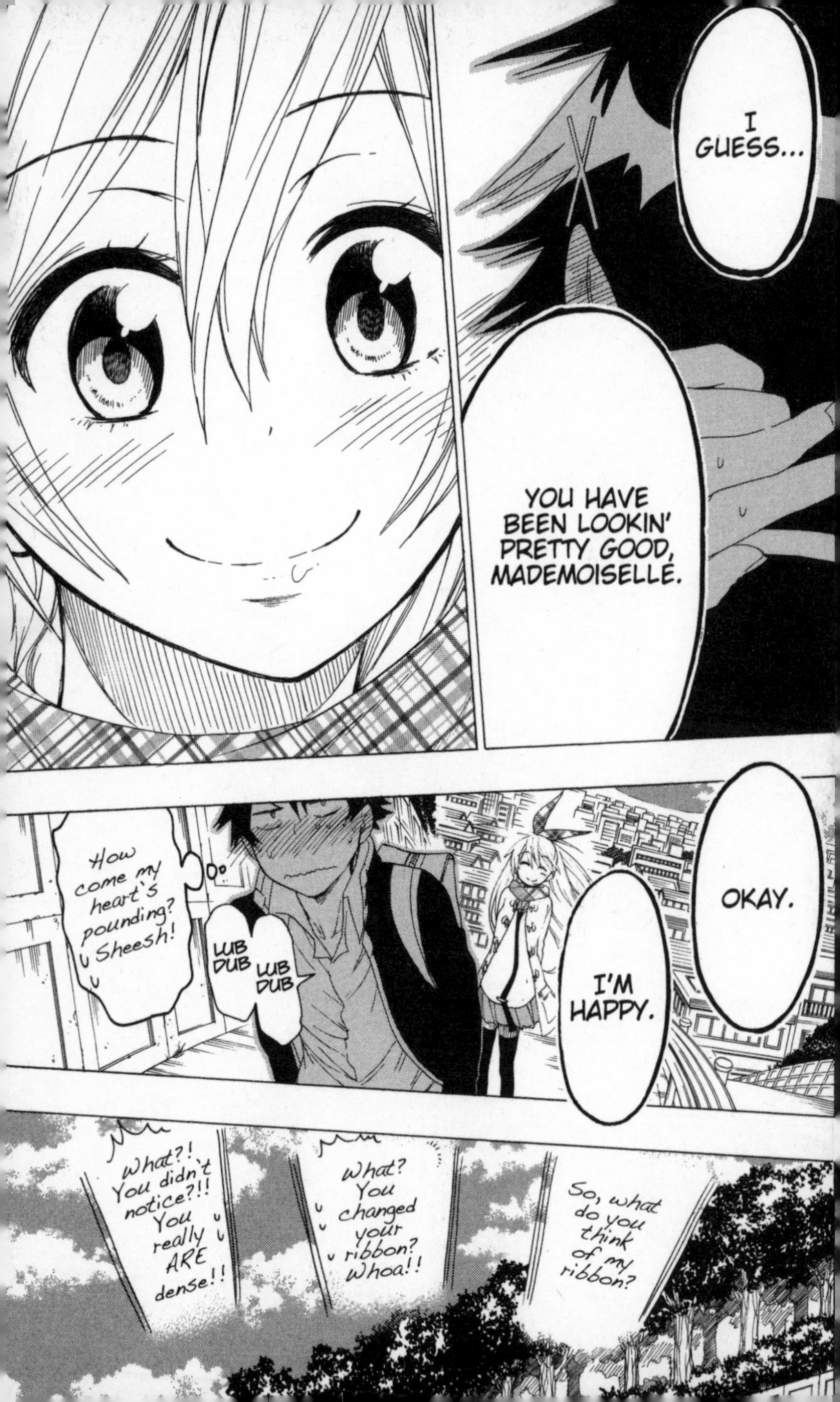
I GUESS...
YOU HAVE BEEN LOOKIN' PRETTY GOOD, MADEMOISELLE.
OKAY.
I'M HAPPY.
LUB DUB LUB DUB
How come my heart's pounding? Sheesh!
So, what do you think of my ribbon?
What? You changed your ribbon? Whoa!!
What?! You didn't notice?!! You really ARE dense!!

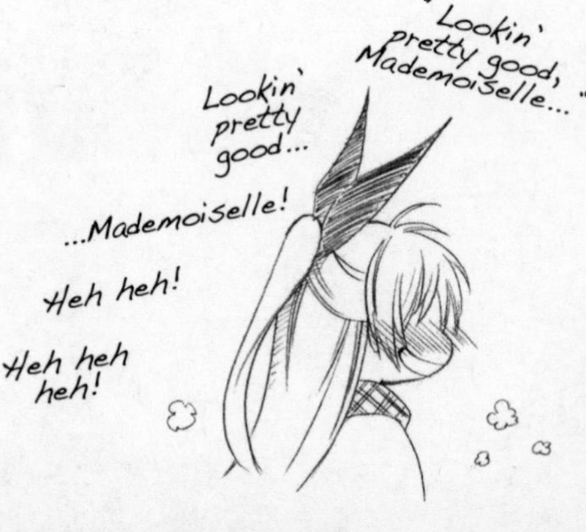
"Lookin' pretty good, Mademoiselle..."
Lookin' pretty good...
...Mademoiselle!
Heh heh!
Heh heh heh!

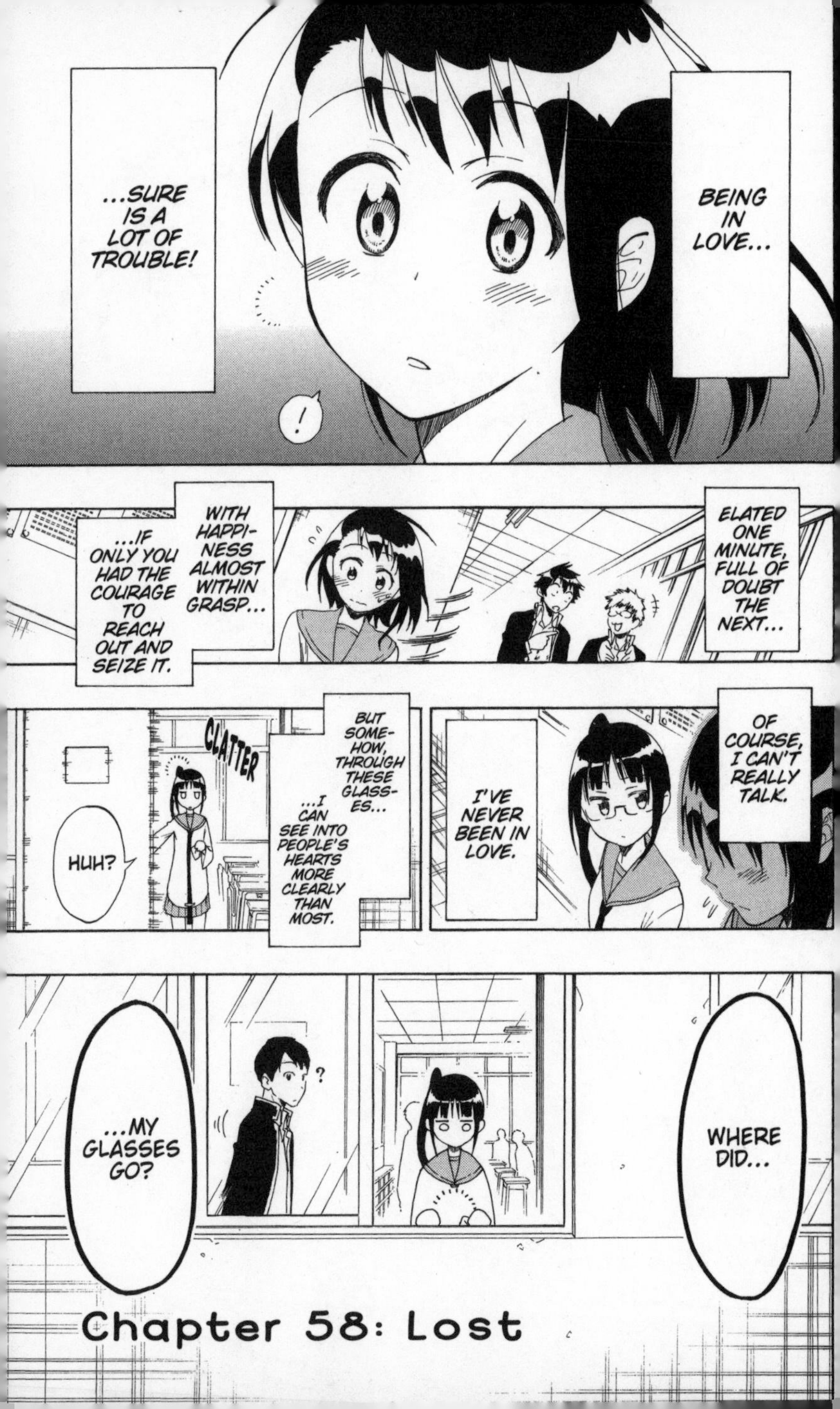
BEING IN LOVE...
...SURE IS A LOT OF TROUBLE!
!
ELATED ONE MINUTE, FULL OF DOUBT THE NEXT...
WITH HAPPINESS ALMOST WITHIN GRASP...
...IF ONLY YOU HAD THE COURAGE TO REACH OUT AND SEIZE IT.
OF COURSE, I CAN'T REALLY TALK.
I'VE NEVER BEEN IN LOVE.
BUT SOMEHOW, THROUGH THESE GLASSES...
...I CAN SEE INTO PEOPLE'S HEARTS MORE CLEARLY THAN MOST.
CLATTER
HUH?
WHERE DID...
...MY GLASSES GO?
Chapter 58: Lost

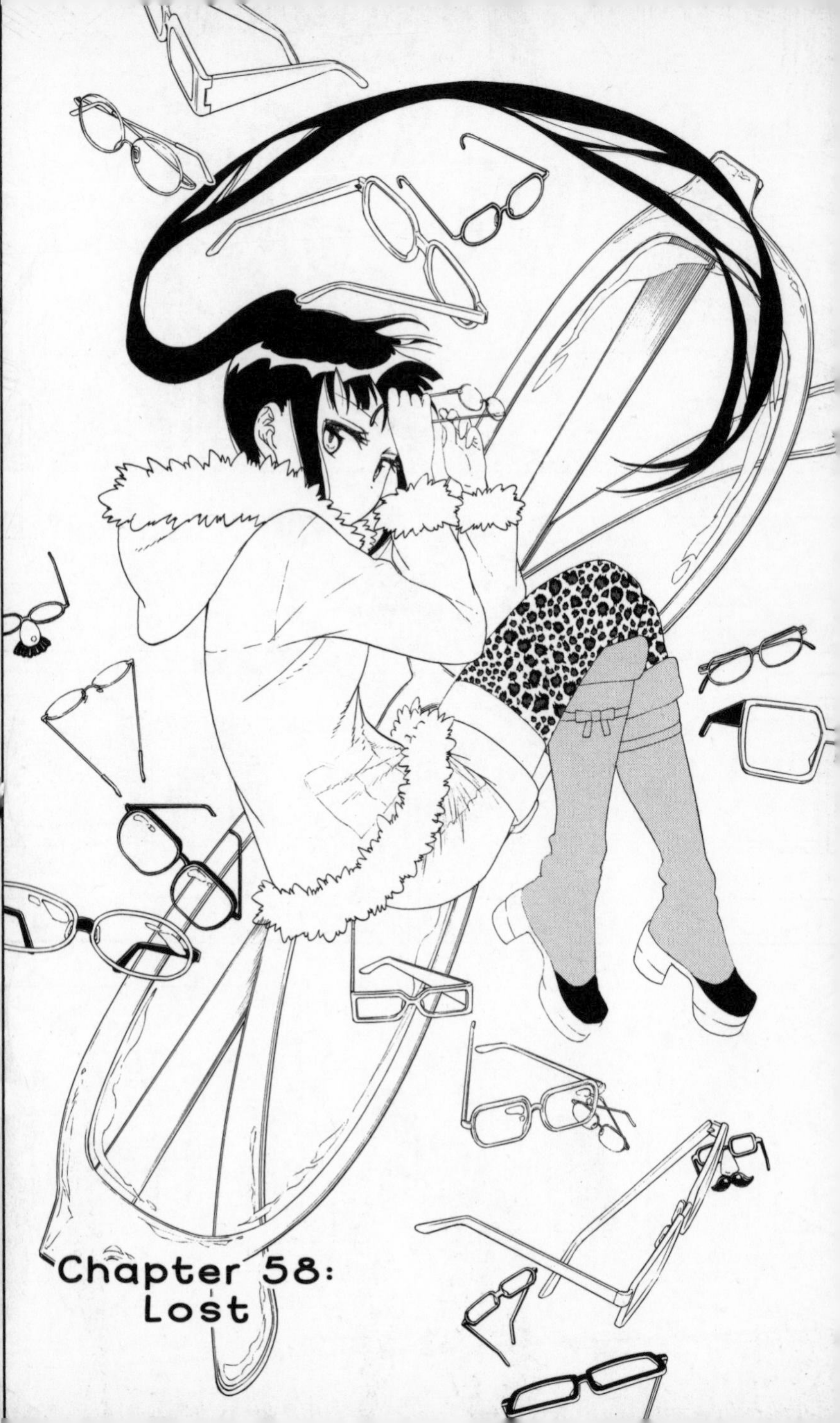
Chapter 58:
Lost

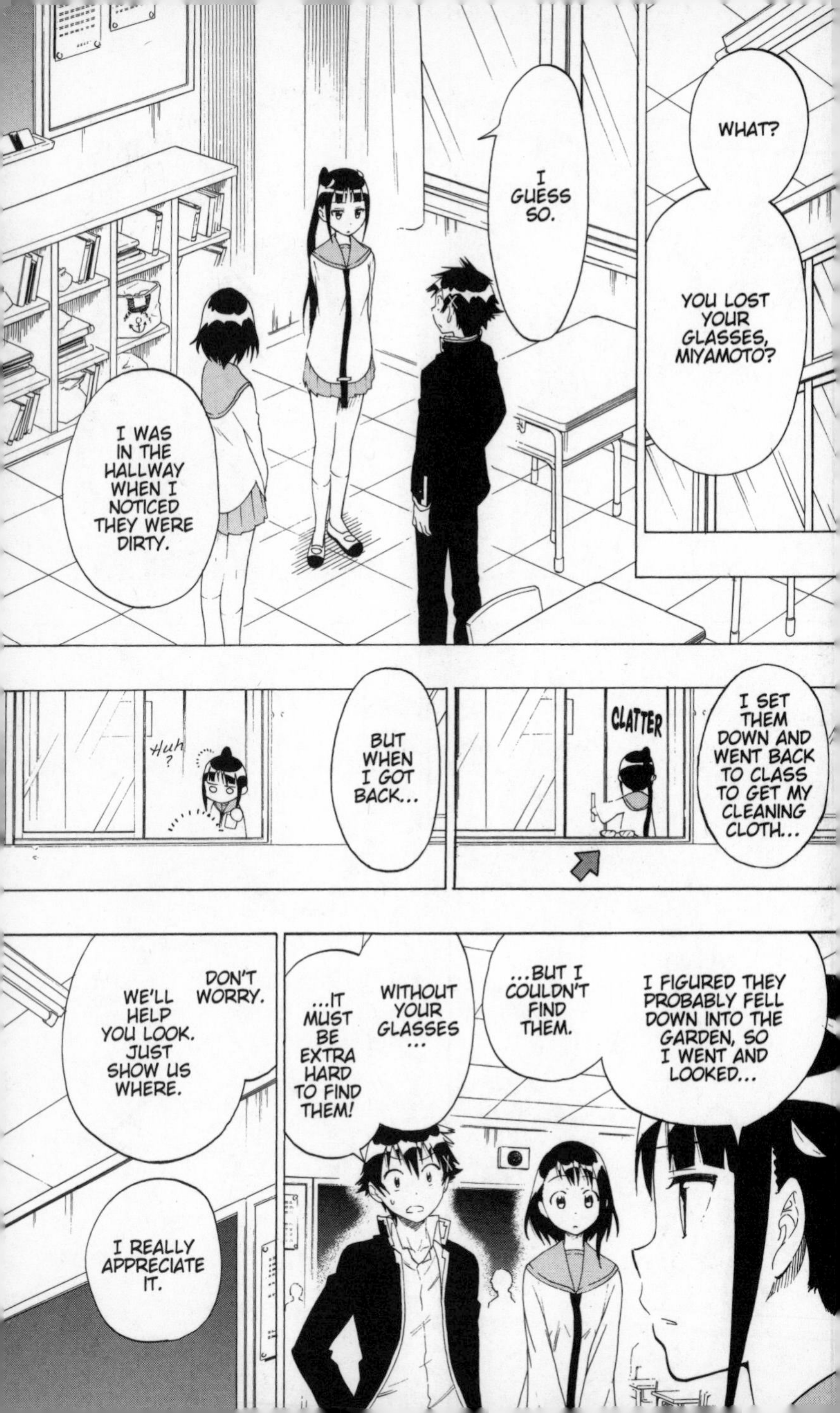
WHAT?
YOU LOST YOUR GLASSES, MIYAMOTO?
I GUESS SO.
I WAS IN THE HALLWAY WHEN I NOTICED THEY WERE DIRTY.
I SET THEM DOWN AND WENT BACK TO CLASS TO GET MY CLEANING CLOTH...
CLATTER
BUT WHEN I GOT BACK...
Huh?
I FIGURED THEY PROBABLY FELL DOWN INTO THE GARDEN, SO I WENT AND LOOKED...
...BUT I COULDN'T FIND THEM.
WITHOUT YOUR GLASSES...
...IT MUST BE EXTRA HARD TO FIND THEM!
DON'T WORRY.
WE'LL HELP YOU LOOK. JUST SHOW US WHERE.
I REALLY APPRECIATE IT.

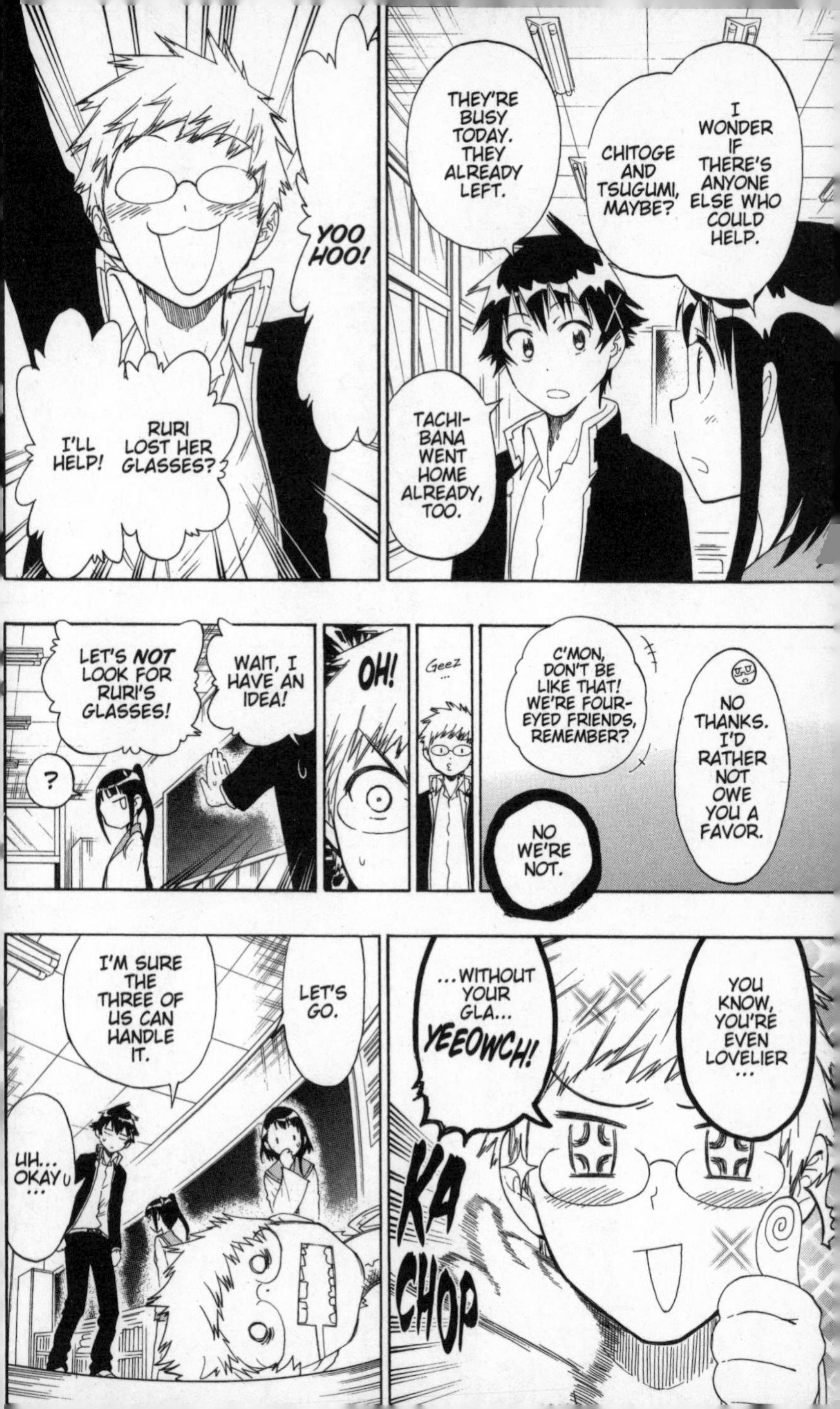
I WONDER IF THERE'S ANYONE ELSE WHO COULD HELP.
CHITOGE AND TSUGUMI, MAYBE?
THEY'RE BUSY TODAY. THEY ALREADY LEFT.
TACHIBANA WENT HOME ALREADY, TOO.
YOO HOO!
RURI LOST HER GLASSES?
I'LL HELP!
NO THANKS. I'D RATHER NOT OWE YOU A FAVOR.
C'MON, DON'T BE LIKE THAT! WE'RE FOUR-EYED FRIENDS, REMEMBER?
NO WE'RE NOT.
GEEZ...
OH!
WAIT, I HAVE AN IDEA!
LET'S **NOT** LOOK FOR RURI'S GLASSES!
?
YOU KNOW, YOU'RE EVEN LOVELIER...
...WITHOUT YOUR GLA... YEEOWCH!
KA CHOP
LET'S GO.
I'M SURE THE THREE OF US CAN HANDLE IT.
UH... OKAY...

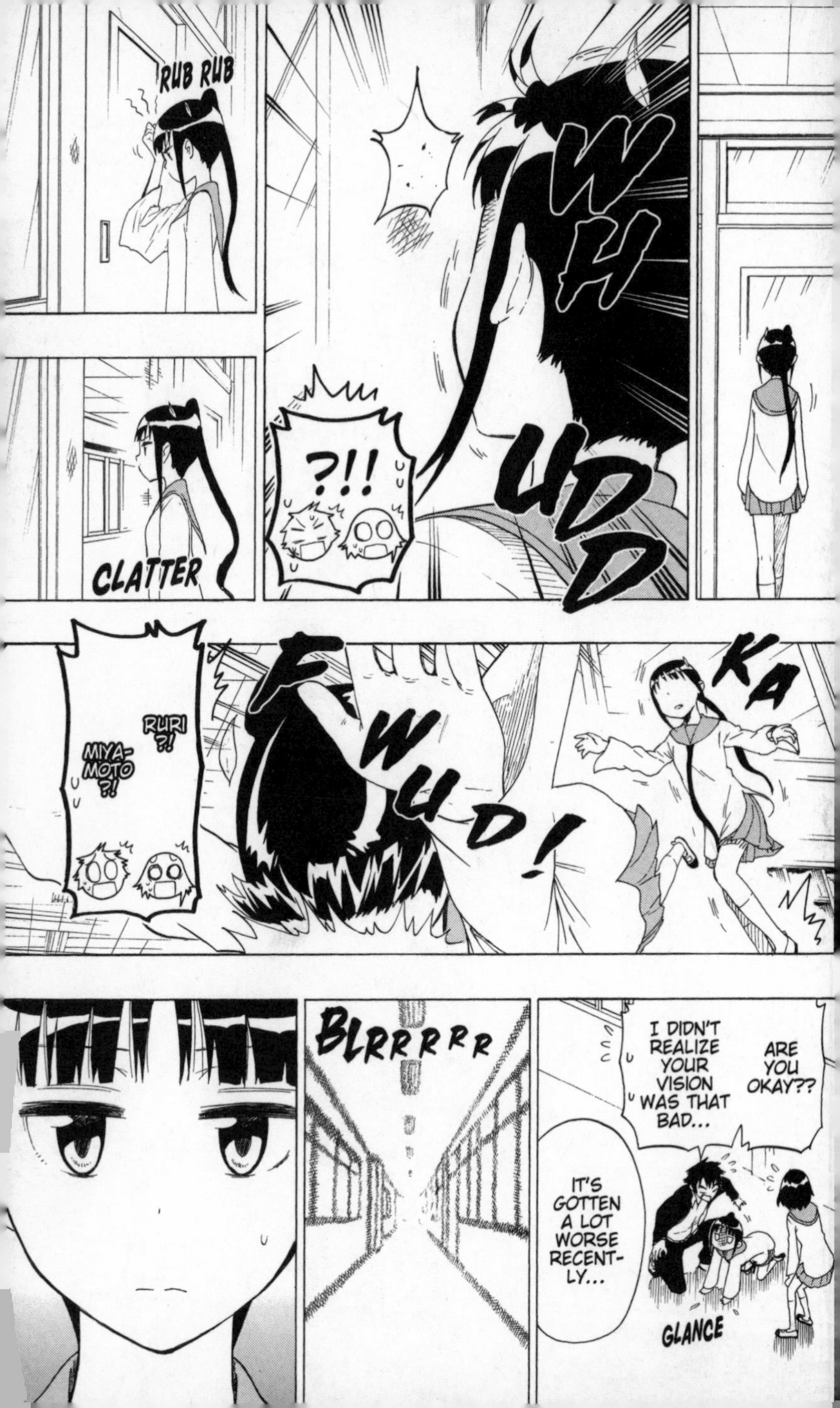
WHUD
?!!
RUB RUB
CLATTER
KA
FWUD!
RURI ?!
MIYA-MOTO ?!
ARE YOU OKAY??
I DIDN'T REALIZE YOUR VISION WAS THAT BAD...
IT'S GOTTEN A LOT WORSE RECENT-LY...
GLANCE
BLRRRRRR

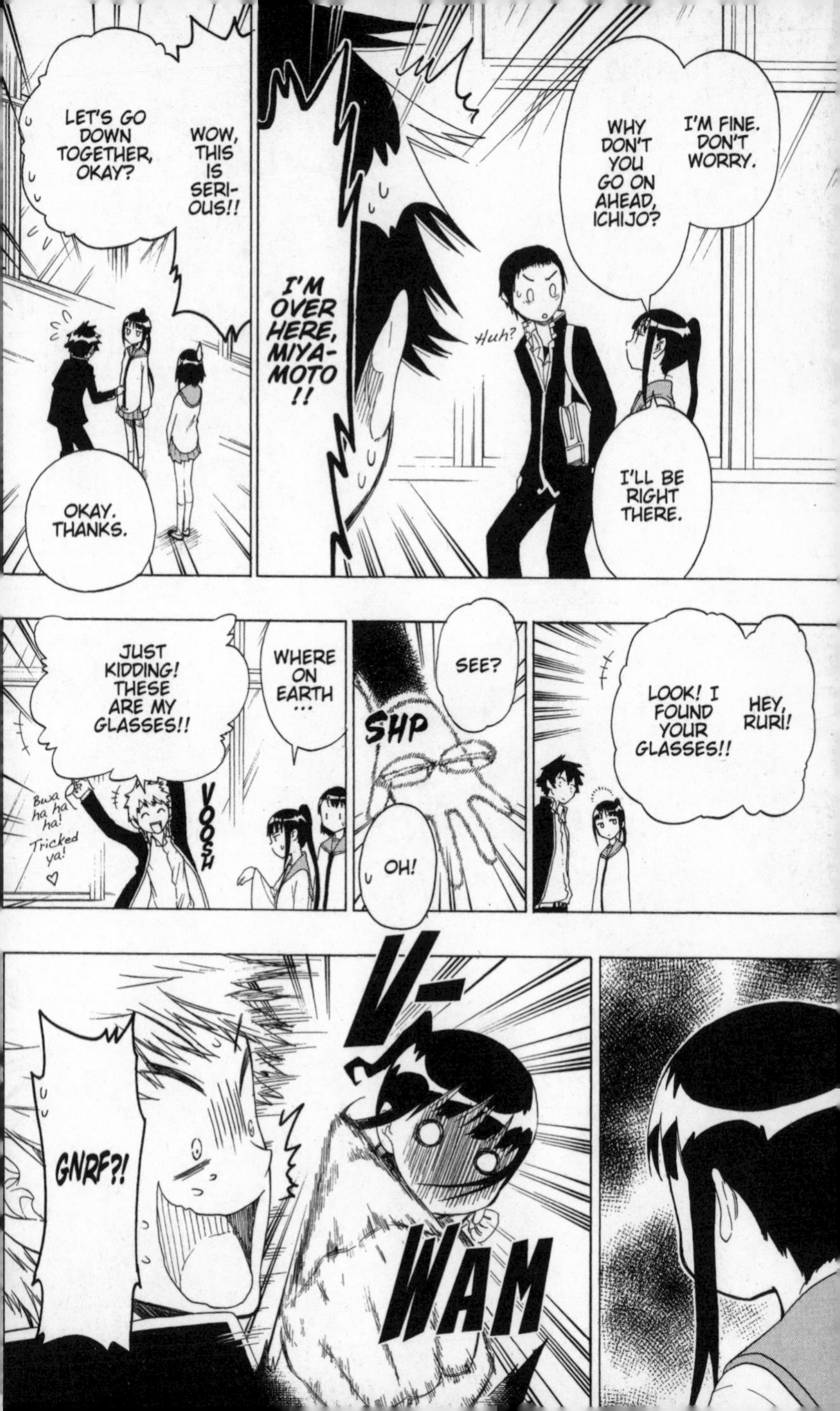
I'M FINE. DON'T WORRY.
WHY DON'T YOU GO ON AHEAD, ICHIJO?
Huh?
I'LL BE RIGHT THERE.
I'M OVER HERE, MIYAMOTO!!
WOW, THIS IS SERI-OUS!!
LET'S GO DOWN TOGETHER, OKAY?
OKAY. THANKS.
HEY, RURI!
LOOK! I FOUND YOUR GLASSES!!
SEE?
SHP
OH!
WHERE ON EARTH ...
JUST KIDDING! THESE ARE MY GLASSES!!
VOOSH
Bwa ha ha ha! Tricked ya! ♡
V-WAM
GNRF?!

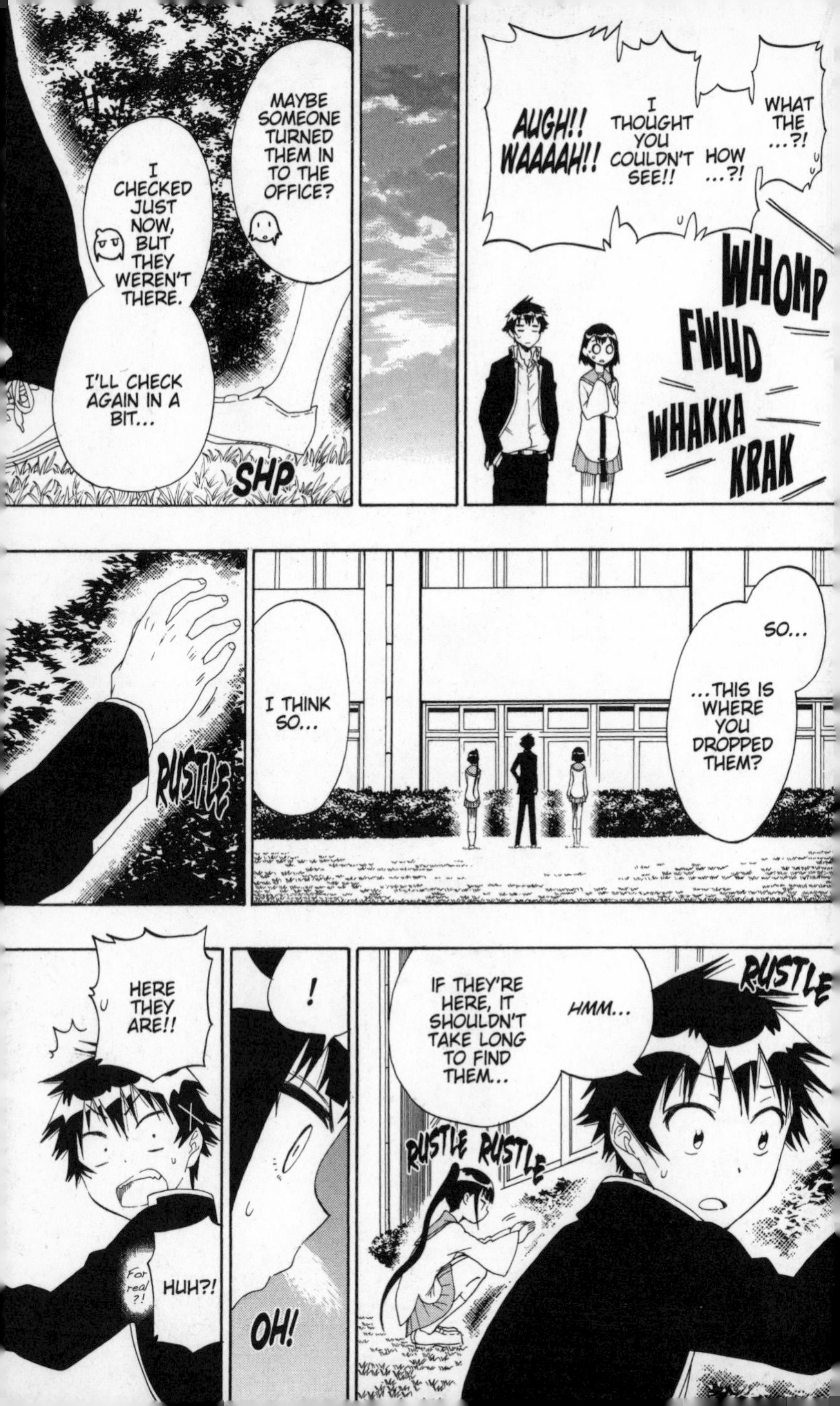
WHAT THE ...?!
HOW ...?!
I THOUGHT YOU COULDN'T SEE!!
AUGH!! WAAAAH!!
WHOMP
FWUD
WHAKKA
KRAK
MAYBE SOMEONE TURNED THEM IN TO THE OFFICE?
I CHECKED JUST NOW, BUT THEY WEREN'T THERE.
I'LL CHECK AGAIN IN A BIT...
SHP
SO...
...THIS IS WHERE YOU DROPPED THEM?
I THINK SO...
RUSTLE
RUSTLE
HMM...
IF THEY'RE HERE, IT SHOULDN'T TAKE LONG TO FIND THEM...
RUSTLE RUSTLE
!
OH!
HERE THEY ARE!!
HUH?!
For real?!

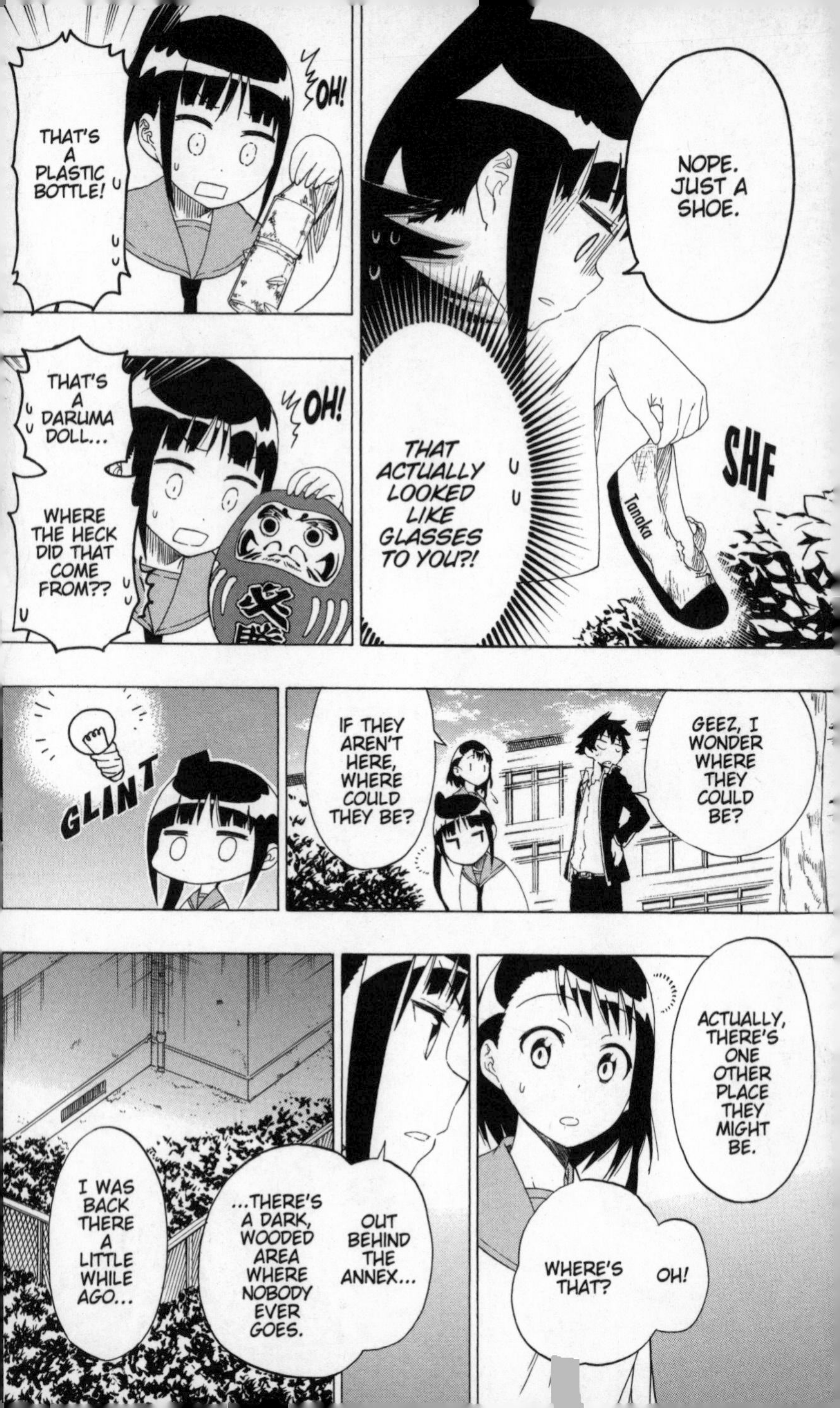
NOPE. JUST A SHOE.
THAT ACTUALLY LOOKED LIKE GLASSES TO YOU?!
SHF
Tanaka
OH!
THAT'S A PLASTIC BOTTLE!
OH!
THAT'S A DARUMA DOLL...
WHERE THE HECK DID THAT COME FROM??
GEEZ, I WONDER WHERE THEY COULD BE?
IF THEY AREN'T HERE, WHERE COULD THEY BE?
GLINT
ACTUALLY, THERE'S ONE OTHER PLACE THEY MIGHT BE.
OH!
WHERE'S THAT?
OUT BEHIND THE ANNEX...
...THERE'S A DARK, WOODED AREA WHERE NOBODY EVER GOES.
I WAS BACK THERE A LITTLE WHILE AGO...

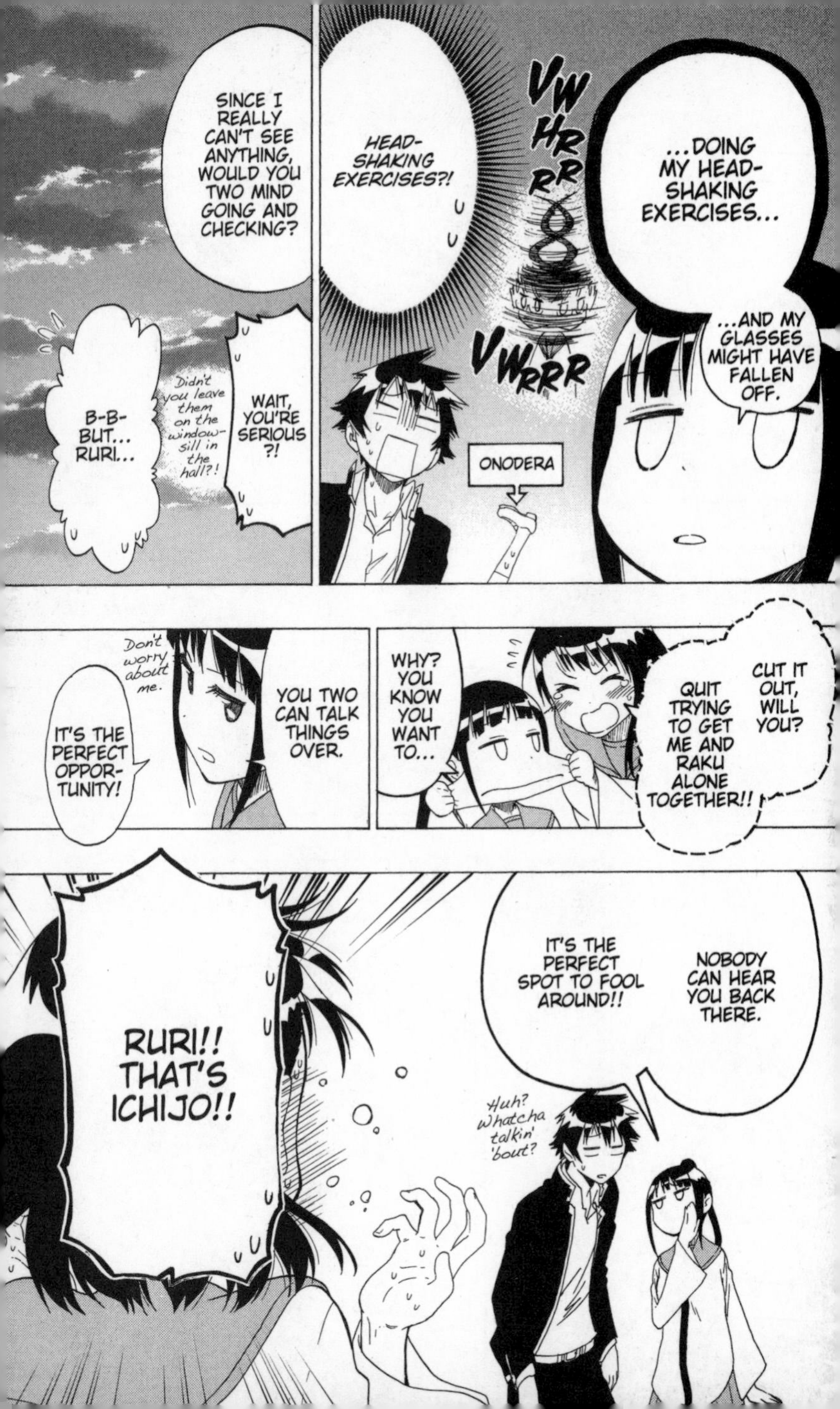
...DOING MY HEAD-SHAKING EXERCISES...
VWHRRR
...AND MY GLASSES MIGHT HAVE FALLEN OFF.
VWRRR
ONODERA
HEAD-SHAKING EXERCISES?!
SINCE I REALLY CAN'T SEE ANYTHING, WOULD YOU TWO MIND GOING AND CHECKING?
WAIT, YOU'RE SERIOUS?!
Didn't you leave them on the window-sill in the hall?!
B-B-BUT... RURI...
CUT IT OUT, WILL YOU?
QUIT TRYING TO GET ME AND RAKU ALONE TOGETHER!!
WHY? YOU KNOW YOU WANT TO...
YOU TWO CAN TALK THINGS OVER.
Don't worry about me.
IT'S THE PERFECT OPPORTUNITY!
NOBODY CAN HEAR YOU BACK THERE.
IT'S THE PERFECT SPOT TO FOOL AROUND!!
Huh? Whatcha talkin' 'bout?
RURI!! THAT'S ICHIJO!!

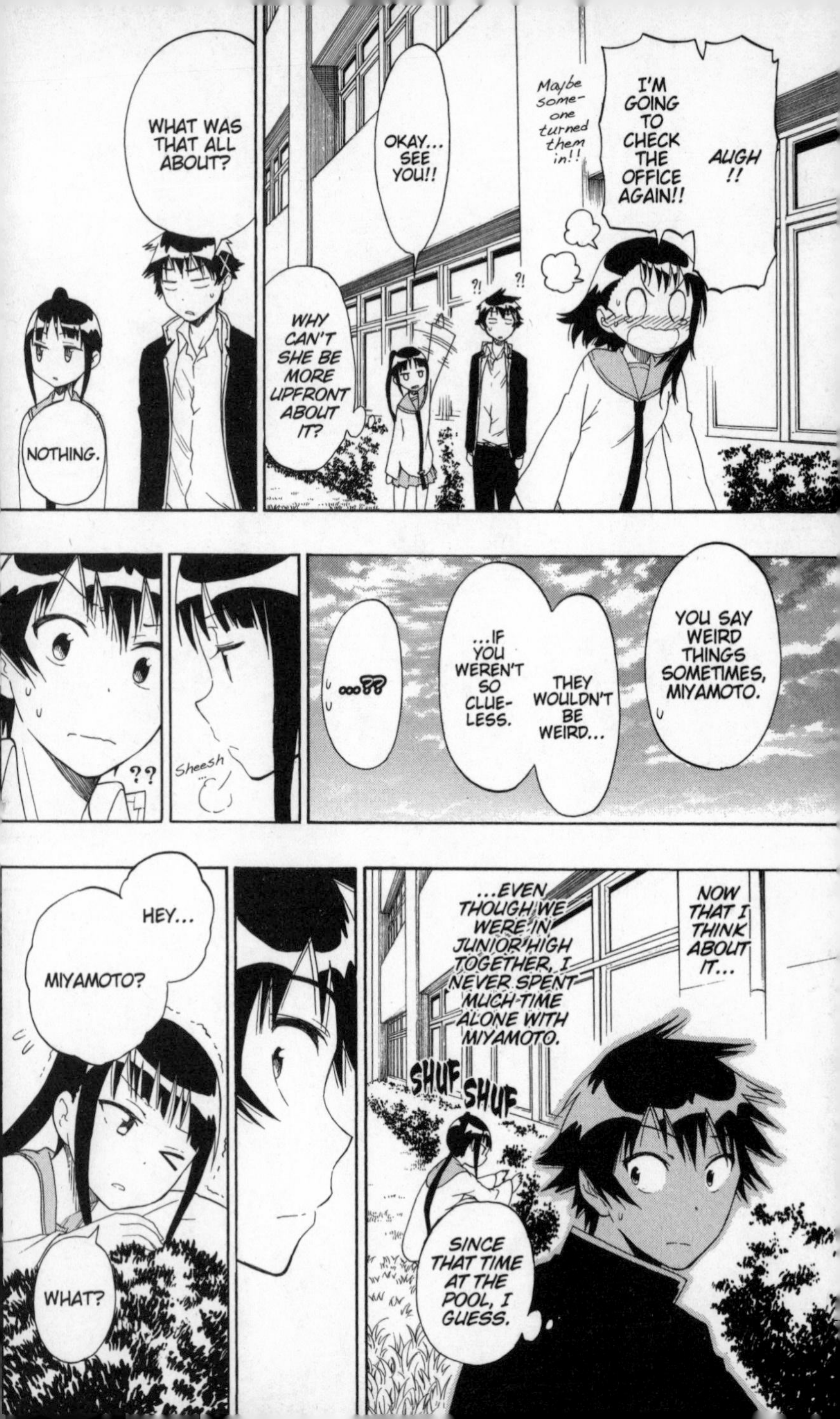
AUGH!!
I'M GOING TO CHECK THE OFFICE AGAIN!!
Maybe someone turned them in!!
?!
?!
OKAY... SEE YOU!!
WHY CAN'T SHE BE MORE UPFRONT ABOUT IT?
WHAT WAS THAT ALL ABOUT?
NOTHING.
YOU SAY WEIRD THINGS SOMETIMES, MIYAMOTO.
THEY WOULDN'T BE WEIRD...
...IF YOU WEREN'T SO CLUELESS.
...??
Sheesh...
??
NOW THAT I THINK ABOUT IT...
...EVEN THOUGH WE WERE IN JUNIOR HIGH TOGETHER, I NEVER SPENT MUCH TIME ALONE WITH MIYAMOTO.
SHUF SHUF
SINCE THAT TIME AT THE POOL, I GUESS.
HEY... MIYAMOTO?
WHAT?

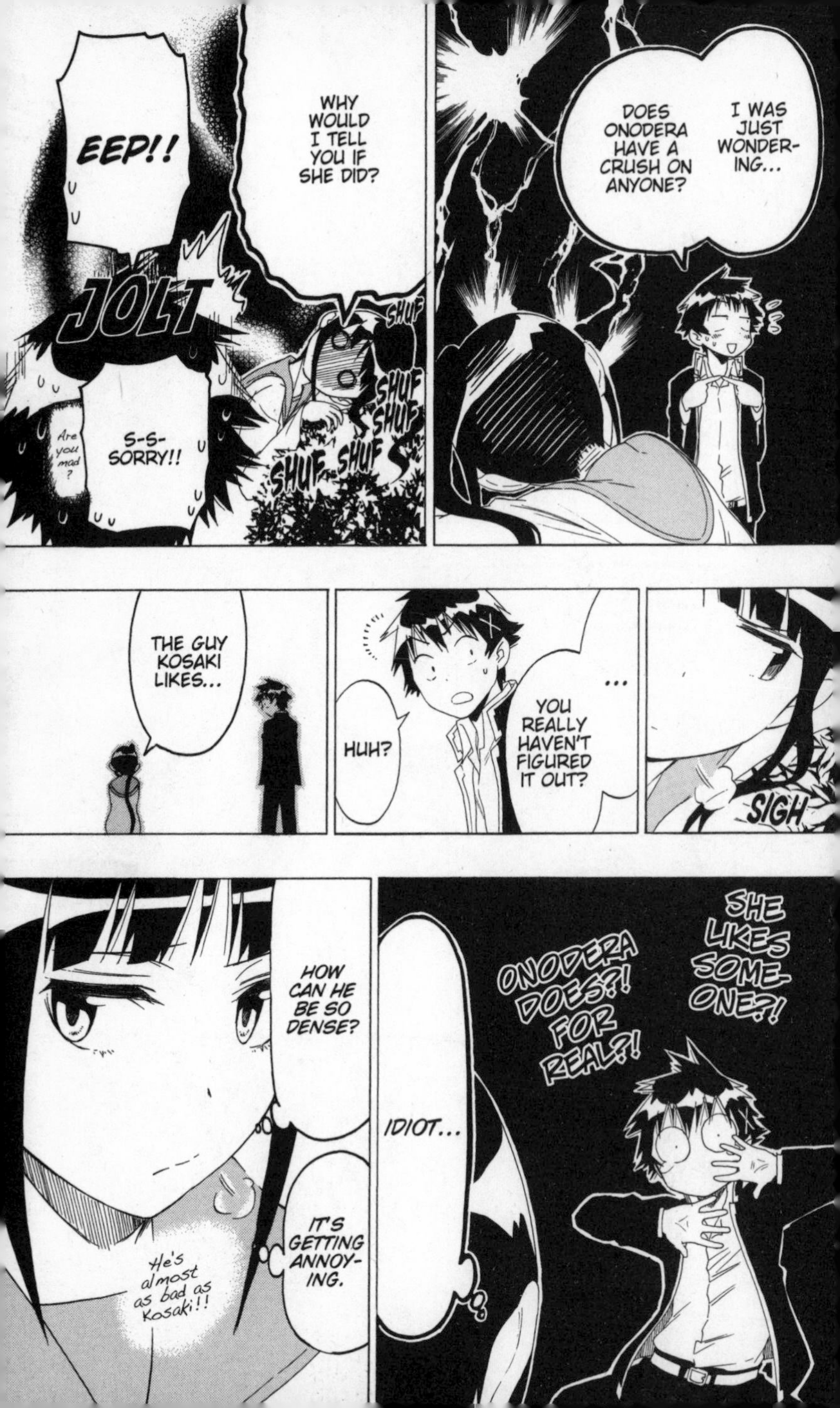
I WAS JUST WONDERING...
DOES ONODERA HAVE A CRUSH ON ANYONE?
WHY WOULD I TELL YOU IF SHE DID?
SHUF SHUF SHUF SHUF SHUF
EEP!!
JOLT
S-S-SORRY!!
Are you mad?
SIGH
...
YOU REALLY HAVEN'T FIGURED IT OUT?
HUH?
THE GUY KOSAKI LIKES...
SHE LIKES SOME-ONE?!
ONODERA DOES?! FOR REAL?!
IDIOT...
HOW CAN HE BE SO DENSE?
IT'S GETTING ANNOY-ING.
He's almost as bad as Kosaki!!

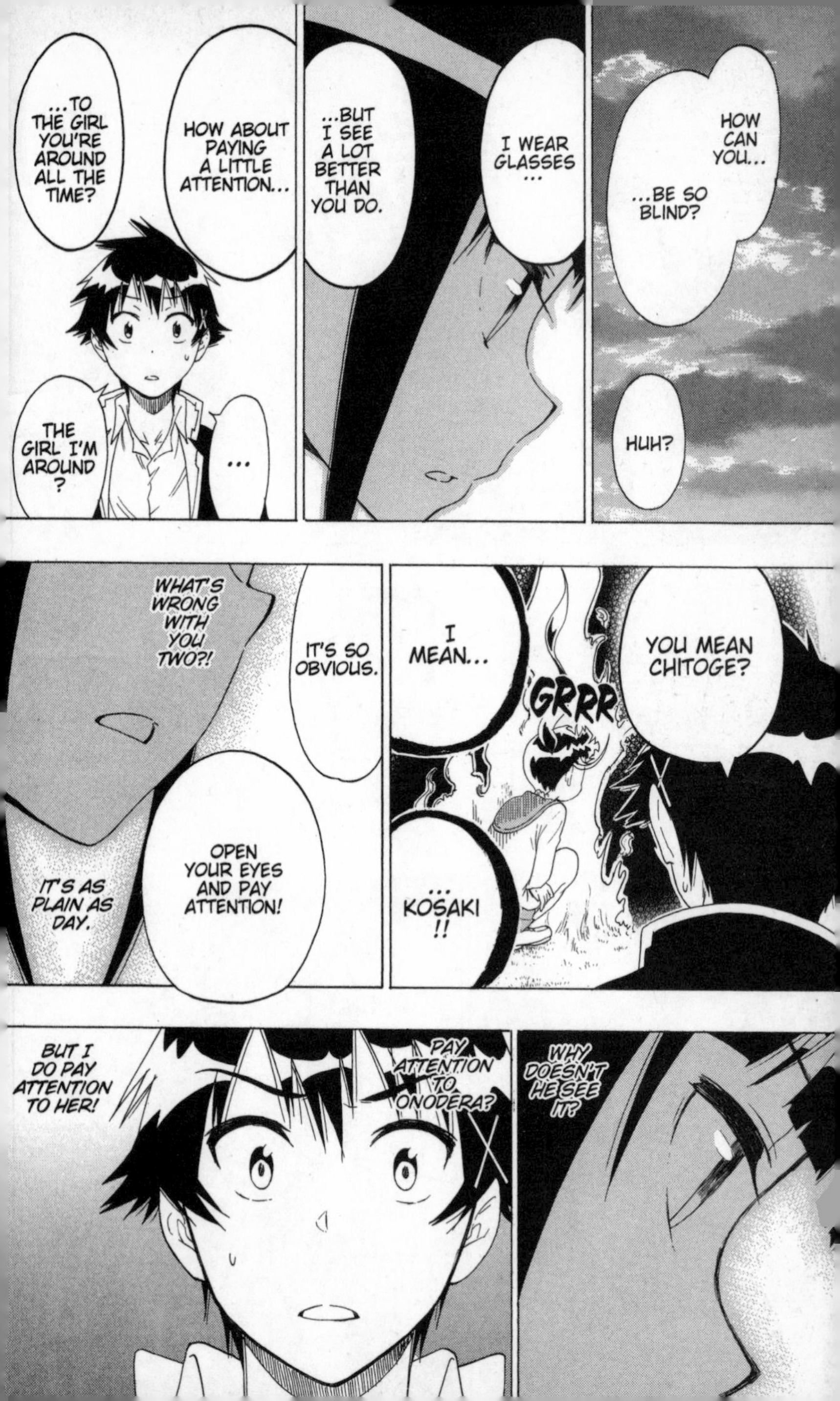
HOW CAN YOU...
...BE SO BLIND?
HUH?
I WEAR GLASSES...
...BUT I SEE A LOT BETTER THAN YOU DO.
HOW ABOUT PAYING A LITTLE ATTENTION...
...TO THE GIRL YOU'RE AROUND ALL THE TIME?
...
THE GIRL I'M AROUND?
YOU MEAN CHITOGE?
GRRR
I MEAN...
...KOSAKI!!
IT'S SO OBVIOUS.
WHAT'S WRONG WITH YOU TWO?!
OPEN YOUR EYES AND PAY ATTENTION!
IT'S AS PLAIN AS DAY.
WHY DOESN'T HE SEE IT?
PAY ATTENTION TO ONODERA?
BUT I DO PAY ATTENTION TO HER!

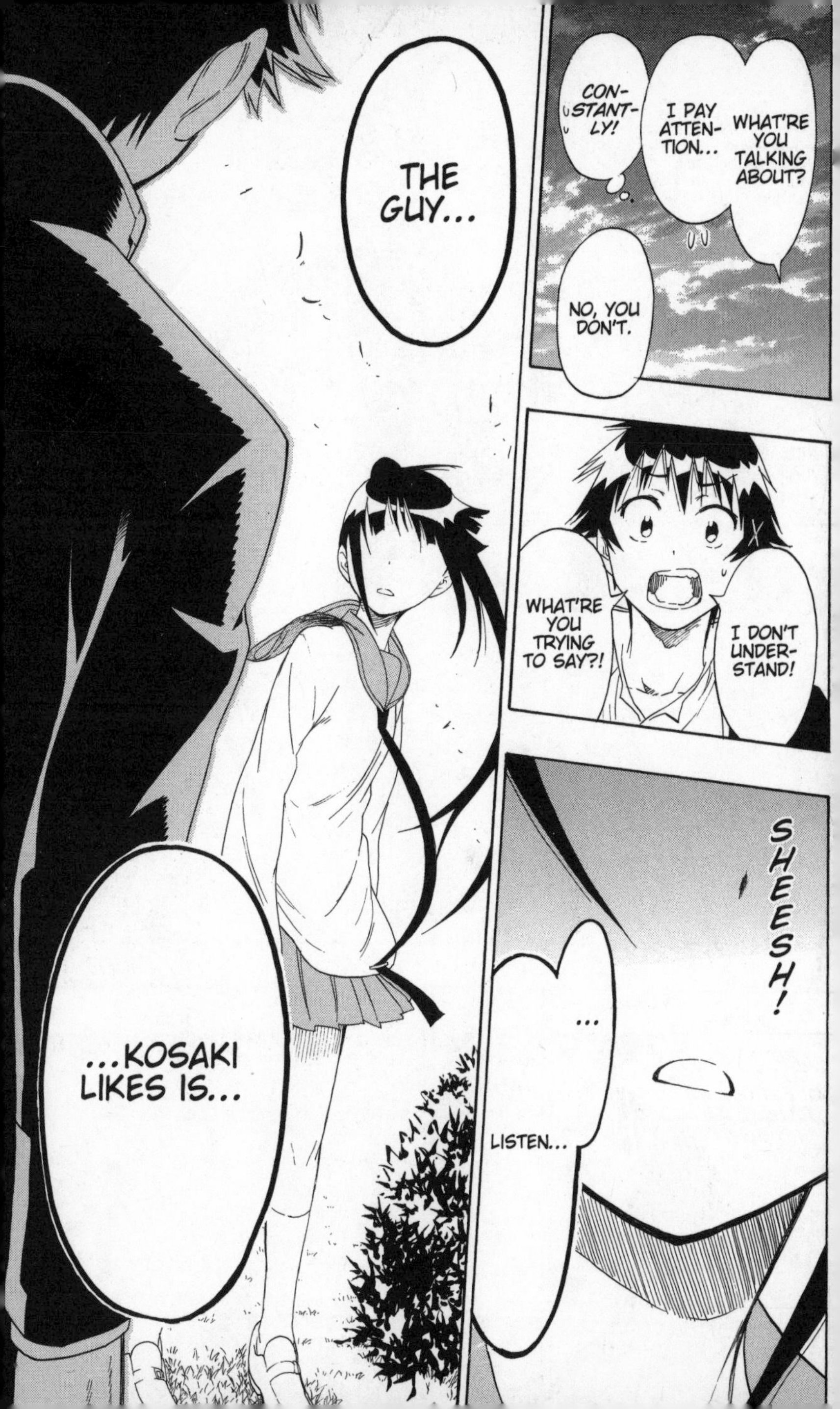
WHAT'RE YOU TALKING ABOUT?
I PAY ATTEN-TION...
CON-STANT-LY!
NO, YOU DON'T.
I DON'T UNDER-STAND!
WHAT'RE YOU TRYING TO SAY?!
SHEESH!
...
LISTEN...
THE GUY...
...KOSAKI LIKES IS...

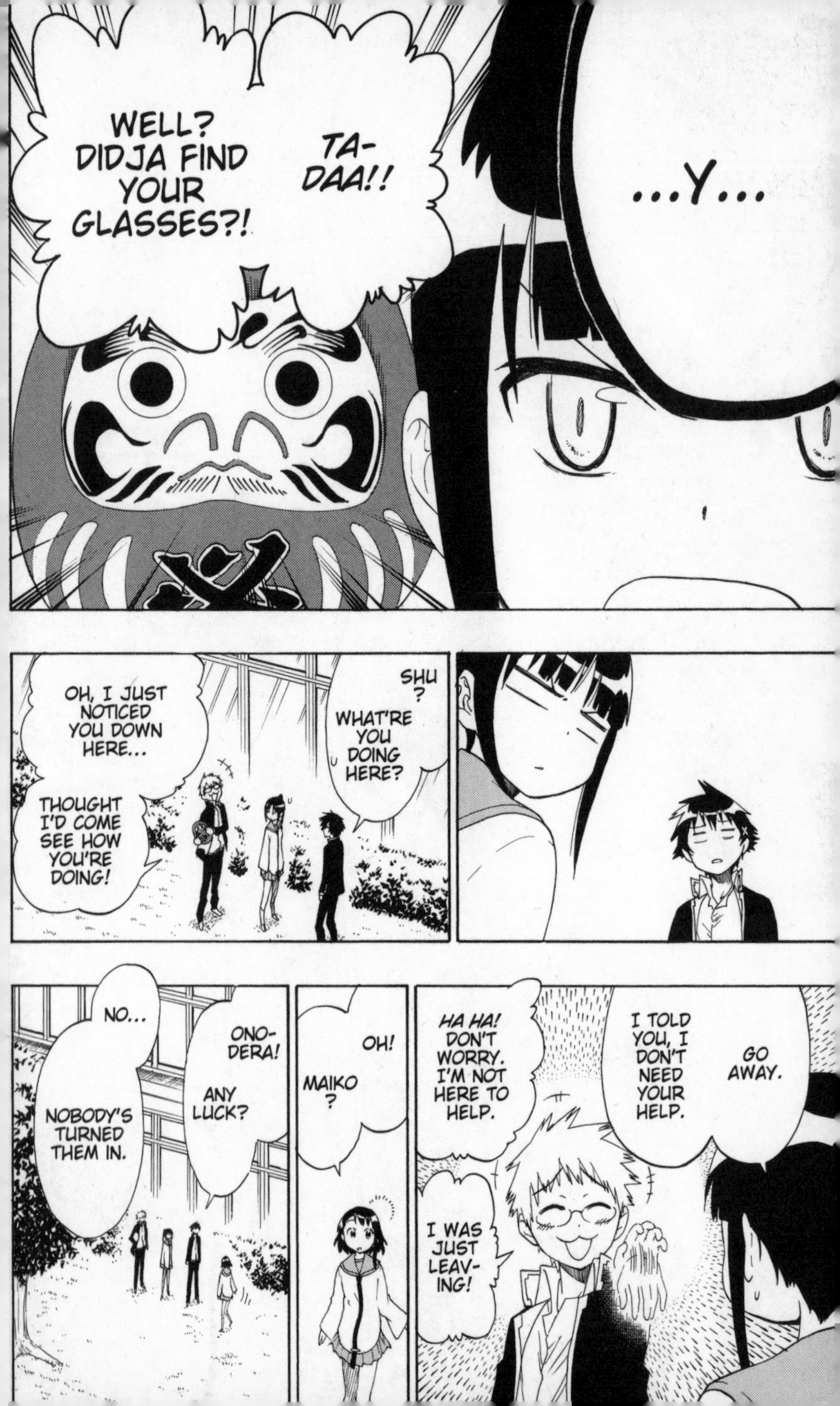
TA-DAA!!
WELL? DIDJA FIND YOUR GLASSES?!
...Y...
SHU? WHAT'RE YOU DOING HERE?
OH, I JUST NOTICED YOU DOWN HERE...
THOUGHT I'D COME SEE HOW YOU'RE DOING!
GO AWAY.
I TOLD YOU, I DON'T NEED YOUR HELP.
HA HA! DON'T WORRY. I'M NOT HERE TO HELP.
I WAS JUST LEAVING!
OH!
MAIKO?
ONO-DERA!
ANY LUCK?
NO...
NOBODY'S TURNED THEM IN.

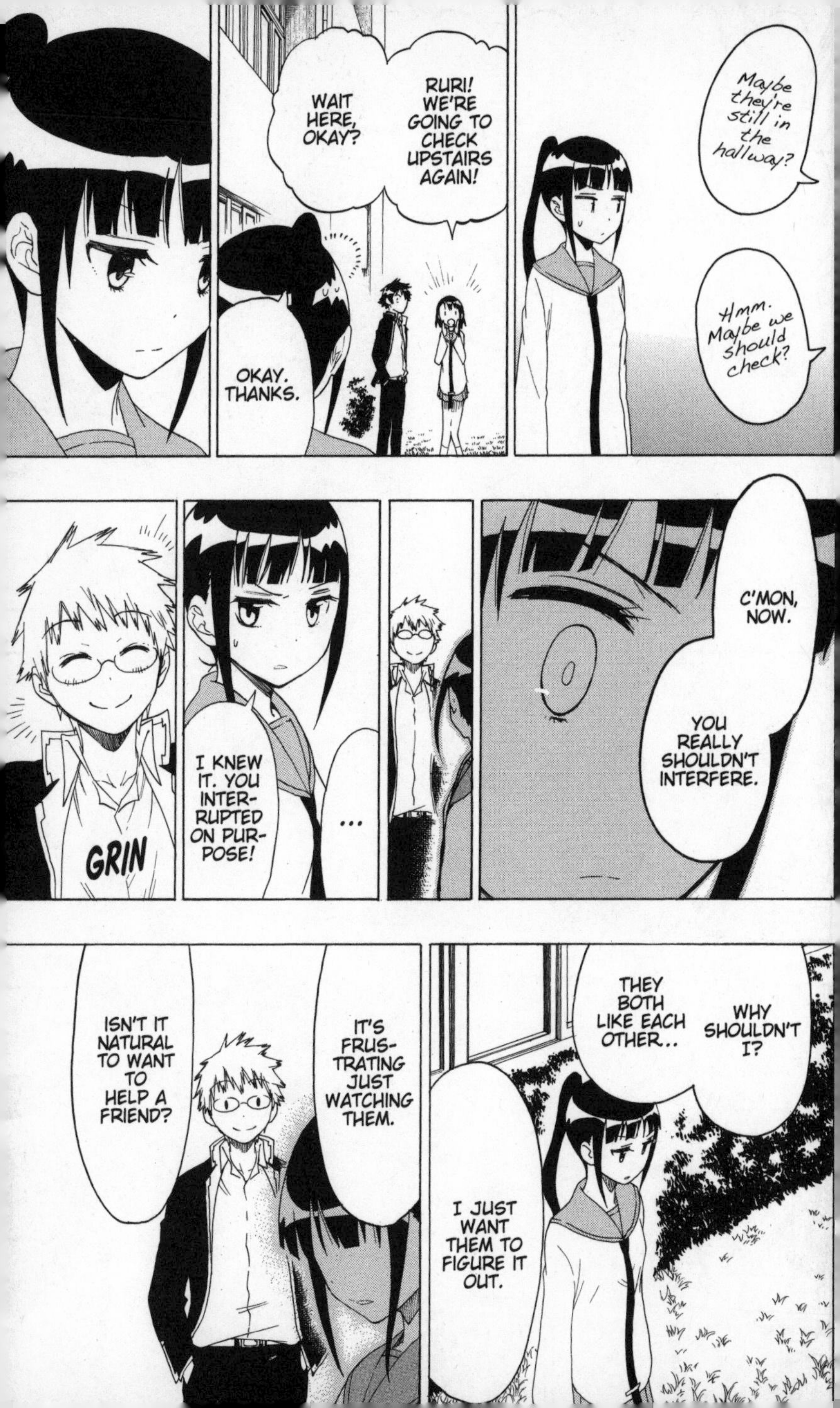

Maybe they're still in the hallway?
Hmm. Maybe we should check?
RURI! WE'RE GOING TO CHECK UPSTAIRS AGAIN!
WAIT HERE, OKAY?
OKAY. THANKS.
C'MON, NOW.
YOU REALLY SHOULDN'T INTERFERE.
...
I KNEW IT. YOU INTERRUPTED ON PURPOSE!
GRIN
WHY SHOULDN'T I?
THEY BOTH LIKE EACH OTHER...
I JUST WANT THEM TO FIGURE IT OUT.
IT'S FRUSTRATING JUST WATCHING THEM.
ISN'T IT NATURAL TO WANT TO HELP A FRIEND?

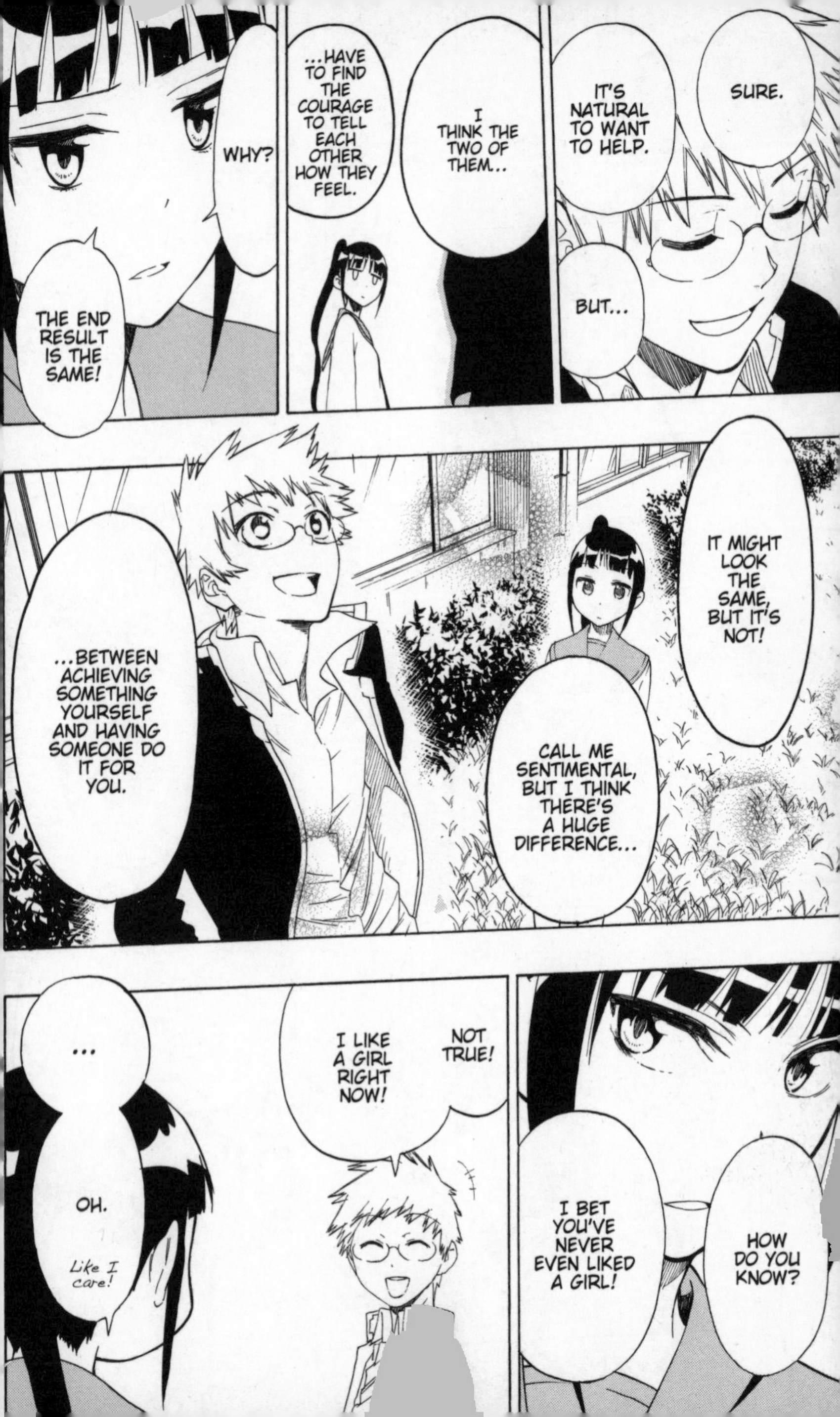
SURE.
IT'S NATURAL TO WANT TO HELP.
BUT...
I THINK THE TWO OF THEM...
...HAVE TO FIND THE COURAGE TO TELL EACH OTHER HOW THEY FEEL.
WHY?
THE END RESULT IS THE SAME!
IT MIGHT LOOK THE SAME, BUT IT'S NOT!
CALL ME SENTIMENTAL, BUT I THINK THERE'S A HUGE DIFFERENCE...
...BETWEEN ACHIEVING SOMETHING YOURSELF AND HAVING SOMEONE DO IT FOR YOU.
HOW DO YOU KNOW?
I BET YOU'VE NEVER EVEN LIKED A GIRL!
NOT TRUE!
I LIKE A GIRL RIGHT NOW!
...
OH.
Like I care!

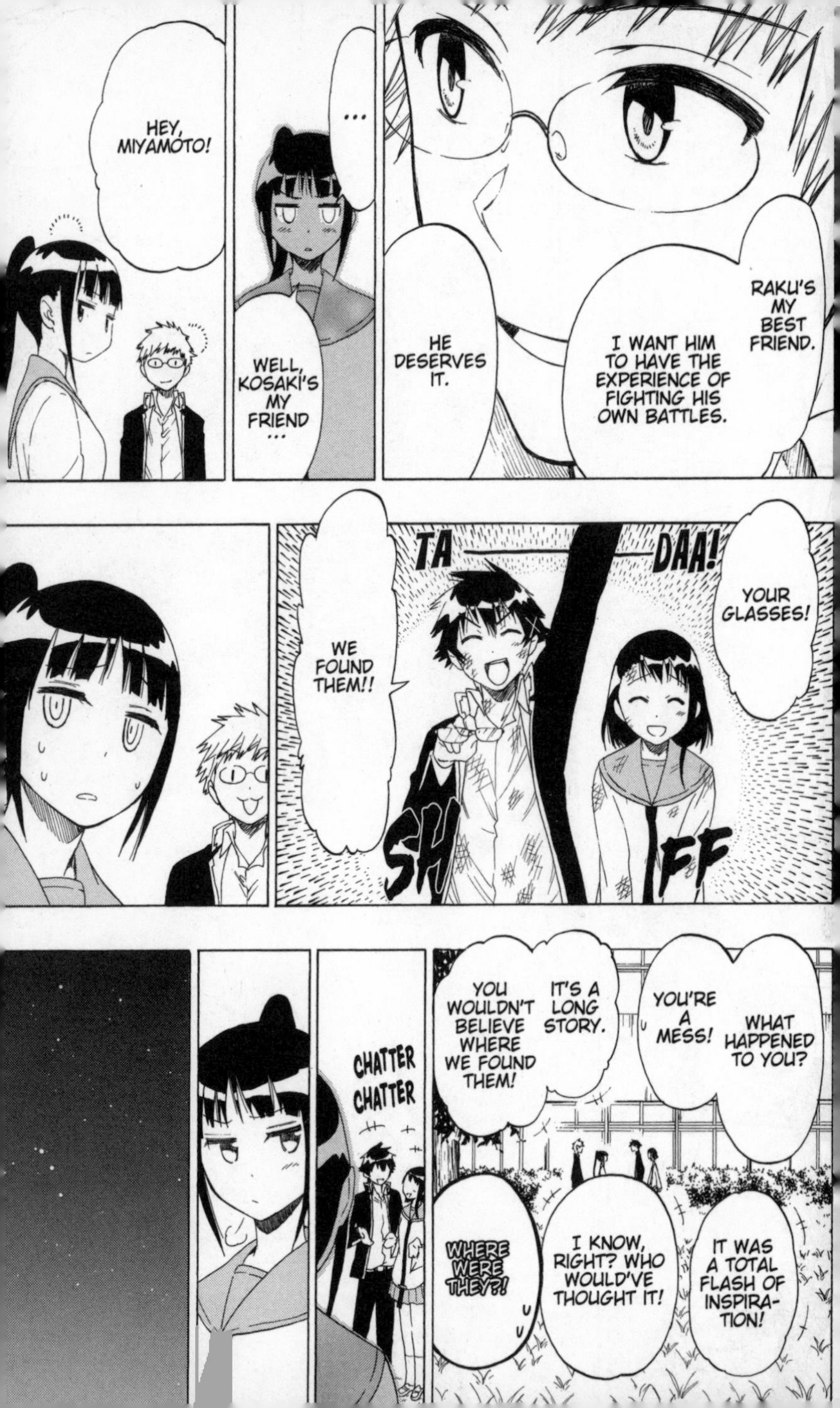
RAKU'S MY BEST FRIEND.
I WANT HIM TO HAVE THE EXPERIENCE OF FIGHTING HIS OWN BATTLES.
HE DESERVES IT.
...
WELL, KOSAKI'S MY FRIEND ...
HEY, MIYAMOTO!
TA——DAA!
YOUR GLASSES!
WE FOUND THEM!!
SHFF
WHAT HAPPENED TO YOU?
YOU'RE A MESS!
IT'S A LONG STORY.
YOU WOULDN'T BELIEVE WHERE WE FOUND THEM!
IT WAS A TOTAL FLASH OF INSPIRATION!
I KNOW, RIGHT? WHO WOULD'VE THOUGHT IT!
WHERE WERE THEY?!
CHATTER CHATTER

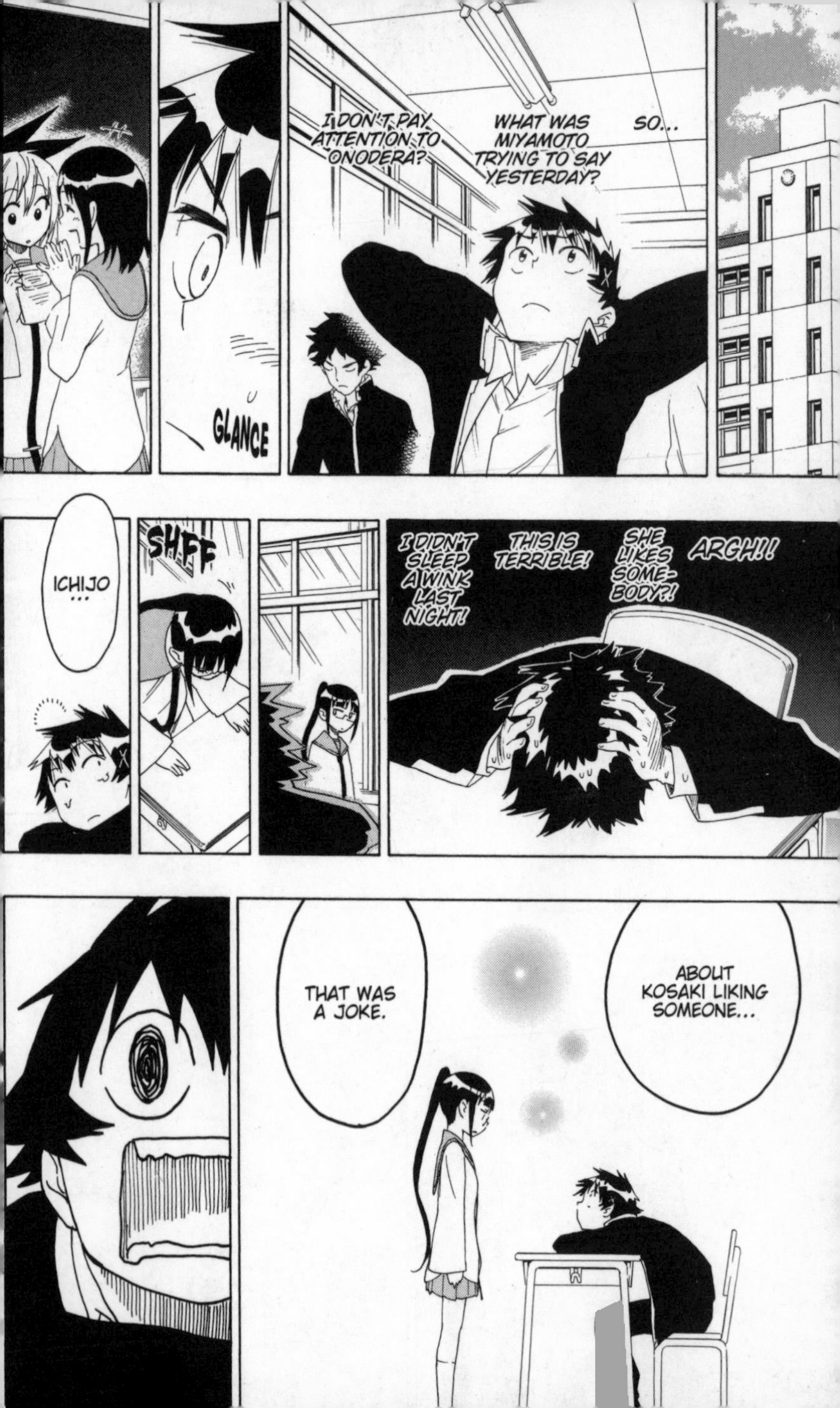
SO...
WHAT WAS MIYAMOTO TRYING TO SAY YESTERDAY?
I DON'T PAY ATTENTION TO ONODERA?
GLANCE
ARGH!!
SHE LIKES SOMEBODY?!
THIS IS TERRIBLE!
I DIDN'T SLEEP A WINK LAST NIGHT!
SHFF
ICHIJO...
ABOUT KOSAKI LIKING SOMEONE...
THAT WAS A JOKE.

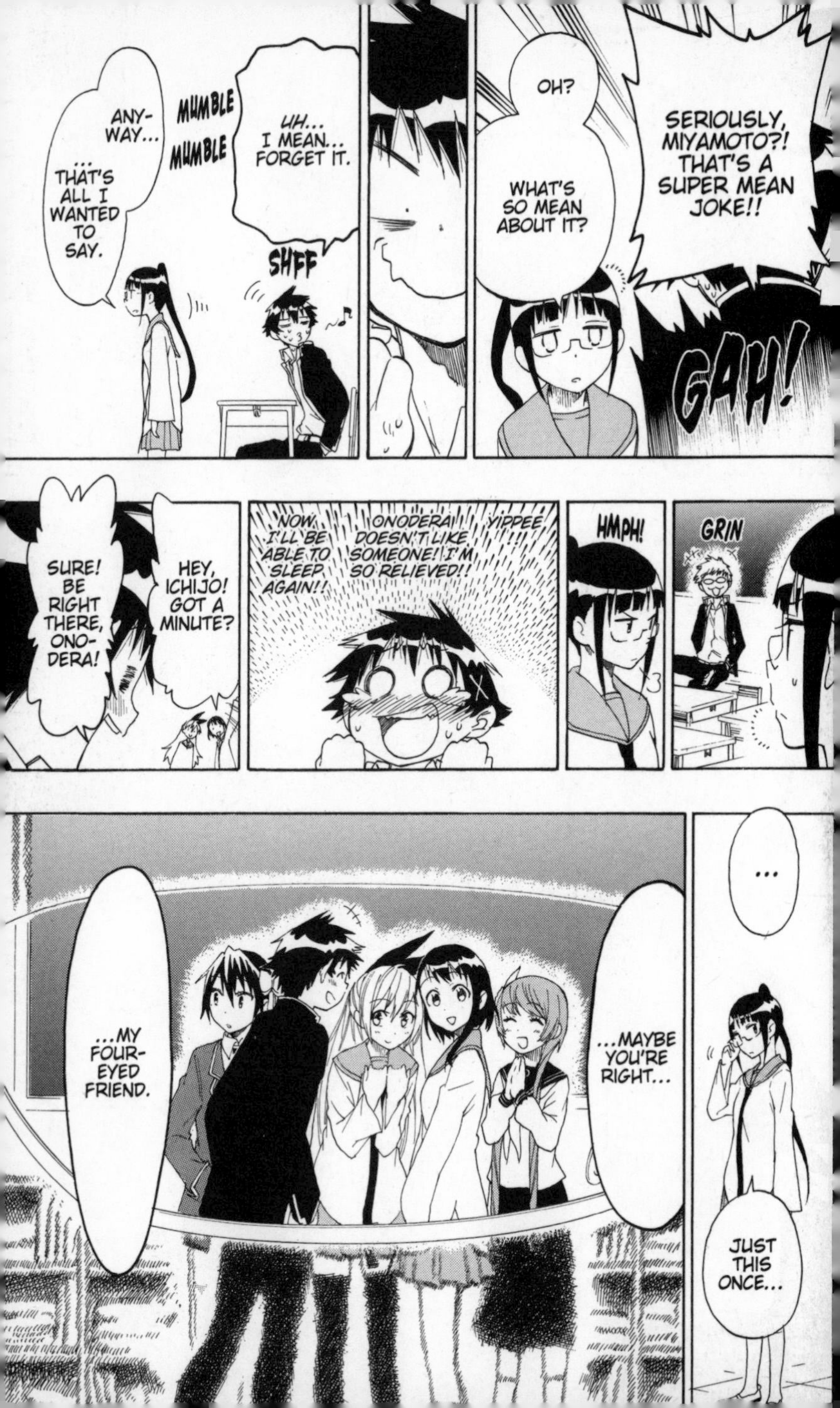
SERIOUSLY, MIYAMOTO?! THAT'S A SUPER MEAN JOKE!!
GAH!
OH?
WHAT'S SO MEAN ABOUT IT?
UH... I MEAN... FORGET IT.
MUMBLE MUMBLE
SHFF
ANY-WAY...
...THAT'S ALL I WANTED TO SAY.
GRIN
HMPH!
YIPPEE!!!
ONODERA DOESN'T LIKE SOMEONE! I'M SO RELIEVED!!
NOW I'LL BE ABLE TO SLEEP AGAIN!!
HEY, ICHIJO! GOT A MINUTE?
SURE! BE RIGHT THERE, ONO-DERA!
...
JUST THIS ONCE...
...MAYBE YOU'RE RIGHT...
...MY FOUR-EYED FRIEND.

Secretly, he was helping.

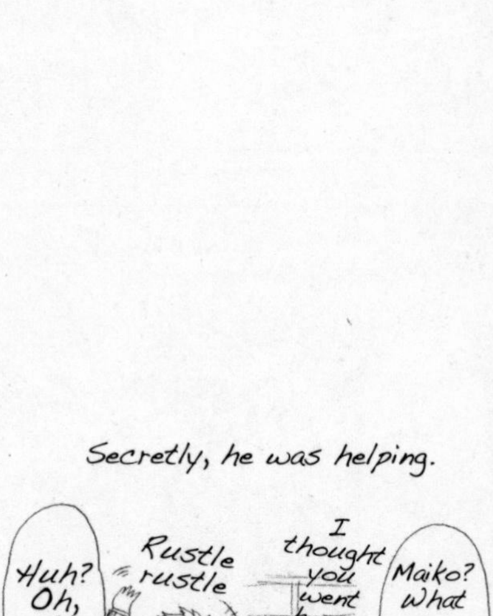
Maiko? What are you doing?
I thought you went home.
Rustle rustle
Huh? Oh, nothing!

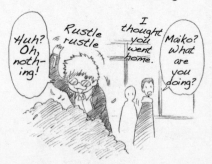

Chapter 59: Long Time No See

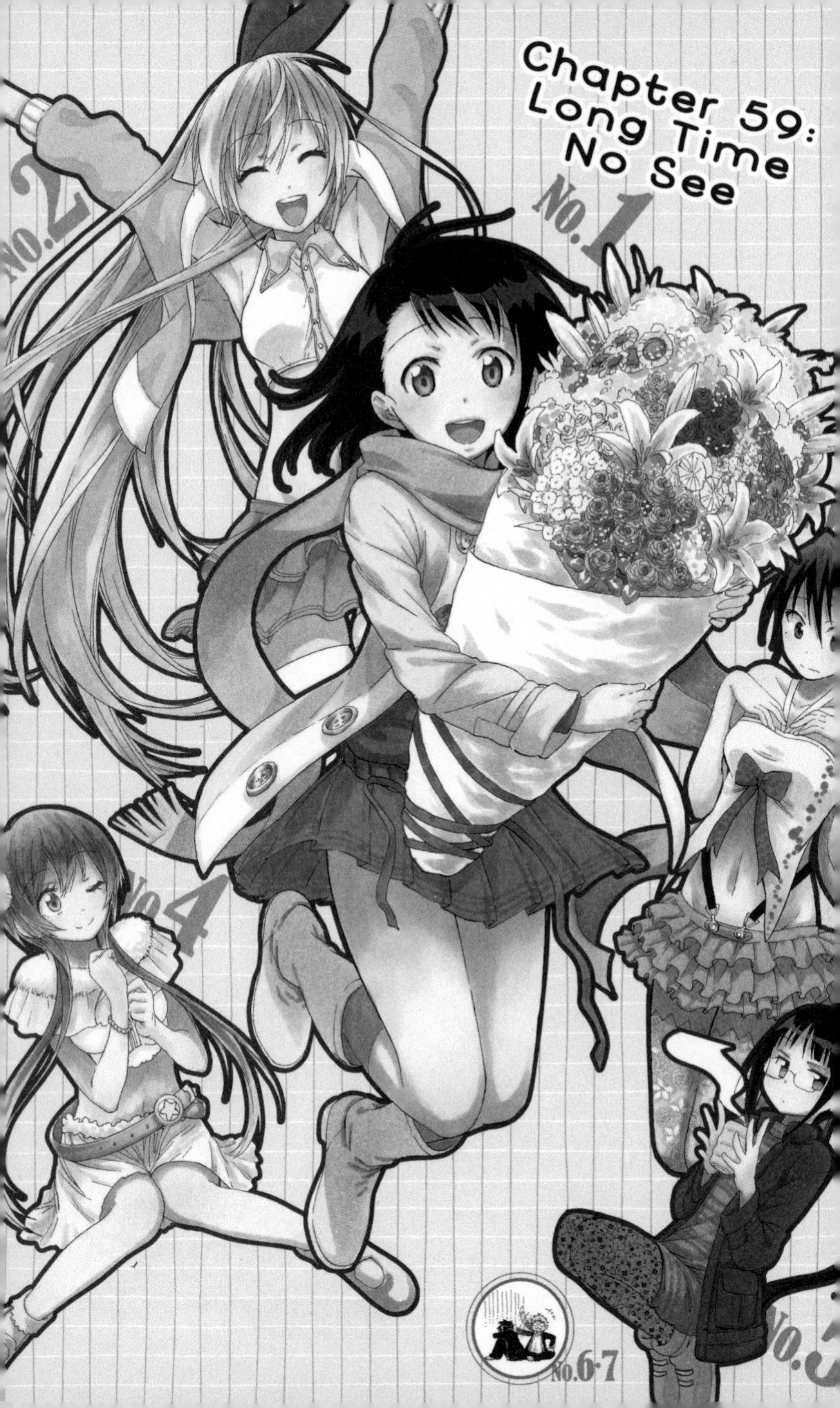

No.1
No.2
No.4
No.3
No.6·7

NISEKOI
False Love

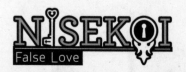

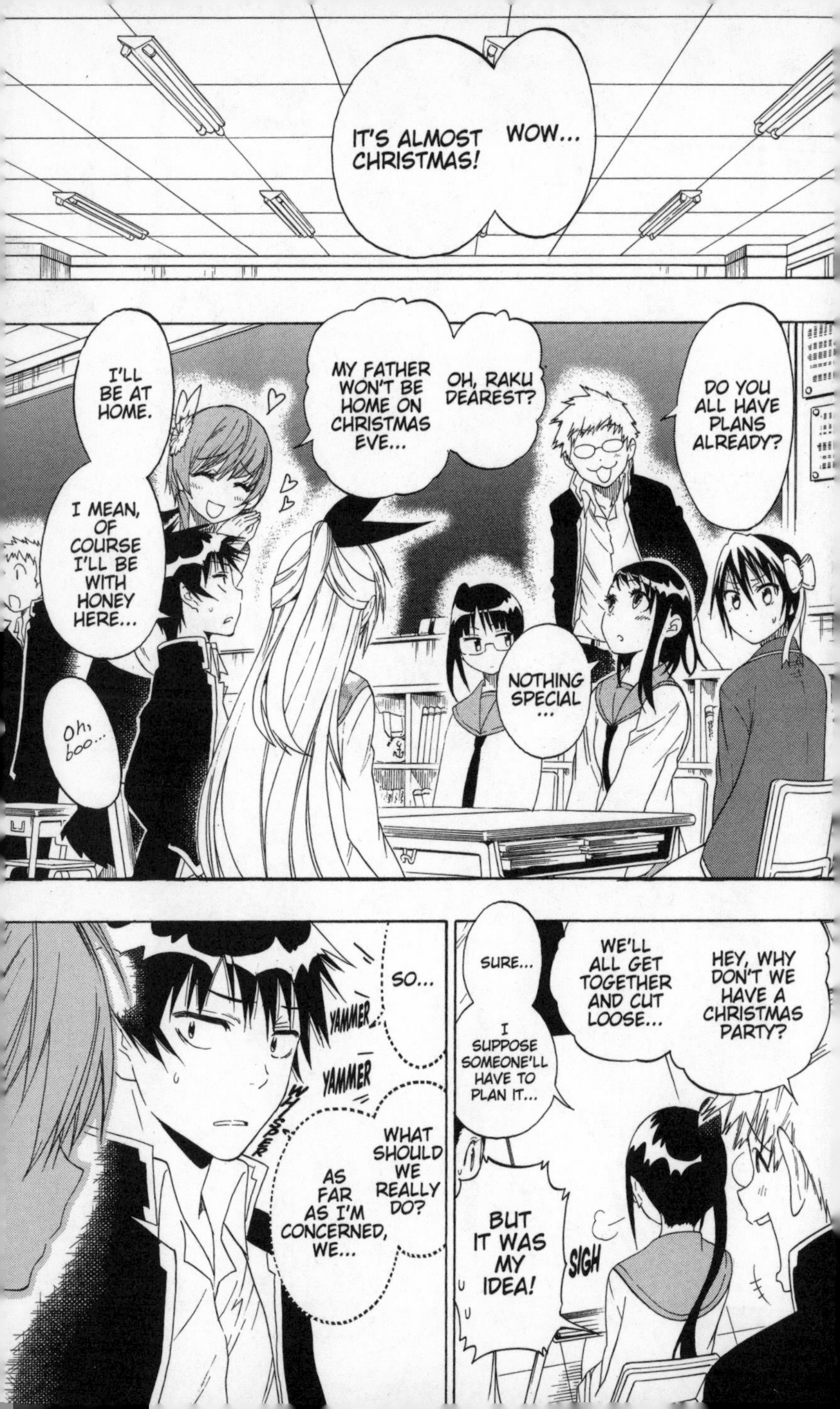
WOW...
IT'S ALMOST CHRISTMAS!
DO YOU ALL HAVE PLANS ALREADY?
OH, RAKU DEAREST?
MY FATHER WON'T BE HOME ON CHRISTMAS EVE...
NOTHING SPECIAL ...
I'LL BE AT HOME.
I MEAN, OF COURSE I'LL BE WITH HONEY HERE...
Oh, boo...
HEY, WHY DON'T WE HAVE A CHRISTMAS PARTY?
WE'LL ALL GET TOGETHER AND CUT LOOSE...
SURE...
I SUPPOSE SOMEONE'LL HAVE TO PLAN IT...
BUT IT WAS MY IDEA!
SIGH
SO...
YAMMER
YAMMER
WHISPER
WHAT SHOULD WE REALLY DO?
AS FAR AS I'M CONCERNED, WE...

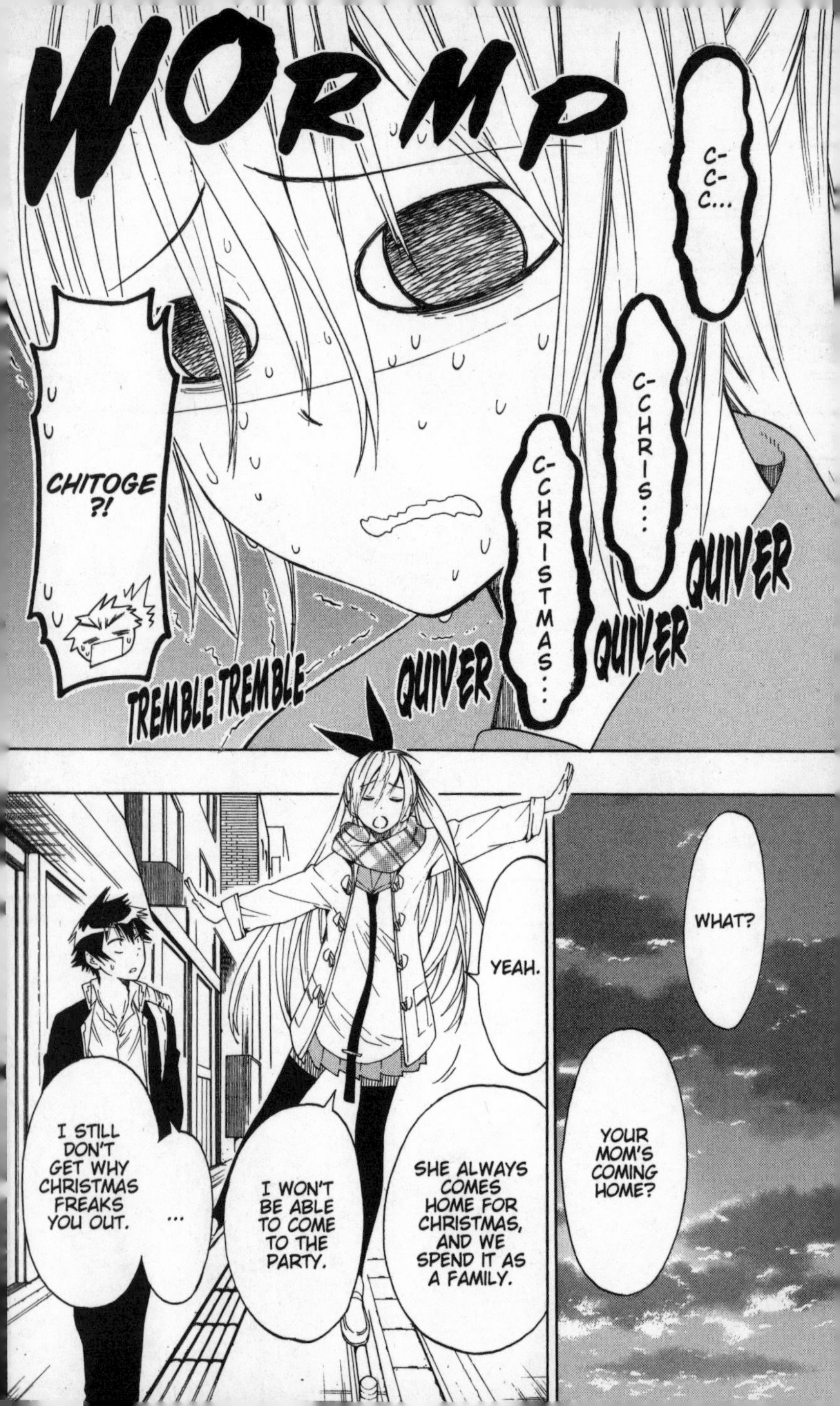

WORMP
C-C-C...
C-CHRIS...
C-CHRISTMAS...
QUIVER
QUIVER
QUIVER
TREMBLE TREMBLE
CHITOGE?!
WHAT?
YOUR MOM'S COMING HOME?
YEAH.
SHE ALWAYS COMES HOME FOR CHRISTMAS, AND WE SPEND IT AS A FAMILY.
I WON'T BE ABLE TO COME TO THE PARTY.
...
I STILL DON'T GET WHY CHRISTMAS FREAKS YOU OUT.

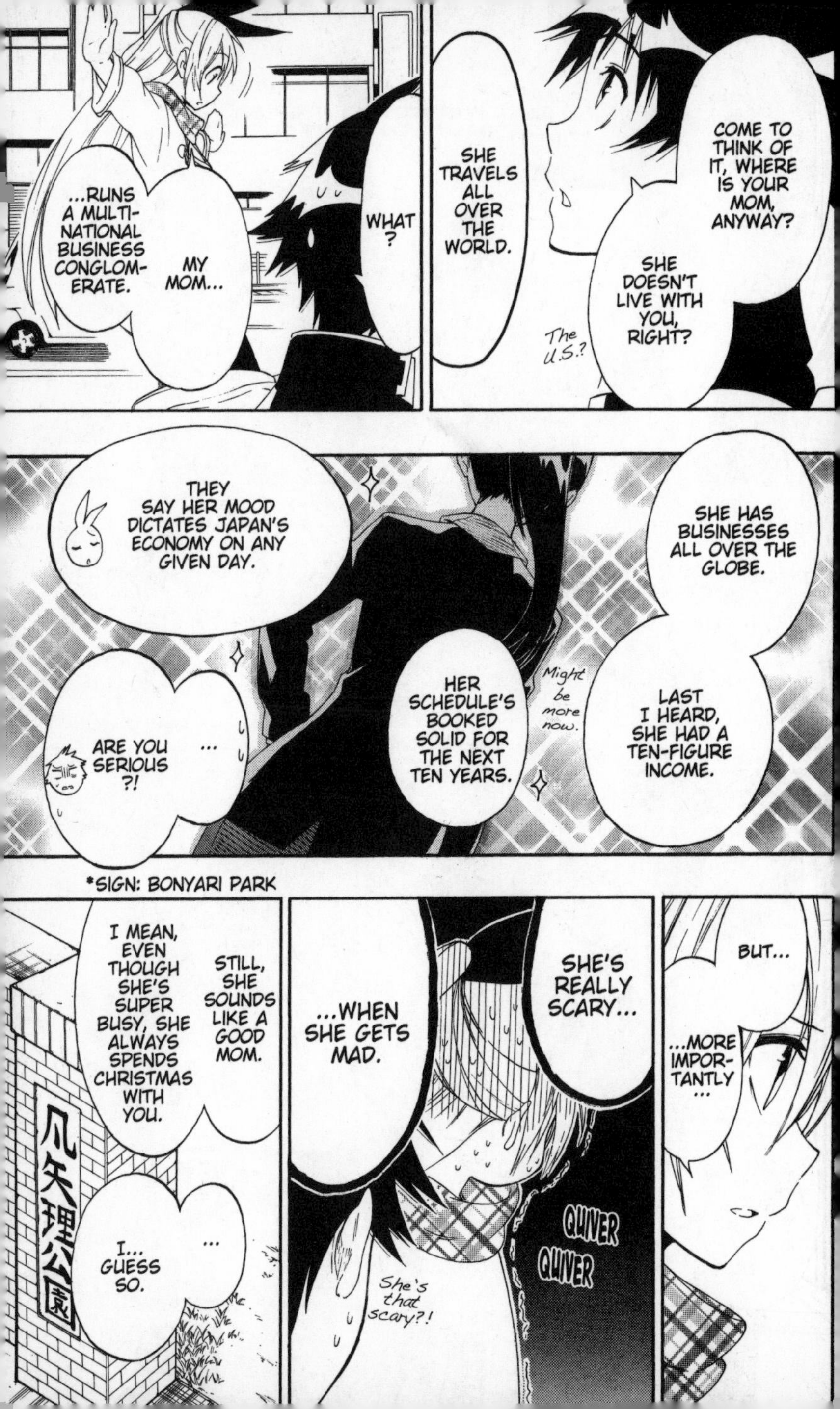
COME TO THINK OF IT, WHERE IS YOUR MOM, ANYWAY?
SHE DOESN'T LIVE WITH YOU, RIGHT?
The U.S.?
SHE TRAVELS ALL OVER THE WORLD.
WHAT?
MY MOM...
...RUNS A MULTI-NATIONAL BUSINESS CONGLOMERATE.
SHE HAS BUSINESSES ALL OVER THE GLOBE.
LAST I HEARD, SHE HAD A TEN-FIGURE INCOME.
Might be more now.
THEY SAY HER MOOD DICTATES JAPAN'S ECONOMY ON ANY GIVEN DAY.
HER SCHEDULE'S BOOKED SOLID FOR THE NEXT TEN YEARS.
...
ARE YOU SERIOUS?!
BUT...
...MORE IMPORTANTLY...
SHE'S REALLY SCARY...
...WHEN SHE GETS MAD.
QUIVER
QUIVER
She's that scary?!
STILL, SHE SOUNDS LIKE A GOOD MOM.
I MEAN, EVEN THOUGH SHE'S SUPER BUSY, SHE ALWAYS SPENDS CHRISTMAS WITH YOU.
...
I... GUESS SO.
凡矢理公園
*SIGN: BONYARI PARK

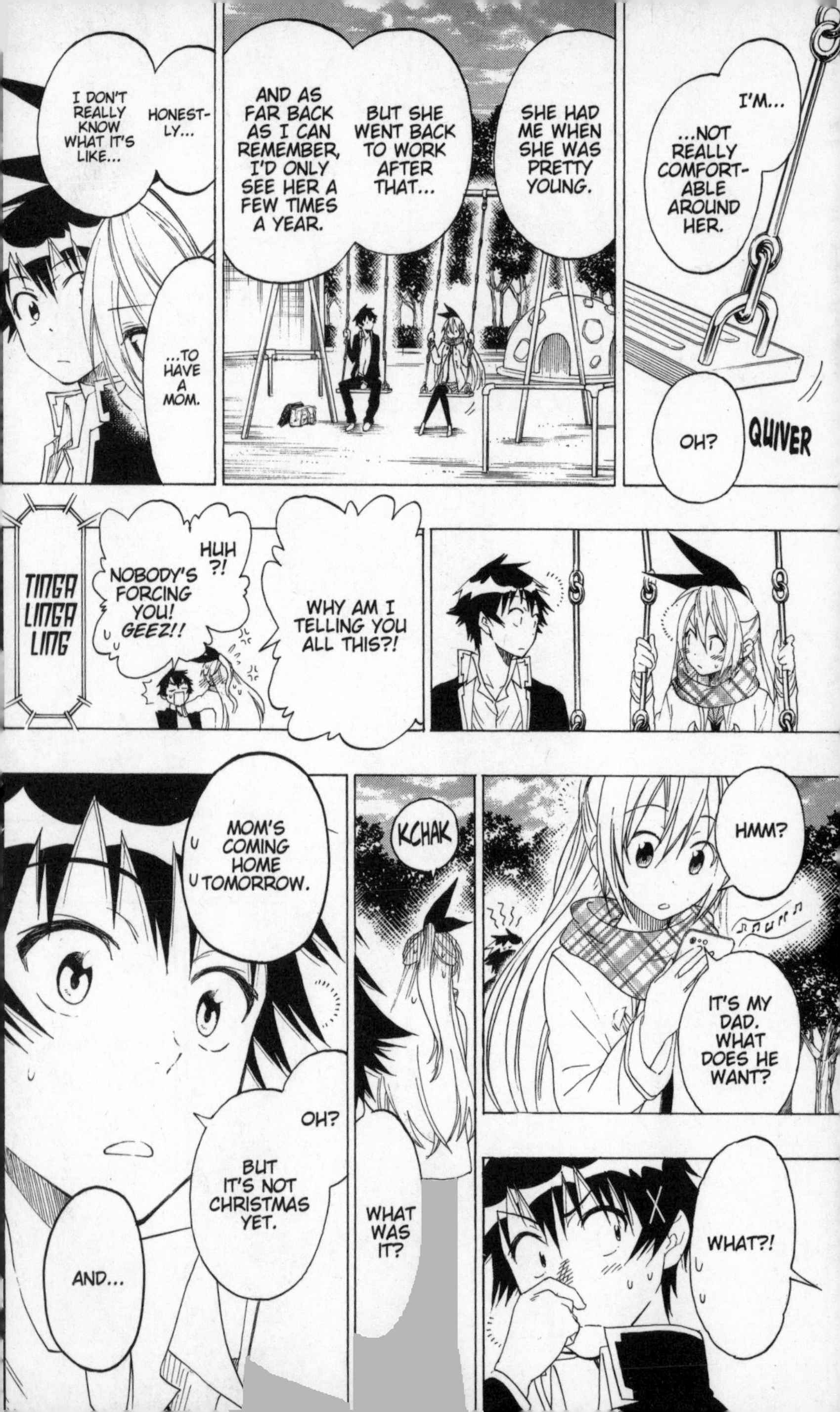
I'M...
...NOT REALLY COMFORTABLE AROUND HER.
OH?
QUIVER
SHE HAD ME WHEN SHE WAS PRETTY YOUNG.
BUT SHE WENT BACK TO WORK AFTER THAT...
AND AS FAR BACK AS I CAN REMEMBER, I'D ONLY SEE HER A FEW TIMES A YEAR.
HONESTLY...
I DON'T REALLY KNOW WHAT IT'S LIKE...
...TO HAVE A MOM.
WHY AM I TELLING YOU ALL THIS?!
HUH?!
NOBODY'S FORCING YOU! GEEZ!!
TINGA LINGA LING
HMM?
IT'S MY DAD. WHAT DOES HE WANT?
WHAT?!
KCHAK
WHAT WAS IT?
MOM'S COMING HOME TOMORROW.
OH?
BUT IT'S NOT CHRISTMAS YET.
AND...

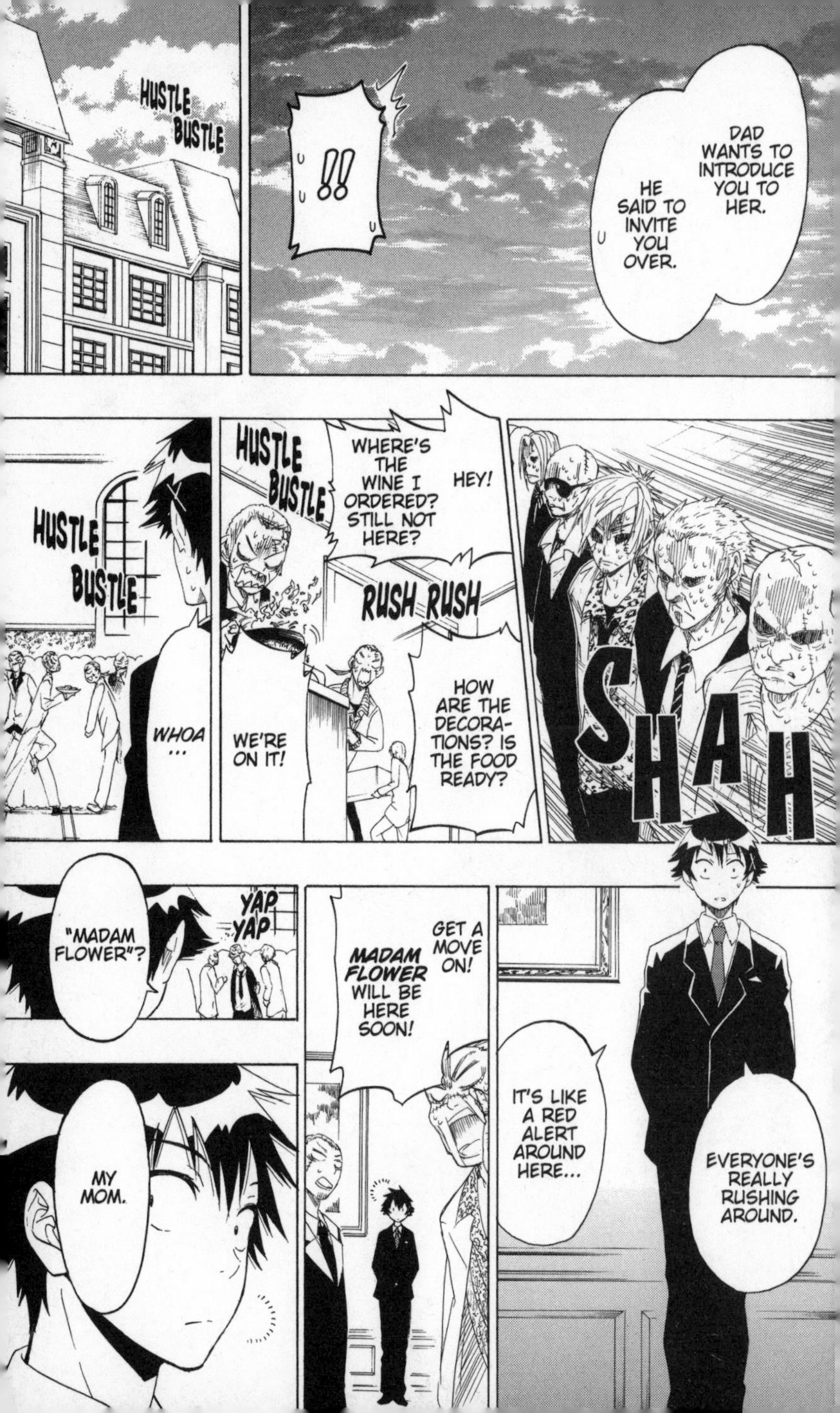
DAD WANTS TO INTRODUCE YOU TO HER.
HE SAID TO INVITE YOU OVER.
!!
HUSTLE BUSTLE
SHAH
HEY!
WHERE'S THE WINE I ORDERED? STILL NOT HERE?
HUSTLE BUSTLE
RUSH RUSH
HOW ARE THE DECORATIONS? IS THE FOOD READY?
WE'RE ON IT!
HUSTLE BUSTLE
WHOA...
EVERYONE'S REALLY RUSHING AROUND.
IT'S LIKE A RED ALERT AROUND HERE...
GET A MOVE ON!
MADAM FLOWER WILL BE HERE SOON!
YAP YAP
"MADAM FLOWER"?
MY MOM.

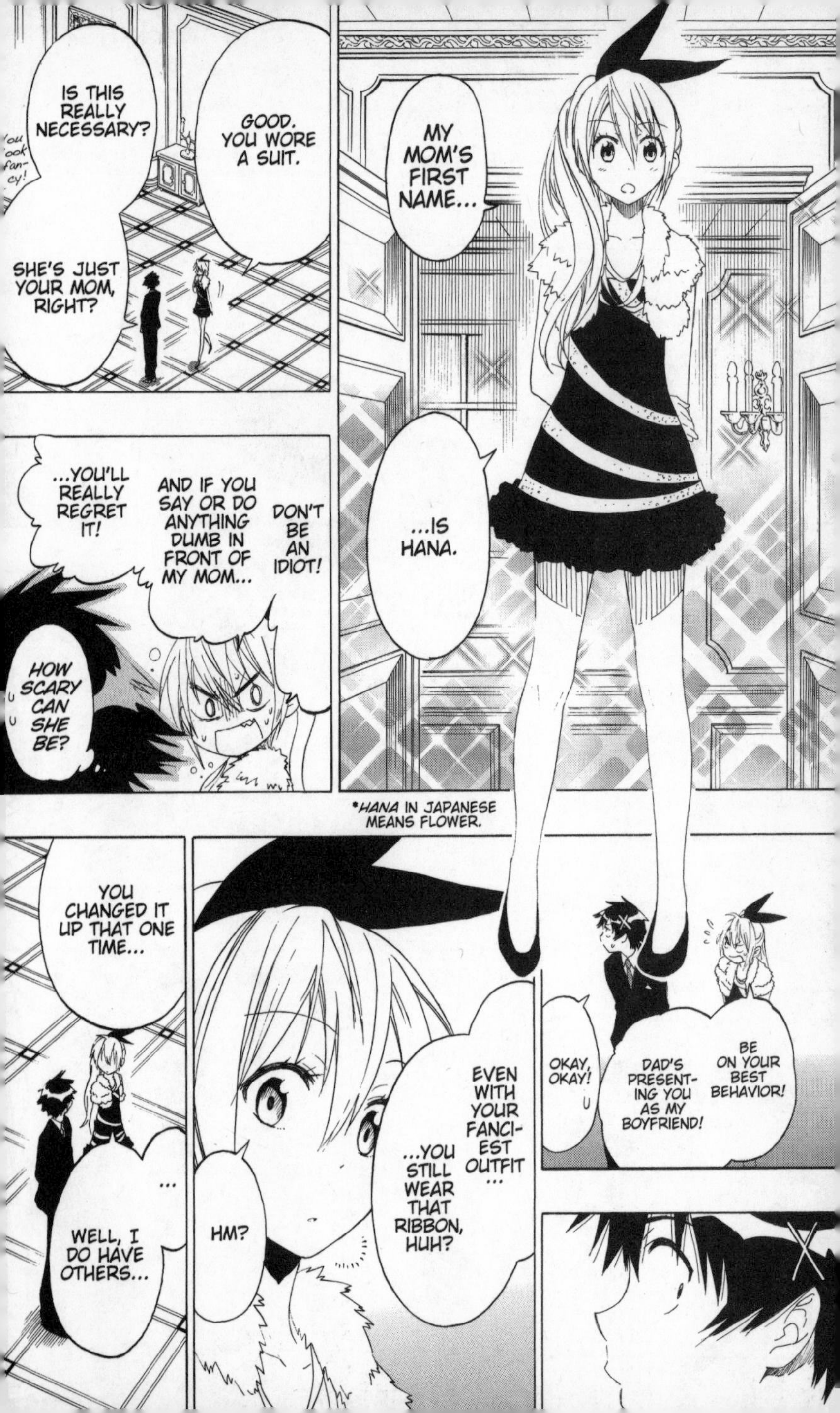
MY MOM'S FIRST NAME...
...IS HANA.
*HANA IN JAPANESE MEANS FLOWER.
GOOD. YOU WORE A SUIT.
IS THIS REALLY NECESSARY?
You look fancy!
SHE'S JUST YOUR MOM, RIGHT?
DON'T BE AN IDIOT!
AND IF YOU SAY OR DO ANYTHING DUMB IN FRONT OF MY MOM...
...YOU'LL REALLY REGRET IT!
HOW SCARY CAN SHE BE?
BE ON YOUR BEST BEHAVIOR!
DAD'S PRESENTING YOU AS MY BOYFRIEND!
OKAY, OKAY!
EVEN WITH YOUR FANCIEST OUTFIT...
...YOU STILL WEAR THAT RIBBON, HUH?
HM?
YOU CHANGED IT UP THAT ONE TIME...
...
WELL, I DO HAVE OTHERS...

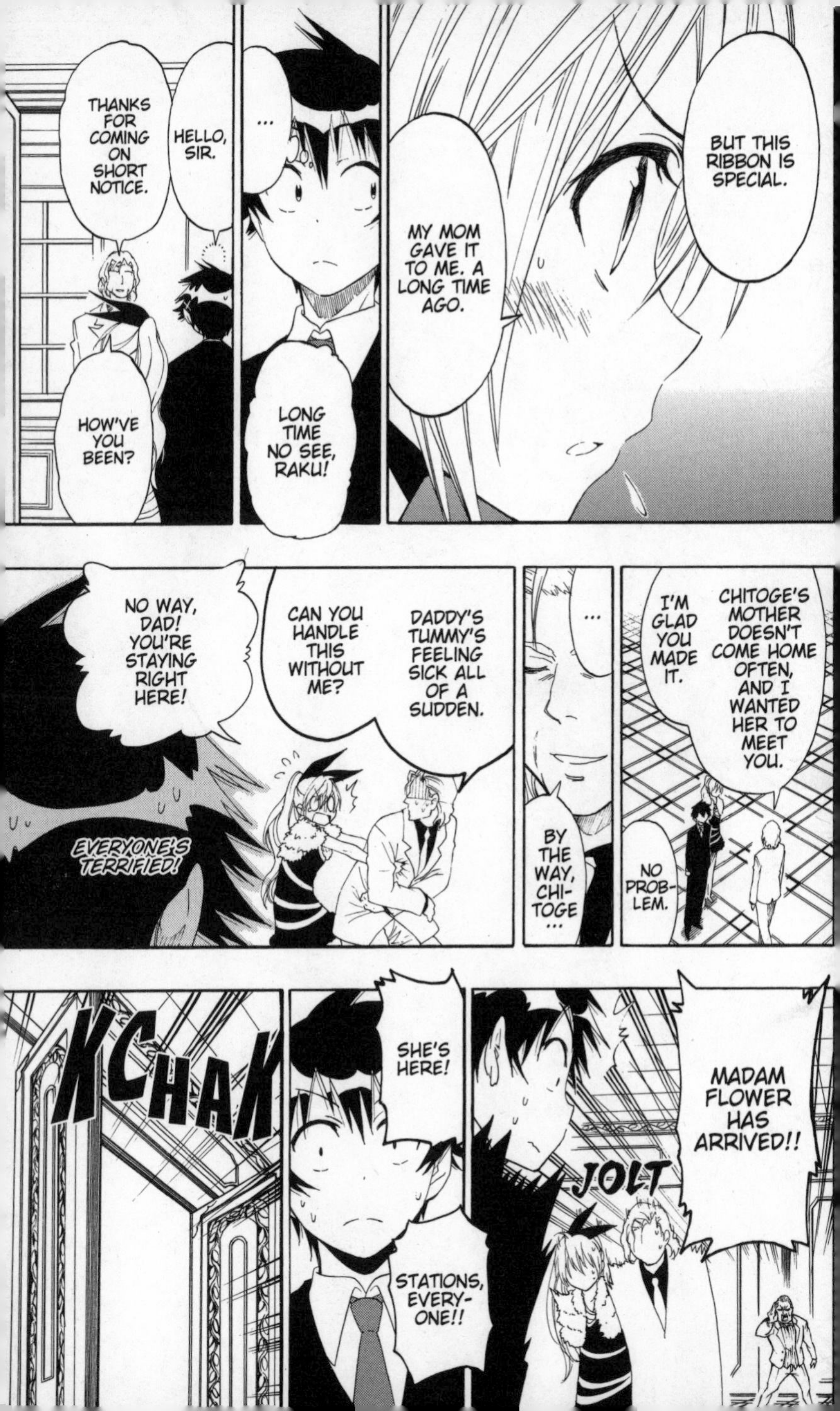
BUT THIS RIBBON IS SPECIAL.
MY MOM GAVE IT TO ME. A LONG TIME AGO.
...
LONG TIME NO SEE, RAKU!
HELLO, SIR.
THANKS FOR COMING ON SHORT NOTICE.
HOW'VE YOU BEEN?
CHITOGE'S MOTHER DOESN'T COME HOME OFTEN, AND I WANTED HER TO MEET YOU.
I'M GLAD YOU MADE IT.
NO PROBLEM.
...
BY THE WAY, CHITOGE...
DADDY'S TUMMY'S FEELING SICK ALL OF A SUDDEN.
CAN YOU HANDLE THIS WITHOUT ME?
NO WAY, DAD! YOU'RE STAYING RIGHT HERE!
EVERYONE'S TERRIFIED!
MADAM FLOWER HAS ARRIVED!!
JOLT
SHE'S HERE!
STATIONS, EVERYONE!!
KCHAK

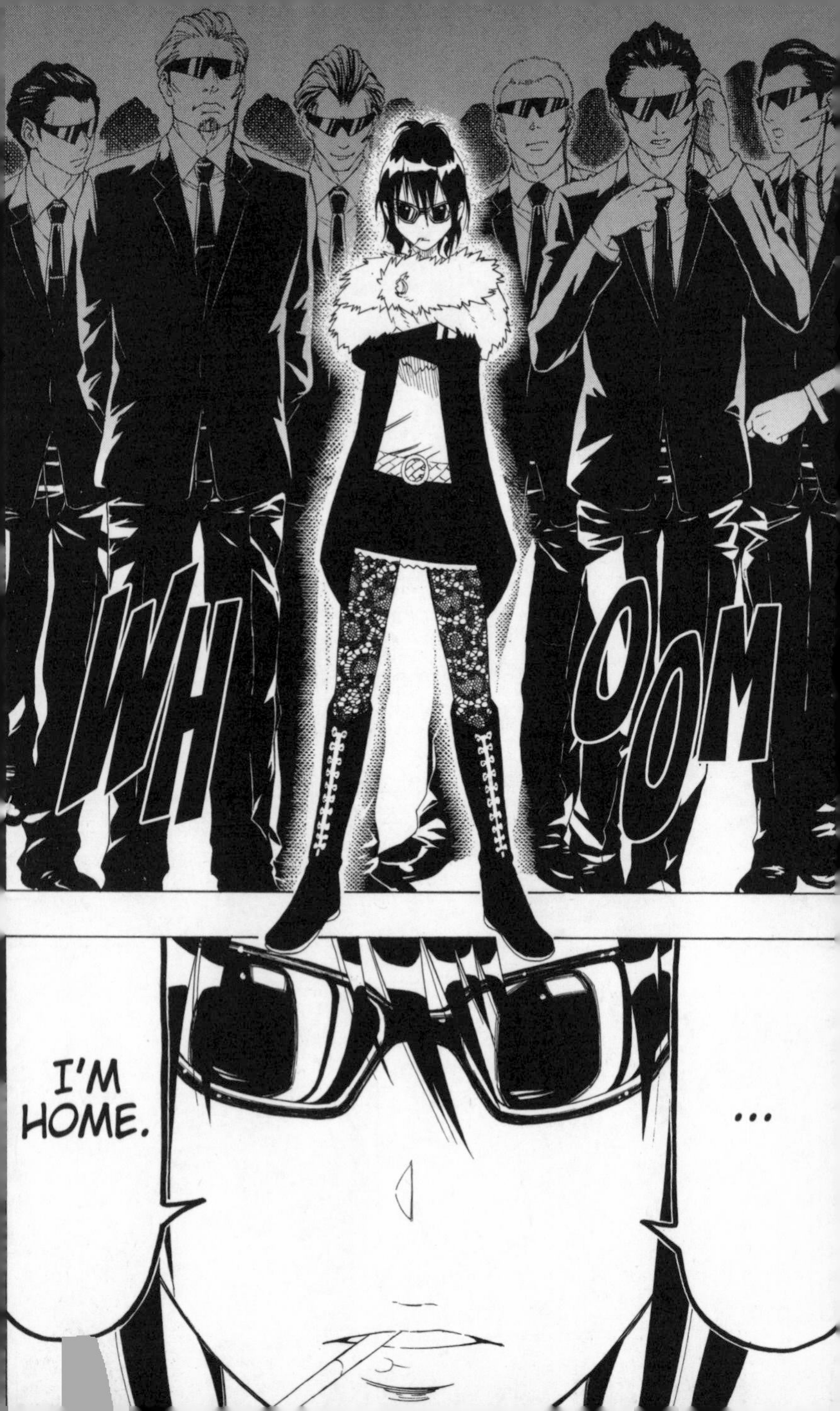
WHOOM
...
I'M HOME.

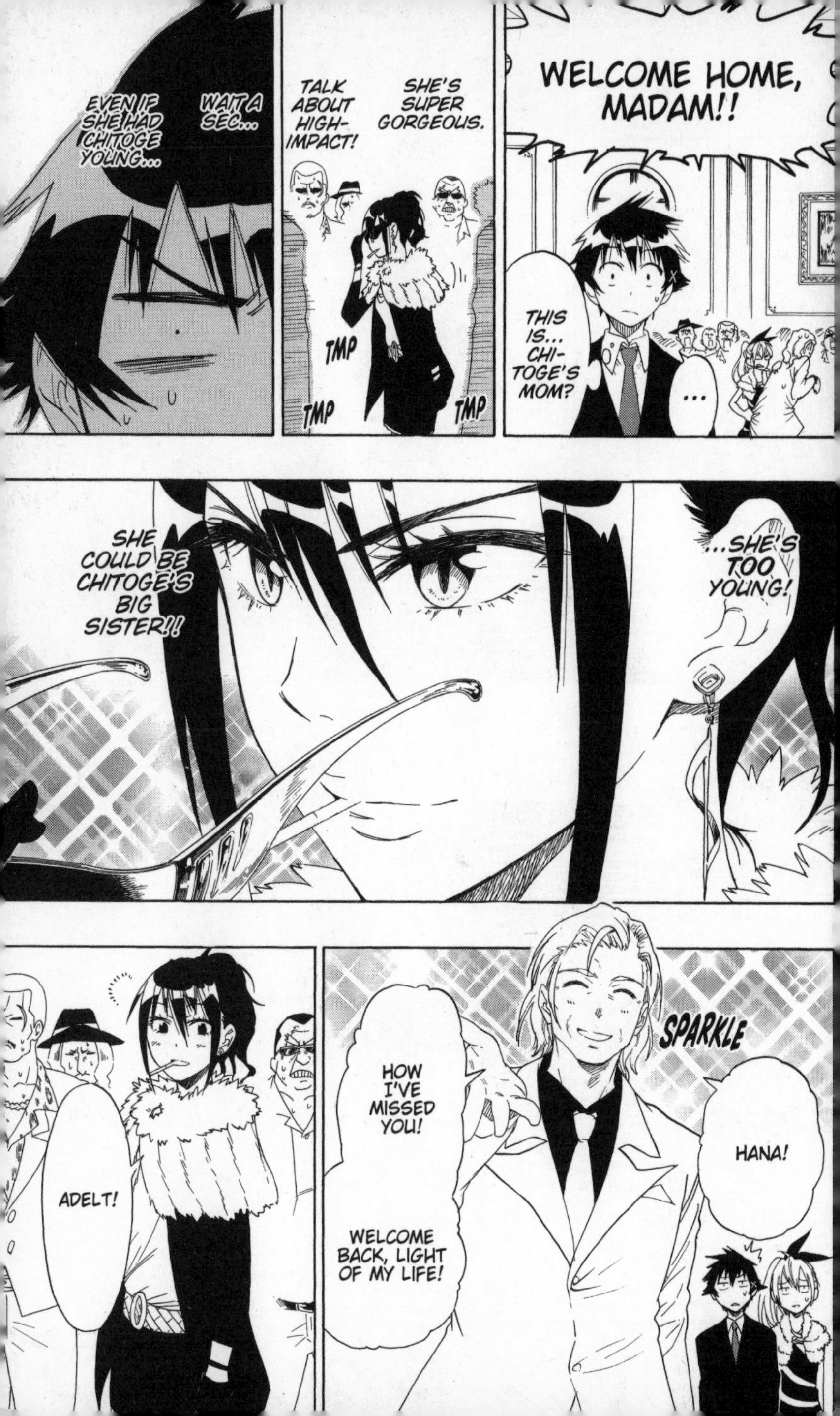
WELCOME HOME, MADAM!!
THIS IS... CHI-TOGE'S MOM?
...
SHE'S SUPER GORGEOUS.
TALK ABOUT HIGH-IMPACT!
TMP
TMP
TMP
WAIT A SEC...
EVEN IF SHE HAD CHITOGE YOUNG...
...SHE'S TOO YOUNG!
SHE COULD BE CHITOGE'S BIG SISTER!!
HANA!
SPARKLE
HOW I'VE MISSED YOU!
WELCOME BACK, LIGHT OF MY LIFE!
ADELT!

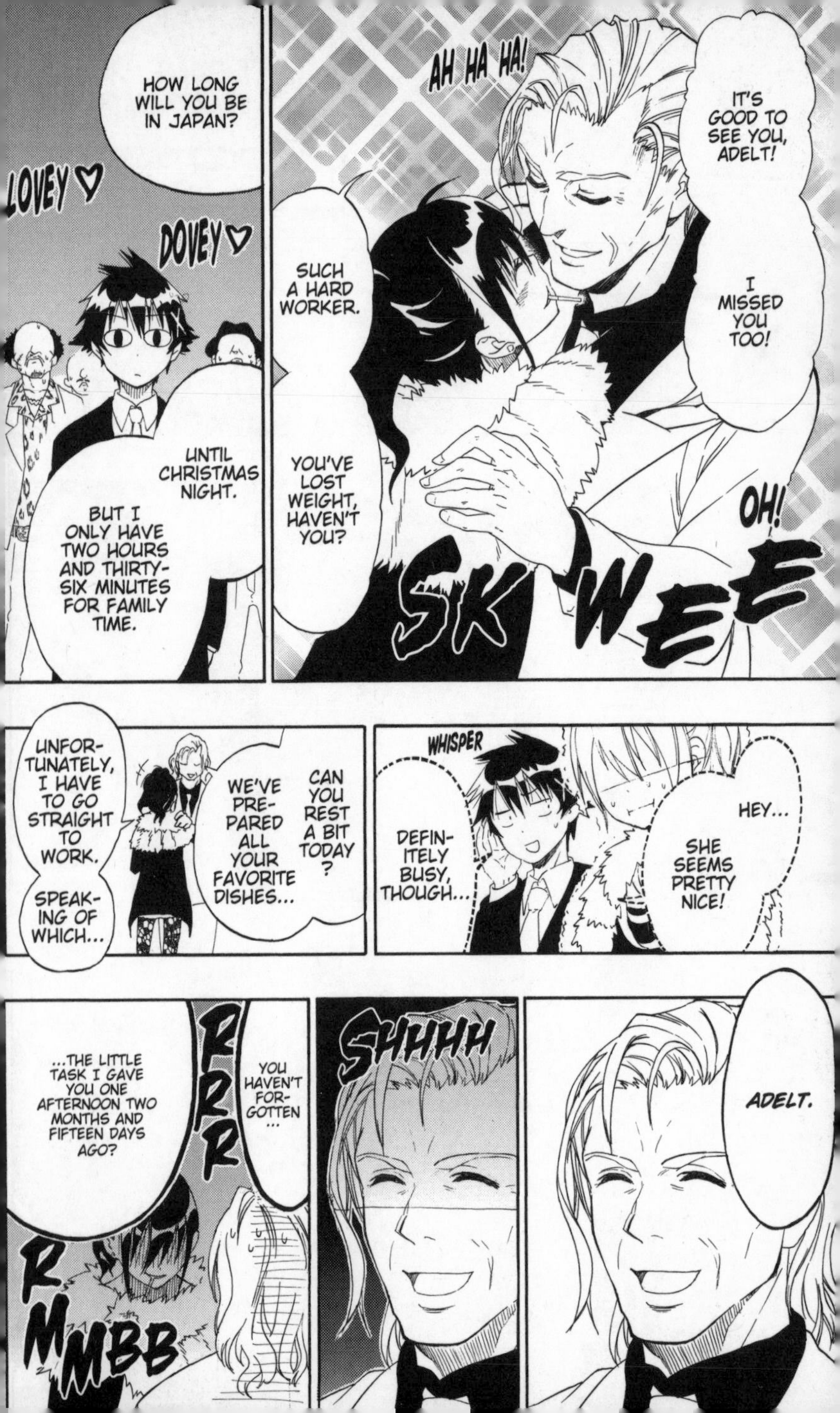
IT'S GOOD TO SEE YOU, ADELT!
AH HA HA!
I MISSED YOU TOO!
SUCH A HARD WORKER.
OH!
YOU'VE LOST WEIGHT, HAVEN'T YOU?
SKWEE
HOW LONG WILL YOU BE IN JAPAN?
LOVEY ♡
DOVEY ♡
UNTIL CHRISTMAS NIGHT.
BUT I ONLY HAVE TWO HOURS AND THIRTY-SIX MINUTES FOR FAMILY TIME.
WHISPER
HEY... SHE SEEMS PRETTY NICE!
DEFINITELY BUSY, THOUGH...
CAN YOU REST A BIT TODAY?
WE'VE PREPARED ALL YOUR FAVORITE DISHES...
UNFORTUNATELY, I HAVE TO GO STRAIGHT TO WORK.
SPEAKING OF WHICH...
ADELT.
SHHHH
YOU HAVEN'T FORGOTTEN...
RRRR
...THE LITTLE TASK I GAVE YOU ONE AFTERNOON TWO MONTHS AND FIFTEEN DAYS AGO?
RRMMBB

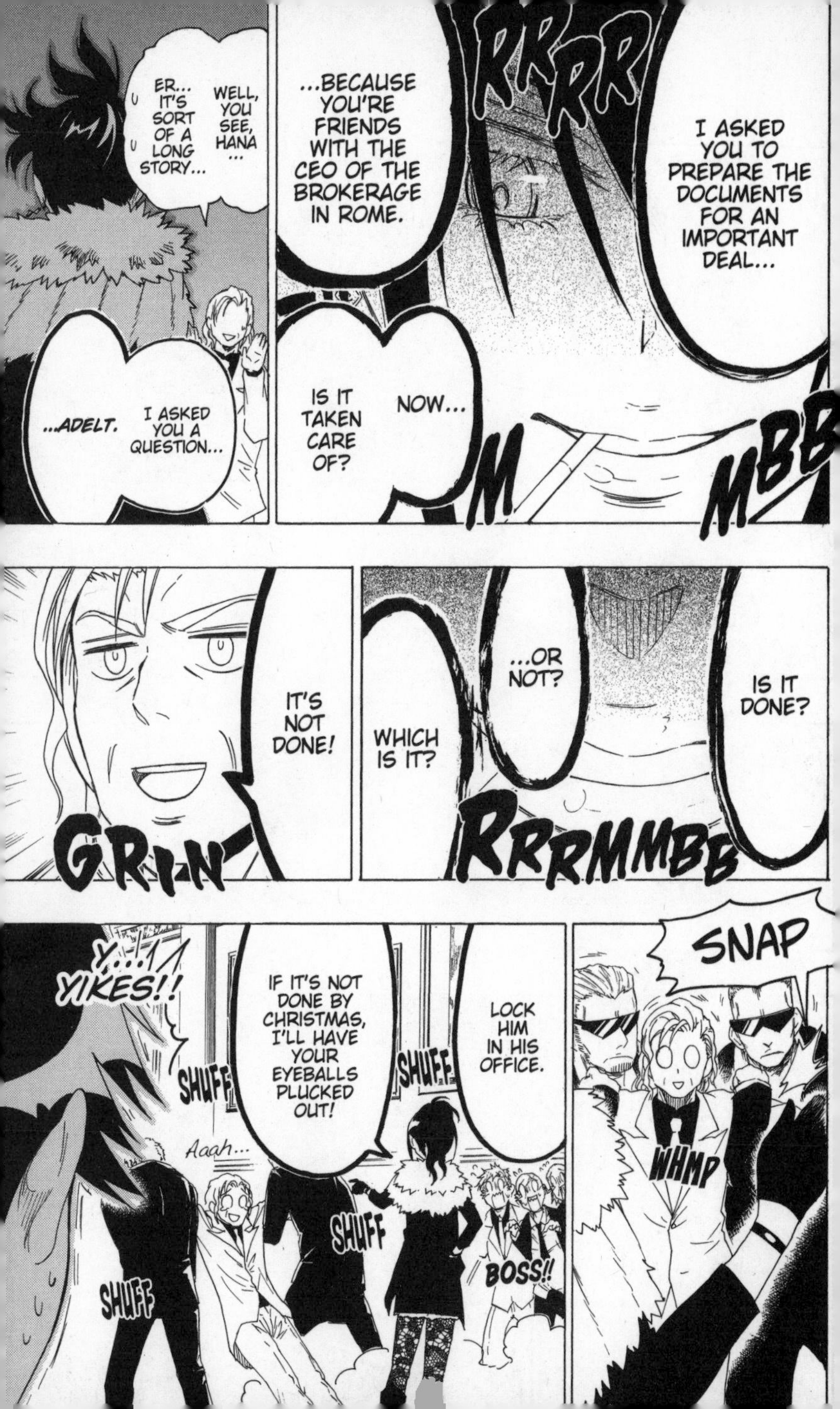
RRRR
I ASKED YOU TO PREPARE THE DOCUMENTS FOR AN IMPORTANT DEAL...
...BECAUSE YOU'RE FRIENDS WITH THE CEO OF THE BROKERAGE IN ROME.
NOW...
IS IT TAKEN CARE OF?
MMBB
WELL, YOU SEE, HANA...
ER... IT'S SORT OF A LONG STORY...
I ASKED YOU A QUESTION...
...ADELT.
IS IT DONE?
...OR NOT?
WHICH IS IT?
RRRMMBB
IT'S NOT DONE!
GRIN
SNAP
WHMP
LOCK HIM IN HIS OFFICE.
SHUFF
IF IT'S NOT DONE BY CHRISTMAS, I'LL HAVE YOUR EYEBALLS PLUCKED OUT!
SHUFF
Y... YIKES!!
SHUFF
SHUFF
Aaah...
BOSS!!

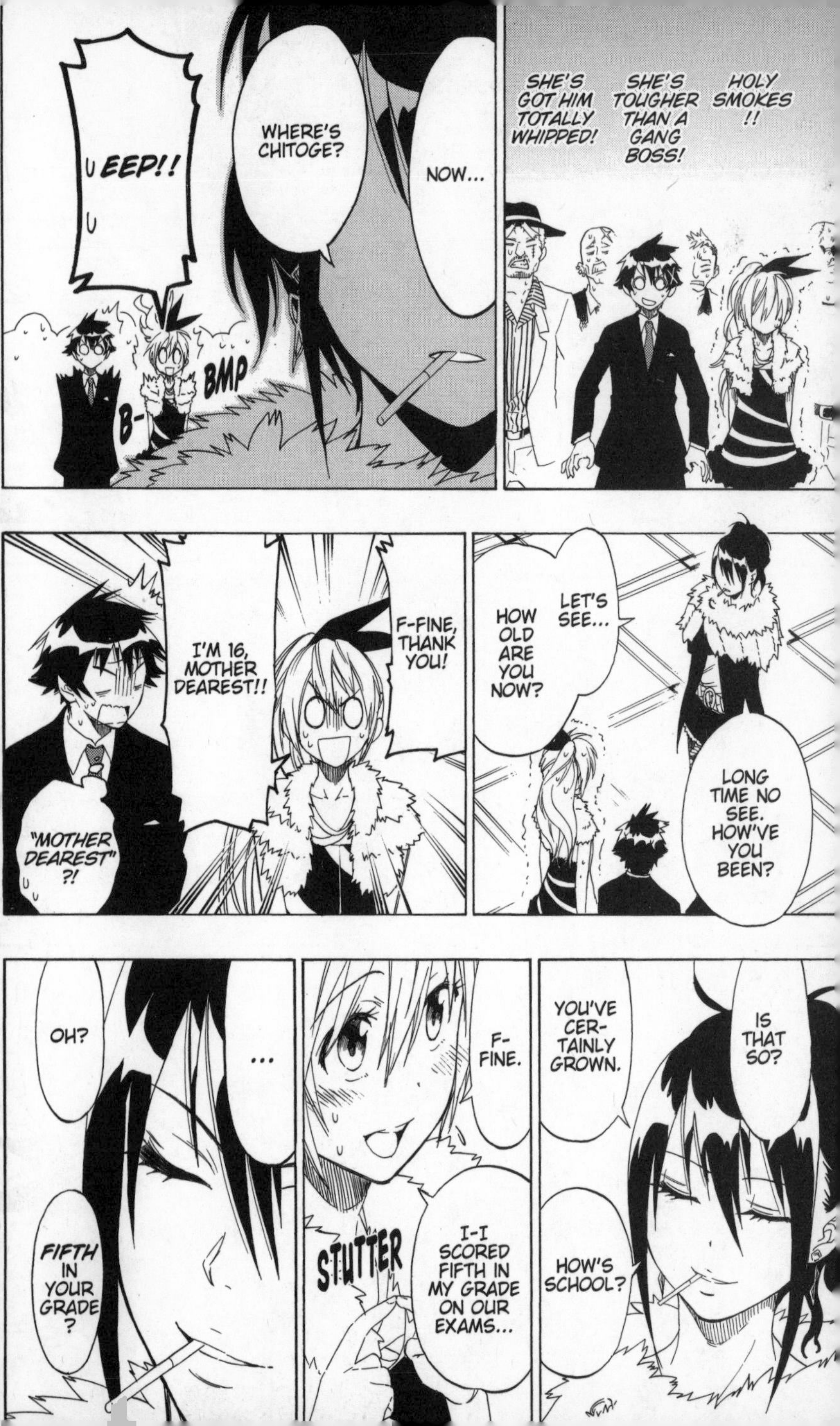
HOLY SMOKES !!
SHE'S TOUGHER THAN A GANG BOSS!
SHE'S GOT HIM TOTALLY WHIPPED!
NOW...
WHERE'S CHITOGE?
EEP!!
BMP
B-
LONG TIME NO SEE. HOW'VE YOU BEEN?
LET'S SEE...
HOW OLD ARE YOU NOW?
F-FINE, THANK YOU!
I'M 16, MOTHER DEAREST!!
"MOTHER DEAREST" ?!
IS THAT SO?
YOU'VE CERTAINLY GROWN.
HOW'S SCHOOL?
F-FINE.
I-I SCORED FIFTH IN MY GRADE ON OUR EXAMS...
STUTTER
...
OH?
FIFTH IN YOUR GRADE ?

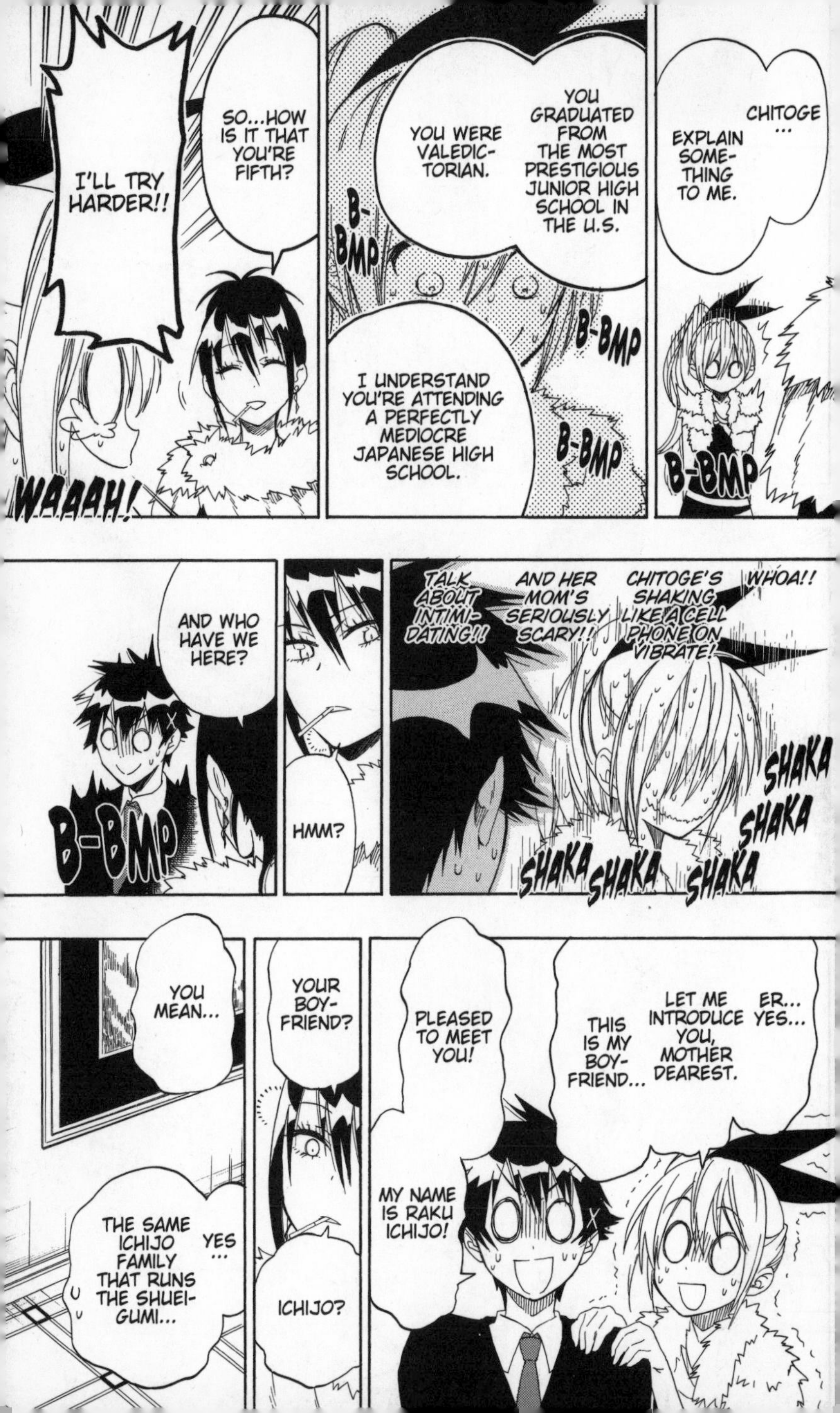
CHITOGE...
EXPLAIN SOMETHING TO ME.
B-BMP
YOU GRADUATED FROM THE MOST PRESTIGIOUS JUNIOR HIGH SCHOOL IN THE U.S.
YOU WERE VALEDICTORIAN.
B-BMP
B-BMP
B-BMP
I UNDERSTAND YOU'RE ATTENDING A PERFECTLY MEDIOCRE JAPANESE HIGH SCHOOL.
SO...HOW IS IT THAT YOU'RE FIFTH?
I'LL TRY HARDER!!
WAAAH!
WHOA!!
CHITOGE'S SHAKING LIKE A CELL PHONE ON VIBRATE!
AND HER MOM'S SERIOUSLY SCARY!!
TALK ABOUT INTIMIDATING!!
SHAKA
SHAKA
SHAKA
SHAKA
SHAKA
HMM?
AND WHO HAVE WE HERE?
B-BMP
ER... YES...
LET ME INTRODUCE YOU, MOTHER DEAREST.
THIS IS MY BOYFRIEND...
PLEASED TO MEET YOU!
MY NAME IS RAKU ICHIJO!
YOUR BOYFRIEND?
ICHIJO?
YOU MEAN...
YES...
THE SAME ICHIJO FAMILY THAT RUNS THE SHUEI-GUMI...

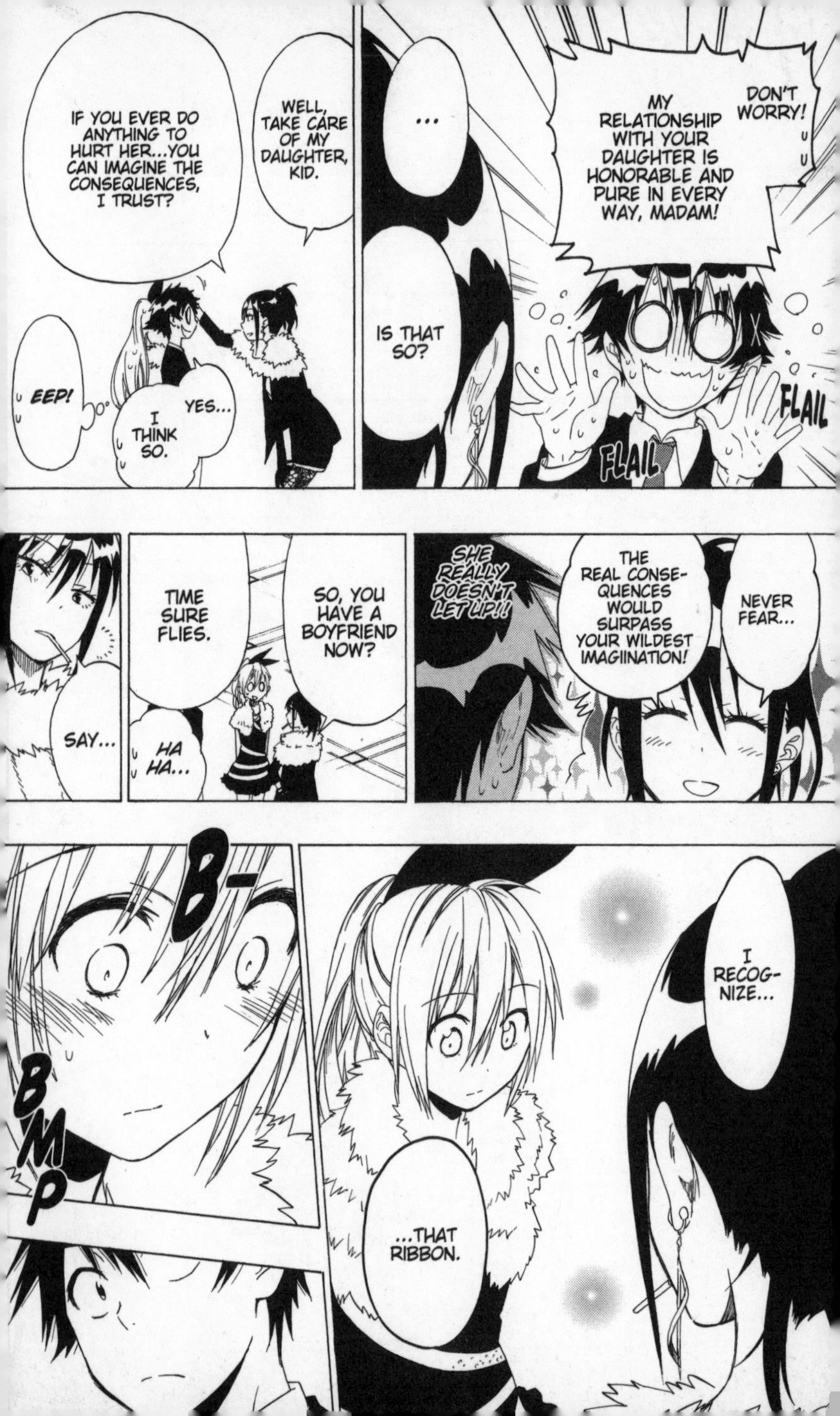

DON'T WORRY!
MY RELATIONSHIP WITH YOUR DAUGHTER IS HONORABLE AND PURE IN EVERY WAY, MADAM!
FLAIL
FLAIL
...
IS THAT SO?
WELL, TAKE CARE OF MY DAUGHTER, KID.
IF YOU EVER DO ANYTHING TO HURT HER...YOU CAN IMAGINE THE CONSEQUENCES, I TRUST?
YES... I THINK SO.
EEP!
NEVER FEAR...
THE REAL CONSE-QUENCES WOULD SURPASS YOUR WILDEST IMAGIINATION!
SHE REALLY DOESN'T LET UP!!
SO, YOU HAVE A BOYFRIEND NOW?
TIME SURE FLIES.
HA HA...
SAY...
I RECOG-NIZE...
...THAT RIBBON.
B-
BMP

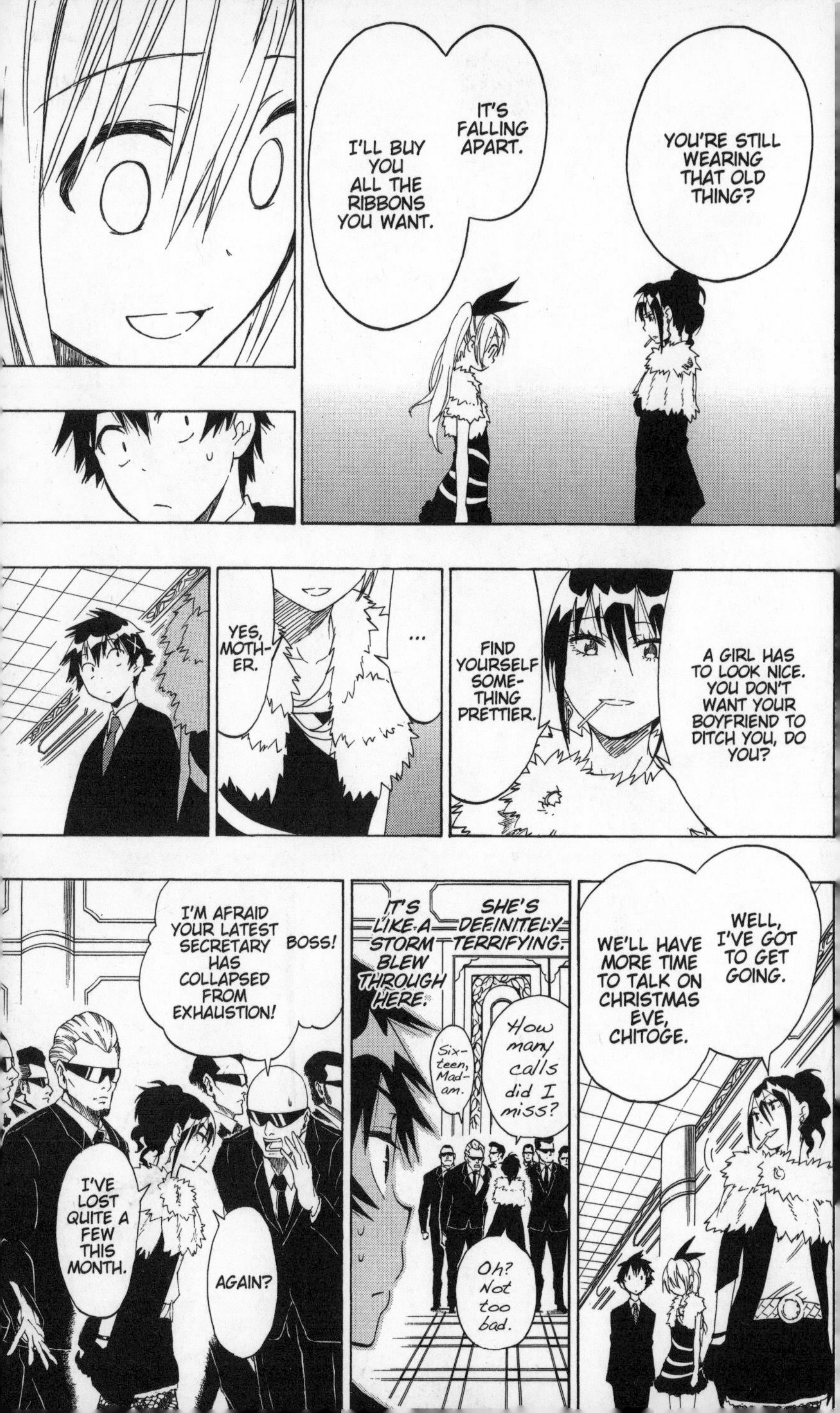
YOU'RE STILL WEARING THAT OLD THING?
IT'S FALLING APART.
I'LL BUY YOU ALL THE RIBBONS YOU WANT.
A GIRL HAS TO LOOK NICE. YOU DON'T WANT YOUR BOYFRIEND TO DITCH YOU, DO YOU?
FIND YOURSELF SOMETHING PRETTIER.
...
YES, MOTHER.
WELL, I'VE GOT TO GET GOING.
WE'LL HAVE MORE TIME TO TALK ON CHRISTMAS EVE, CHITOGE.
SHE'S DEFINITELY TERRIFYING.
IT'S LIKE A STORM BLEW THROUGH HERE.
How many calls did I miss?
Sixteen, Madam.
Oh? Not too bad.
BOSS!
I'M AFRAID YOUR LATEST SECRETARY HAS COLLAPSED FROM EXHAUSTION!
AGAIN?
I'VE LOST QUITE A FEW THIS MONTH.

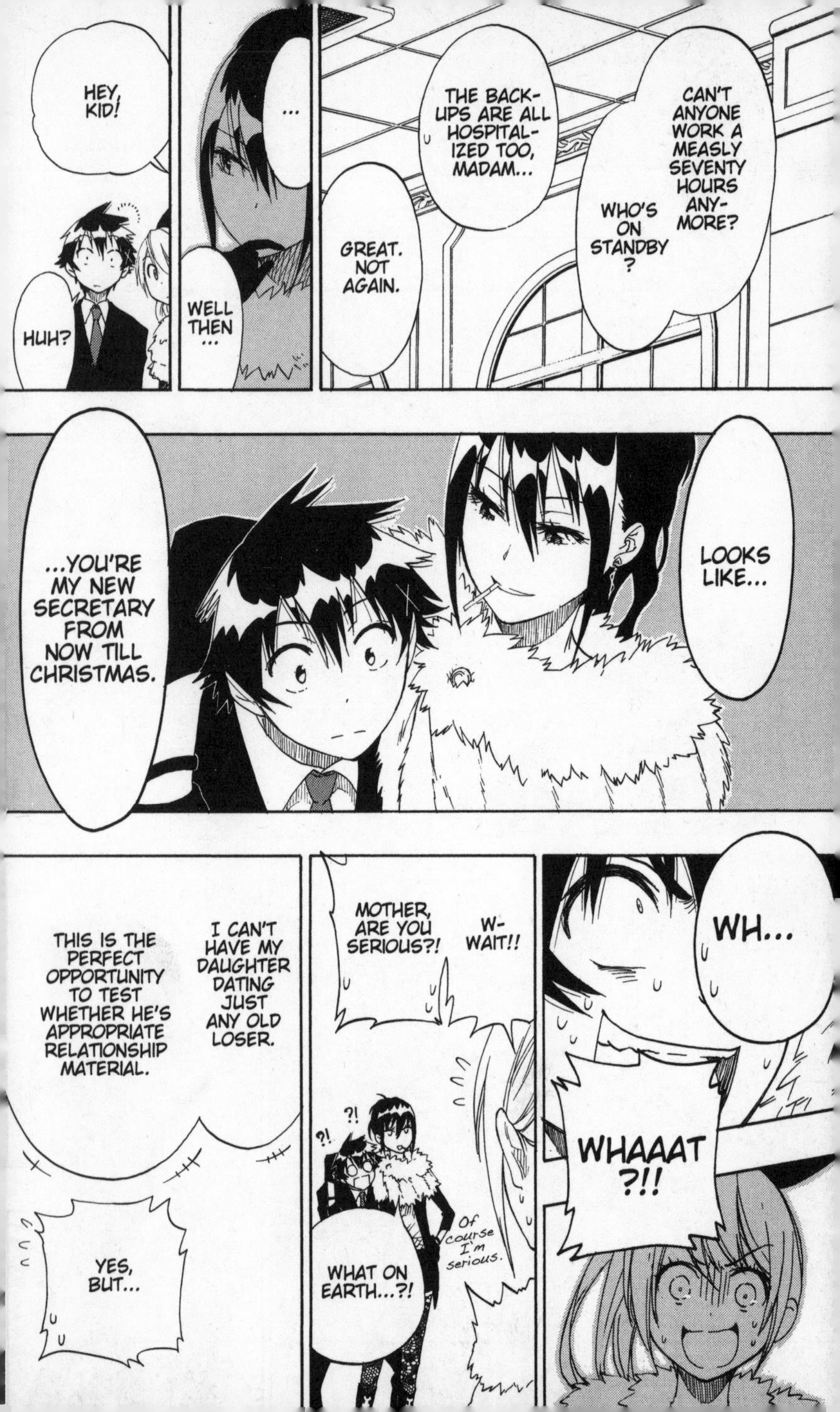
CAN'T ANYONE WORK A MEASLY SEVENTY HOURS ANYMORE?
WHO'S ON STANDBY?
THE BACK-UPS ARE ALL HOSPITALIZED TOO, MADAM...
GREAT. NOT AGAIN.
...
WELL THEN...
HEY, KID!
HUH?
LOOKS LIKE...
...YOU'RE MY NEW SECRETARY FROM NOW TILL CHRISTMAS.
WH...
WHAAAT?!!
W-WAIT!!
MOTHER, ARE YOU SERIOUS?!
Of course I'm serious.
?!
?!
WHAT ON EARTH...?!
I CAN'T HAVE MY DAUGHTER DATING JUST ANY OLD LOSER.
THIS IS THE PERFECT OPPORTUNITY TO TEST WHETHER HE'S APPROPRIATE RELATIONSHIP MATERIAL.
YES, BUT...

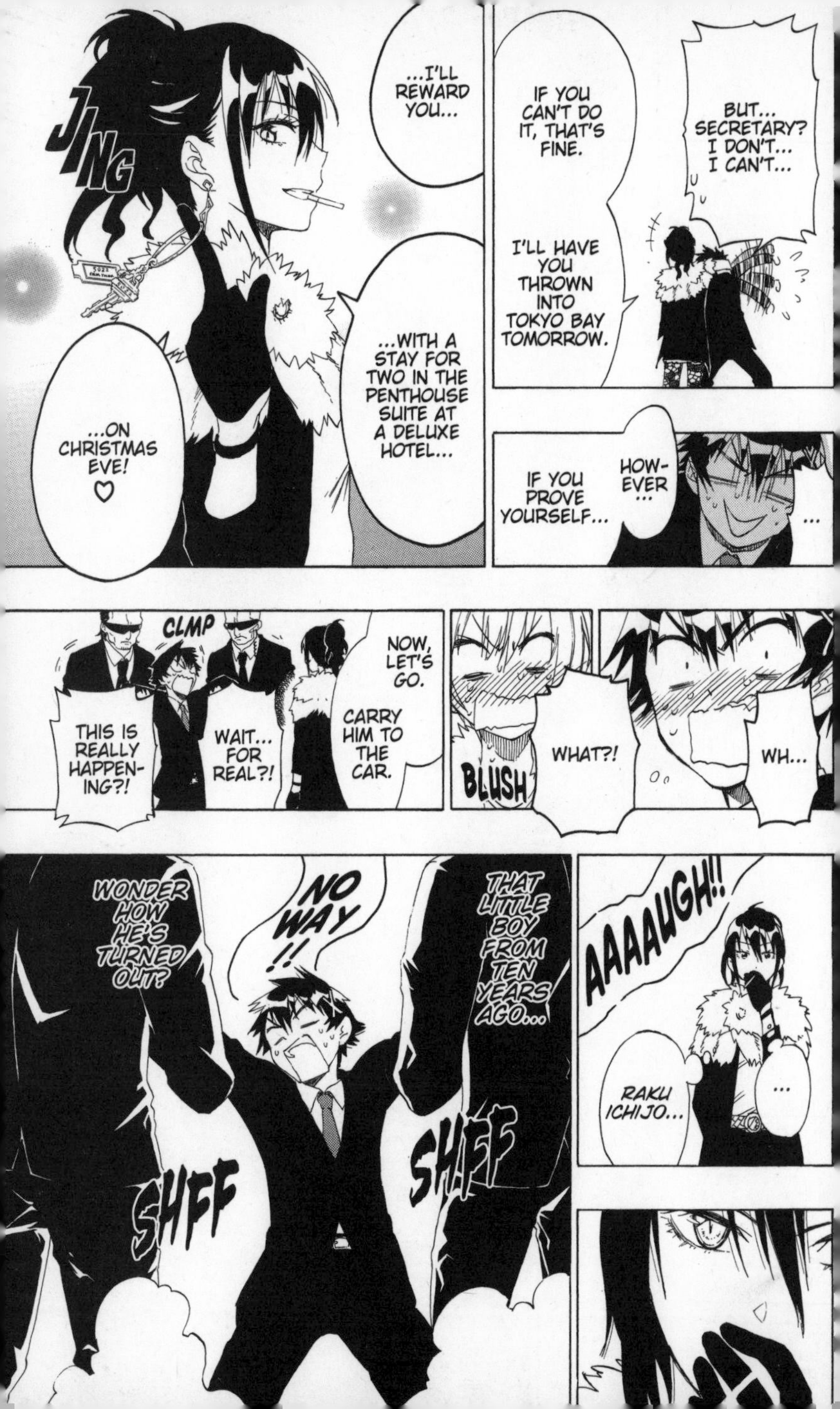
BUT... SECRETARY? I DON'T... I CAN'T...
IF YOU CAN'T DO IT, THAT'S FINE.
I'LL HAVE YOU THROWN INTO TOKYO BAY TOMORROW.
...
HOW-EVER...
IF YOU PROVE YOURSELF...
JING
...I'LL REWARD YOU...
...WITH A STAY FOR TWO IN THE PENTHOUSE SUITE AT A DELUXE HOTEL...
...ON CHRISTMAS EVE! ♡
WH...
WHAT?!
BLUSH
NOW, LET'S GO.
CARRY HIM TO THE CAR.
CLMP
WAIT... FOR REAL?!
THIS IS REALLY HAPPENING?!
AAAAUGH!!
...
RAKU ICHIJO...
THAT LITTLE BOY FROM TEN YEARS AGO...
NO WAY!!
WONDER HOW HE'S TURNED OUT?
SHFF
SHFF

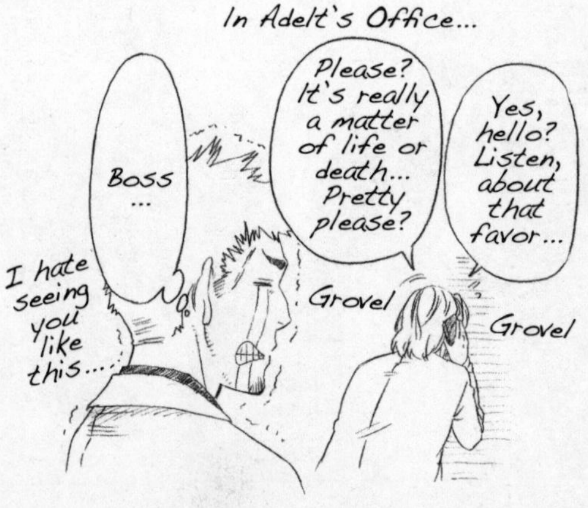
In Adelt's Office...
Yes, hello? Listen, about that favor...
Grovel
Please? It's really a matter of life or death... Pretty please?
Grovel
Boss...
I hate seeing you like this....

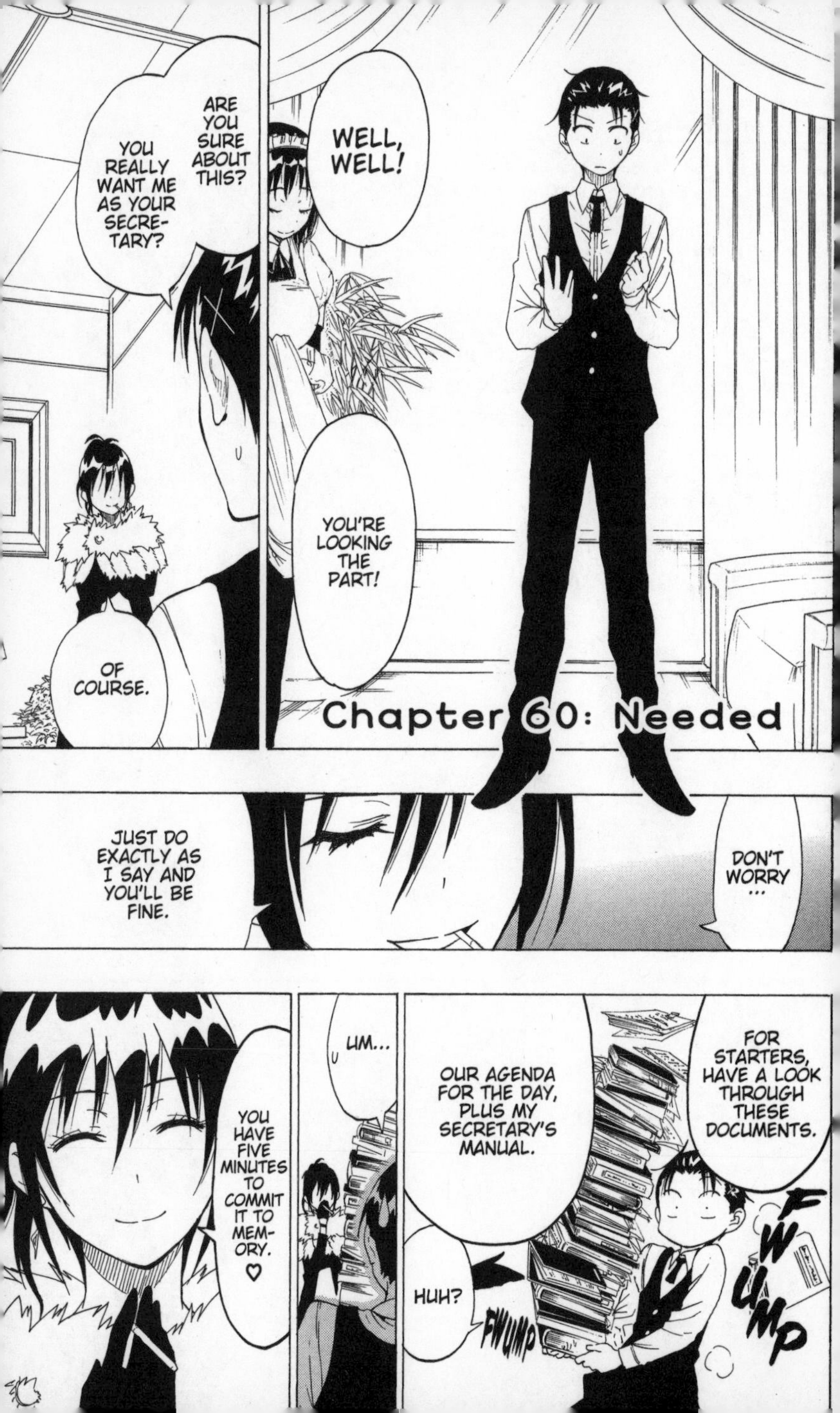
WELL, WELL!
YOU'RE LOOKING THE PART!
Chapter 60: Needed
ARE YOU SURE ABOUT THIS?
YOU REALLY WANT ME AS YOUR SECRETARY?
OF COURSE.
DON'T WORRY...
JUST DO EXACTLY AS I SAY AND YOU'LL BE FINE.
FOR STARTERS, HAVE A LOOK THROUGH THESE DOCUMENTS.
FWUMP
OUR AGENDA FOR THE DAY, PLUS MY SECRETARY'S MANUAL.
HUH?
FWUMP
UM...
YOU HAVE FIVE MINUTES TO COMMIT IT TO MEMORY. ♡

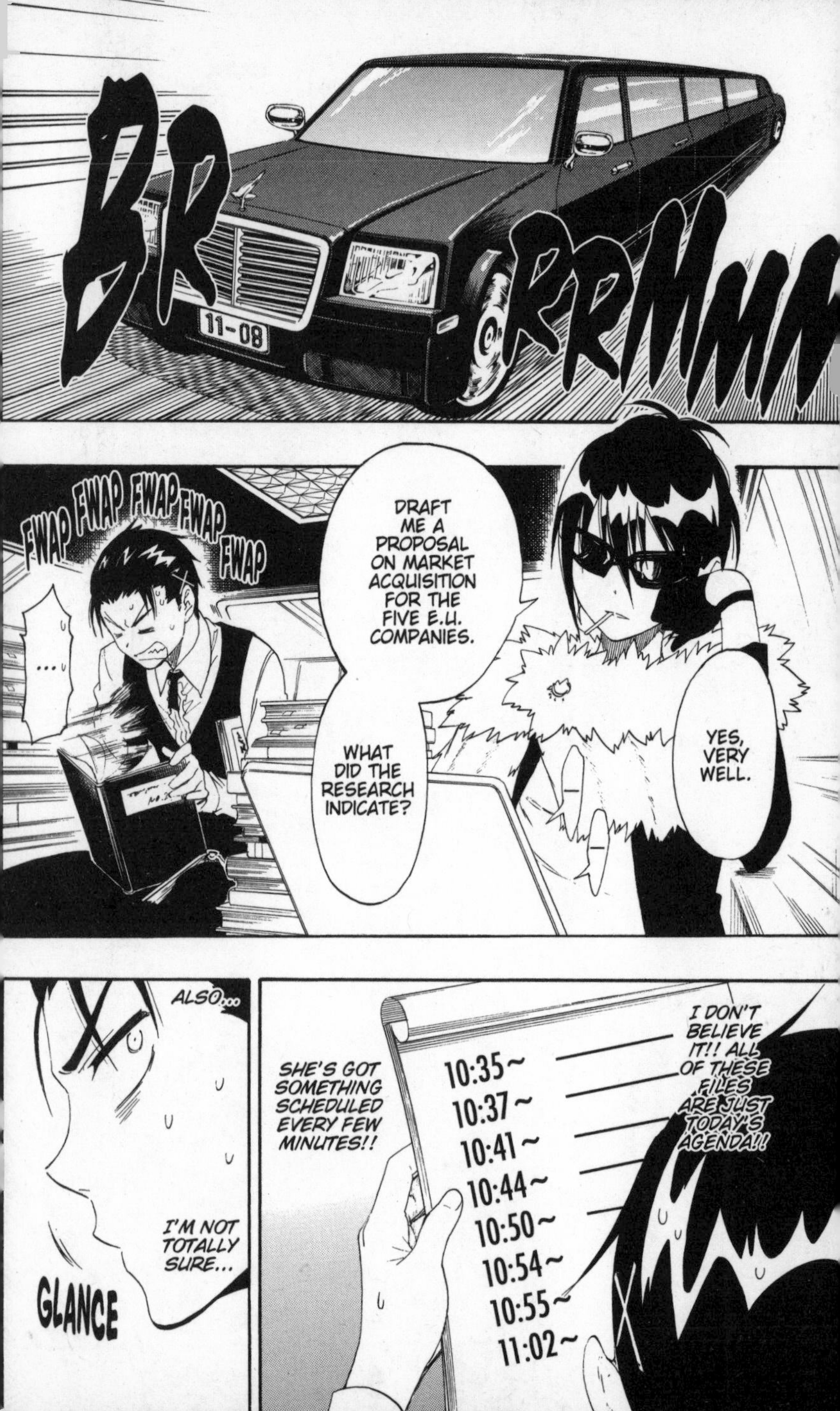
BR
RRMMM
11-08
DRAFT ME A PROPOSAL ON MARKET ACQUISITION FOR THE FIVE E.U. COMPANIES.
YES, VERY WELL.
WHAT DID THE RESEARCH INDICATE?
FWAP FWAP FWAP FWAP FWAP
...
I DON'T BELIEVE IT!! ALL OF THESE FILES ARE JUST TODAY'S AGENDA!!
10:35~
10:37~
10:41~
10:44~
10:50~
10:54~
10:55~
11:02~
SHE'S GOT SOMETHING SCHEDULED EVERY FEW MINUTES!!
ALSO...
I'M NOT TOTALLY SURE...
GLANCE

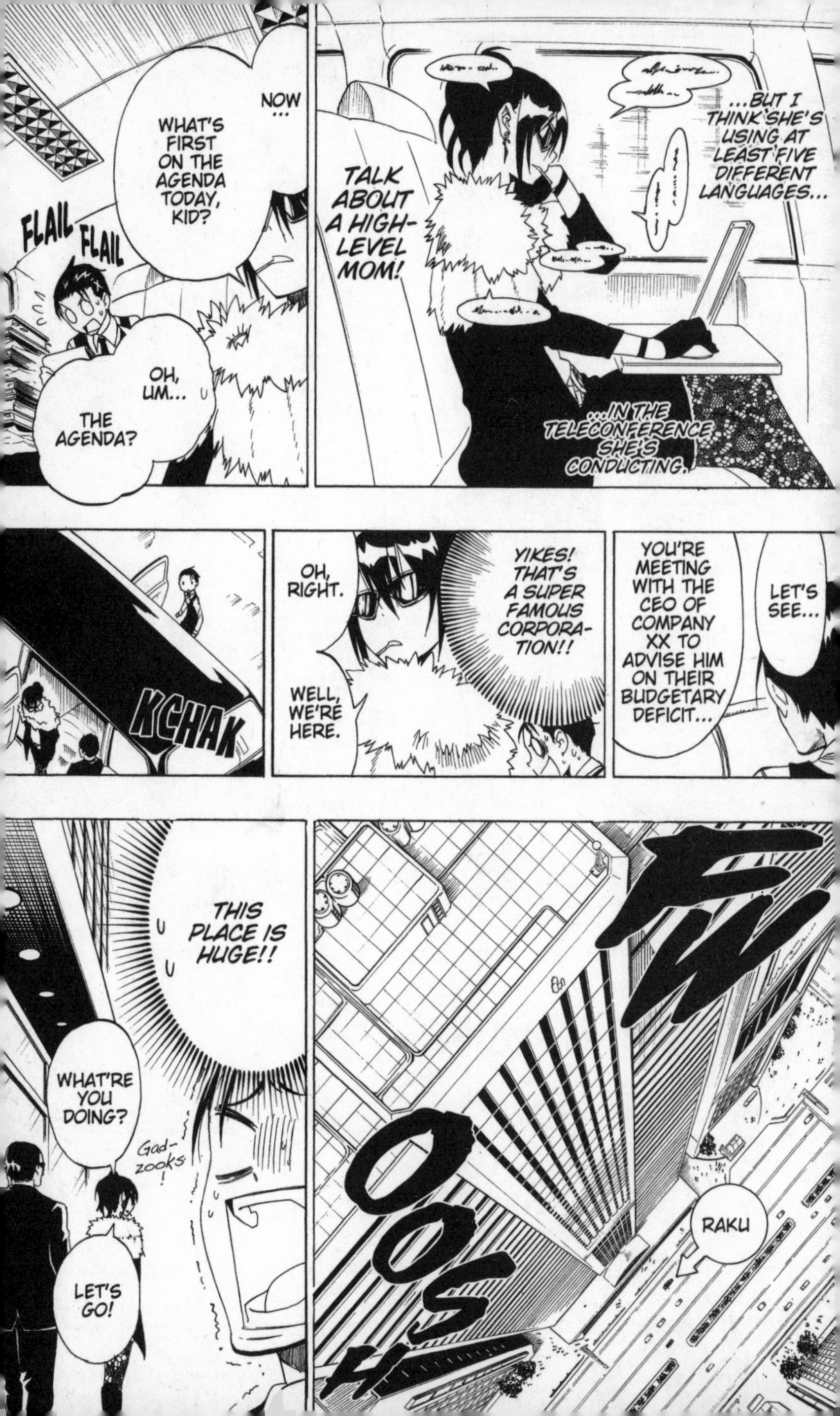

...BUT I THINK SHE'S USING AT LEAST FIVE DIFFERENT LANGUAGES...
...IN THE TELECONFERENCE SHE'S CONDUCTING.
TALK ABOUT A HIGH-LEVEL MOM!
NOW...
WHAT'S FIRST ON THE AGENDA TODAY, KID?
FLAIL FLAIL
OH, UM...
THE AGENDA?
LET'S SEE...
YOU'RE MEETING WITH THE CEO OF COMPANY XX TO ADVISE HIM ON THEIR BUDGETARY DEFICIT...
YIKES! THAT'S A SUPER FAMOUS CORPORATION!!
OH, RIGHT.
WELL, WE'RE HERE.
KCHAK
FWOOSH
RAKU
THIS PLACE IS HUGE!!
WHAT'RE YOU DOING?
Gad-zooks!
LET'S GO!

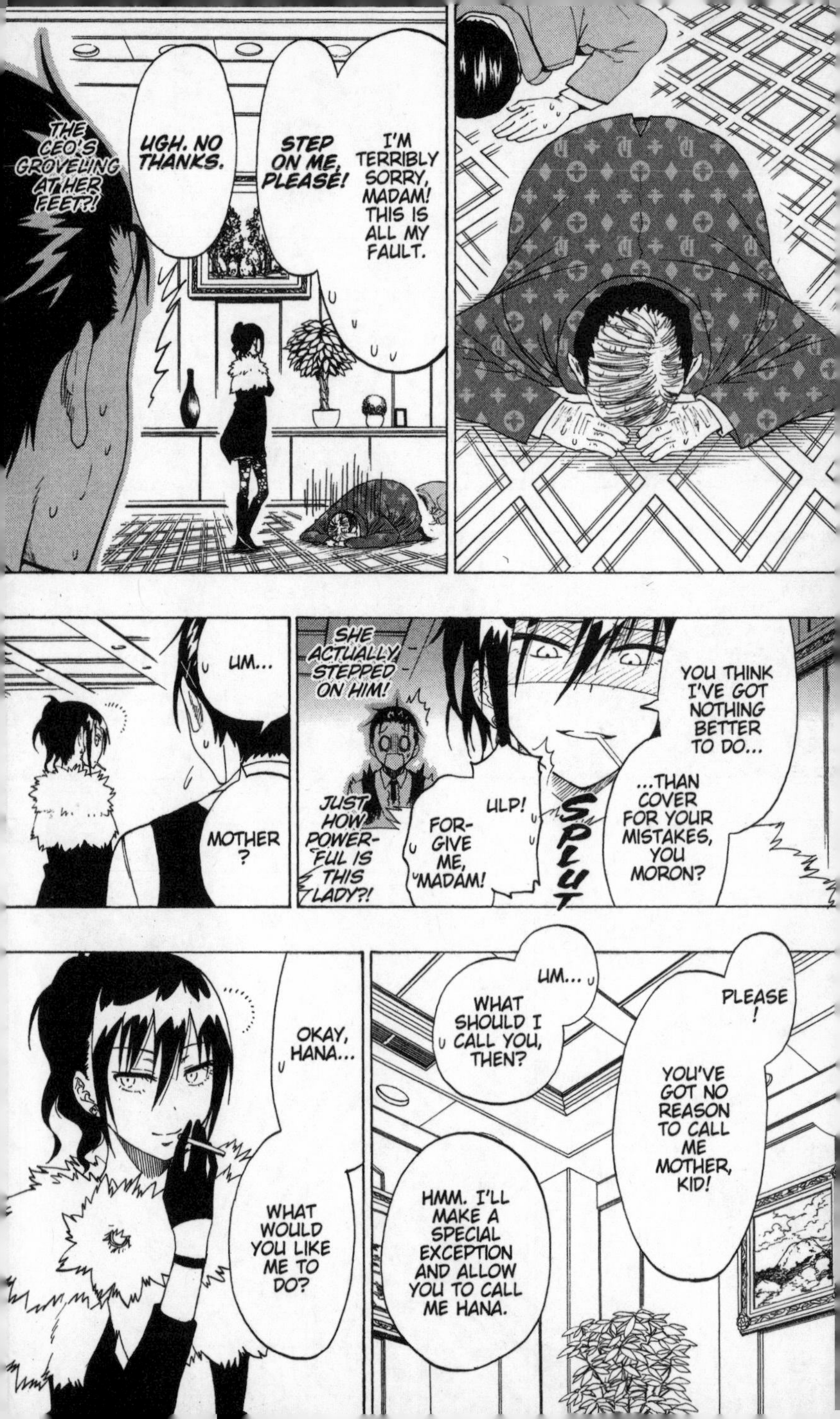
I'M TERRIBLY SORRY, MADAM! THIS IS ALL MY FAULT.
STEP ON ME, PLEASE!
UGH. NO THANKS.
THE CEO'S GROVELING AT HER FEET?!
YOU THINK I'VE GOT NOTHING BETTER TO DO...
...THAN COVER FOR YOUR MISTAKES, YOU MORON?
SPLUT
ULP!
FOR-GIVE ME, MADAM!
SHE ACTUALLY STEPPED ON HIM!
JUST HOW POWER-FUL IS THIS LADY?!
UM...
MOTHER?
PLEASE!
YOU'VE GOT NO REASON TO CALL ME MOTHER, KID!
UM...
WHAT SHOULD I CALL YOU, THEN?
HMM. I'LL MAKE A SPECIAL EXCEPTION AND ALLOW YOU TO CALL ME HANA.
OKAY, HANA...
WHAT WOULD YOU LIKE ME TO DO?

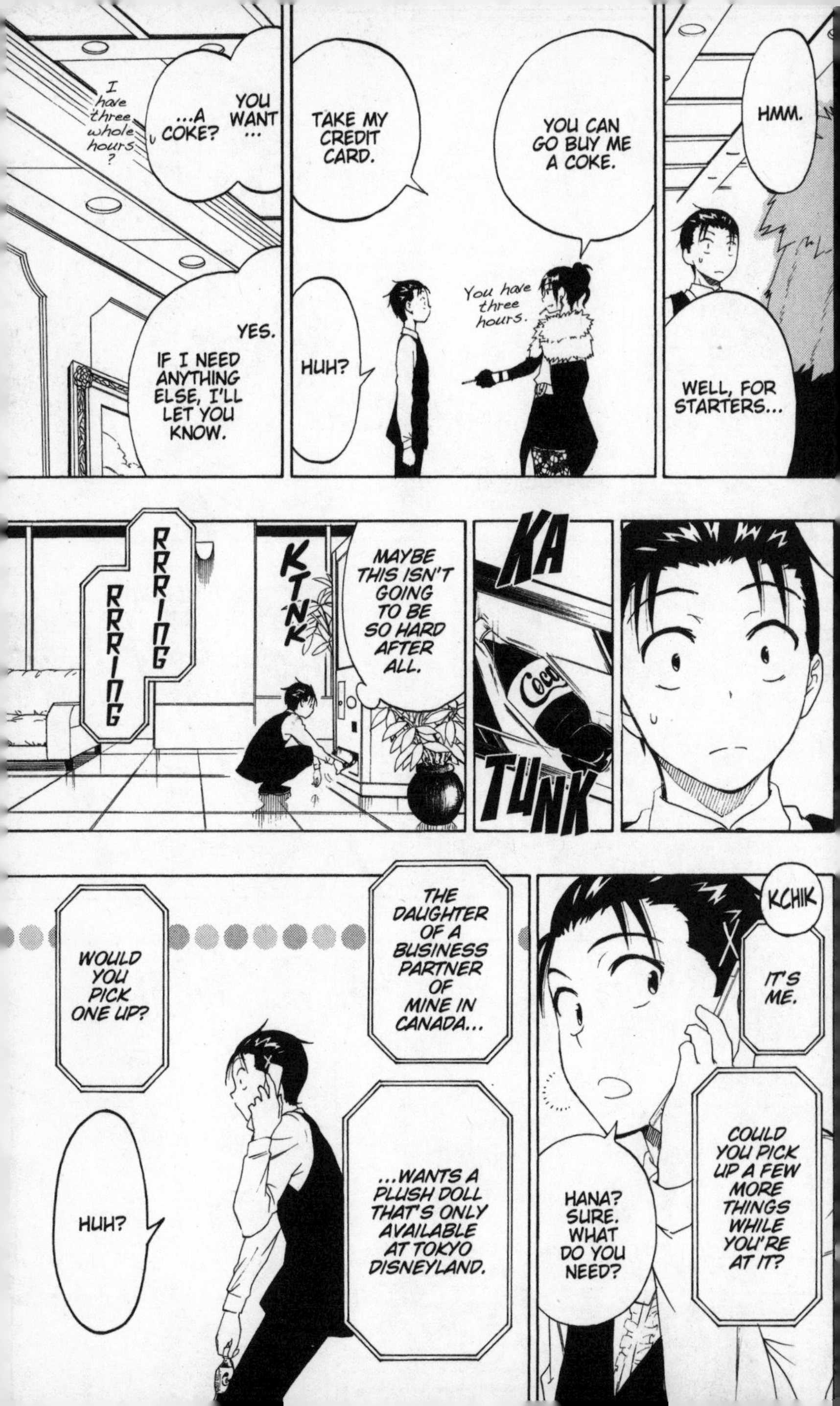
HMM.
WELL, FOR STARTERS...
YOU CAN GO BUY ME A COKE.
You have three hours.
TAKE MY CREDIT CARD.
HUH?
YOU WANT...
...A COKE?
I have three whole hours?
YES.
IF I NEED ANYTHING ELSE, I'LL LET YOU KNOW.
KA
TUNK
MAYBE THIS ISN'T GOING TO BE SO HARD AFTER ALL.
KTNK
RRRING
RRRING
KCHIK
IT'S ME.
COULD YOU PICK UP A FEW MORE THINGS WHILE YOU'RE AT IT?
HANA? SURE. WHAT DO YOU NEED?
THE DAUGHTER OF A BUSINESS PARTNER OF MINE IN CANADA...
...WANTS A PLUSH DOLL THAT'S ONLY AVAILABLE AT TOKYO DISNEYLAND.
WOULD YOU PICK ONE UP?
HUH?

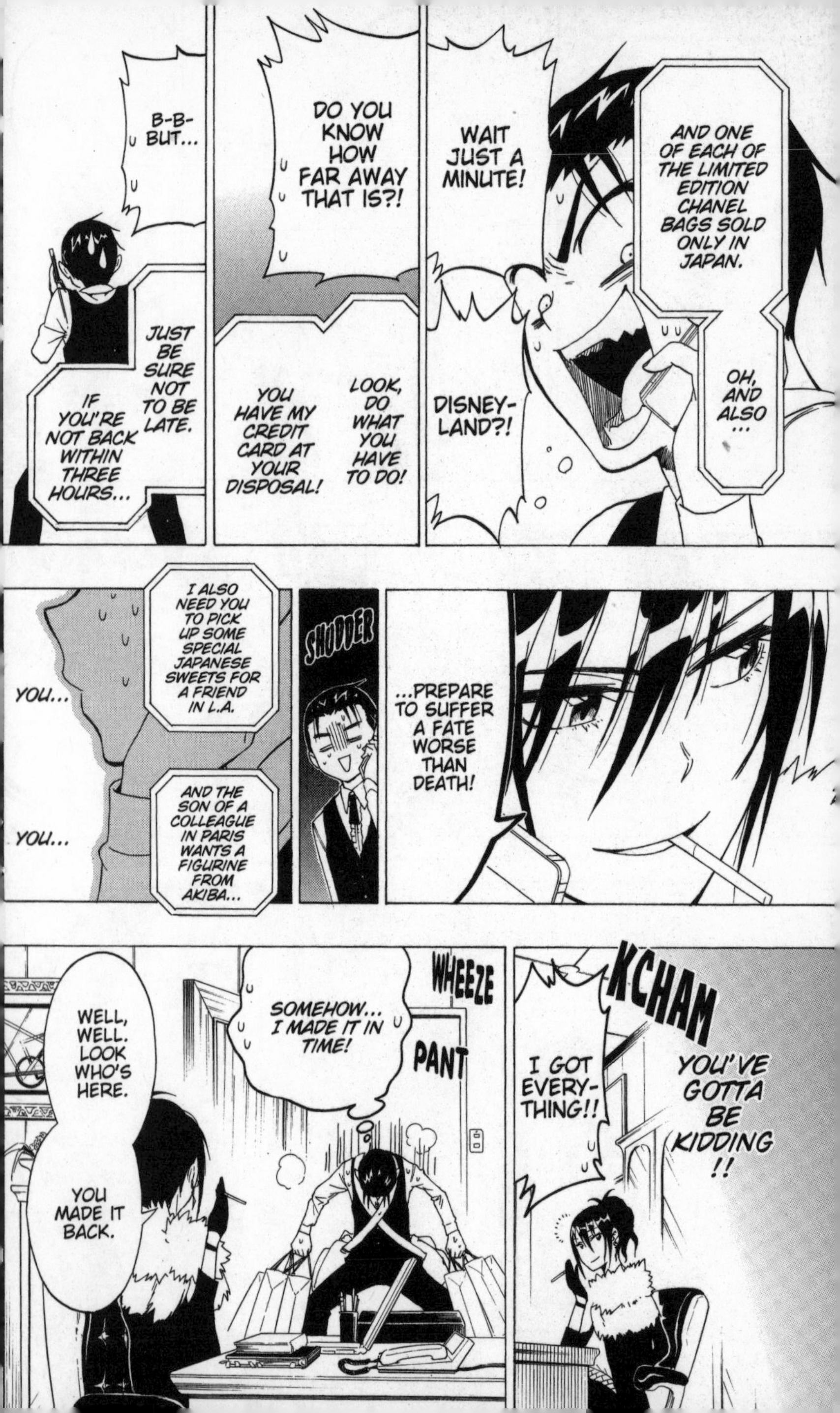
AND ONE OF EACH OF THE LIMITED EDITION CHANEL BAGS SOLD ONLY IN JAPAN.
WAIT JUST A MINUTE!
OH, AND ALSO ...
DISNEY-LAND?!
DO YOU KNOW HOW FAR AWAY THAT IS?!
LOOK, DO WHAT YOU HAVE TO DO!
YOU HAVE MY CREDIT CARD AT YOUR DISPOSAL!
B-B-BUT...
JUST BE SURE NOT TO BE LATE.
IF YOU'RE NOT BACK WITHIN THREE HOURS...
...PREPARE TO SUFFER A FATE WORSE THAN DEATH!
SHUDDER
I ALSO NEED YOU TO PICK UP SOME SPECIAL JAPANESE SWEETS FOR A FRIEND IN L.A.
YOU...
AND THE SON OF A COLLEAGUE IN PARIS WANTS A FIGURINE FROM AKIBA...
YOU...
KCHAM
YOU'VE GOTTA BE KIDDING!!
I GOT EVERY-THING!!
WHEEZE
SOMEHOW... I MADE IT IN TIME!
PANT
WELL, WELL. LOOK WHO'S HERE.
YOU MADE IT BACK.

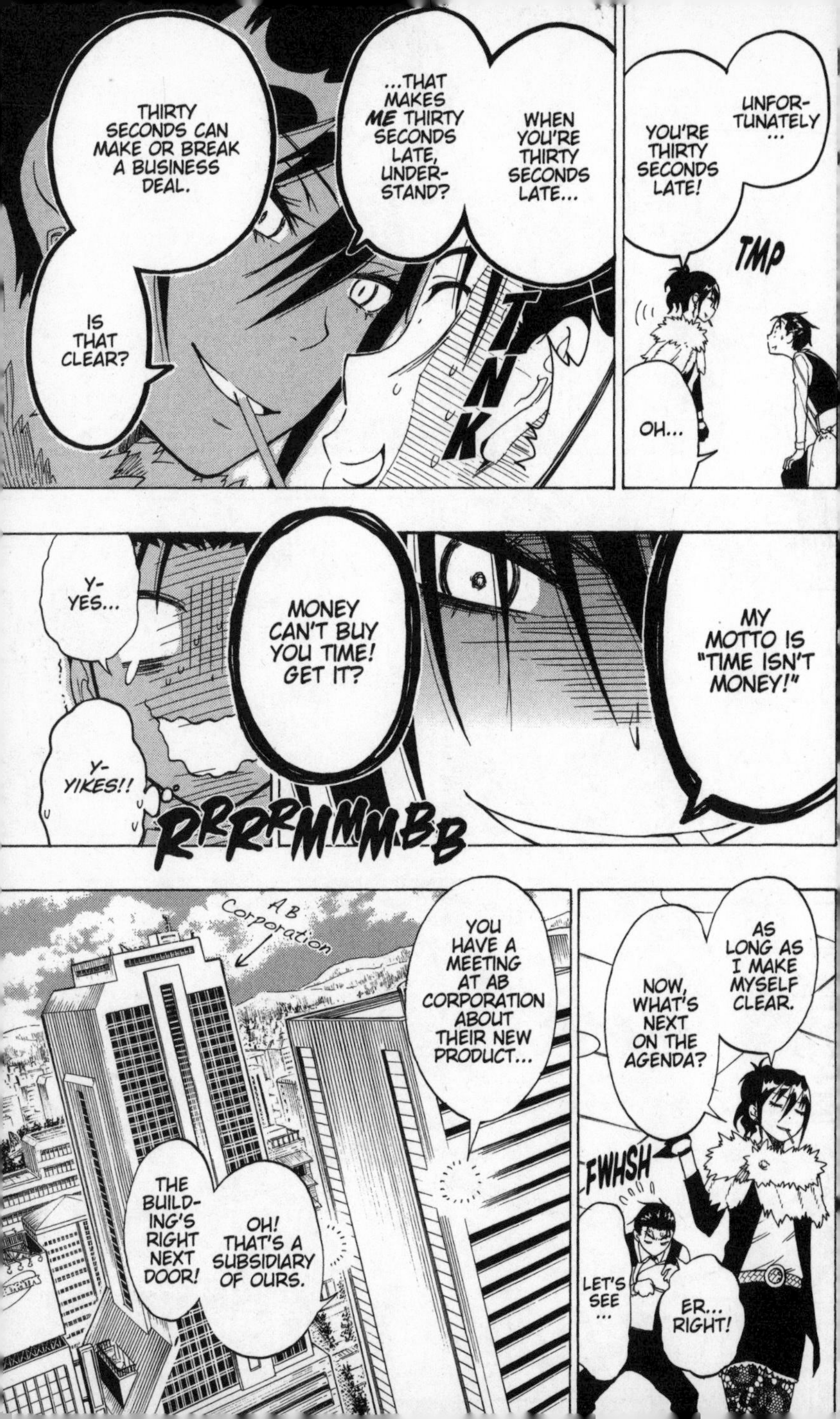

UNFOR-TUNATELY...
YOU'RE THIRTY SECONDS LATE!
TMP
OH...
WHEN YOU'RE THIRTY SECONDS LATE...
...THAT MAKES *ME* THIRTY SECONDS LATE, UNDER-STAND?
TINK
THIRTY SECONDS CAN MAKE OR BREAK A BUSINESS DEAL.
IS THAT CLEAR?
MY MOTTO IS "TIME ISN'T MONEY!"
MONEY CAN'T BUY YOU TIME! GET IT?
Y-YES...
Y-YIKES!!
RRRRMMMBB
AS LONG AS I MAKE MYSELF CLEAR.
NOW, WHAT'S NEXT ON THE AGENDA?
FWHSH
ER... RIGHT!
LET'S SEE...
YOU HAVE A MEETING AT AB CORPORATION ABOUT THEIR NEW PRODUCT...
AB Corporation
OH! THAT'S A SUBSIDIARY OF OURS.
THE BUILD-ING'S RIGHT NEXT DOOR!

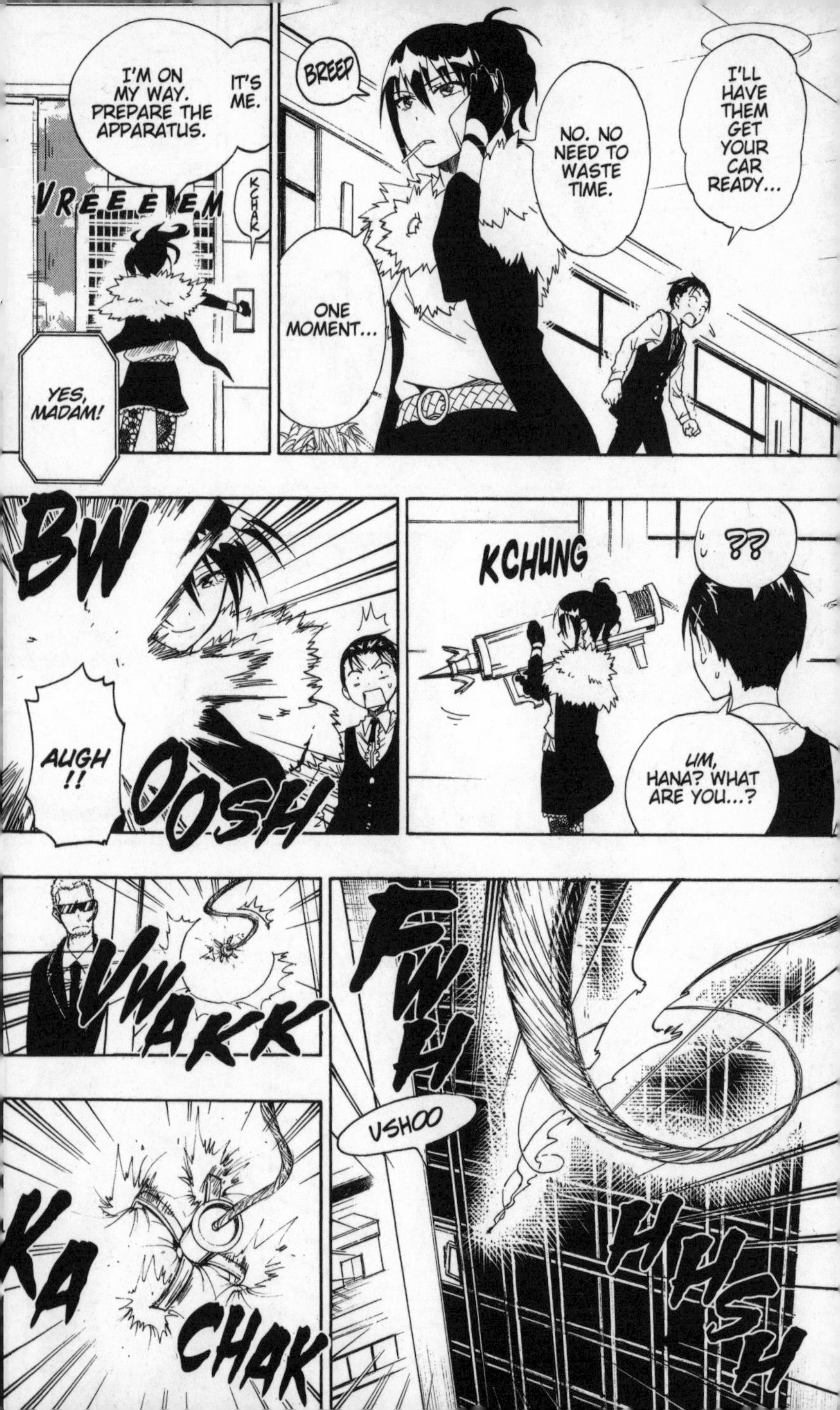
I'LL HAVE THEM GET YOUR CAR READY...
NO. NO NEED TO WASTE TIME.
BREEP
ONE MOMENT...
IT'S ME.
I'M ON MY WAY. PREPARE THE APPARATUS.
KCHAK
VREEEEVEM
YES, MADAM!
??
KCHUNG
UM, HANA? WHAT ARE YOU...?
BW
OOSH
AUGH !!
FWH
VSHOO
WHSH
VWAKK
KA
CHAK

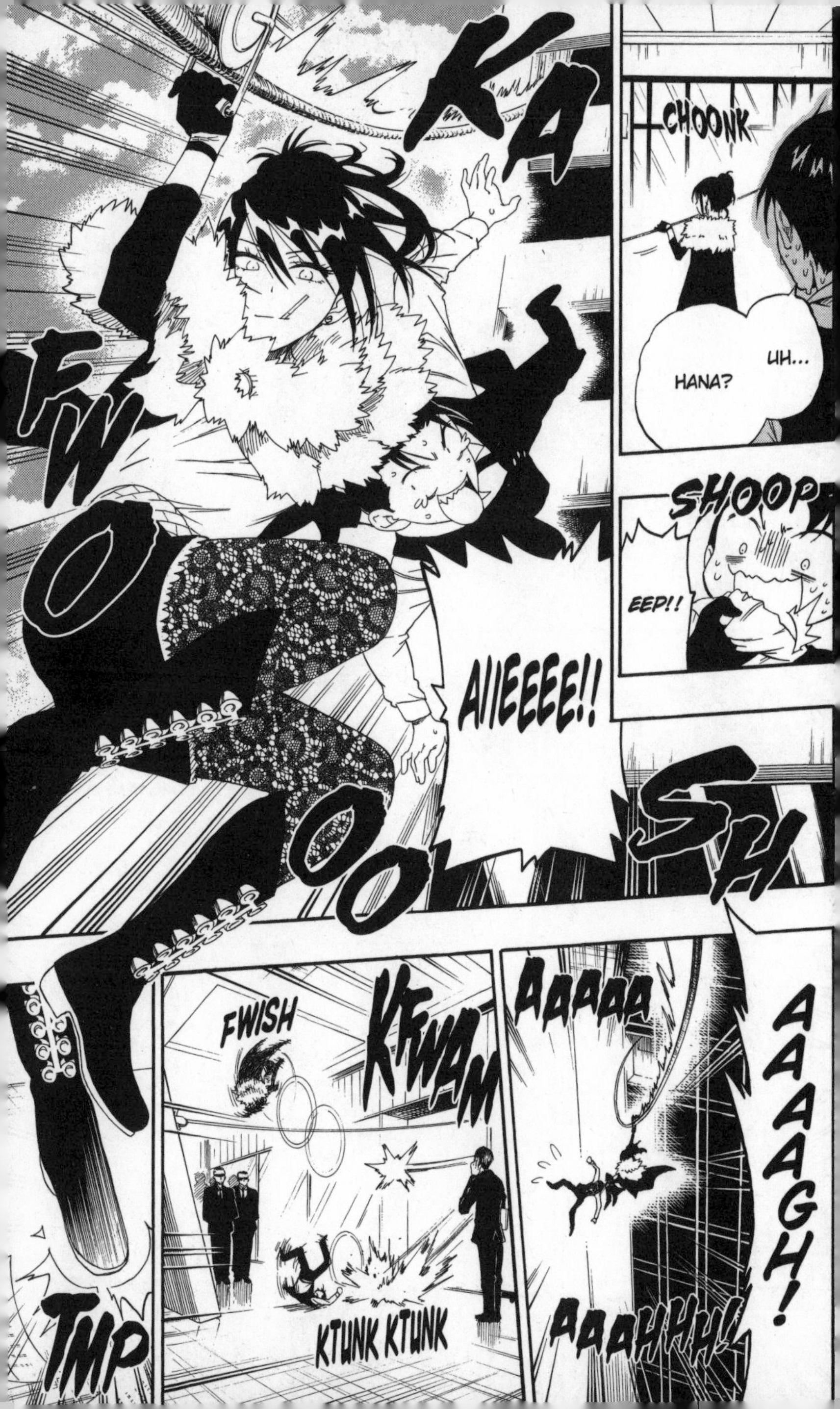
CHOONK
UH...
HANA?
SHOOP
EEP!!
KA
FWOOOOSH
AIIEEEE!!
AAAAA
AAAAGH!
AAAHHH!
KFWAM
FWISH
KTUNK KTUNK
TMP

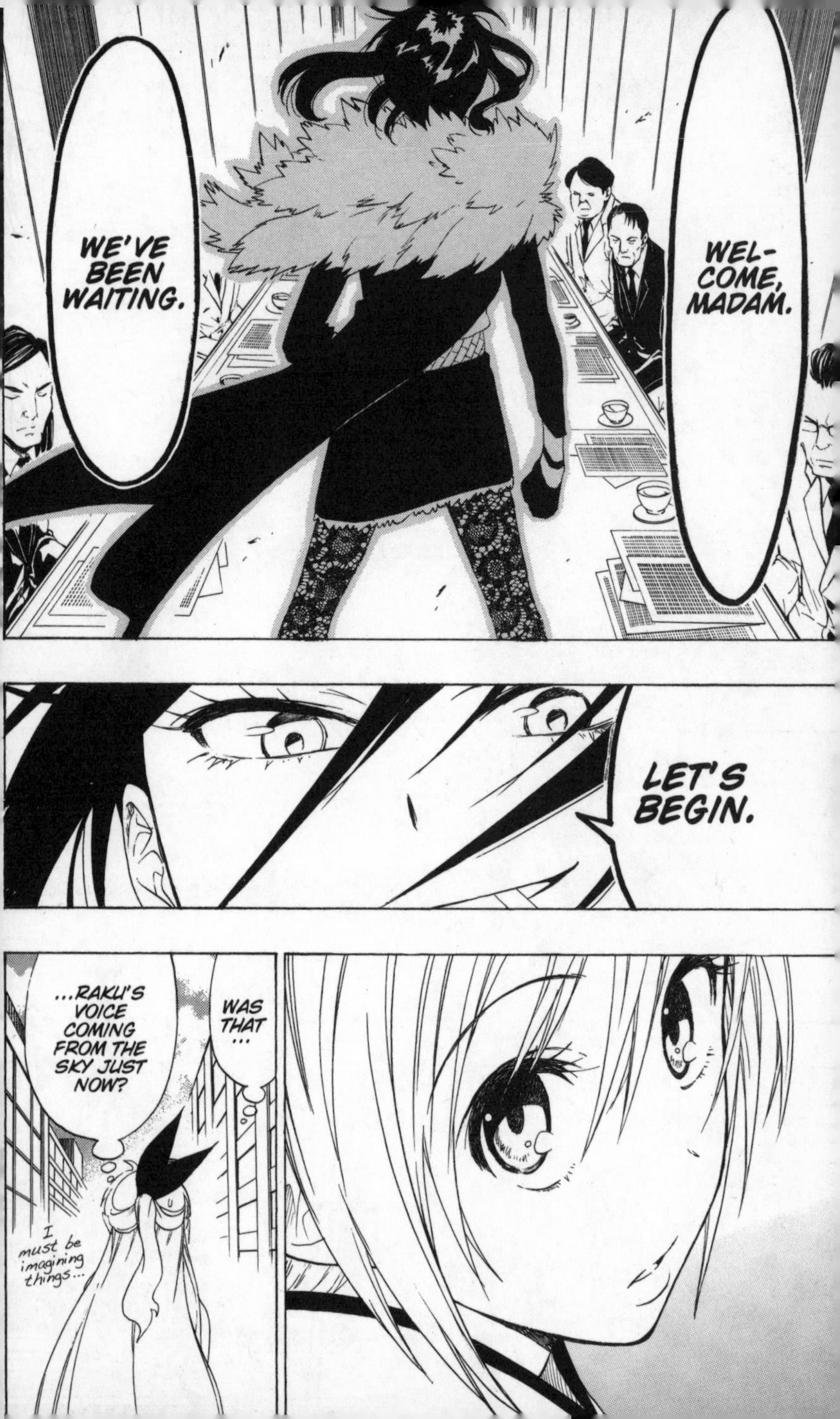
WEL-COME, MADAM.
WE'VE BEEN WAITING.
LET'S BEGIN.
WAS THAT ...
...RAKU'S VOICE COMING FROM THE SKY JUST NOW?
I must be imagining things...

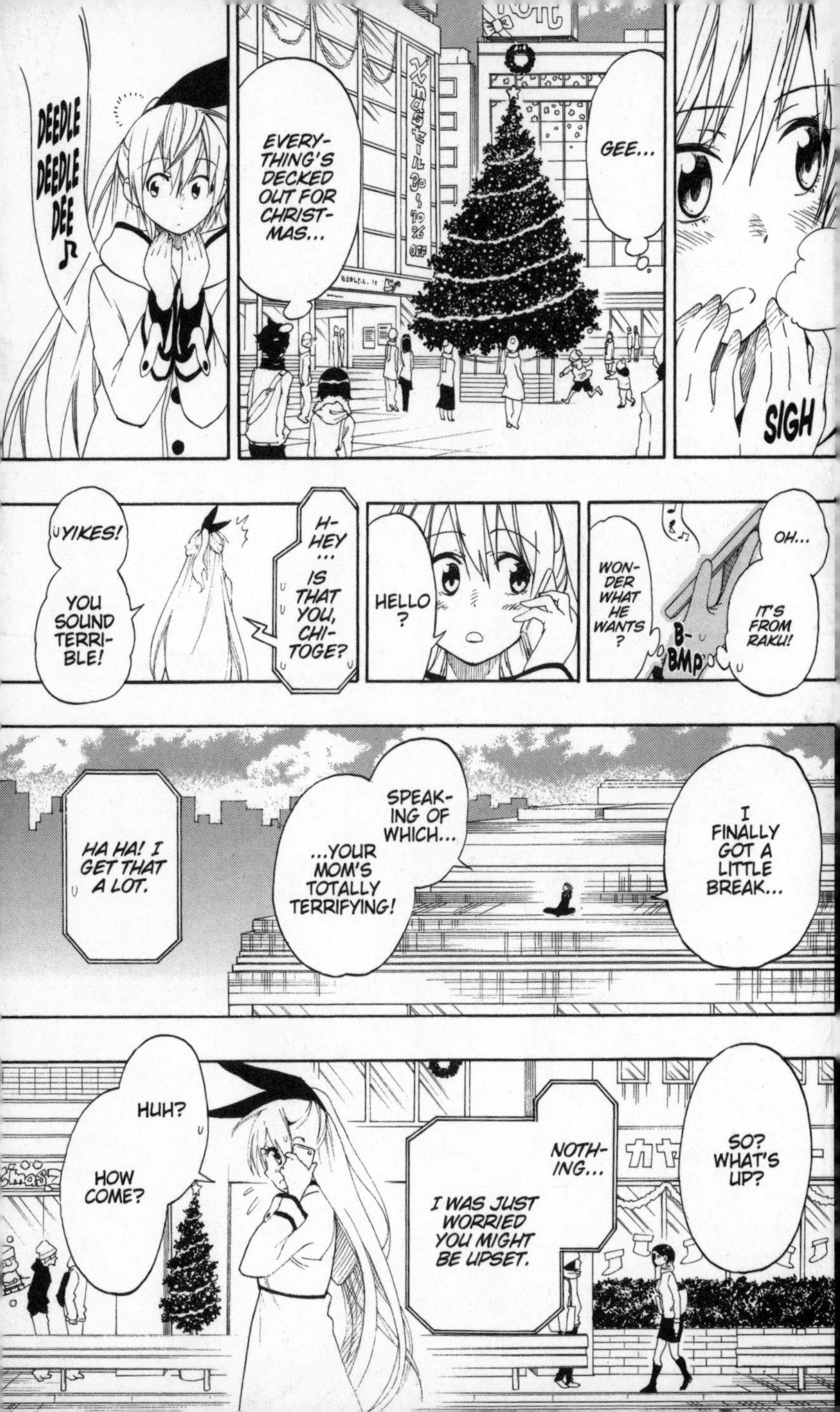
GEE...
SIGH
EVERY-THING'S DECKED OUT FOR CHRIST-MAS...
DEEDLE DEEDLE DEE ♪
OH...
IT'S FROM RAKU!
WON-DER WHAT HE WANTS?
B-BMP
HELLO?
H-HEY... IS THAT YOU, CHI-TOGE?
YIKES!
YOU SOUND TERRI-BLE!
I FINALLY GOT A LITTLE BREAK...
SPEAK-ING OF WHICH...
...YOUR MOM'S TOTALLY TERRIFYING!
HA HA! I GET THAT A LOT.
SO? WHAT'S UP?
NOTH-ING...
I WAS JUST WORRIED YOU MIGHT BE UPSET.
HUH?
HOW COME?

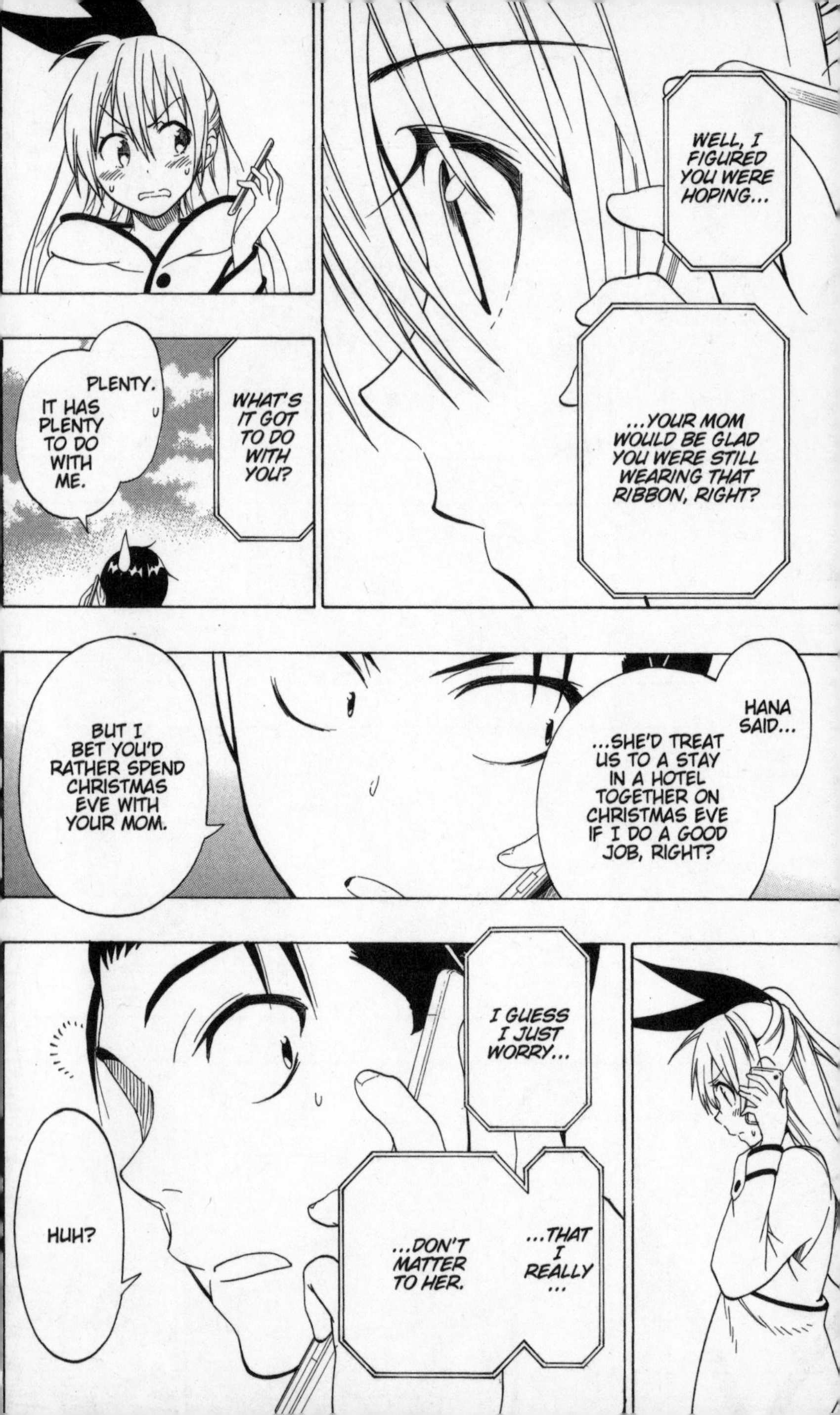
WELL, I FIGURED YOU WERE HOPING...
...YOUR MOM WOULD BE GLAD YOU WERE STILL WEARING THAT RIBBON, RIGHT?
WHAT'S IT GOT TO DO WITH YOU?
PLENTY. IT HAS PLENTY TO DO WITH ME.
HANA SAID... ...SHE'D TREAT US TO A STAY IN A HOTEL TOGETHER ON CHRISTMAS EVE IF I DO A GOOD JOB, RIGHT?
BUT I BET YOU'D RATHER SPEND CHRISTMAS EVE WITH YOUR MOM.
I GUESS I JUST WORRY...
...THAT I REALLY ... ...DON'T MATTER TO HER.
HUH?

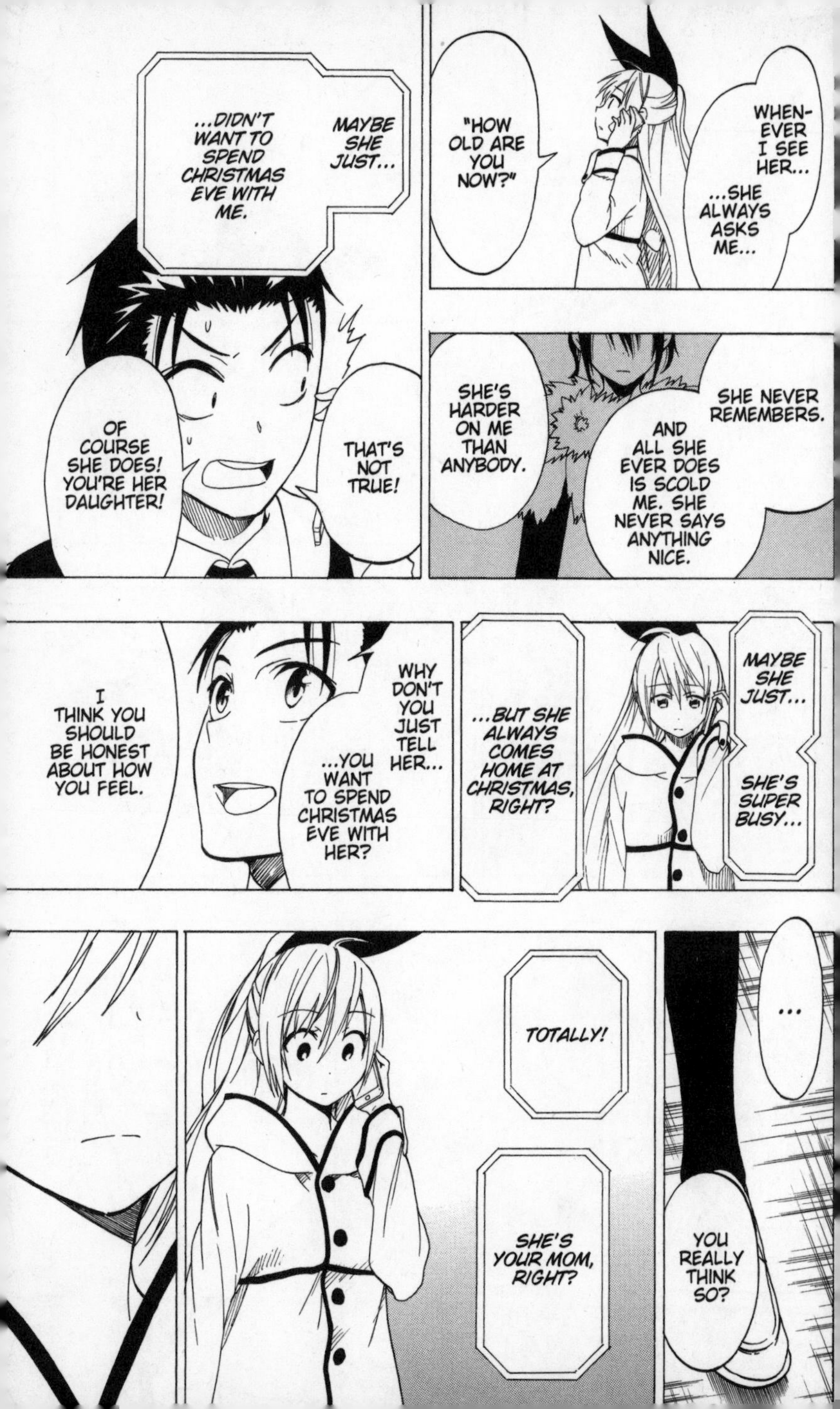
WHEN-EVER I SEE HER...
...SHE ALWAYS ASKS ME...
"HOW OLD ARE YOU NOW?"
SHE NEVER REMEMBERS.
AND ALL SHE EVER DOES IS SCOLD ME. SHE NEVER SAYS ANYTHING NICE.
SHE'S HARDER ON ME THAN ANYBODY.
MAYBE SHE JUST...
...DIDN'T WANT TO SPEND CHRISTMAS EVE WITH ME.
THAT'S NOT TRUE!
OF COURSE SHE DOES! YOU'RE HER DAUGHTER!
MAYBE SHE JUST...
SHE'S SUPER BUSY...
...BUT SHE ALWAYS COMES HOME AT CHRISTMAS, RIGHT?
WHY DON'T YOU JUST TELL HER...
...YOU WANT TO SPEND CHRISTMAS EVE WITH HER?
I THINK YOU SHOULD BE HONEST ABOUT HOW YOU FEEL.
...
YOU REALLY THINK SO?
TOTALLY!
SHE'S YOUR MOM, RIGHT?

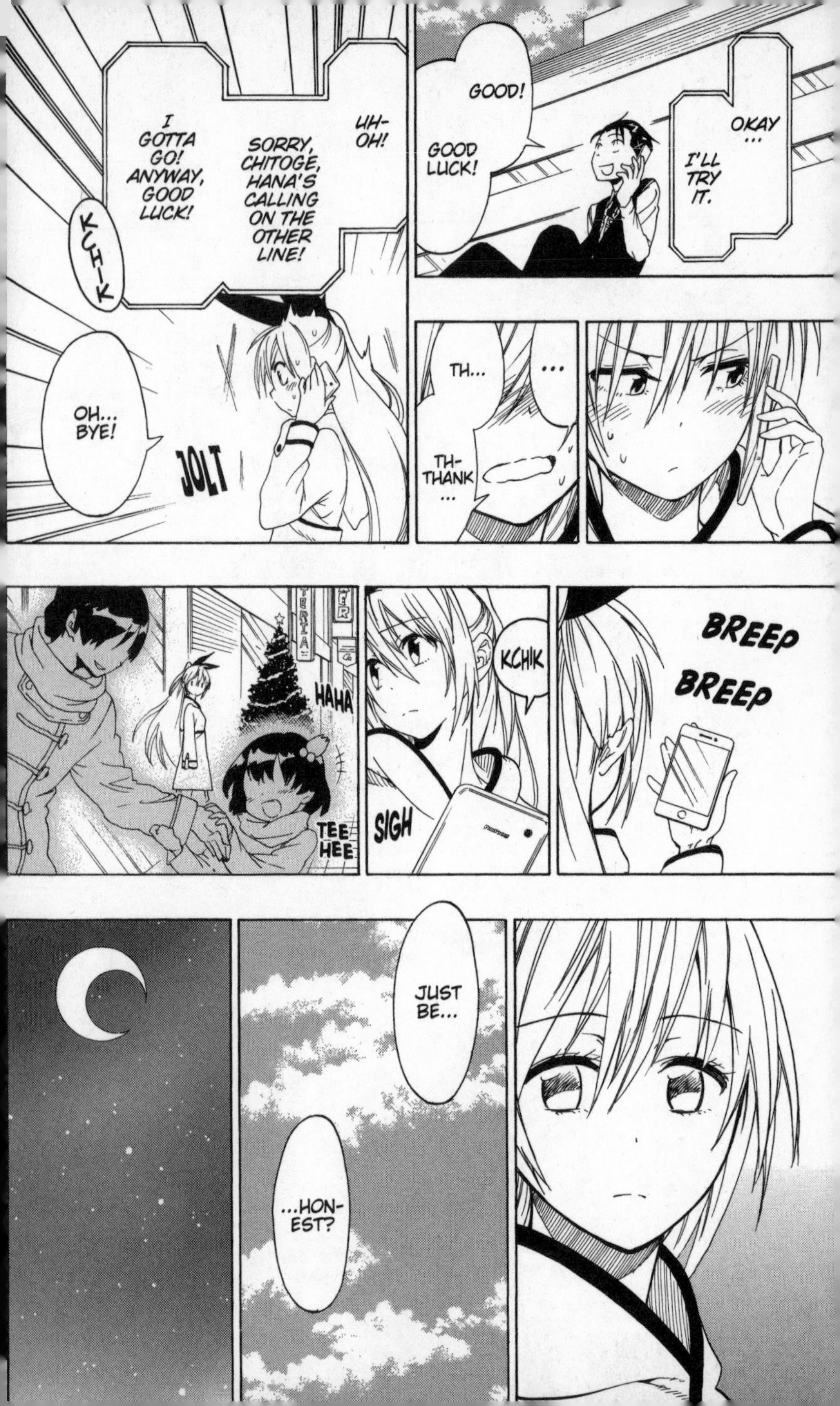

OKAY... I'LL TRY IT.
GOOD! GOOD LUCK!
...
TH... TH-THANK...
UH-OH!
SORRY, CHITOGE, HANA'S CALLING ON THE OTHER LINE!
I GOTTA GO! ANYWAY, GOOD LUCK!
KCHIK
OH... BYE!
JOLT
BREEP
BREEP
KCHIK
SIGH
HAHA
TEE HEE
JUST BE...
...HON-EST?

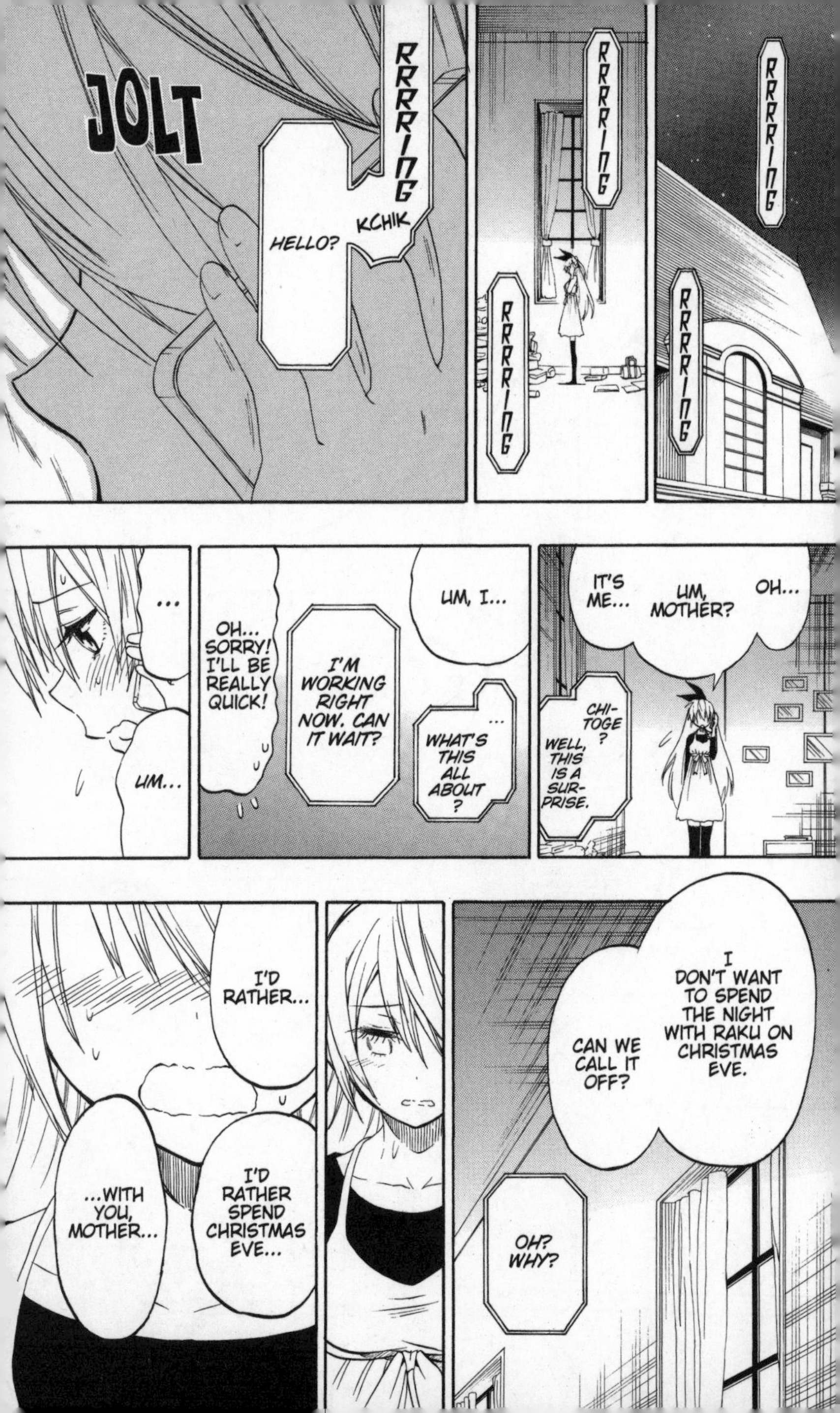
RRRRING
RRRRING
RRRRING
RRRRING
JOLT
RRRRING
KCHIK
HELLO?
OH...
UM, MOTHER?
IT'S ME...
CHITOGE? WELL, THIS IS A SURPRISE.
UM, I...
...WHAT'S THIS ALL ABOUT?
I'M WORKING RIGHT NOW. CAN IT WAIT?
OH... SORRY! I'LL BE REALLY QUICK!
...
UM...
I DON'T WANT TO SPEND THE NIGHT WITH RAKU ON CHRISTMAS EVE.
CAN WE CALL IT OFF?
OH? WHY?
I'D RATHER...
I'D RATHER SPEND CHRISTMAS EVE...
...WITH YOU, MOTHER...

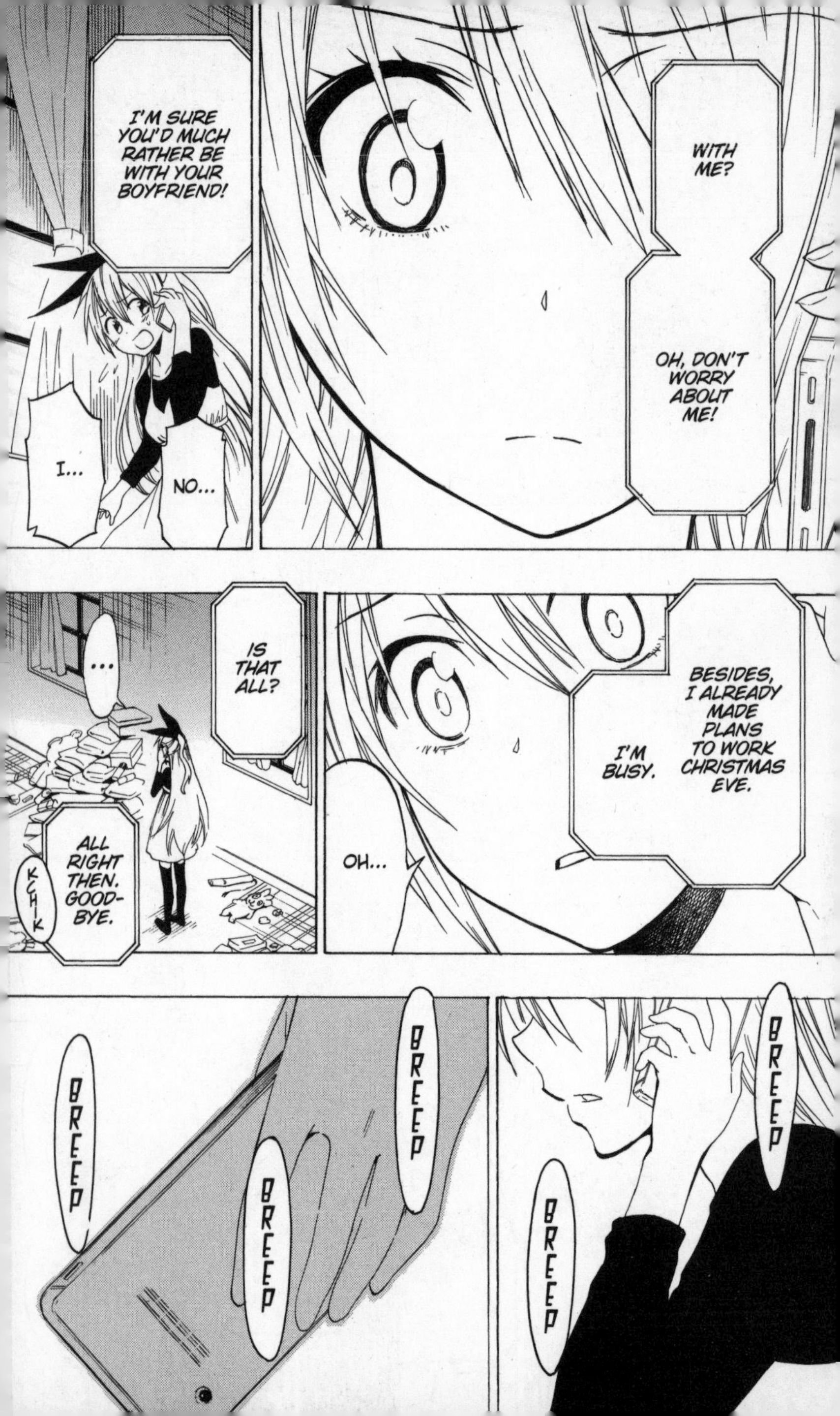
WITH ME?
OH, DON'T WORRY ABOUT ME!
I'M SURE YOU'D MUCH RATHER BE WITH YOUR BOYFRIEND!
NO...
I...
BESIDES, I ALREADY MADE PLANS TO WORK CHRISTMAS EVE.
I'M BUSY.
OH...
IS THAT ALL?
...
ALL RIGHT THEN. GOOD-BYE.
KCHIK
BREEP
BREEP
BREEP
BREEP
BREEP

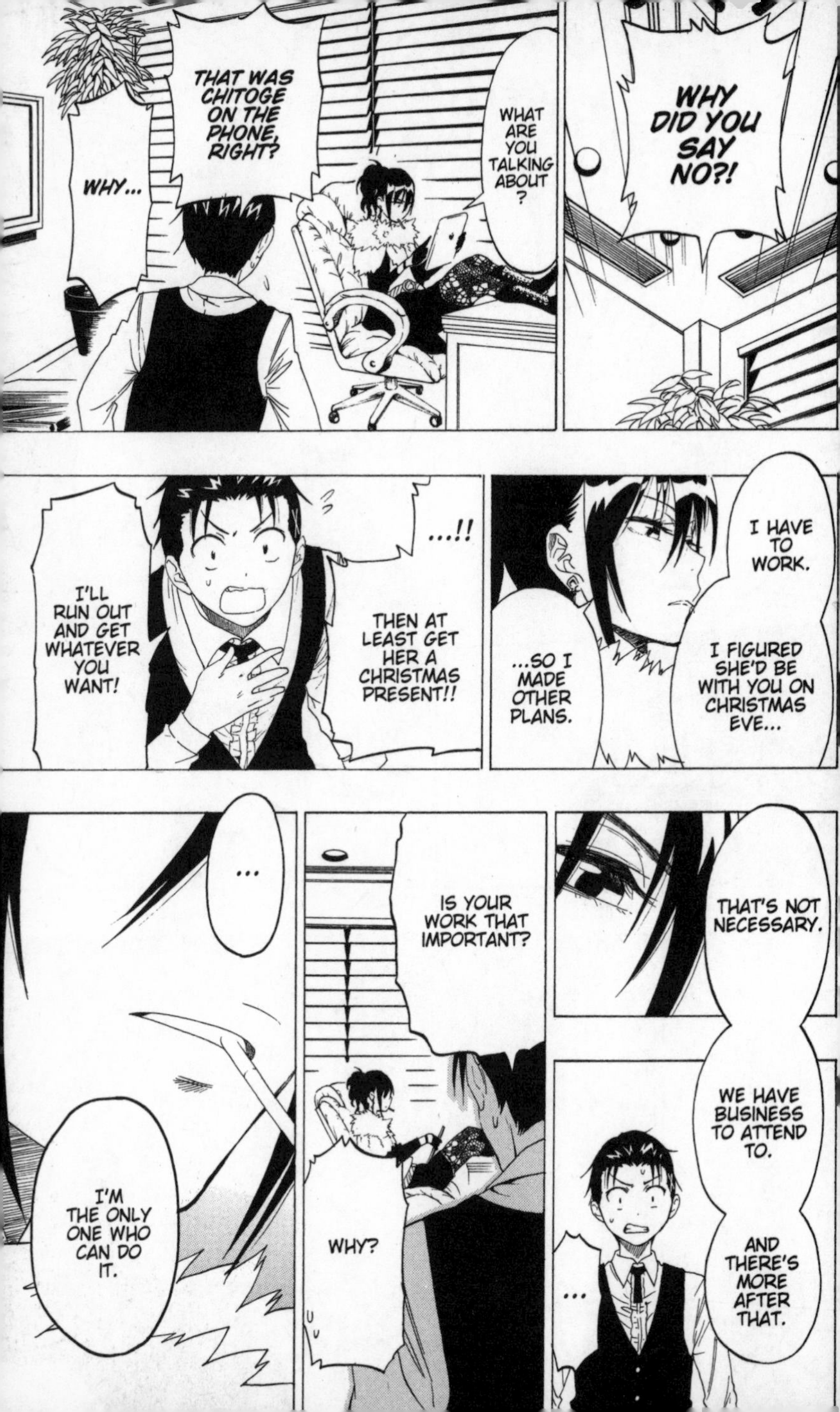
WHY DID YOU SAY NO?!
WHAT ARE YOU TALKING ABOUT?
THAT WAS CHITOGE ON THE PHONE, RIGHT?
WHY...
I HAVE TO WORK.
I FIGURED SHE'D BE WITH YOU ON CHRISTMAS EVE...
...SO I MADE OTHER PLANS.
...!!
THEN AT LEAST GET HER A CHRISTMAS PRESENT!!
I'LL RUN OUT AND GET WHATEVER YOU WANT!
THAT'S NOT NECESSARY.
WE HAVE BUSINESS TO ATTEND TO.
AND THERE'S MORE AFTER THAT.
...
IS YOUR WORK THAT IMPORTANT?
WHY?
...
I'M THE ONLY ONE WHO CAN DO IT.

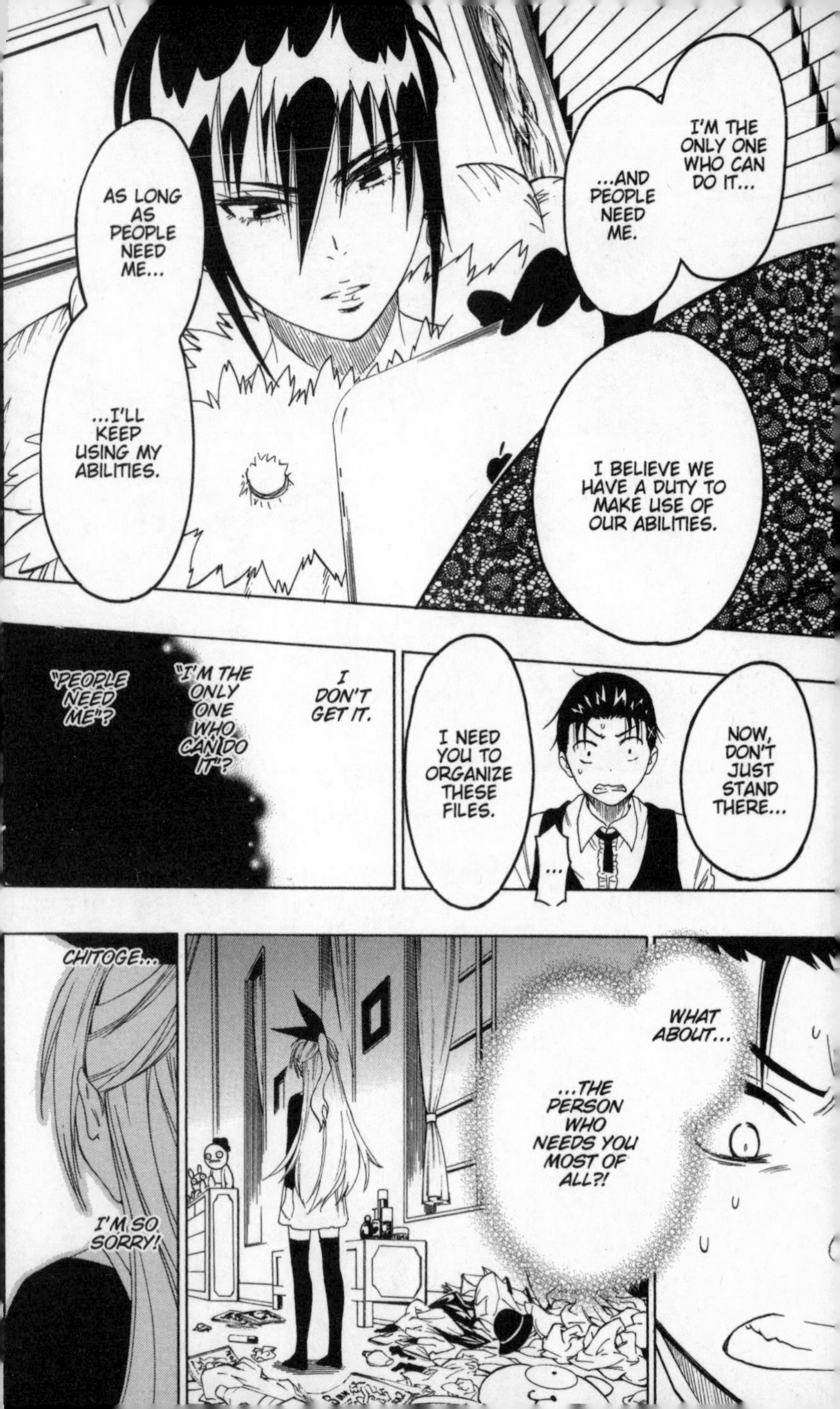
I'M THE ONLY ONE WHO CAN DO IT...
...AND PEOPLE NEED ME.
I BELIEVE WE HAVE A DUTY TO MAKE USE OF OUR ABILITIES.
AS LONG AS PEOPLE NEED ME...
...I'LL KEEP USING MY ABILITIES.
NOW, DON'T JUST STAND THERE...
I NEED YOU TO ORGANIZE THESE FILES.
...
I DON'T GET IT.
"I'M THE ONLY ONE WHO CAN DO IT"?
"PEOPLE NEED ME"?
WHAT ABOUT...
...THE PERSON WHO NEEDS YOU MOST OF ALL?!
CHITOGE...
I'M SO SORRY!

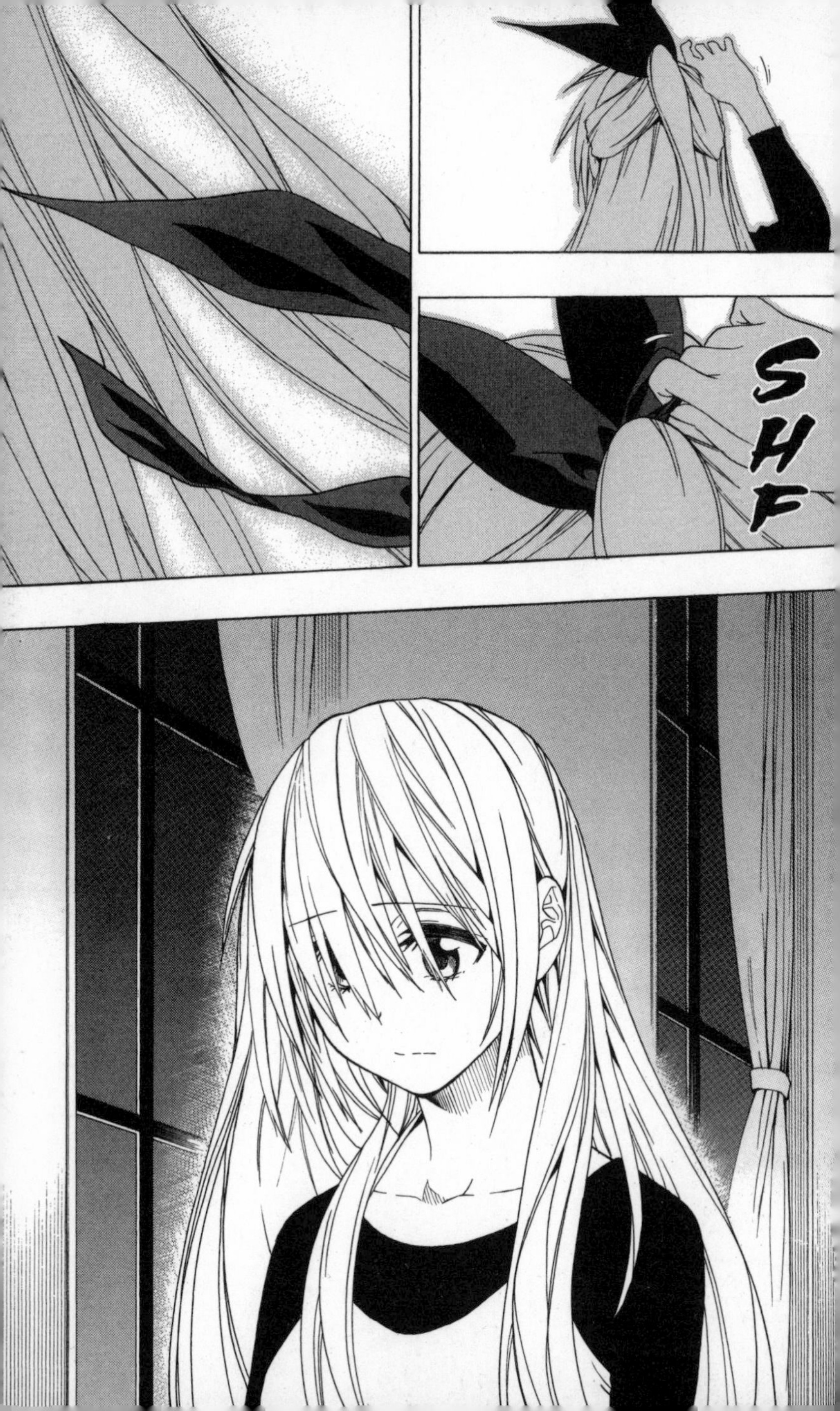
SHF

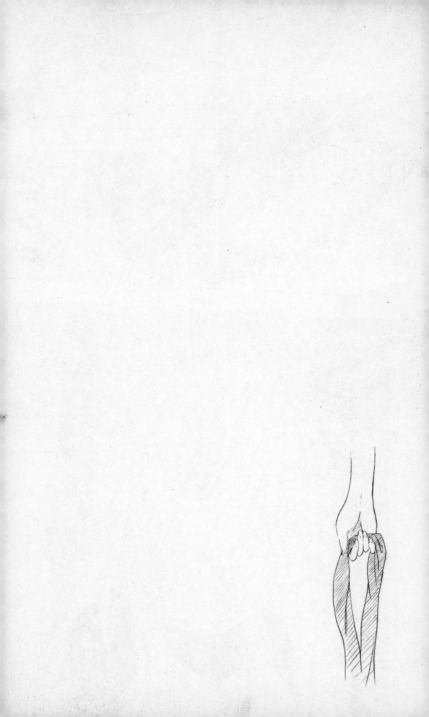

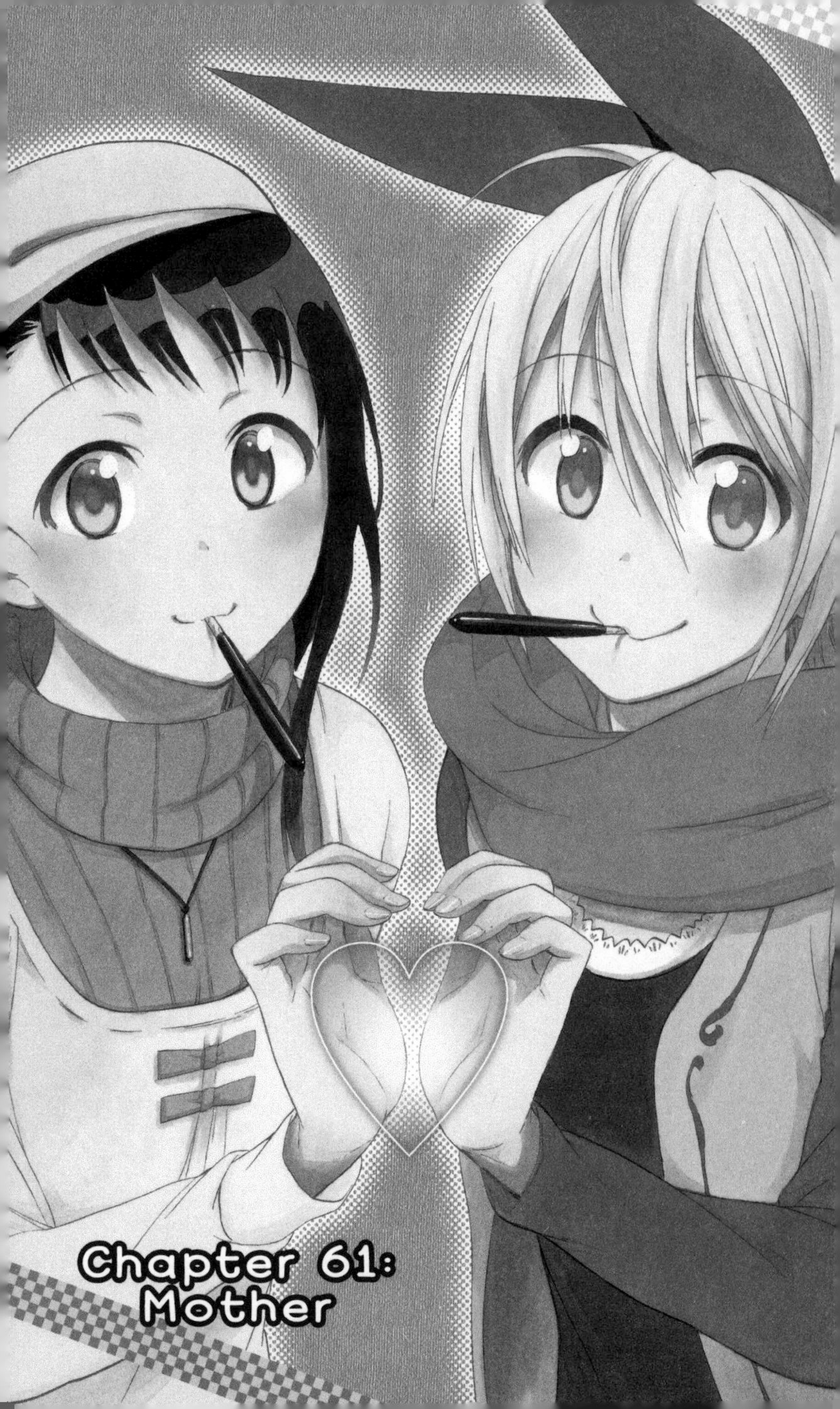
Chapter 61:
Mother

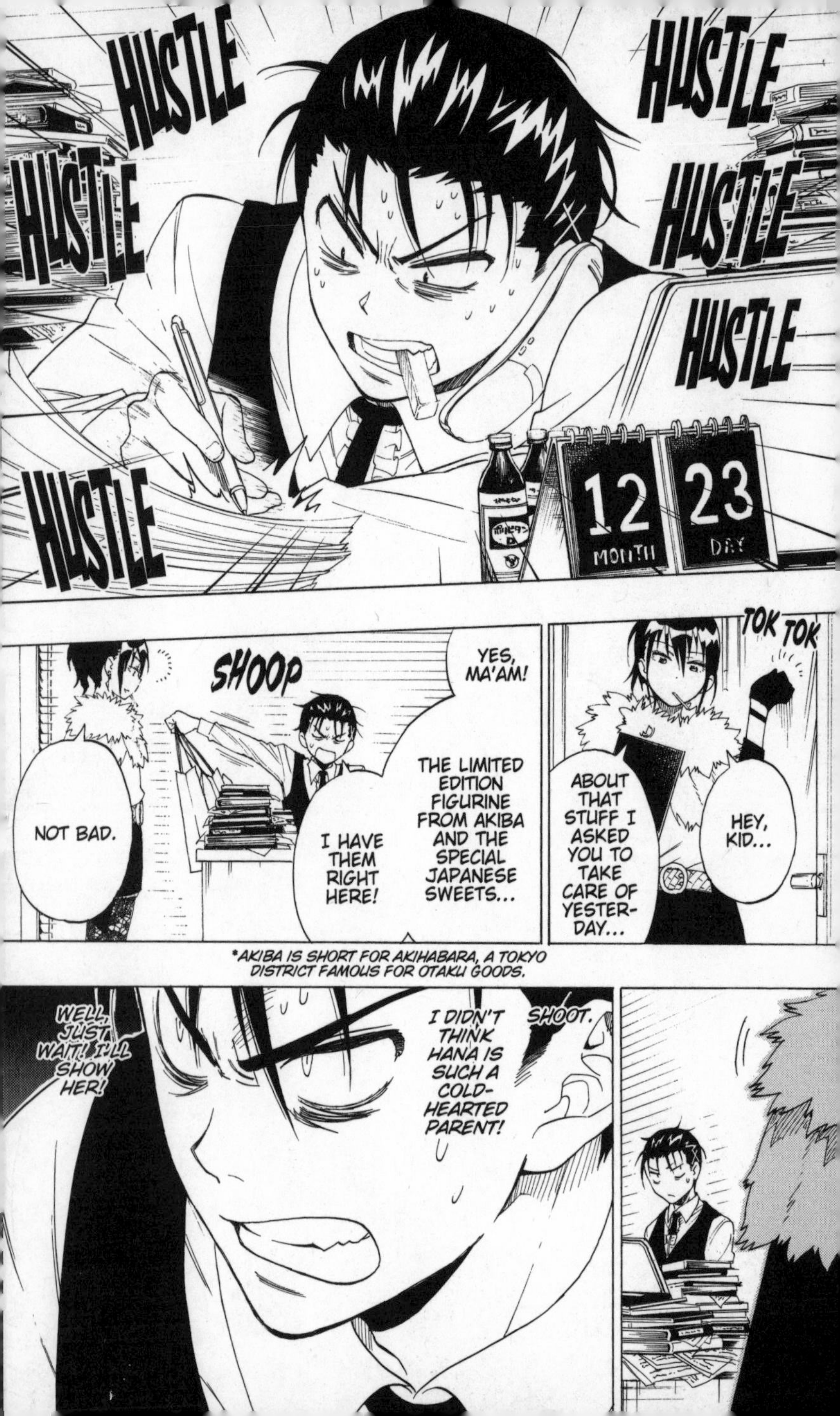
HUSTLE
HUSTLE
HUSTLE
12 MONTH
23 DAY
HUSTLE
HUSTLE
HUSTLE
TOK TOK
HEY, KID...
ABOUT THAT STUFF I ASKED YOU TO TAKE CARE OF YESTERDAY...
YES, MA'AM!
THE LIMITED EDITION FIGURINE FROM AKIBA AND THE SPECIAL JAPANESE SWEETS...
SHOOP
I HAVE THEM RIGHT HERE!
NOT BAD.
*AKIBA IS SHORT FOR AKIHABARA, A TOKYO DISTRICT FAMOUS FOR OTAKU GOODS.
SHOOT.
I DIDN'T THINK HANA IS SUCH A COLD-HEARTED PARENT!
WELL, JUST WAIT! I'LL SHOW HER!

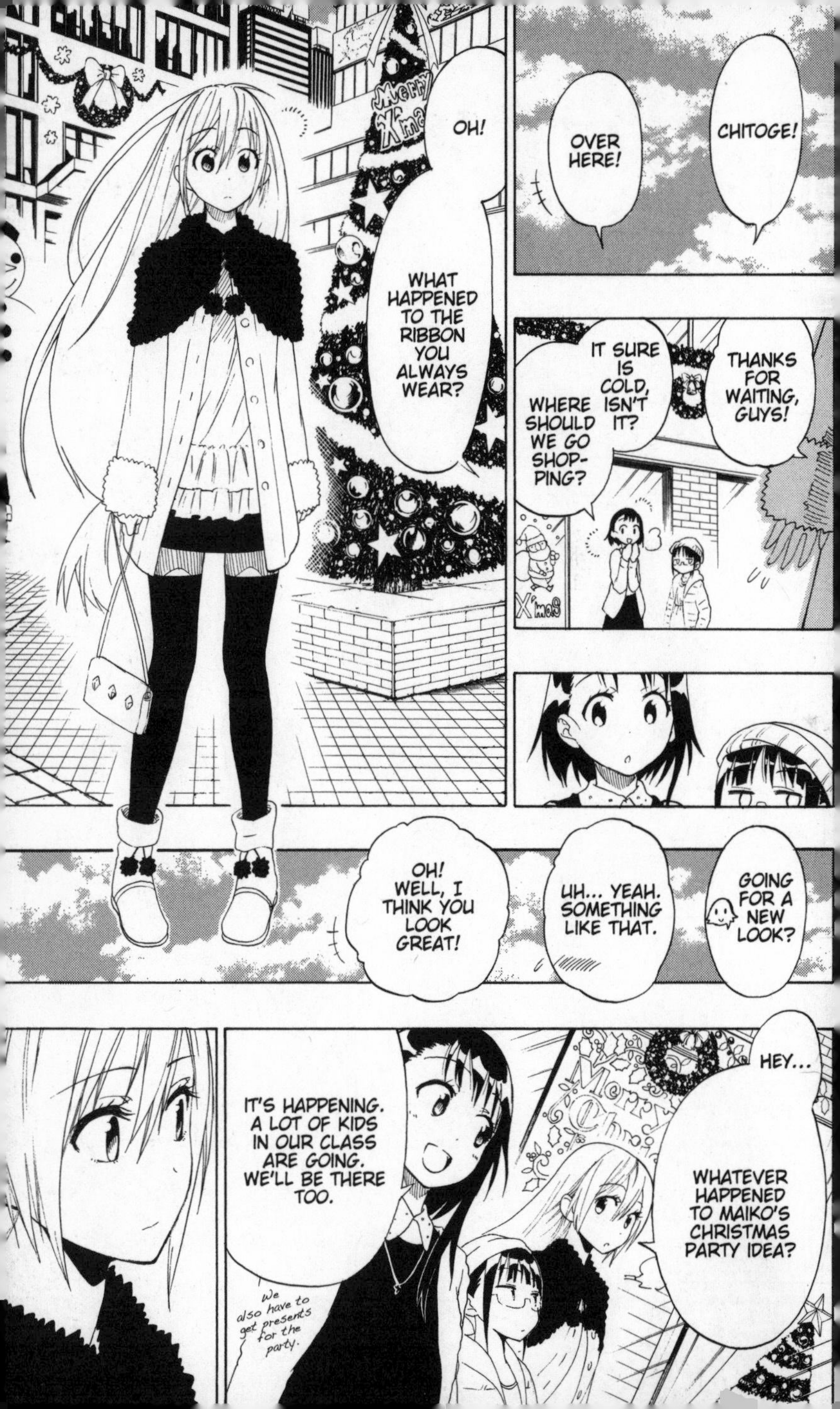
CHITOGE!
OVER HERE!
THANKS FOR WAITING, GUYS!
IT SURE IS COLD, ISN'T IT?
WHERE SHOULD WE GO SHOPPING?
X'mas
Merry X'mas
OH!
WHAT HAPPENED TO THE RIBBON YOU ALWAYS WEAR?
GOING FOR A NEW LOOK?
UH... YEAH. SOMETHING LIKE THAT.
OH! WELL, I THINK YOU LOOK GREAT!
HEY...
WHATEVER HAPPENED TO MAIKO'S CHRISTMAS PARTY IDEA?
IT'S HAPPENING. A LOT OF KIDS IN OUR CLASS ARE GOING. WE'LL BE THERE TOO.
We also have to get presents for the party.

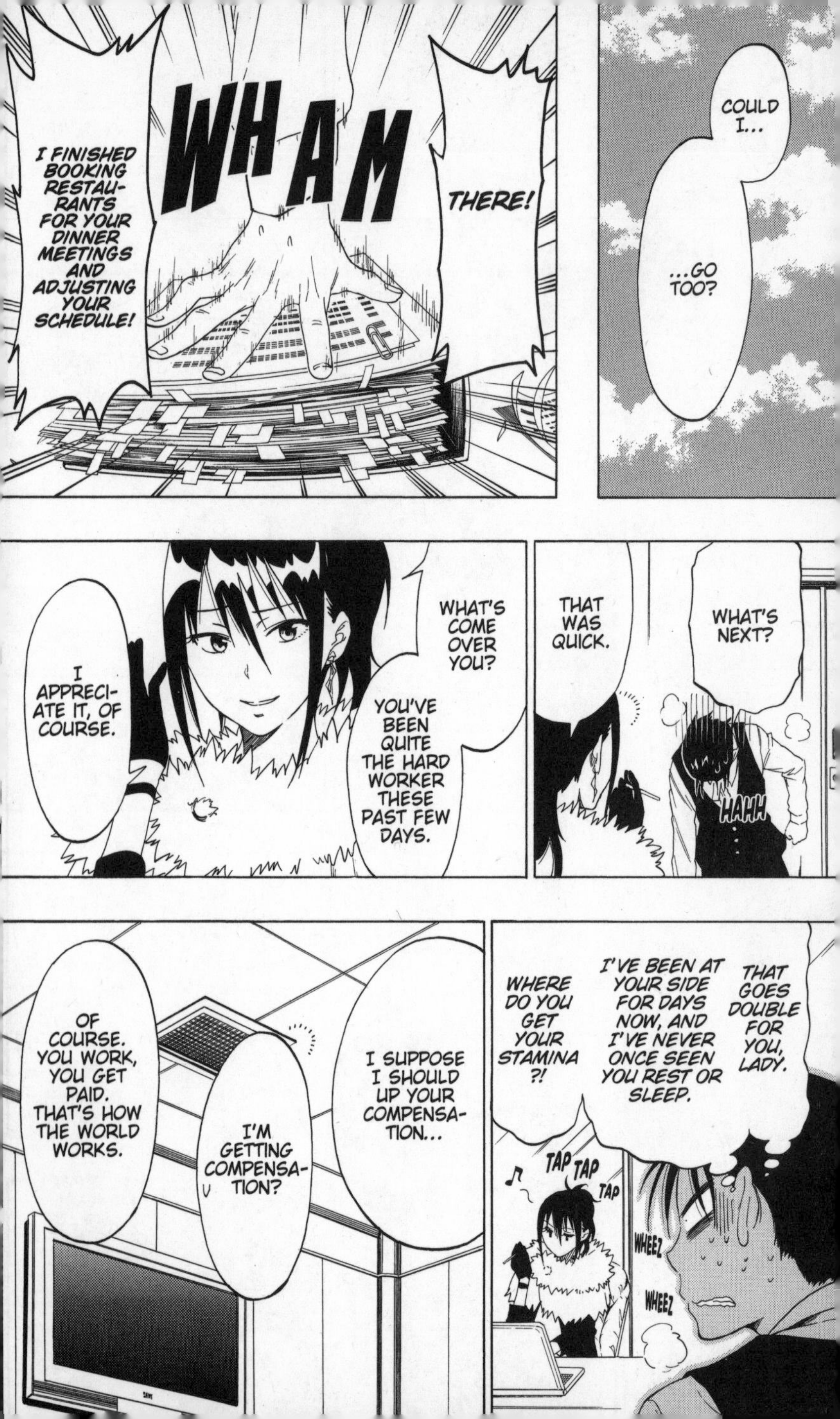
COULD I...
...GO TOO?
THERE!
WHAM
I FINISHED BOOKING RESTAU-RANTS FOR YOUR DINNER MEETINGS AND ADJUSTING YOUR SCHEDULE!
WHAT'S NEXT?
HAHH
THAT WAS QUICK.
WHAT'S COME OVER YOU?
YOU'VE BEEN QUITE THE HARD WORKER THESE PAST FEW DAYS.
I APPRECI-ATE IT, OF COURSE.
THAT GOES DOUBLE FOR YOU, LADY.
I'VE BEEN AT YOUR SIDE FOR DAYS NOW, AND I'VE NEVER ONCE SEEN YOU REST OR SLEEP.
WHERE DO YOU GET YOUR STAMINA?!
TAP TAP TAP
WHEEZ
WHEEZ
I SUPPOSE I SHOULD UP YOUR COMPENSA-TION...
I'M GETTING COMPENSA-TION?
OF COURSE. YOU WORK, YOU GET PAID. THAT'S HOW THE WORLD WORKS.

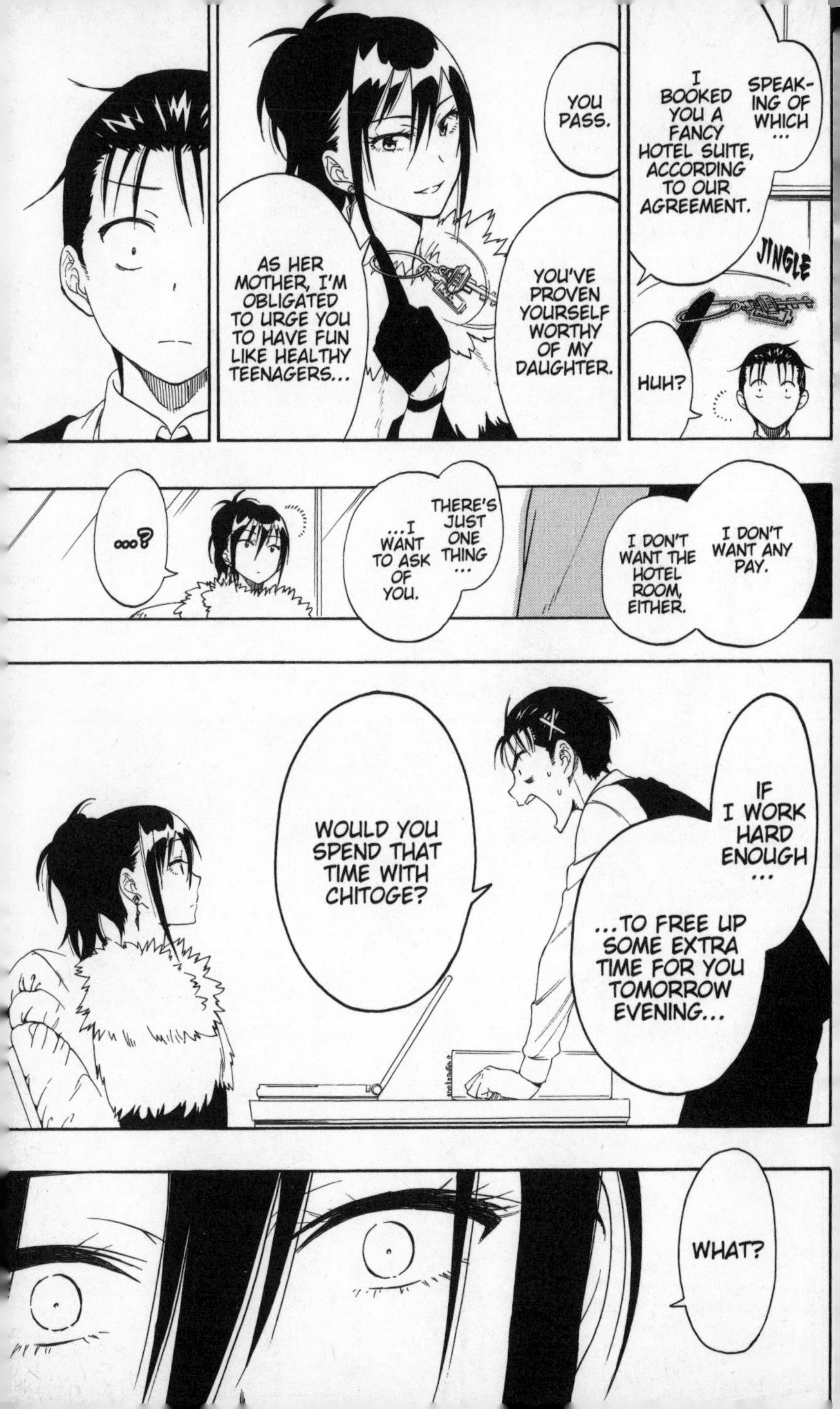
SPEAKING OF WHICH...
I BOOKED YOU A FANCY HOTEL SUITE, ACCORDING TO OUR AGREEMENT.
JINGLE
HUH?
YOU PASS.
YOU'VE PROVEN YOURSELF WORTHY OF MY DAUGHTER.
AS HER MOTHER, I'M OBLIGATED TO URGE YOU TO HAVE FUN LIKE HEALTHY TEENAGERS...
I DON'T WANT ANY PAY.
I DON'T WANT THE HOTEL ROOM, EITHER.
THERE'S JUST ONE THING...
...I WANT TO ASK OF YOU.
...?
IF I WORK HARD ENOUGH...
...TO FREE UP SOME EXTRA TIME FOR YOU TOMORROW EVENING...
WOULD YOU SPEND THAT TIME WITH CHITOGE?
WHAT?

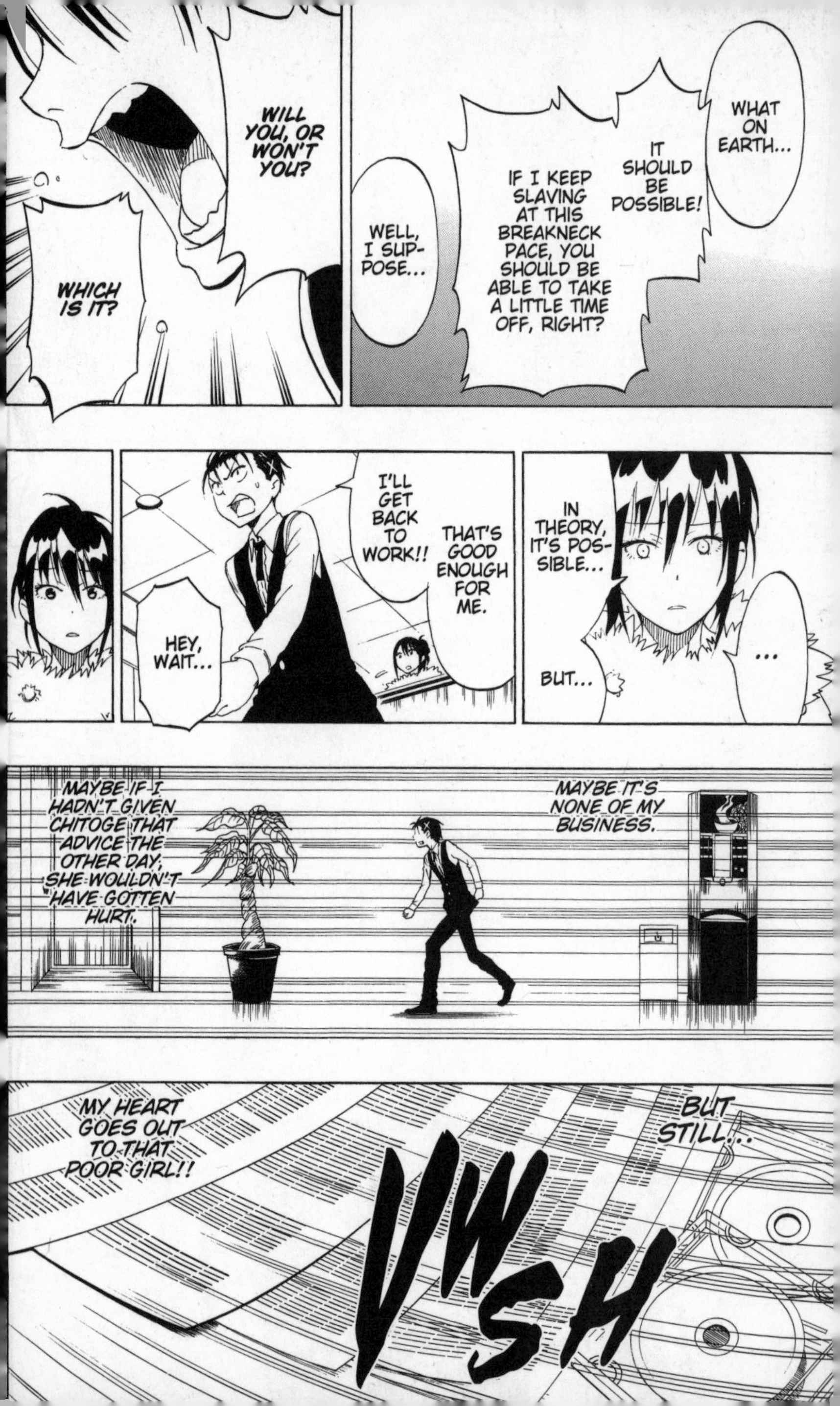

WHAT ON EARTH...
IT SHOULD BE POSSIBLE!
IF I KEEP SLAVING AT THIS BREAKNECK PACE, YOU SHOULD BE ABLE TO TAKE A LITTLE TIME OFF, RIGHT?
WELL, I SUPPOSE...
WILL YOU, OR WON'T YOU?
WHICH IS IT?
IN THEORY, IT'S POSSIBLE...
...
BUT...
THAT'S GOOD ENOUGH FOR ME.
I'LL GET BACK TO WORK!!
HEY, WAIT...
MAYBE IT'S NONE OF MY BUSINESS.
MAYBE IF I HADN'T GIVEN CHITOGE THAT ADVICE THE OTHER DAY, SHE WOULDN'T HAVE GOTTEN HURT.
BUT STILL...
VWSH
MY HEART GOES OUT TO THAT POOR GIRL!!

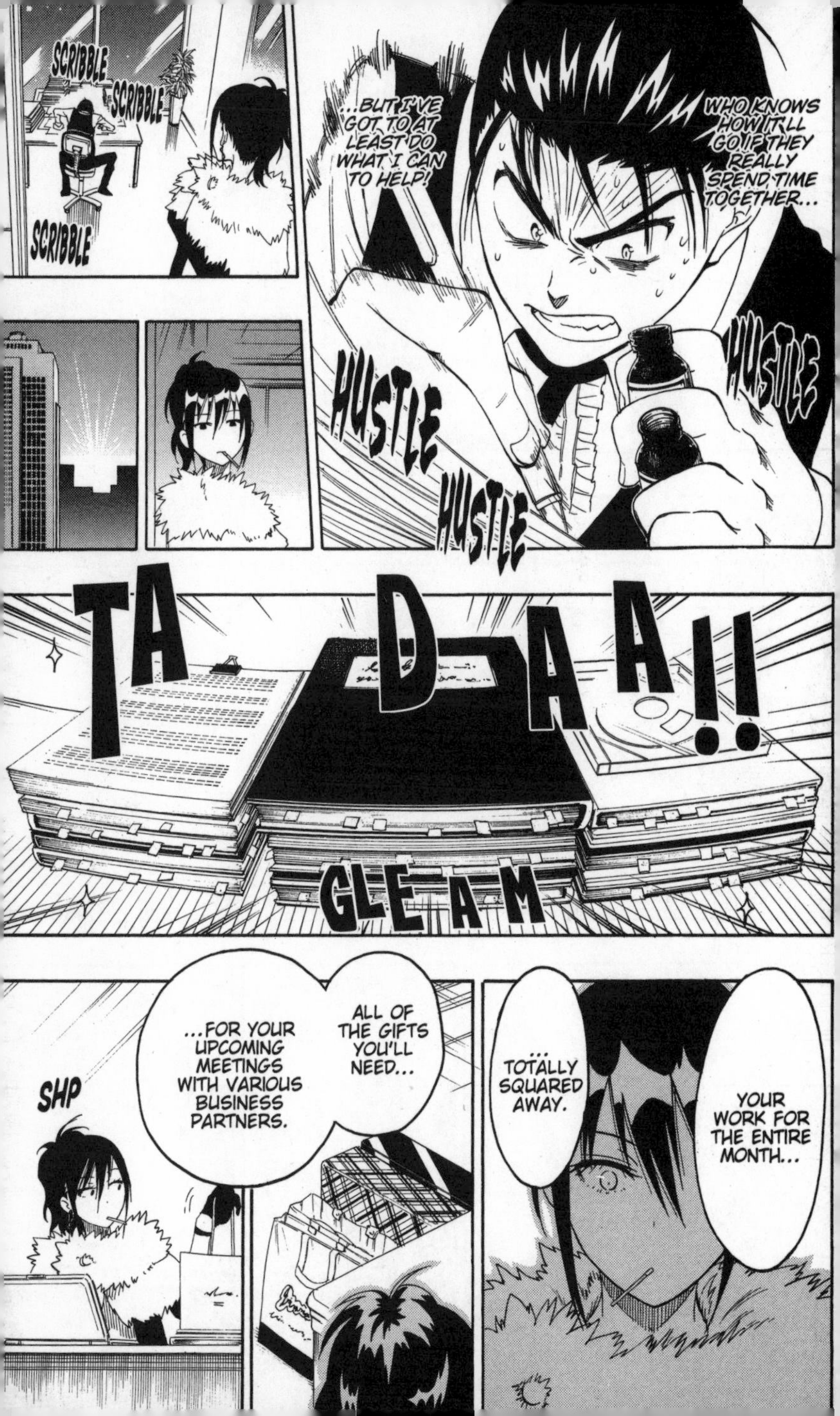
WHO KNOWS HOW IT'LL GO IF THEY REALLY SPEND TIME TOGETHER...
...BUT I'VE GOT TO AT LEAST DO WHAT I CAN TO HELP!
HUSTLE
HUSTLE
HUSTLE
SCRIBBLE
SCRIBBLE
SCRIBBLE
TA-DAA!!
GLEAM
YOUR WORK FOR THE ENTIRE MONTH...
...TOTALLY SQUARED AWAY.
ALL OF THE GIFTS YOU'LL NEED...
...FOR YOUR UPCOMING MEETINGS WITH VARIOUS BUSINESS PARTNERS.
SHP

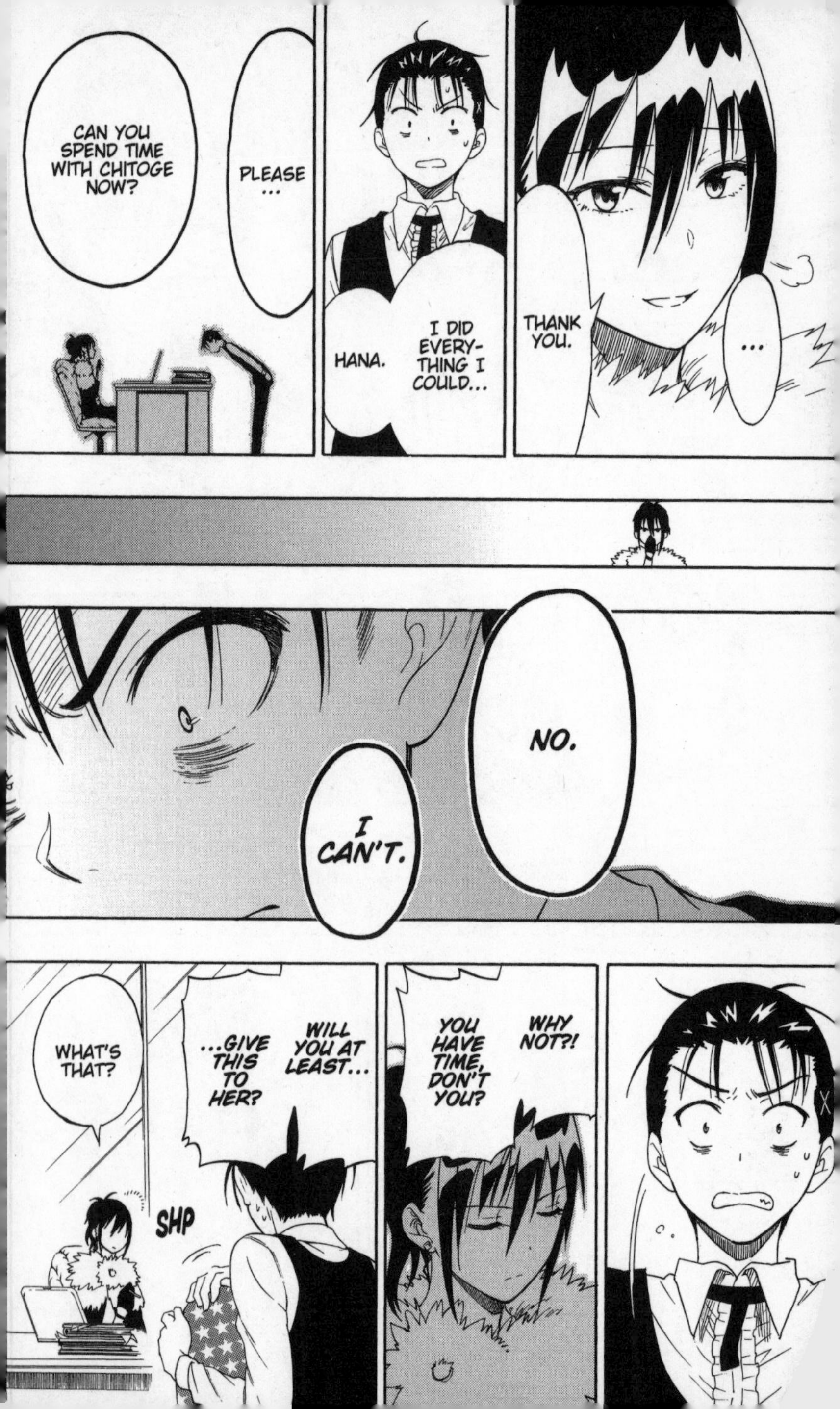
...
THANK YOU.
I DID EVERYTHING I COULD...
HANA.
PLEASE...
CAN YOU SPEND TIME WITH CHITOGE NOW?
NO.
I CAN'T.
WHY NOT?!
YOU HAVE TIME, DON'T YOU?
WILL YOU AT LEAST...
...GIVE THIS TO HER?
WHAT'S THAT?
SHP

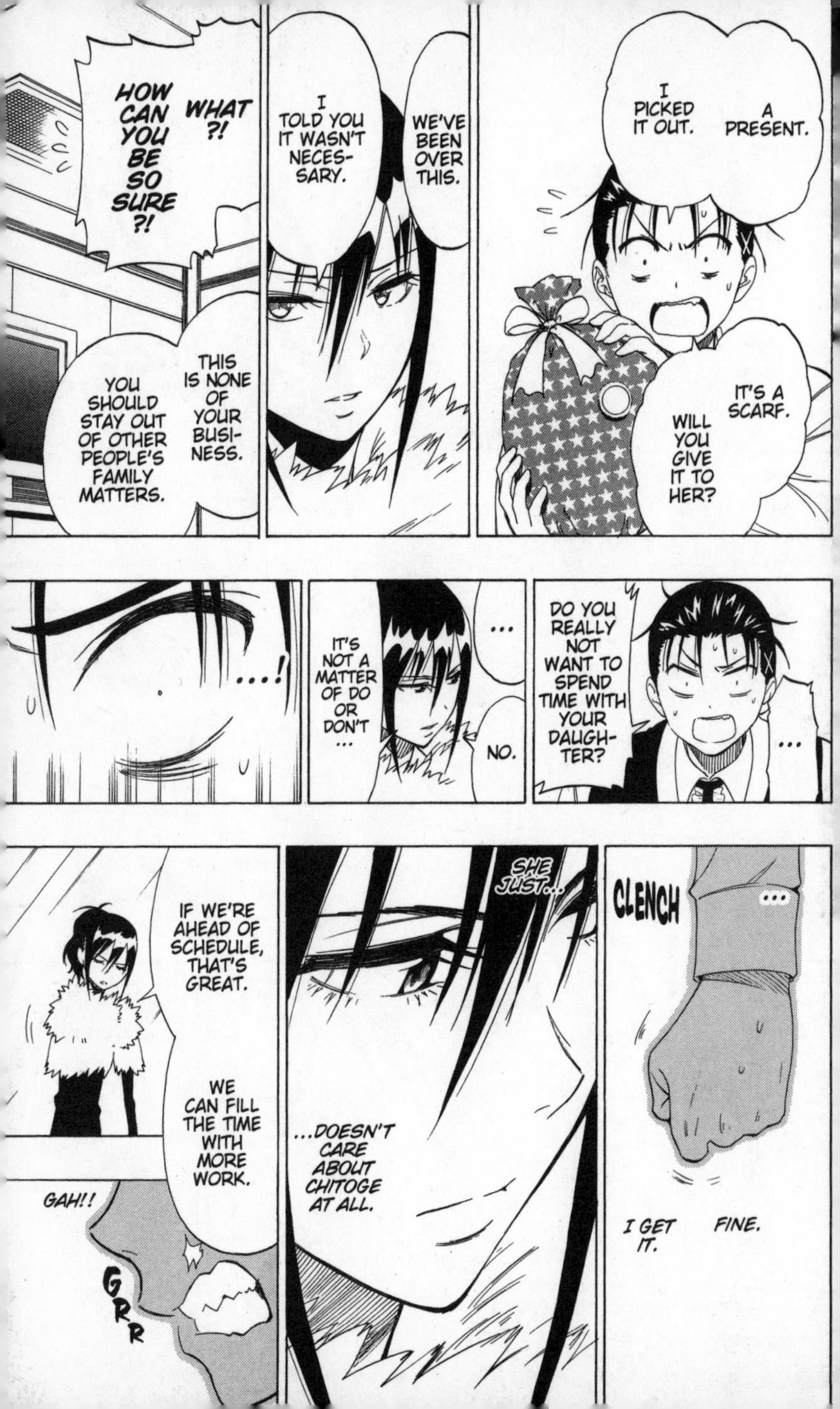
A PRESENT.
I PICKED IT OUT.
IT'S A SCARF.
WILL YOU GIVE IT TO HER?
WE'VE BEEN OVER THIS.
I TOLD YOU IT WASN'T NECES-SARY.
THIS IS NONE OF YOUR BUSI-NESS.
YOU SHOULD STAY OUT OF OTHER PEOPLE'S FAMILY MATTERS.
WHAT?!
HOW CAN YOU BE SO SURE?!
DO YOU REALLY NOT WANT TO SPEND TIME WITH YOUR DAUGHTER?
...
...
NO.
IT'S NOT A MATTER OF DO OR DON'T ...
...!
CLENCH
...
FINE.
I GET IT.
SHE JUST...
...DOESN'T CARE ABOUT CHITOGE AT ALL.
IF WE'RE AHEAD OF SCHEDULE, THAT'S GREAT.
WE CAN FILL THE TIME WITH MORE WORK.
GAH!!
GRR

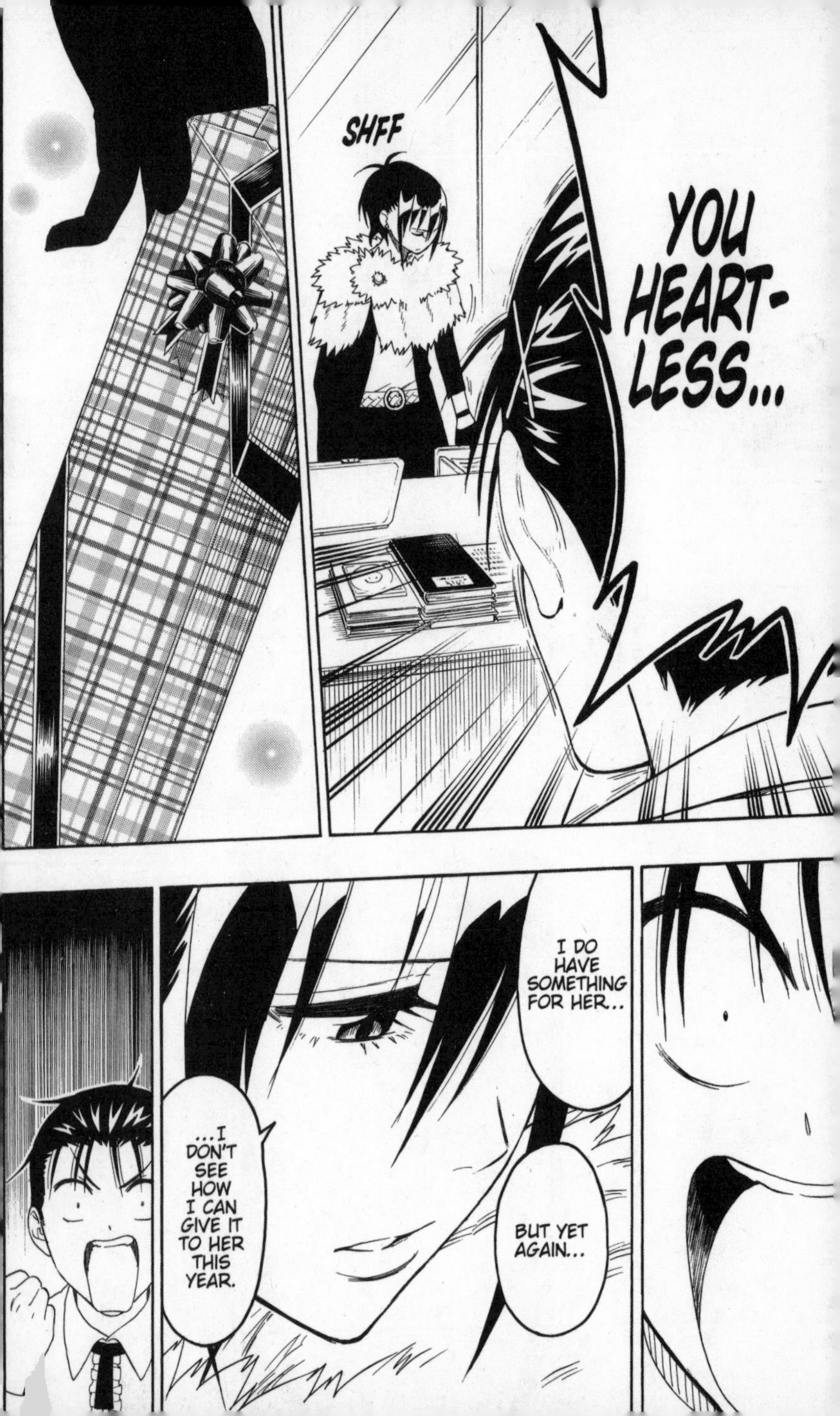
YOU HEARTLESS...
SHFF
I DO HAVE SOMETHING FOR HER...
BUT YET AGAIN...
...I DON'T SEE HOW I CAN GIVE IT TO HER THIS YEAR.

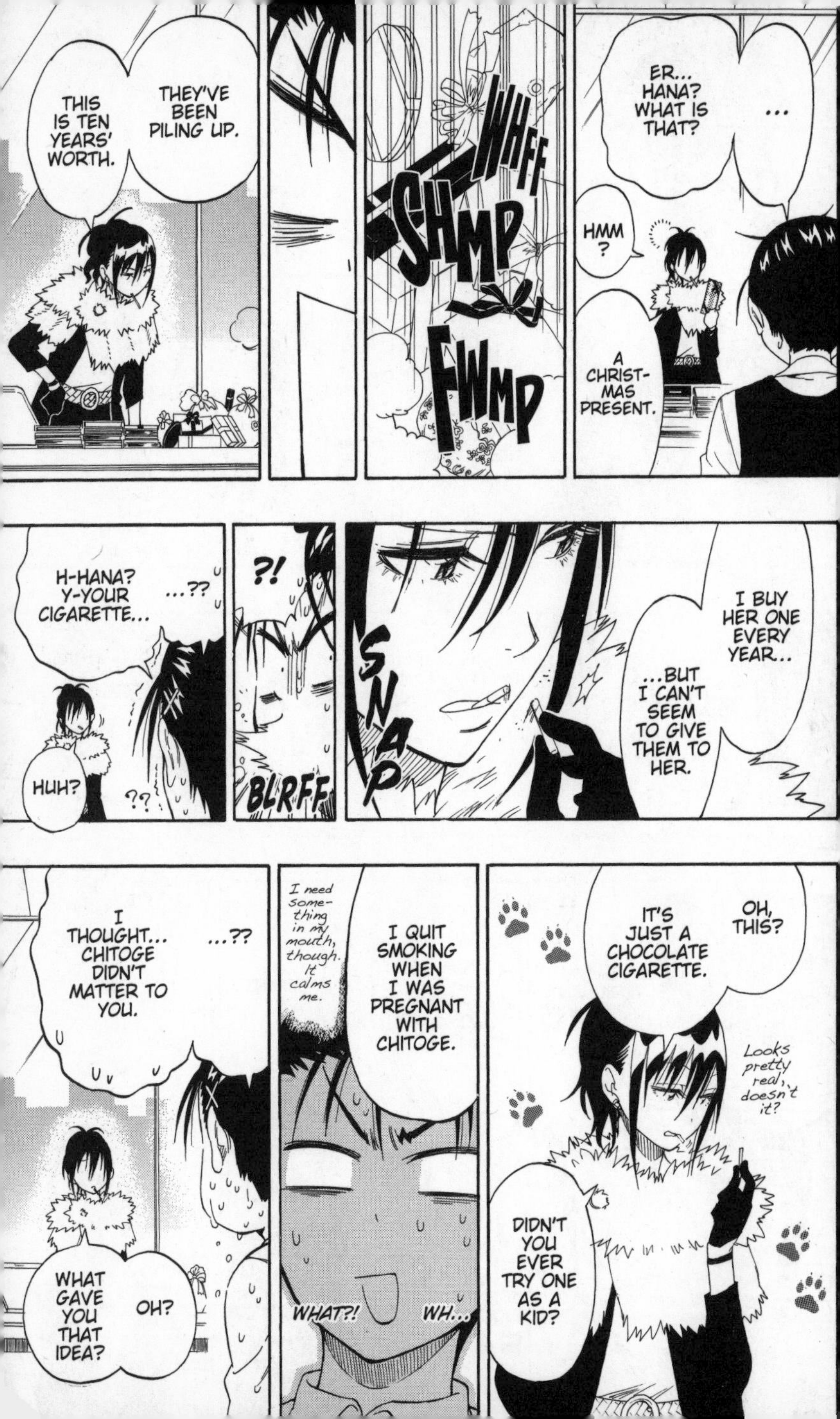
...
ER... HANA? WHAT IS THAT?
HMM ?
A CHRISTMAS PRESENT.
WHFF
SHMP
FWMP
THEY'VE BEEN PILING UP.
THIS IS TEN YEARS' WORTH.
I BUY HER ONE EVERY YEAR...
...BUT I CAN'T SEEM TO GIVE THEM TO HER.
SNAP
?!
BLRFF
...??
H-HANA? Y-YOUR CIGARETTE...
??
HUH?
OH, THIS?
IT'S JUST A CHOCOLATE CIGARETTE.
Looks pretty real, doesn't it?
DIDN'T YOU EVER TRY ONE AS A KID?
I QUIT SMOKING WHEN I WAS PREGNANT WITH CHITOGE.
I need something in my mouth, though. It calms me.
WH...
WHAT?!
...??
I THOUGHT... CHITOGE DIDN'T MATTER TO YOU.
OH?
WHAT GAVE YOU THAT IDEA?

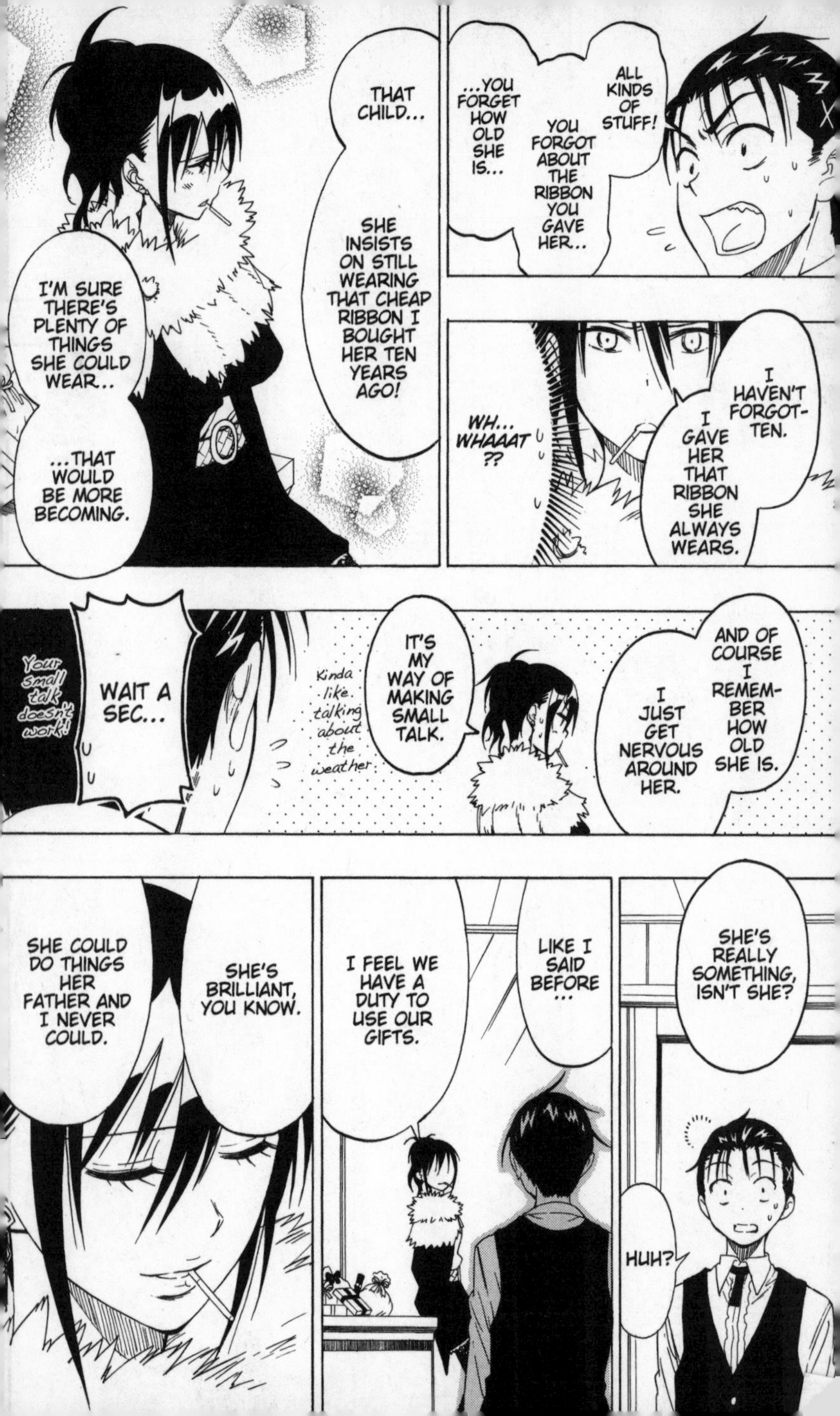

ALL KINDS OF STUFF!
YOU FORGOT ABOUT THE RIBBON YOU GAVE HER...
...YOU FORGET HOW OLD SHE IS...
I HAVEN'T FORGOT-TEN.
I GAVE HER THAT RIBBON SHE ALWAYS WEARS.
WH... WHAAAT??
THAT CHILD...
SHE INSISTS ON STILL WEARING THAT CHEAP RIBBON I BOUGHT HER TEN YEARS AGO!
I'M SURE THERE'S PLENTY OF THINGS SHE COULD WEAR...
...THAT WOULD BE MORE BECOMING.
AND OF COURSE I REMEM-BER HOW OLD SHE IS.
I JUST GET NERVOUS AROUND HER.
IT'S MY WAY OF MAKING SMALL TALK.
Kinda like talking about the weather
WAIT A SEC...
Your small talk doesn't work!
SHE'S REALLY SOMETHING, ISN'T SHE?
HUH?
LIKE I SAID BEFORE...
I FEEL WE HAVE A DUTY TO USE OUR GIFTS.
SHE'S BRILLIANT, YOU KNOW.
SHE COULD DO THINGS HER FATHER AND I NEVER COULD.

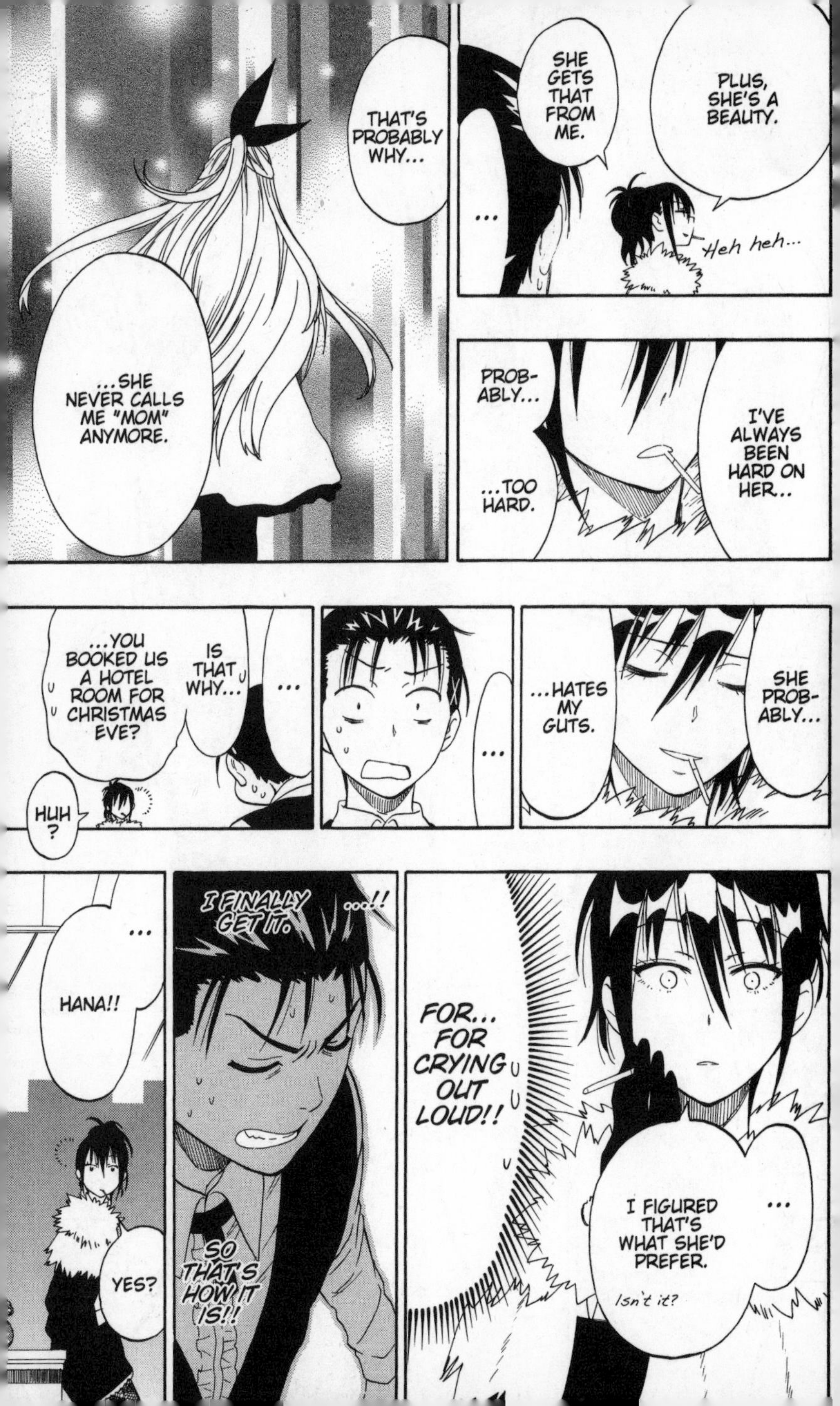
PLUS, SHE'S A BEAUTY.
SHE GETS THAT FROM ME.
...
Heh heh...
I'VE ALWAYS BEEN HARD ON HER...
PROB-ABLY...
...TOO HARD.
THAT'S PROBABLY WHY...
...SHE NEVER CALLS ME "MOM" ANYMORE.
SHE PROB-ABLY...
...HATES MY GUTS.
...
...
IS THAT WHY...
...YOU BOOKED US A HOTEL ROOM FOR CHRISTMAS EVE?
HUH?
...
I FIGURED THAT'S WHAT SHE'D PREFER.
Isn't it?
FOR... FOR CRYING OUT LOUD!!
...!!
I FINALLY GET IT.
SO THAT'S HOW IT IS!!
...
HANA!!
YES?

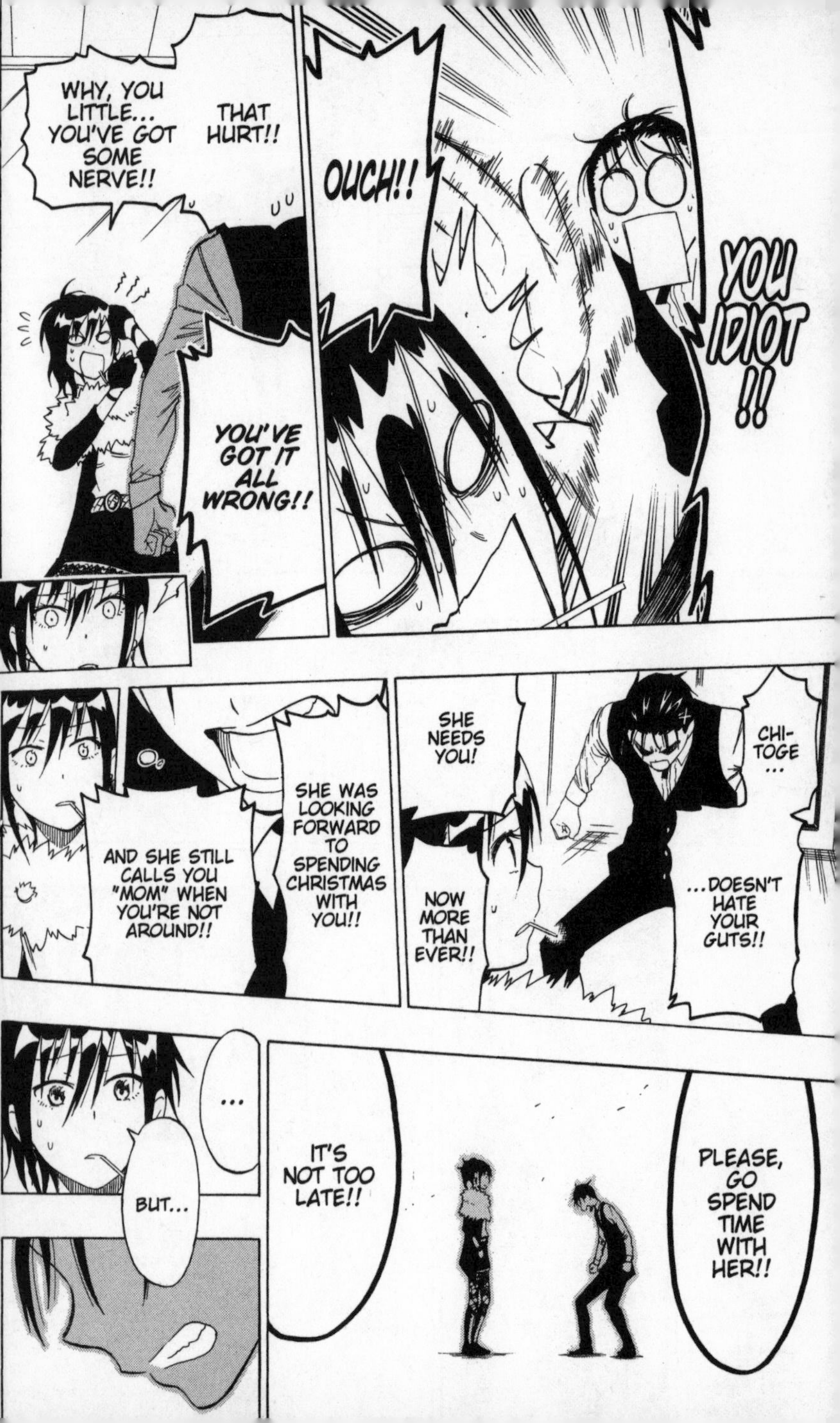
YOU IDIOT!!
OUCH!!
THAT HURT!!
WHY, YOU LITTLE... YOU'VE GOT SOME NERVE!!
YOU'VE GOT IT ALL WRONG!!
CHI-TOGE...
...DOESN'T HATE YOUR GUTS!!
SHE NEEDS YOU!
NOW MORE THAN EVER!!
SHE WAS LOOKING FORWARD TO SPENDING CHRISTMAS WITH YOU!!
AND SHE STILL CALLS YOU "MOM" WHEN YOU'RE NOT AROUND!!
PLEASE, GO SPEND TIME WITH HER!!
IT'S NOT TOO LATE!!
...
BUT...

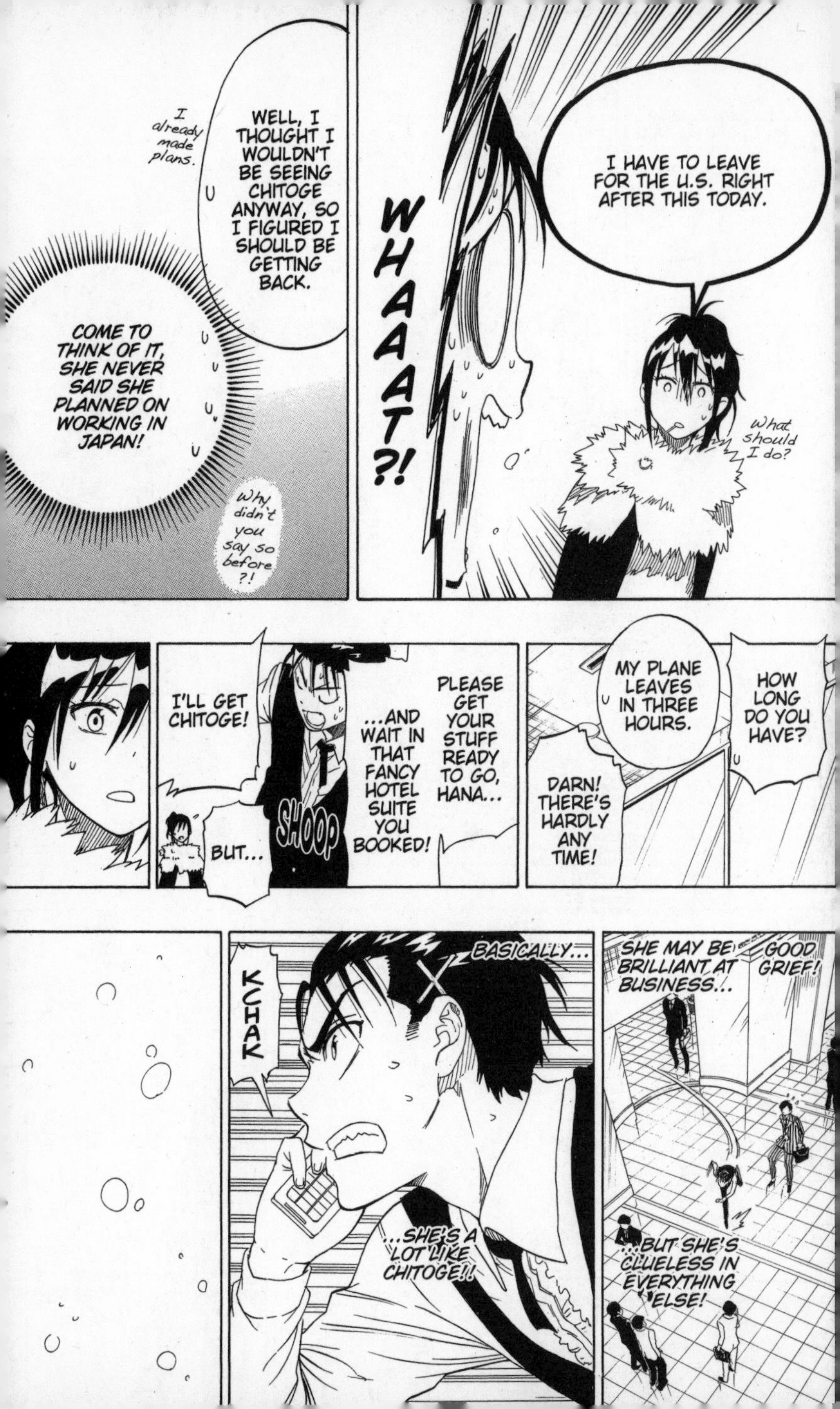
I HAVE TO LEAVE FOR THE U.S. RIGHT AFTER THIS TODAY.
What should I do?
WHAAAAT?!
WELL, I THOUGHT I WOULDN'T BE SEEING CHITOGE ANYWAY, SO I FIGURED I SHOULD BE GETTING BACK.
I already made plans.
COME TO THINK OF IT, SHE NEVER SAID SHE PLANNED ON WORKING IN JAPAN!
Why didn't you say so before?!
HOW LONG DO YOU HAVE?
MY PLANE LEAVES IN THREE HOURS.
DARN! THERE'S HARDLY ANY TIME!
PLEASE GET YOUR STUFF READY TO GO, HANA...
...AND WAIT IN THAT FANCY HOTEL SUITE YOU BOOKED!
SHOOP
I'LL GET CHITOGE!
BUT...
GOOD GRIEF!
SHE MAY BE BRILLIANT AT BUSINESS...
...BUT SHE'S CLUELESS IN EVERYTHING ELSE!
BASICALLY...
KCHAK
...SHE'S A LOT LIKE CHITOGE!!

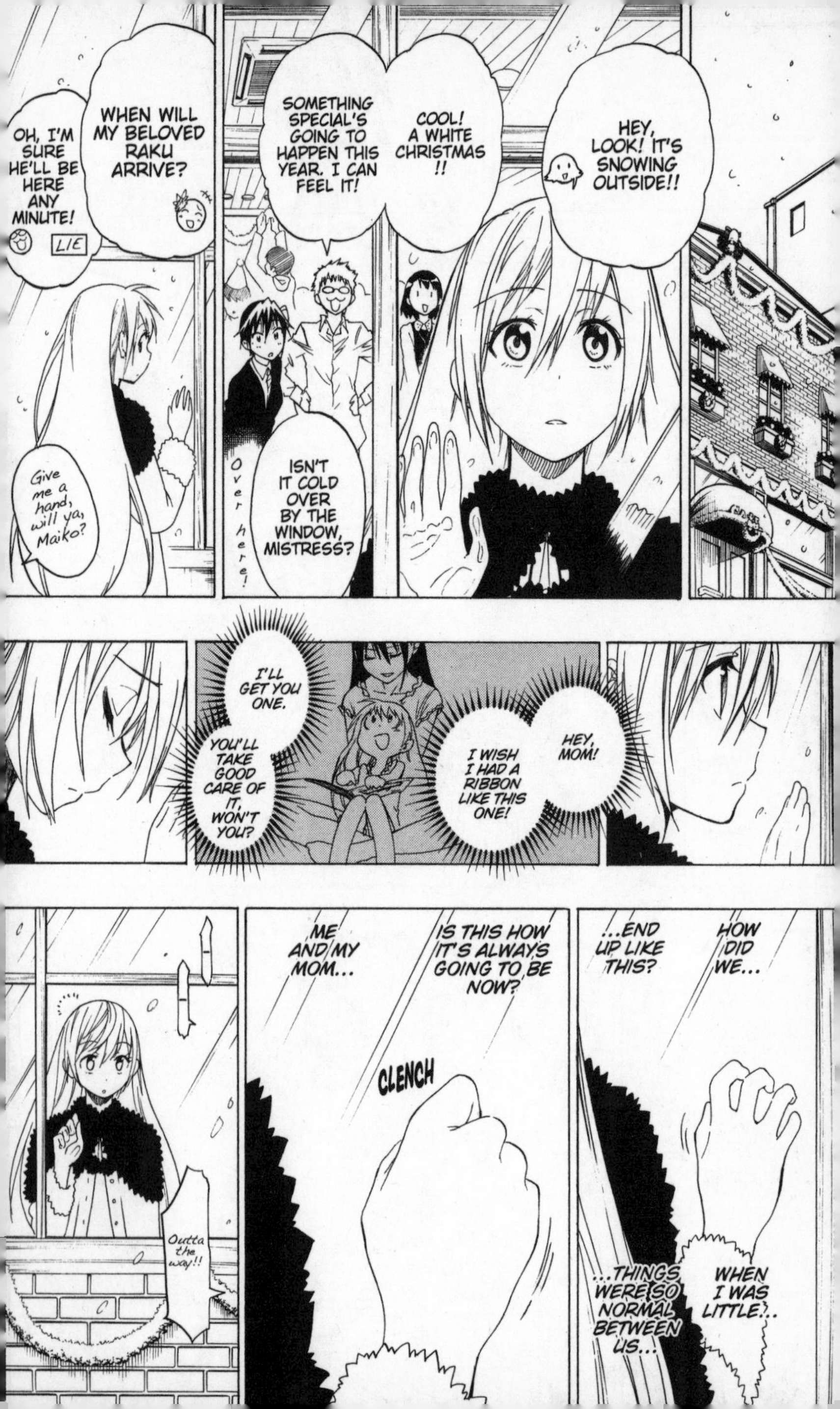
HEY, LOOK! IT'S SNOWING OUTSIDE!!
COOL! A WHITE CHRISTMAS!!
SOMETHING SPECIAL'S GOING TO HAPPEN THIS YEAR. I CAN FEEL IT!
ISN'T IT COLD OVER BY THE WINDOW, MISTRESS?
Over here!
WHEN WILL MY BELOVED RAKU ARRIVE?
OH, I'M SURE HE'LL BE HERE ANY MINUTE!
LIE
Give me a hand, will ya, Maiko?
HEY, MOM!
I WISH I HAD A RIBBON LIKE THIS ONE!
I'LL GET YOU ONE.
YOU'LL TAKE GOOD CARE OF IT, WON'T YOU?
HOW DID WE...
...END UP LIKE THIS?
WHEN I WAS LITTLE...
...THINGS WERE SO NORMAL BETWEEN US...
IS THIS HOW IT'S ALWAYS GOING TO BE NOW?
ME AND MY MOM...
CLENCH
Outta the way!!

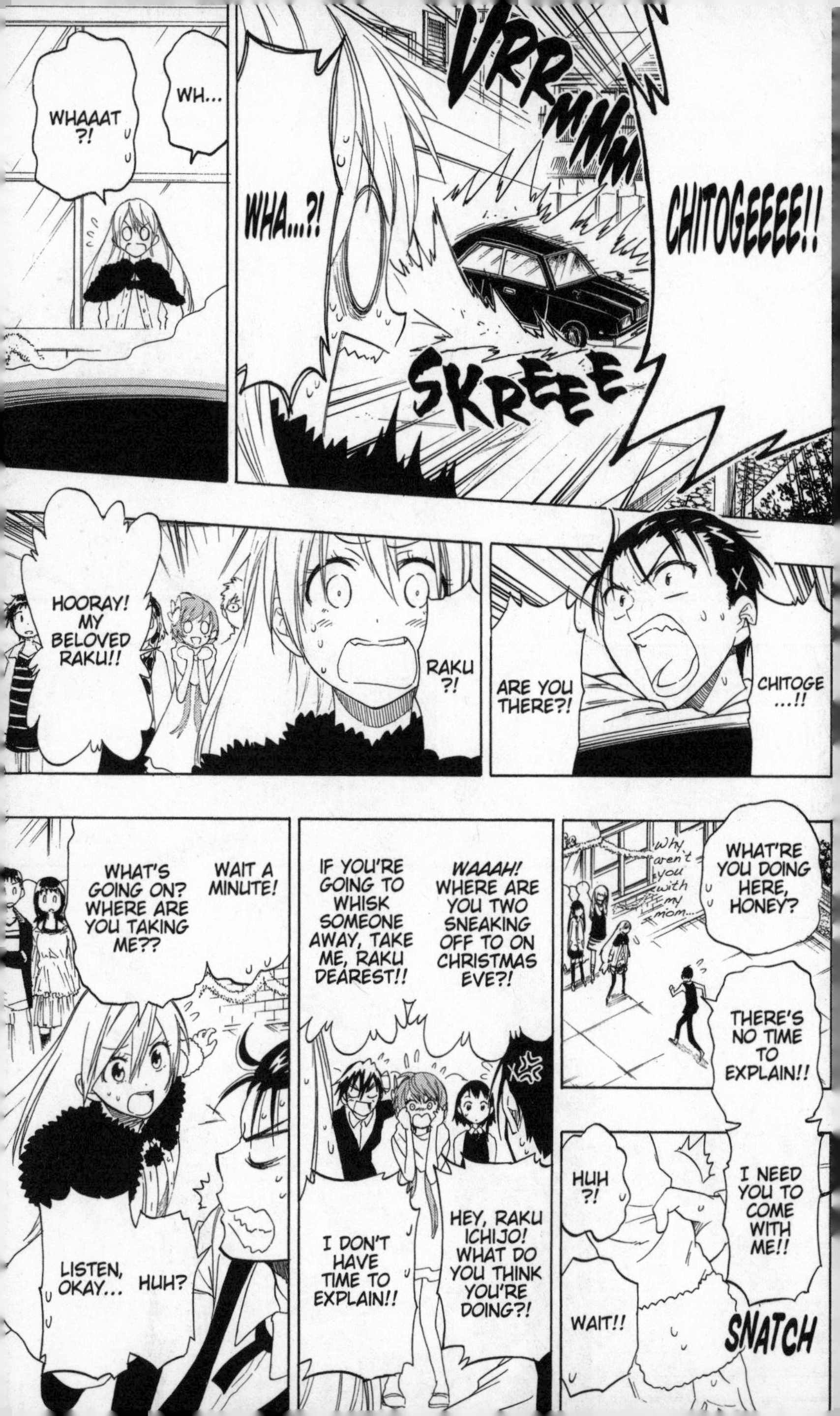
VRRMMMM
CHITOGEEEE!!
WHA...?!
SKREEE
WH...
WHAAAT ?!
CHITOGE ...!!
ARE YOU THERE?!
RAKU ?!
HOORAY! MY BELOVED RAKU!!
WHAT'RE YOU DOING HERE, HONEY?
Why aren't you with my mom...
THERE'S NO TIME TO EXPLAIN!!
I NEED YOU TO COME WITH ME!!
HUH ?!
SNATCH
WAIT!!
WAAAH! WHERE ARE YOU TWO SNEAKING OFF TO ON CHRISTMAS EVE?!
IF YOU'RE GOING TO WHISK SOMEONE AWAY, TAKE ME, RAKU DEAREST!!
HEY, RAKU ICHIJO! WHAT DO YOU THINK YOU'RE DOING?!
I DON'T HAVE TIME TO EXPLAIN!!
WAIT A MINUTE!
WHAT'S GOING ON? WHERE ARE YOU TAKING ME??
HUH?
LISTEN, OKAY...

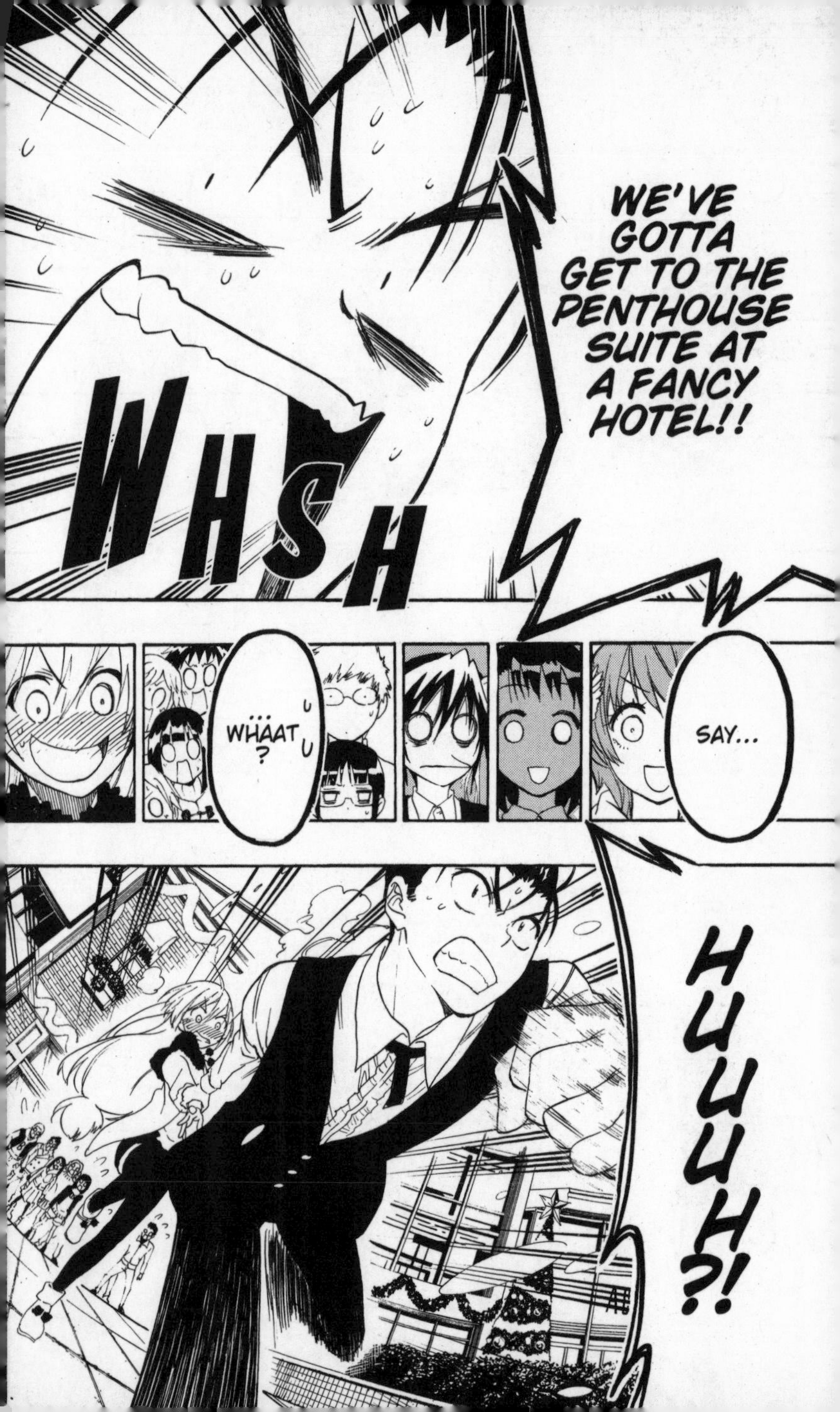
WE'VE GOTTA GET TO THE PENTHOUSE SUITE AT A FANCY HOTEL!!
WHSH
SAY...
WHÄAT?
HUUUH?!

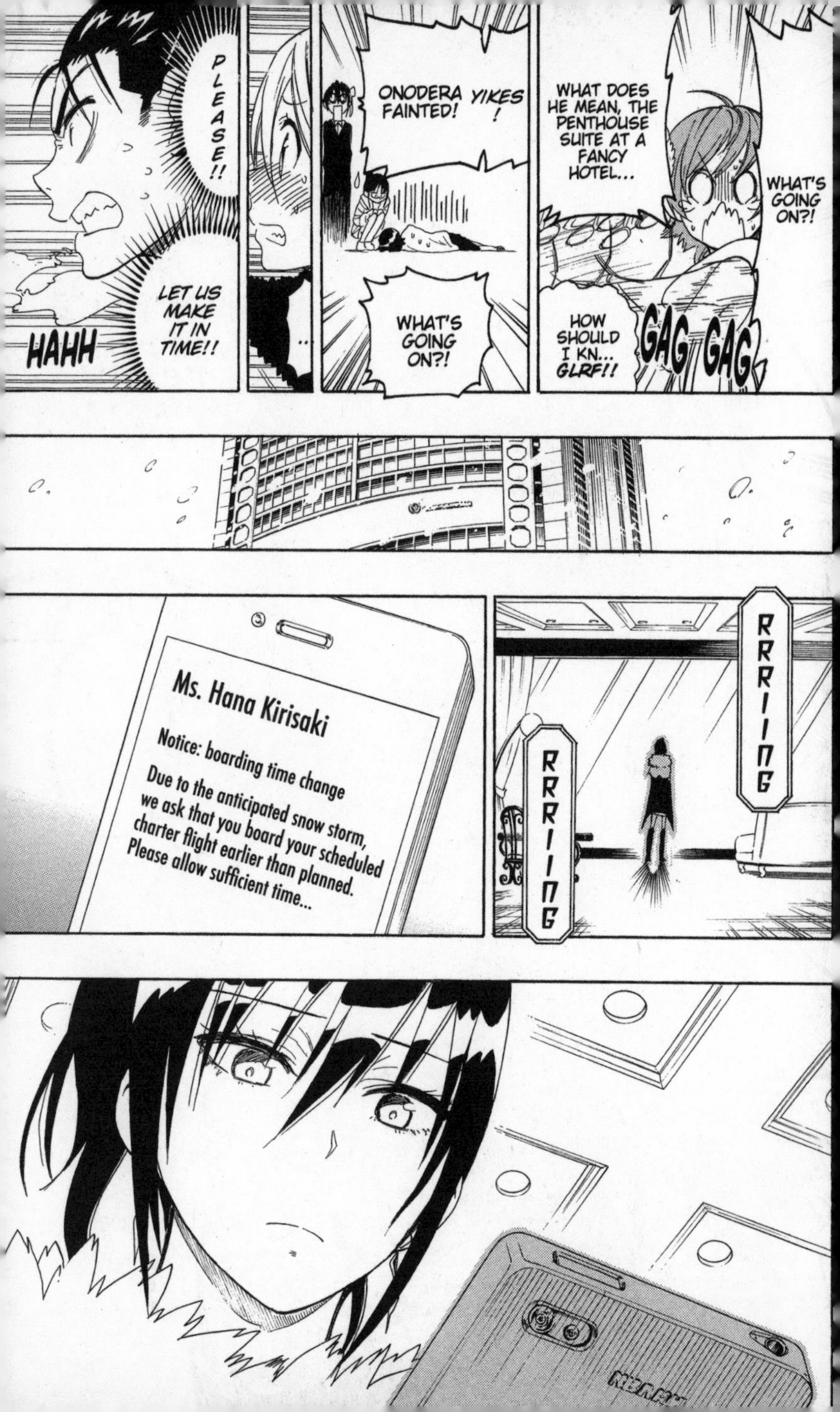
WHAT DOES HE MEAN, THE PENTHOUSE SUITE AT A FANCY HOTEL...
WHAT'S GOING ON?!
GAG GAG
HOW SHOULD I KN... GLRF!!
YIKES!
ONODERA FAINTED!
WHAT'S GOING ON?!
...
PLEASE!!
LET US MAKE IT IN TIME!!
HAHH
RRRIING
RRRIING
Ms. Hana Kirisaki
Notice: boarding time change
Due to the anticipated snow storm, we ask that you board your scheduled charter flight earlier than planned. Please allow sufficient time...

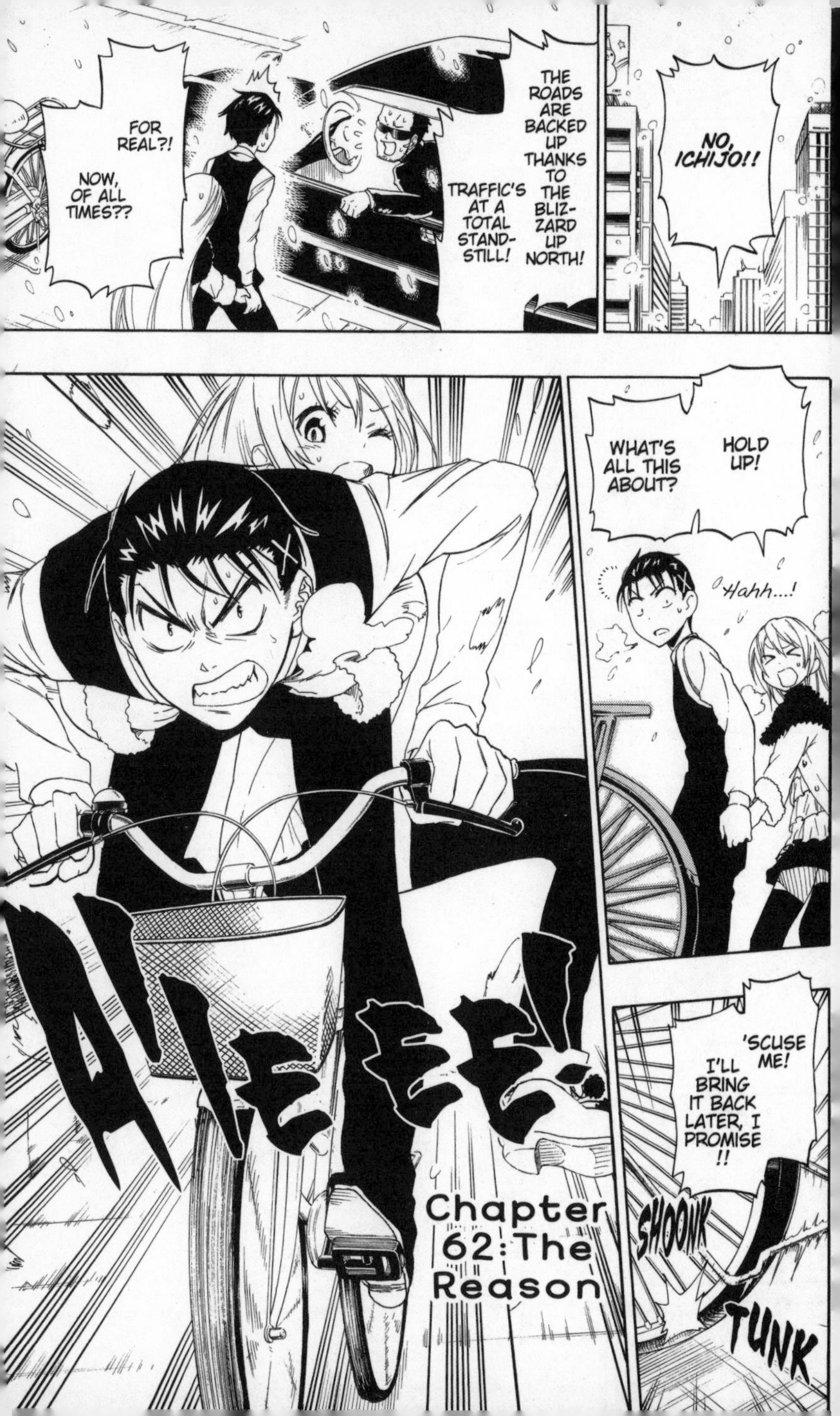
NO, ICHIJO!!
THE ROADS ARE BACKED UP THANKS TO THE BLIZZARD UP NORTH!
TRAFFIC'S AT A TOTAL STANDSTILL!
FOR REAL?!
NOW, OF ALL TIMES??
HOLD UP!
WHAT'S ALL THIS ABOUT?
Hahh...!
'SCUSE ME!
I'LL BRING IT BACK LATER, I PROMISE!!
SHOONK
TUNK
AIEEE!
Chapter 62: The Reason

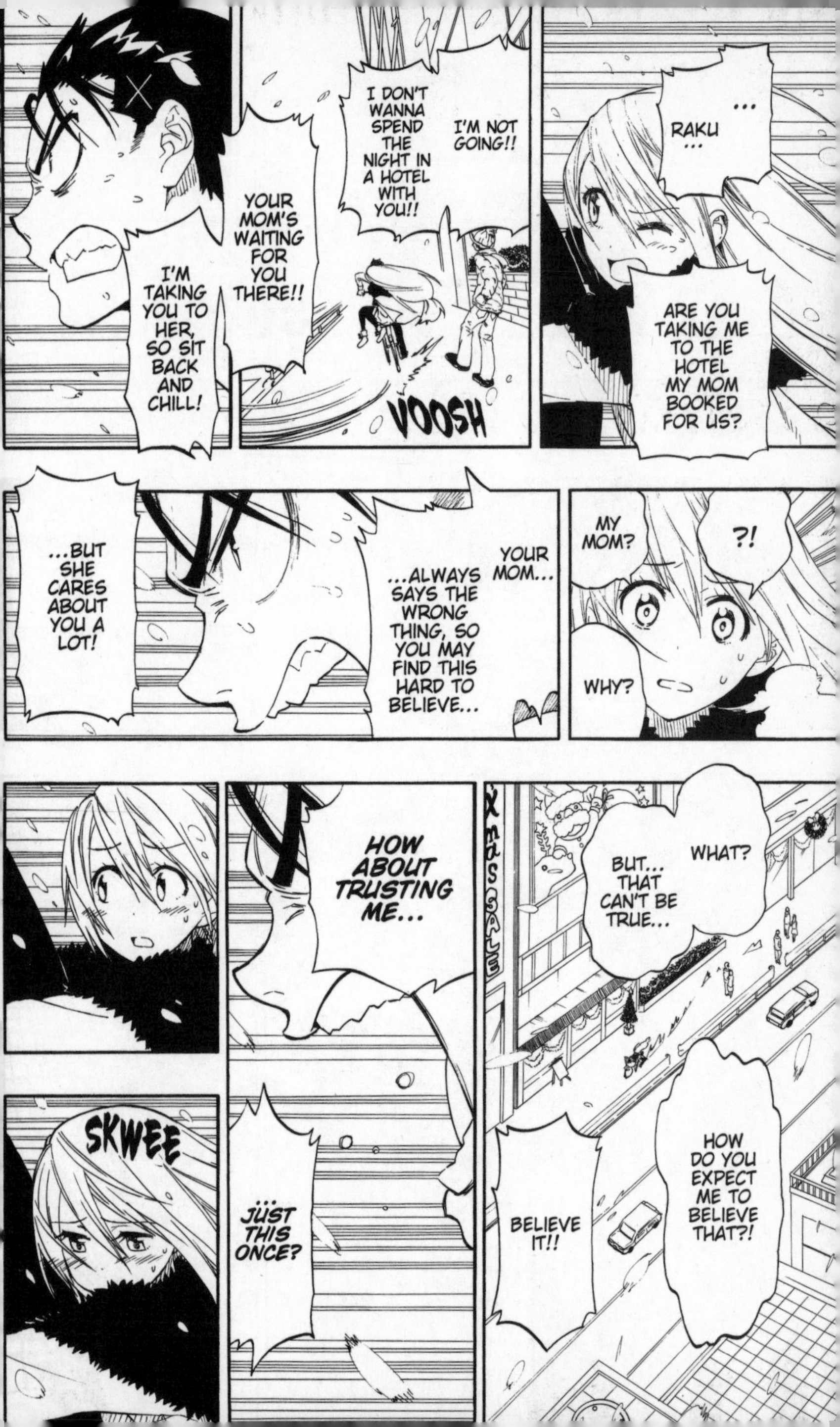
...
RAKU...
ARE YOU TAKING ME TO THE HOTEL MY MOM BOOKED FOR US?
I'M NOT GOING!!
I DON'T WANNA SPEND THE NIGHT IN A HOTEL WITH YOU!!
VOOSH
YOUR MOM'S WAITING FOR YOU THERE!!
I'M TAKING YOU TO HER, SO SIT BACK AND CHILL!
?!
MY MOM?
WHY?
YOUR MOM...
...ALWAYS SAYS THE WRONG THING, SO YOU MAY FIND THIS HARD TO BELIEVE...
...BUT SHE CARES ABOUT YOU A LOT!
WHAT?
BUT... THAT CAN'T BE TRUE...
HOW DO YOU EXPECT ME TO BELIEVE THAT?!
BELIEVE IT!!
HOW ABOUT TRUSTING ME...
...JUST THIS ONCE?
SKWEE

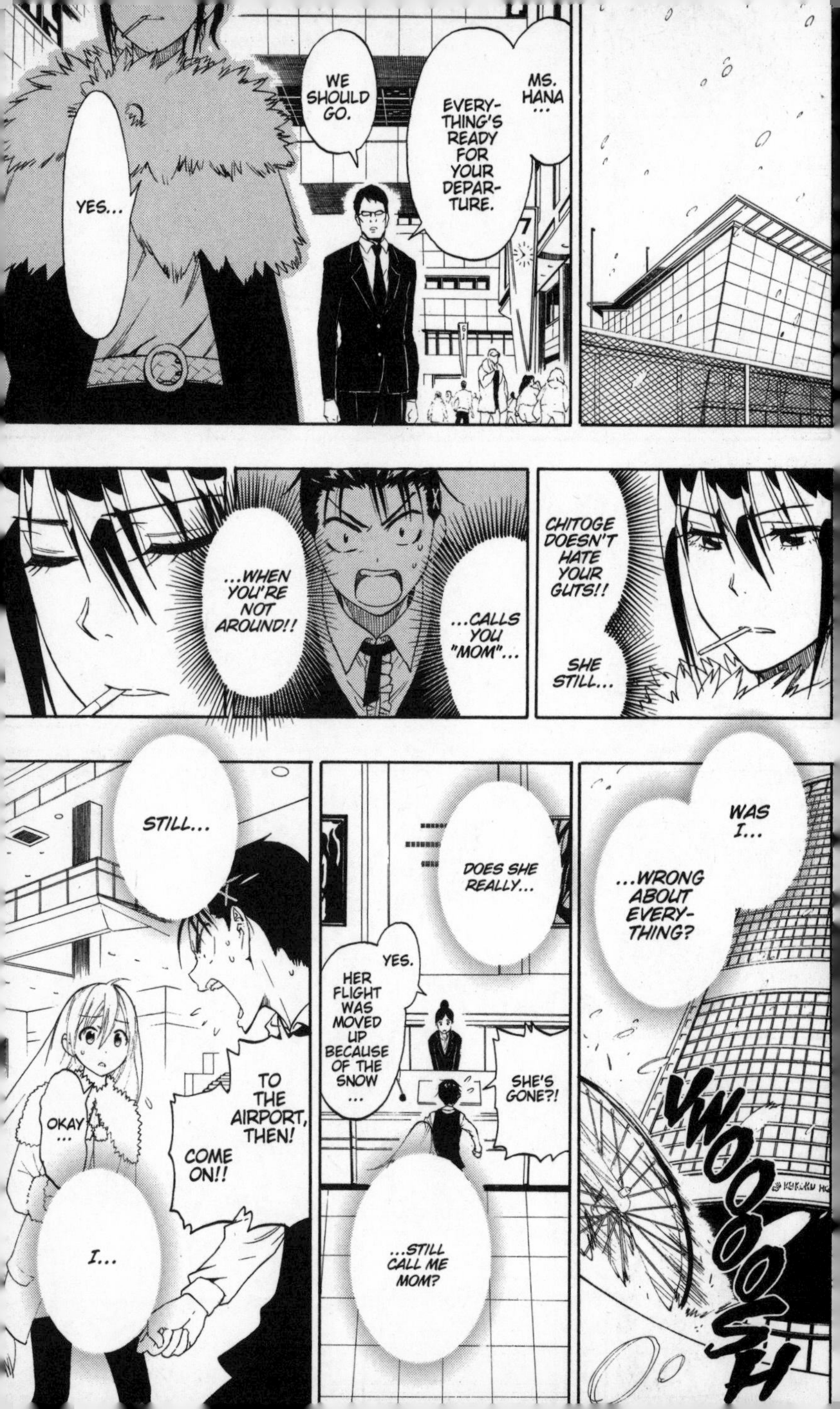
MS. HANA...
EVERYTHING'S READY FOR YOUR DEPARTURE.
WE SHOULD GO.
YES...
CHITOGE DOESN'T HATE YOUR GUTS!!
SHE STILL...
...CALLS YOU "MOM"...
...WHEN YOU'RE NOT AROUND!!
WAS I...
...WRONG ABOUT EVERYTHING?
WOOOOOSH
DOES SHE REALLY...
SHE'S GONE?!
YES. HER FLIGHT WAS MOVED UP BECAUSE OF THE SNOW...
...STILL CALL ME MOM?
STILL...
TO THE AIRPORT, THEN!
COME ON!!
OKAY...
I...

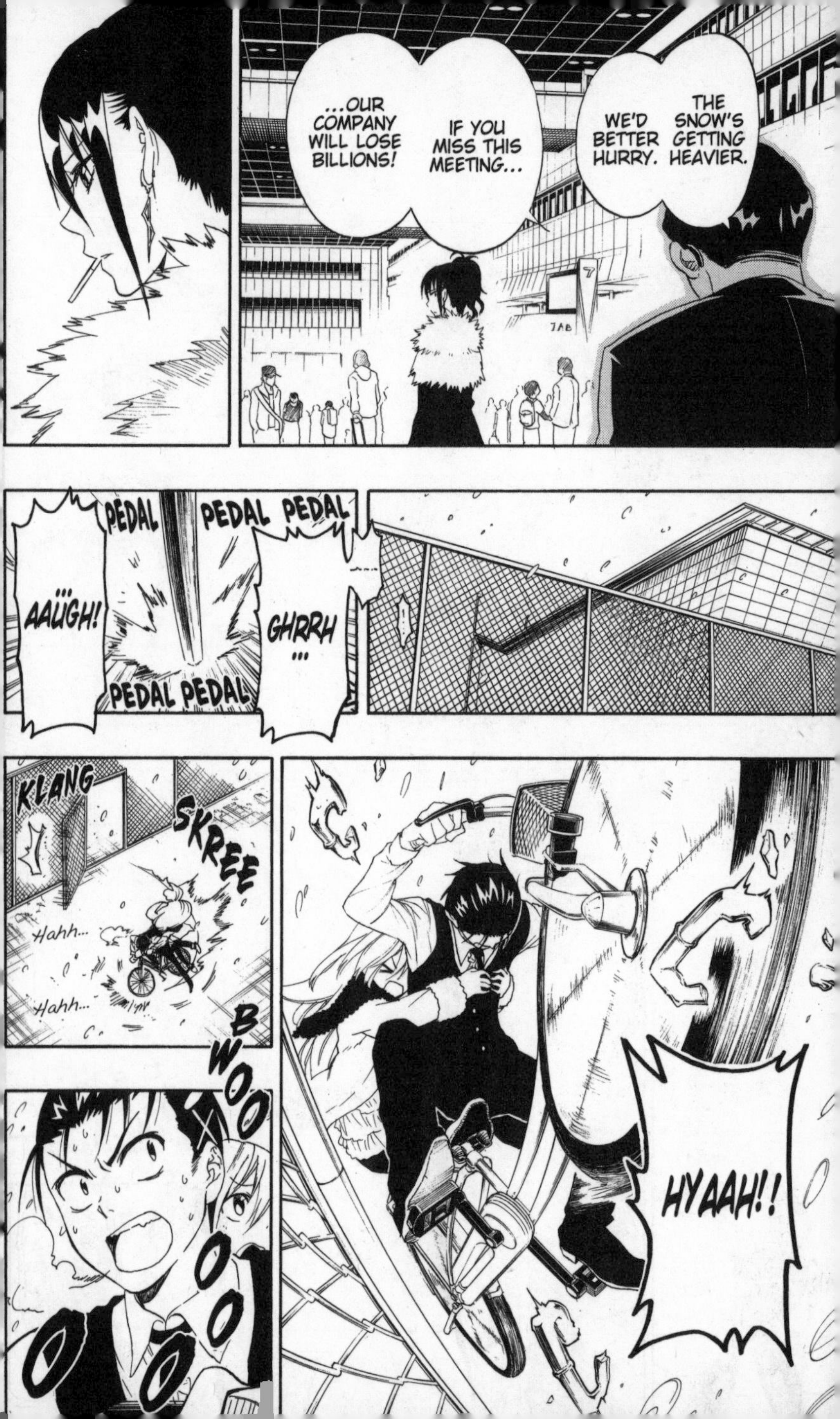
THE SNOW'S GETTING HEAVIER.
WE'D BETTER HURRY.
IF YOU MISS THIS MEETING...
...OUR COMPANY WILL LOSE BILLIONS!
PEDAL PEDAL
GHRRH...
PEDAL
PEDAL PEDAL
AAÜGH!
HYAAH!!
SKREE
KLANG
Hahh...
Hahh...
BWOOO

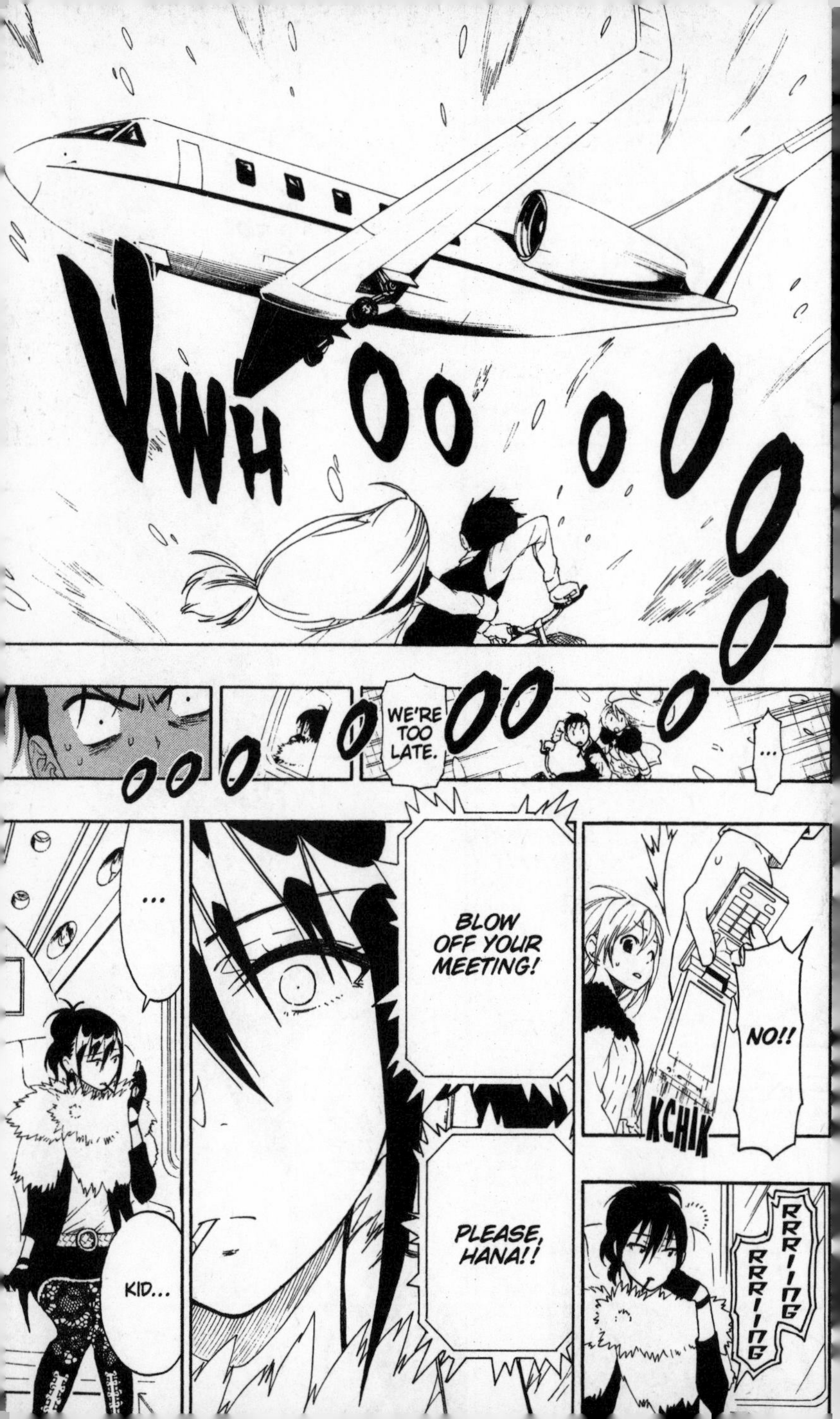
VWHOOOOOOOOOOOOOOO
...
WE'RE TOO LATE.
NO!!
KCHIK
RRRING RRRING
BLOW OFF YOUR MEETING!
PLEASE, HANA!!
...
KID...

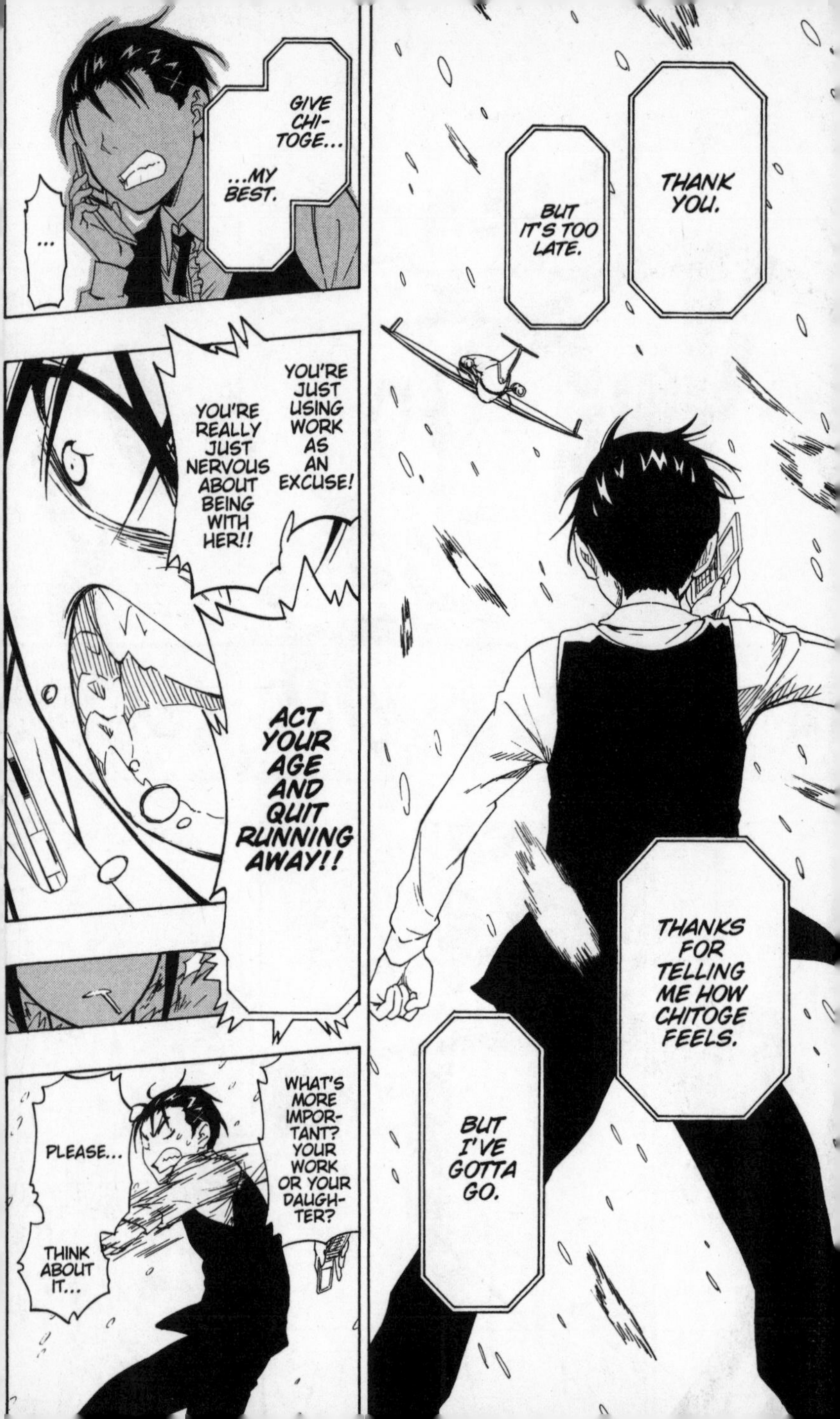
THANK YOU.
BUT IT'S TOO LATE.
THANKS FOR TELLING ME HOW CHITOGE FEELS.
BUT I'VE GOTTA GO.
GIVE CHI-TOGE...
...MY BEST.
...
YOU'RE JUST USING WORK AS AN EXCUSE!
YOU'RE REALLY JUST NERVOUS ABOUT BEING WITH HER!!
ACT YOUR AGE AND QUIT RUNNING AWAY!!
WHAT'S MORE IMPOR-TANT? YOUR WORK OR YOUR DAUGH-TER?
PLEASE...
THINK ABOUT IT...

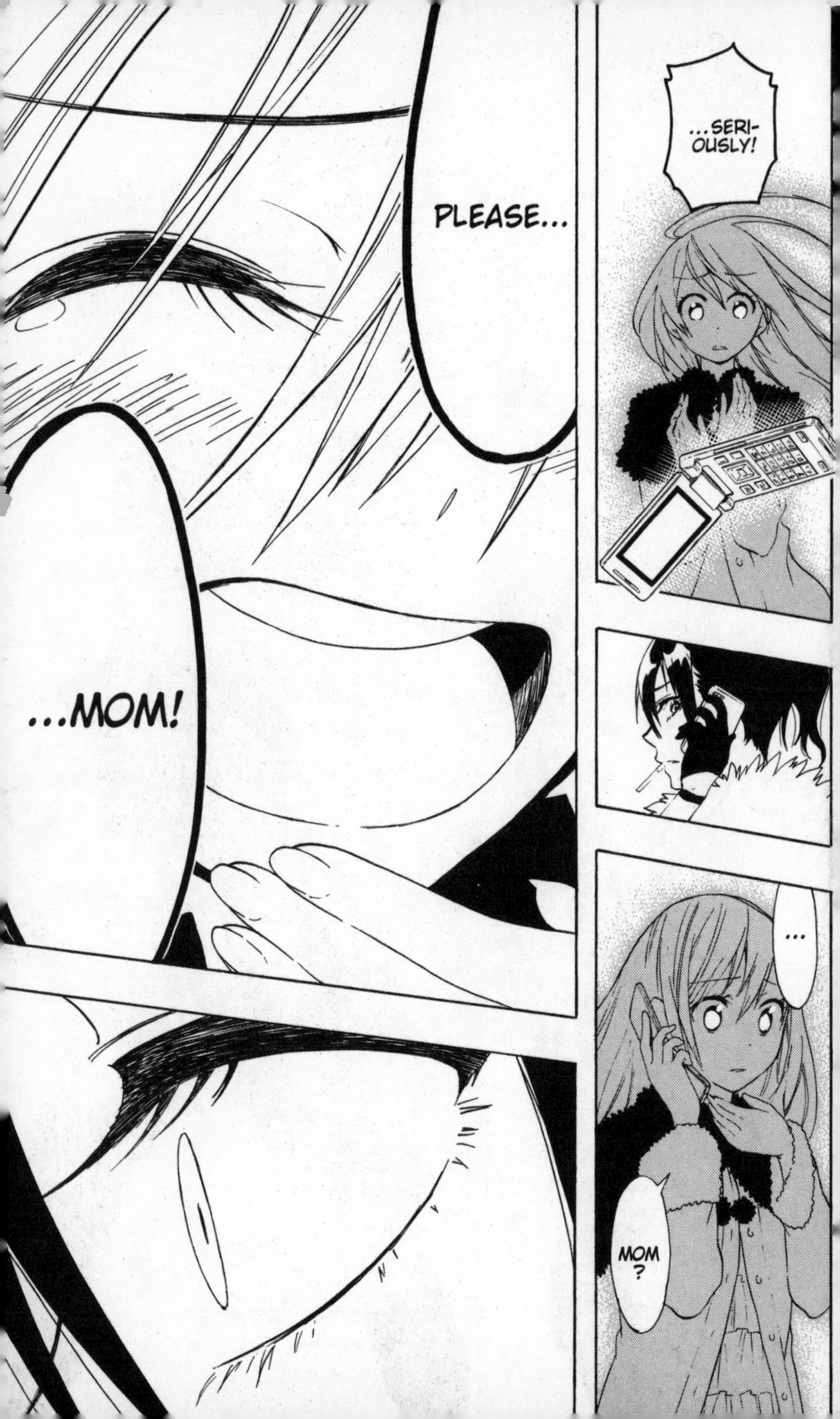
...SERI-
OUSLY!
...
MOM
?
PLEASE...
...MOM!

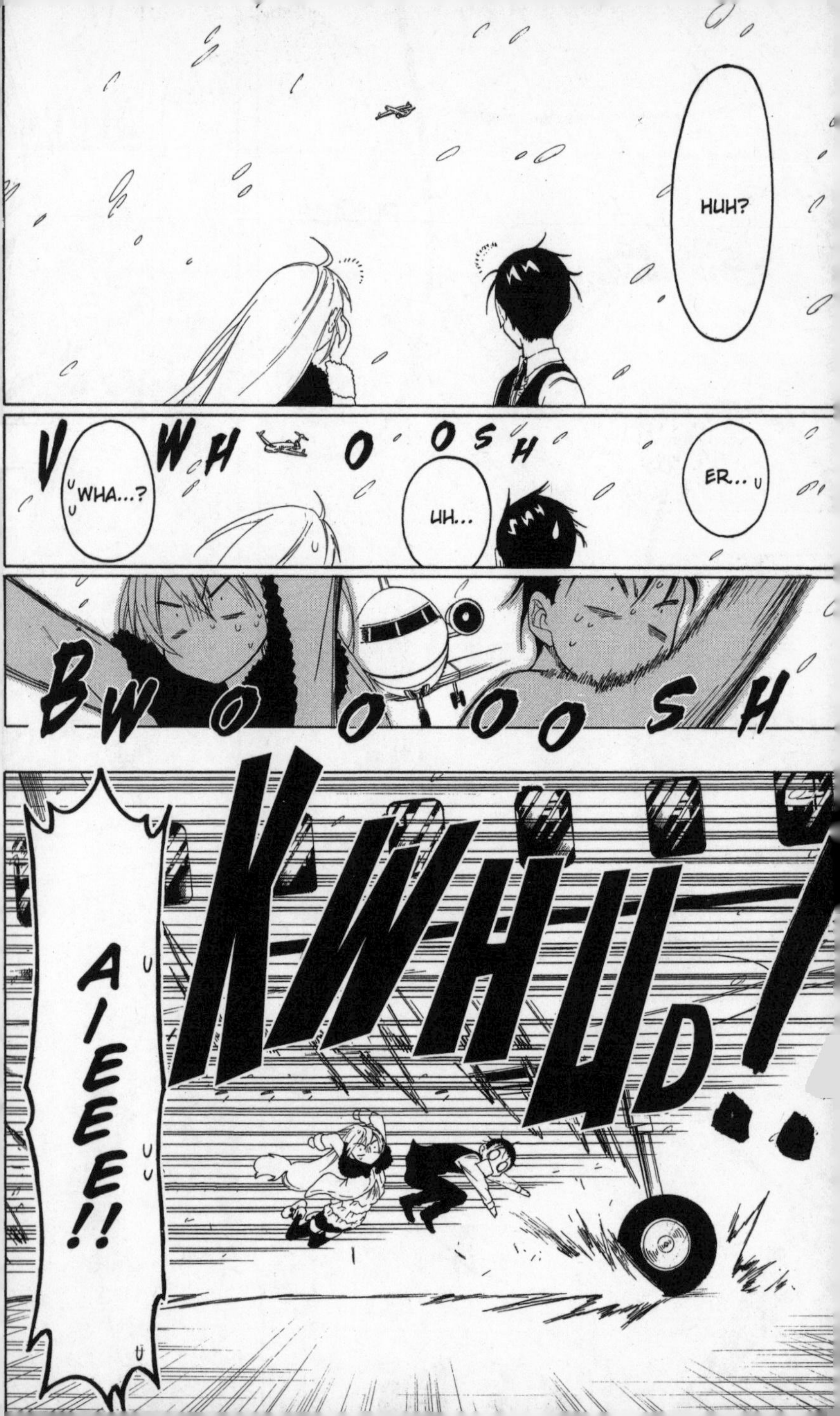
HUH?
VWHOOSH
ER...
UH...
WHA...?
BWOOOOSH
KWHUD!!
AIEEEE!!

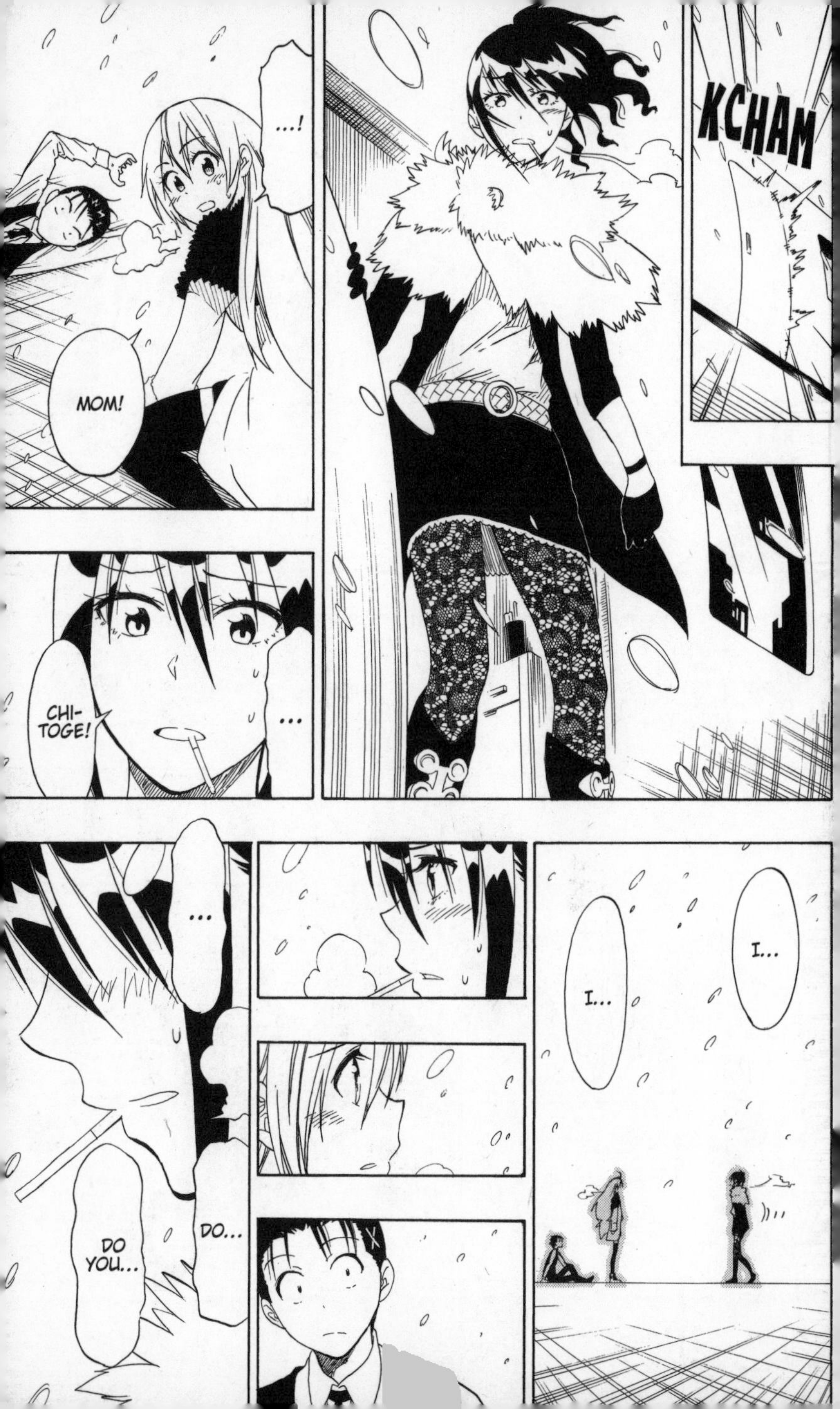

KCHAM
...!
MOM!
CHI-TOGE!
...
I...
I...
...
DO...
DO YOU...

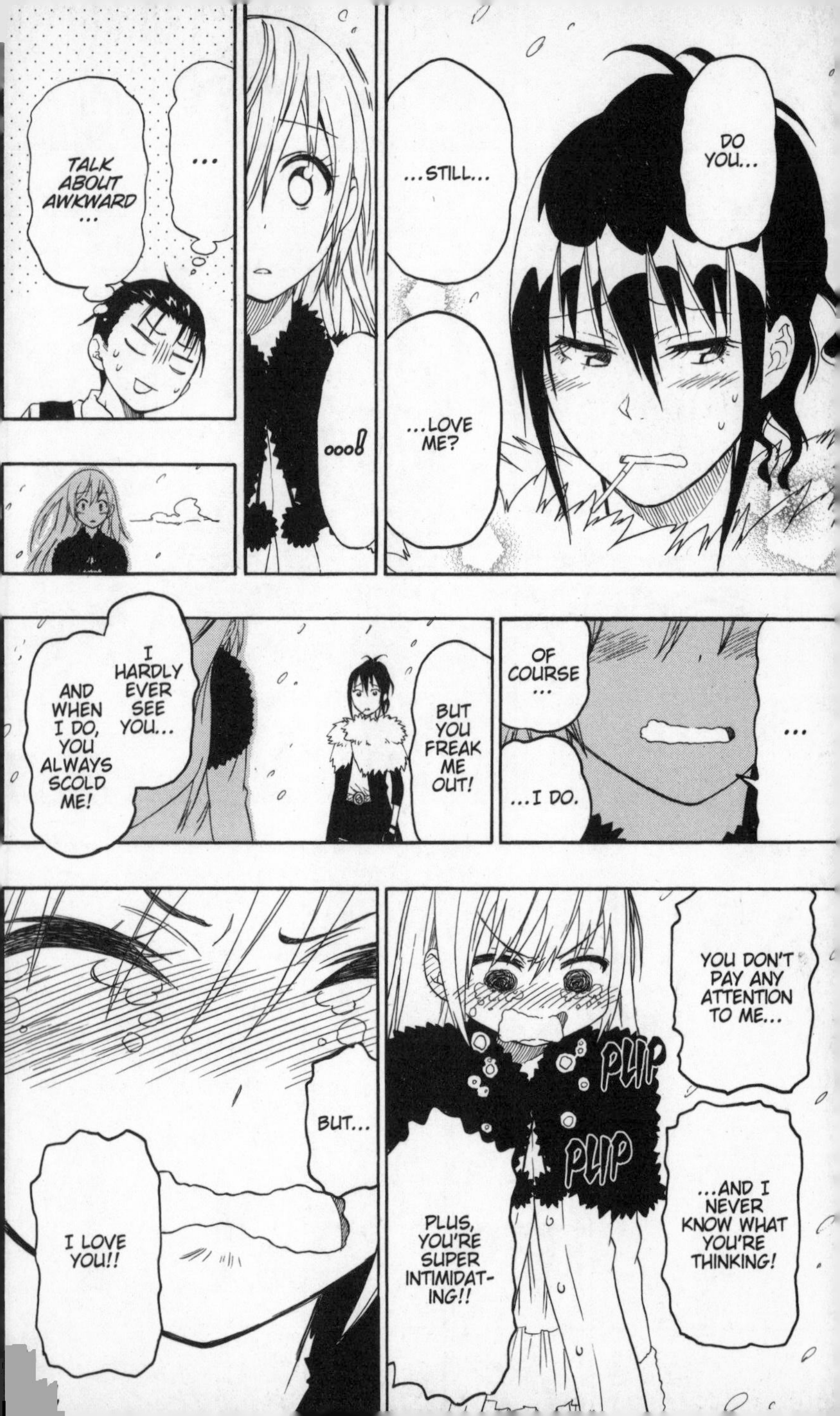
DO YOU...
...STILL...
...LOVE ME?
ooo!
...
TALK ABOUT AWKWARD...
...
OF COURSE...
...I DO.
BUT YOU FREAK ME OUT!
I HARDLY EVER SEE YOU...
AND WHEN I DO, YOU ALWAYS SCOLD ME!
YOU DON'T PAY ANY ATTENTION TO ME...
PLIP
PLIP
...AND I NEVER KNOW WHAT YOU'RE THINKING!
PLUS, YOU'RE SUPER INTIMIDAT-ING!!
BUT...
I LOVE YOU!!

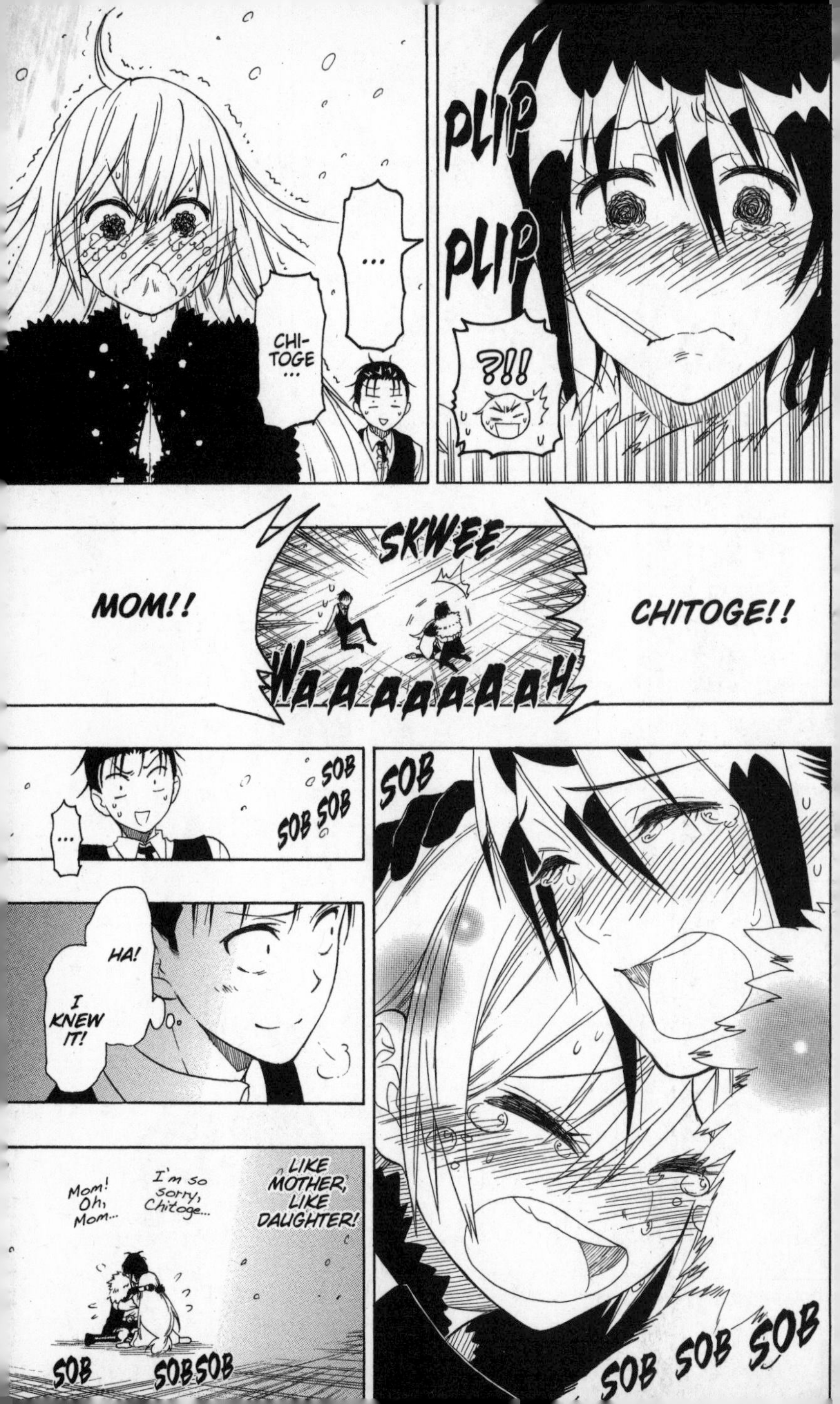
PLIP
PLIP
?!!
...
CHI-TOGE...
CHITOGE!!
SKWEE
WAAAAAAAH
MOM!!
SOB
SOB SOB SOB
...
SOB
SOB SOB
HA!
I KNEW IT!
LIKE MOTHER, LIKE DAUGHTER!
I'm so sorry, Chitoge...
Mom! Oh, Mom...
SOB
SOBSOB

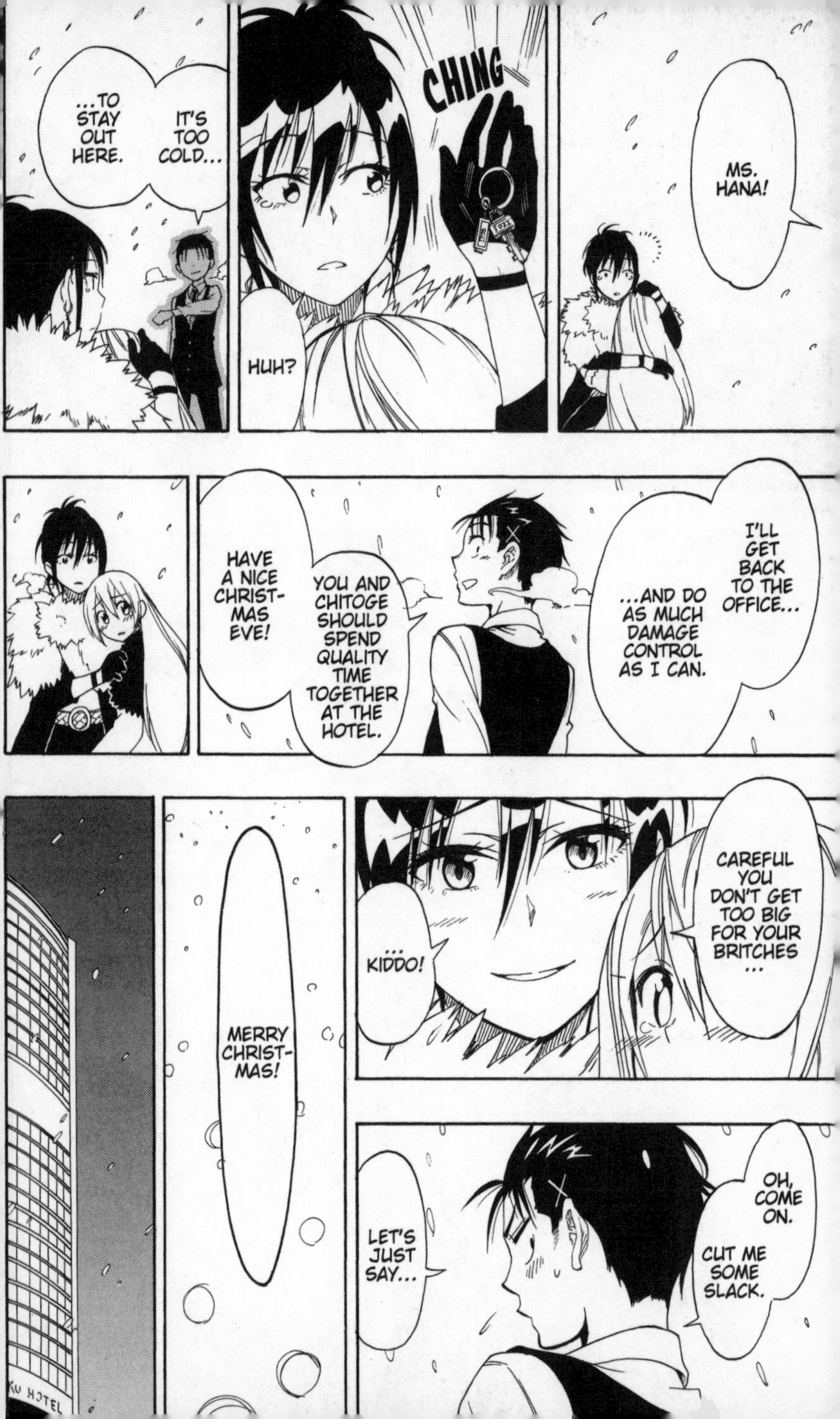
MS. HANA!
CHING
HUH?
IT'S TOO COLD...
...TO STAY OUT HERE.
I'LL GET BACK TO THE OFFICE...
...AND DO AS MUCH DAMAGE CONTROL AS I CAN.
YOU AND CHITOGE SHOULD SPEND QUALITY TIME TOGETHER AT THE HOTEL.
HAVE A NICE CHRISTMAS EVE!
CAREFUL YOU DON'T GET TOO BIG FOR YOUR BRITCHES...
...KIDDO!
OH, COME ON.
CUT ME SOME SLACK.
LET'S JUST SAY...
MERRY CHRISTMAS!
KU HOTEL

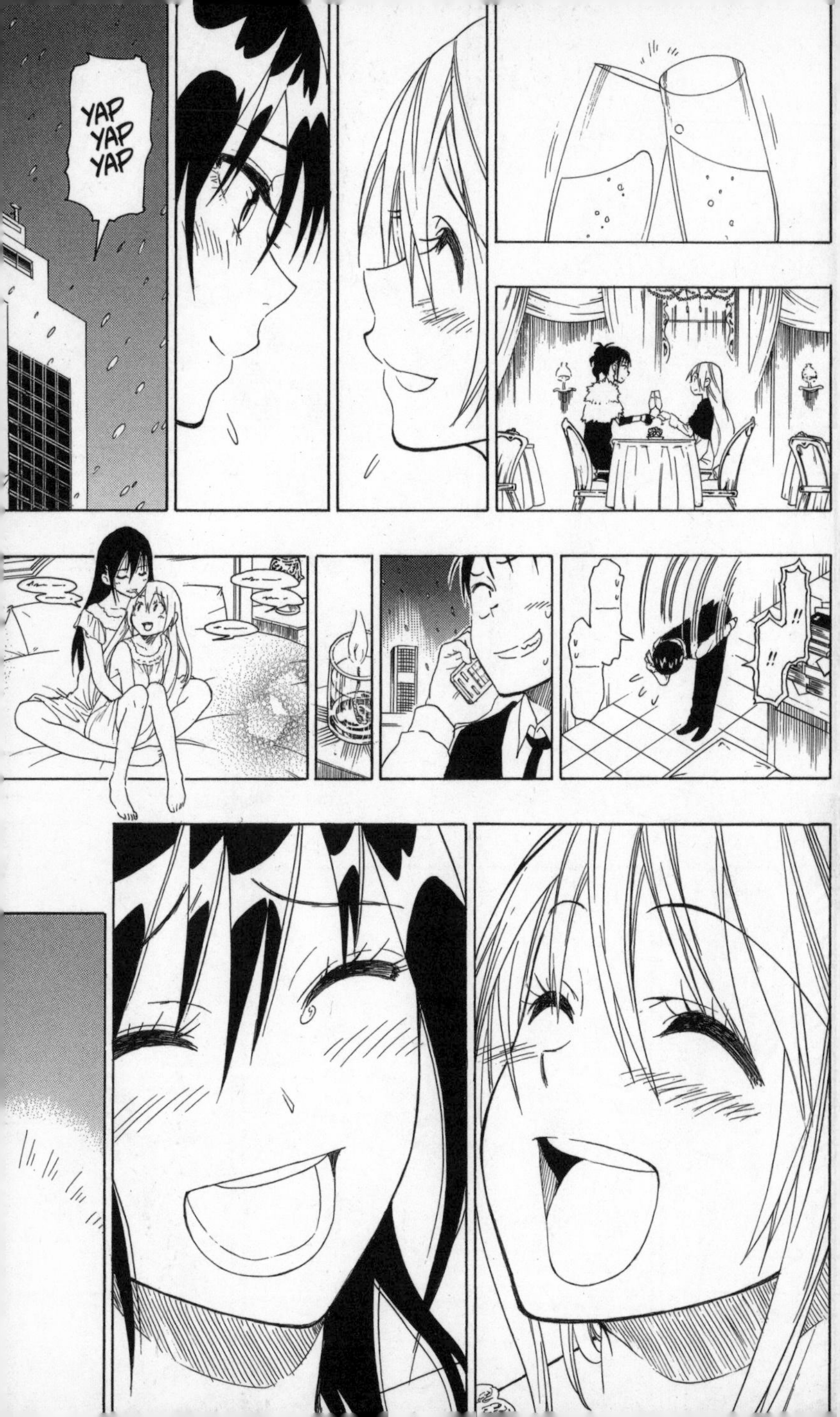
YAP YAP YAP
!!
!!

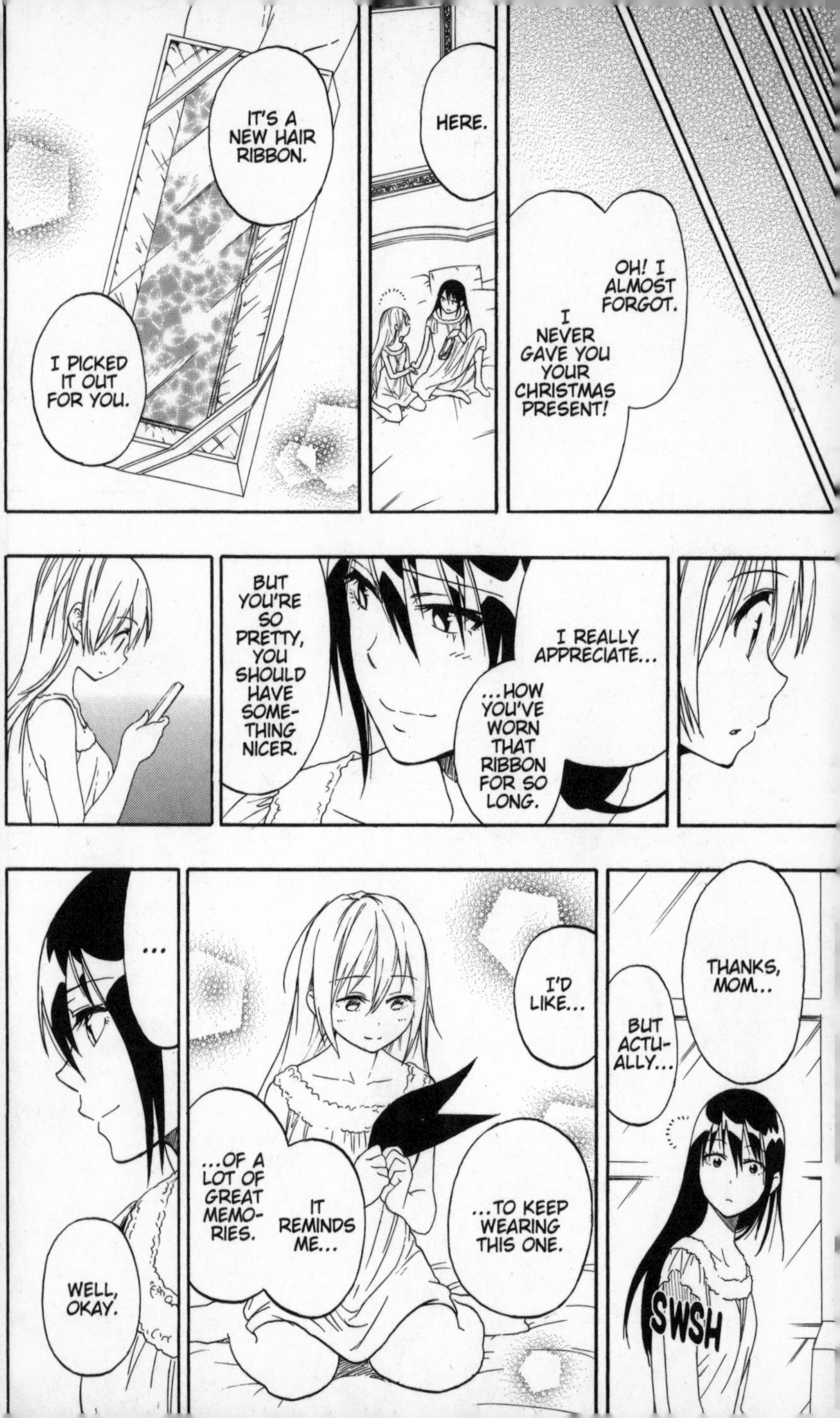
OH! I ALMOST FORGOT.
I NEVER GAVE YOU YOUR CHRISTMAS PRESENT!
HERE.
IT'S A NEW HAIR RIBBON.
I PICKED IT OUT FOR YOU.
I REALLY APPRECIATE...
...HOW YOU'VE WORN THAT RIBBON FOR SO LONG.
BUT YOU'RE SO PRETTY, YOU SHOULD HAVE SOME-THING NICER.
THANKS, MOM..
BUT ACTU-ALLY...
SWSH
I'D LIKE...
...TO KEEP WEARING THIS ONE.
IT REMINDS ME...
...OF A LOT OF GREAT MEMO-RIES.
...
WELL, OKAY.

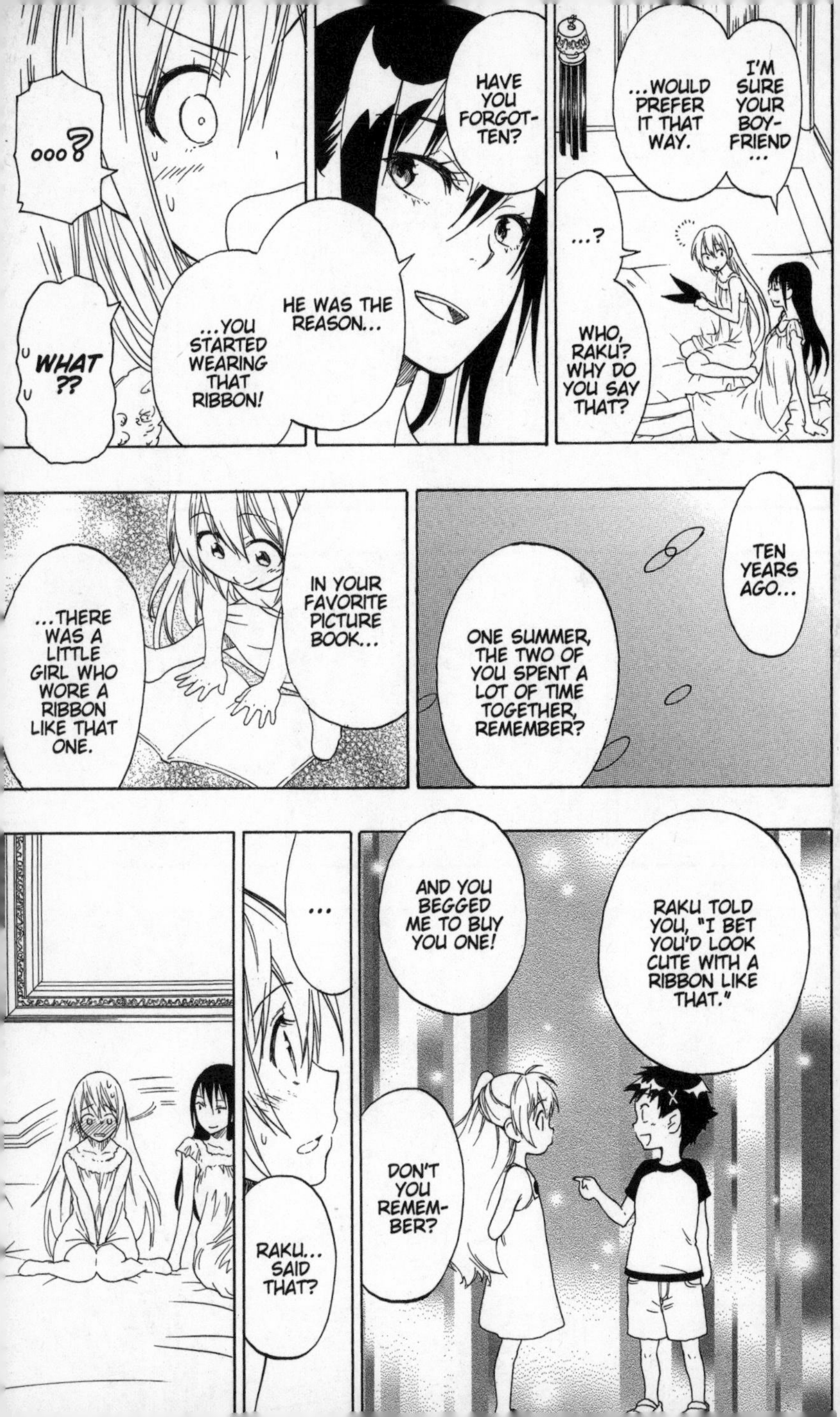
I'M SURE YOUR BOY-FRIEND...
...WOULD PREFER IT THAT WAY.
...?
WHO, RAKU? WHY DO YOU SAY THAT?
HAVE YOU FORGOT-TEN?
HE WAS THE REASON...
...YOU STARTED WEARING THAT RIBBON!
ooo?
WHAT??
TEN YEARS AGO...
ONE SUMMER, THE TWO OF YOU SPENT A LOT OF TIME TOGETHER, REMEMBER?
IN YOUR FAVORITE PICTURE BOOK...
...THERE WAS A LITTLE GIRL WHO WORE A RIBBON LIKE THAT ONE.
RAKU TOLD YOU, "I BET YOU'D LOOK CUTE WITH A RIBBON LIKE THAT."
AND YOU BEGGED ME TO BUY YOU ONE!
DON'T YOU REMEMBER?
...
RAKU... SAID THAT?

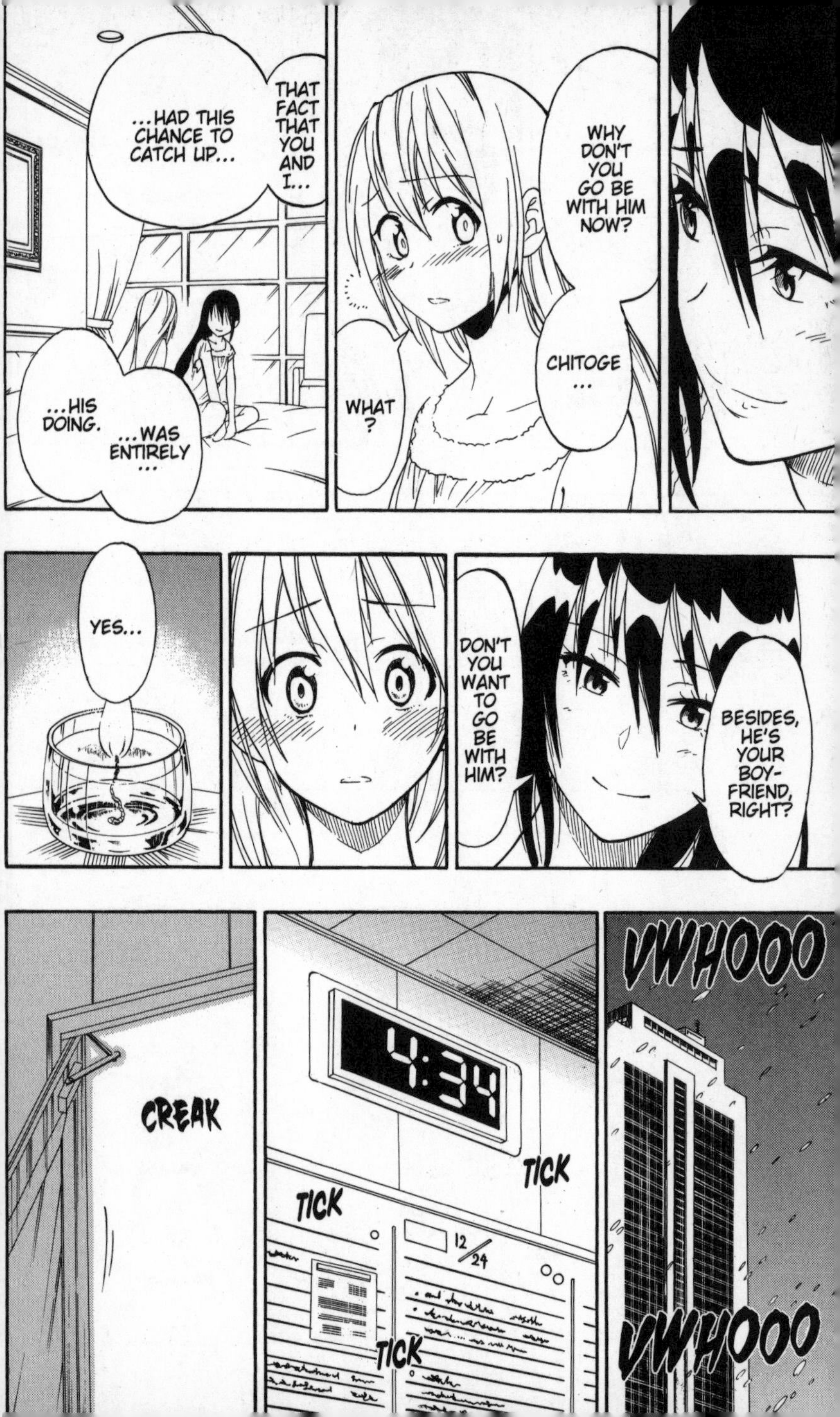
WHY DON'T YOU GO BE WITH HIM NOW?
CHITOGE...
WHAT?
THAT FACT THAT YOU AND I...
...HAD THIS CHANCE TO CATCH UP...
...WAS ENTIRELY...
...HIS DOING.
BESIDES, HE'S YOUR BOY-FRIEND, RIGHT?
DON'T YOU WANT TO GO BE WITH HIM?
YES...
VWHOOO
VWHOOO
4:34
TICK
TICK
12/24
TICK
CREAK

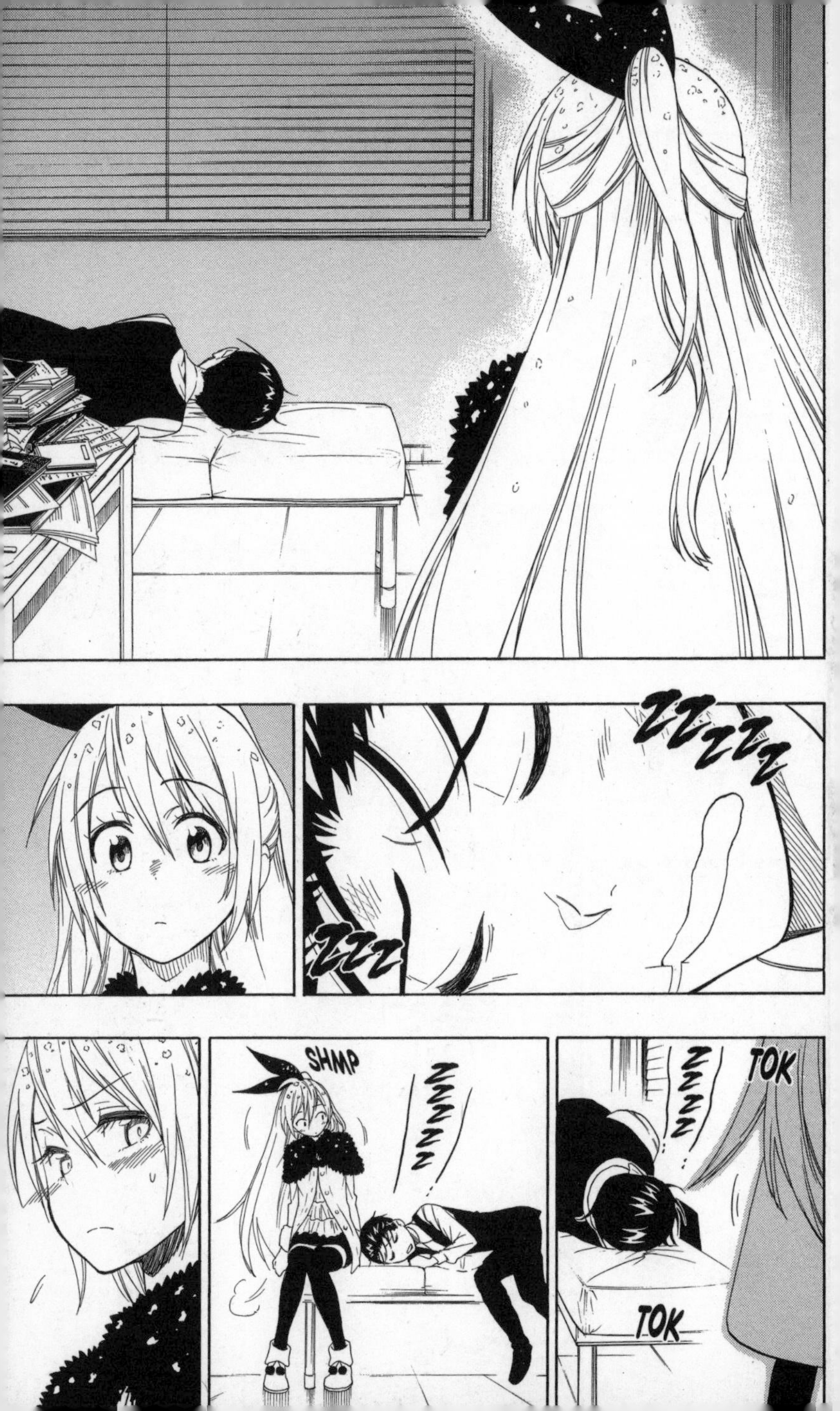
ZZZZZ
ZZZ
TOK
ZZZZ
TOK
SHMP
ZZZZZZ

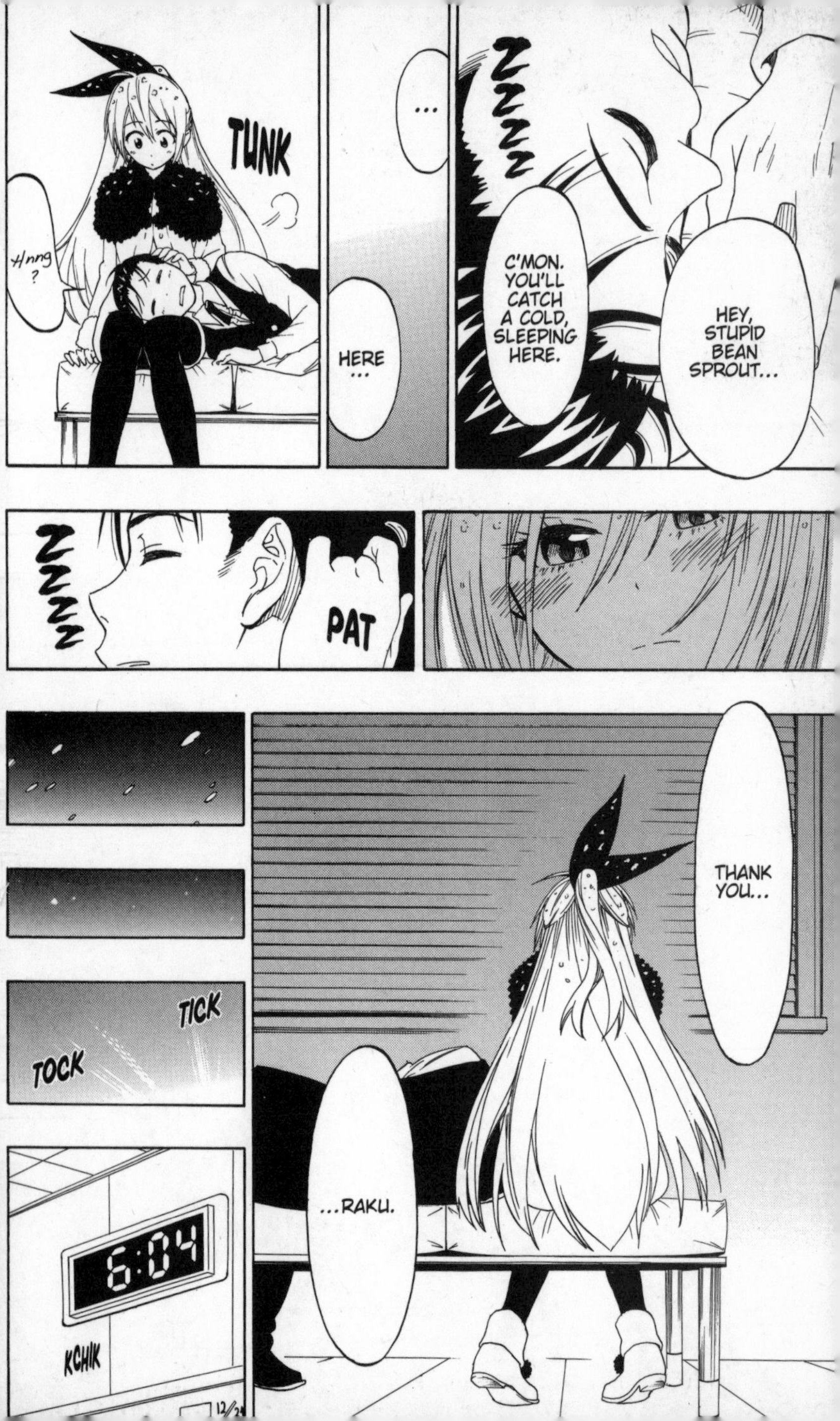
ZZZZ
HEY, STUPID BEAN SPROUT...
C'MON. YOU'LL CATCH A COLD, SLEEPING HERE.
...
HERE ...
TUNK
Hnng ?
ZZZZ
PAT
THANK YOU...
...RAKU.
TICK
TOCK
6:04
KCHIK

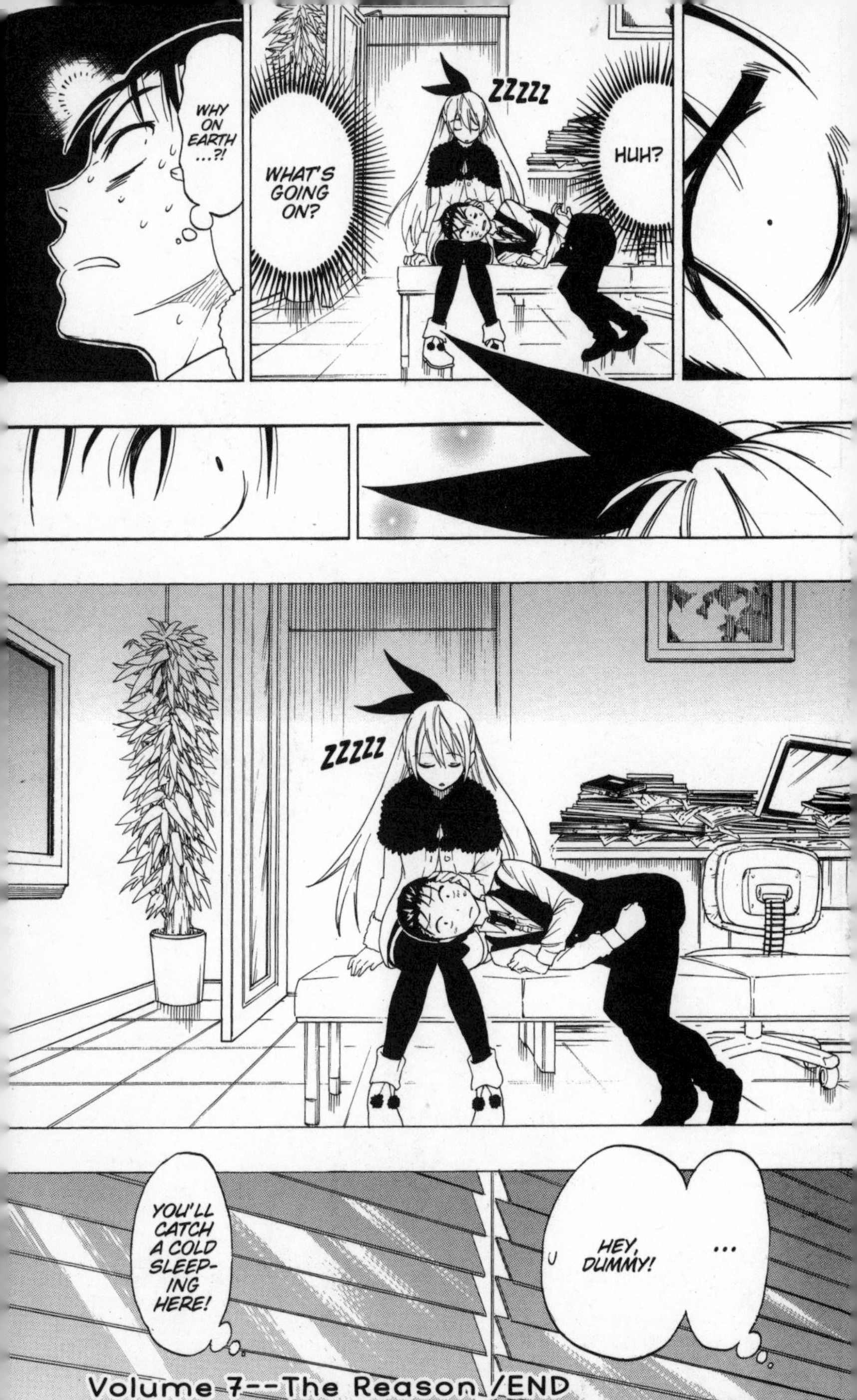
ZZZZZ
HUH?
WHAT'S GOING ON?
WHY ON EARTH ...?!
ZZZZZ
...
HEY, DUMMY!
YOU'LL CATCH A COLD SLEEP-ING HERE!
Volume 7--The Reason /END

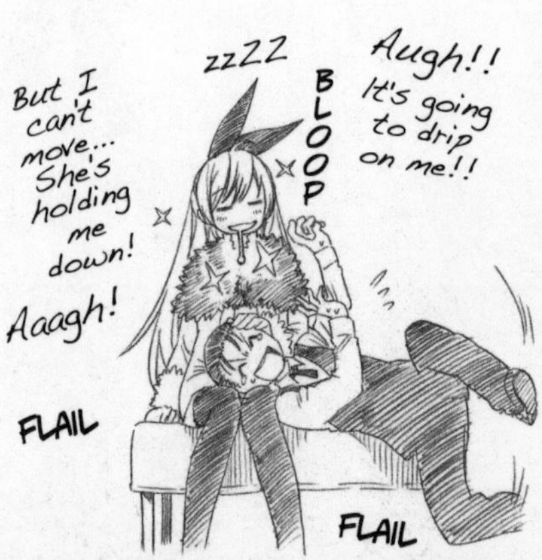
Augh!! It's going to drip on me!!
BLOOP
zzZZ
But I can't move... She's holding me down!
Aaagh!
FLAIL
FLAIL

Artist's Homework

Draw an illustration incorporating the Jump pirate logo in your series.

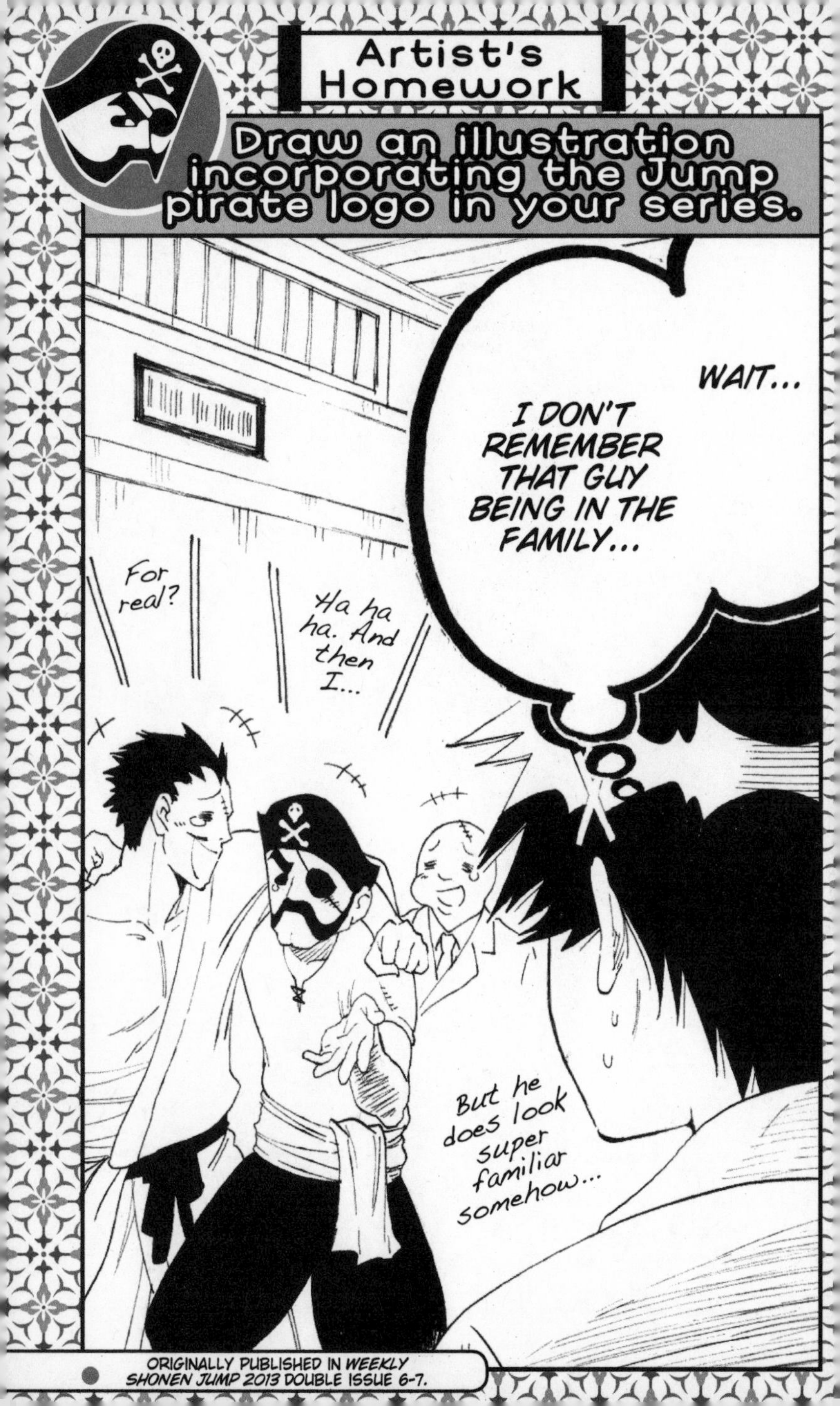
WAIT...
I DON'T REMEMBER THAT GUY BEING IN THE FAMILY...
Ha ha ha. And then I...
For real?
But he does look super familiar somehow...

ORIGINALLY PUBLISHED IN *WEEKLY SHONEN JUMP* 2013 DOUBLE ISSUE 6-7.

Bonus Comic

☆Chapter 57: Intermission☆

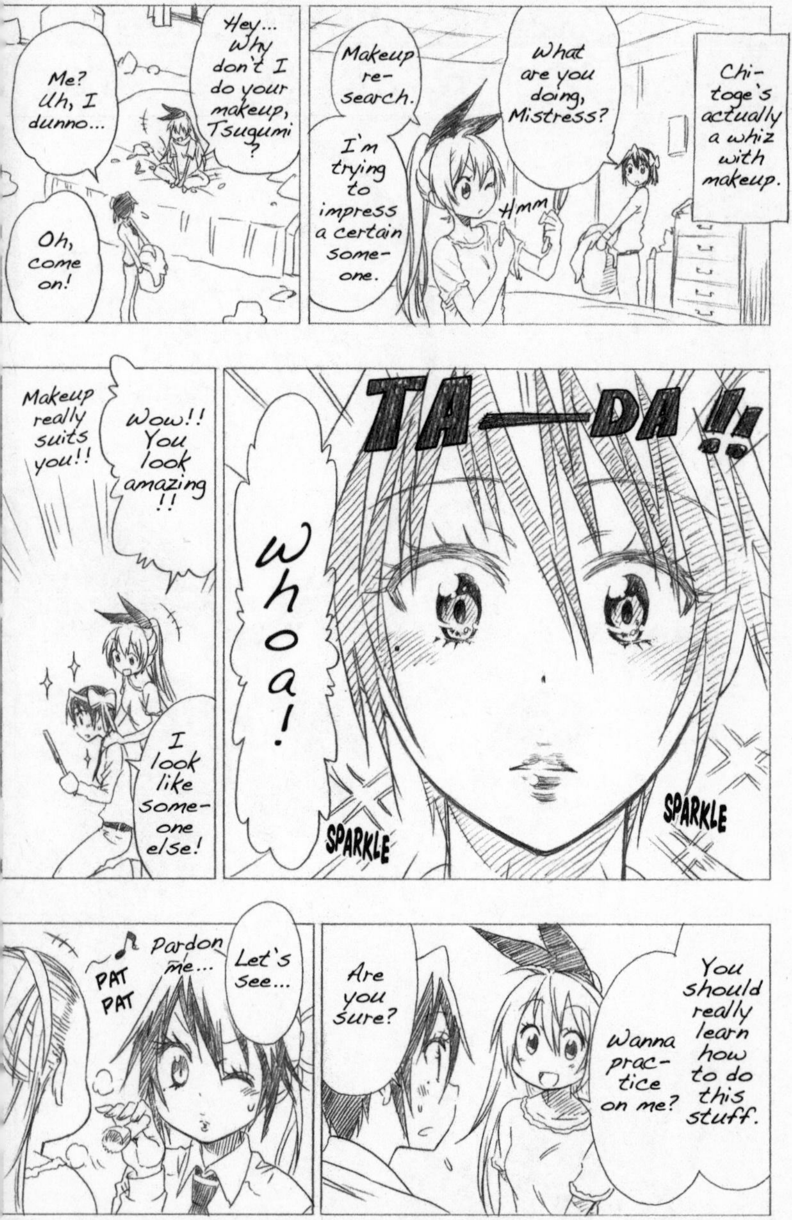
Chitoge's actually a whiz with makeup.
What are you doing, Mistress?
Makeup research.
I'm trying to impress a certain someone.
Hmm
Hey... Why don't I do your makeup, Tsugumi?
Me? Uh, I dunno...
Oh, come on!
TA—DA!!
Whoa!
SPARKLE
SPARKLE
Wow!! You look amazing!!
Makeup really suits you!!
I look like someone else!
You should really learn how to do this stuff.
Wanna practice on me?
Are you sure?
Let's see...
Pardon me...
PAT PAT

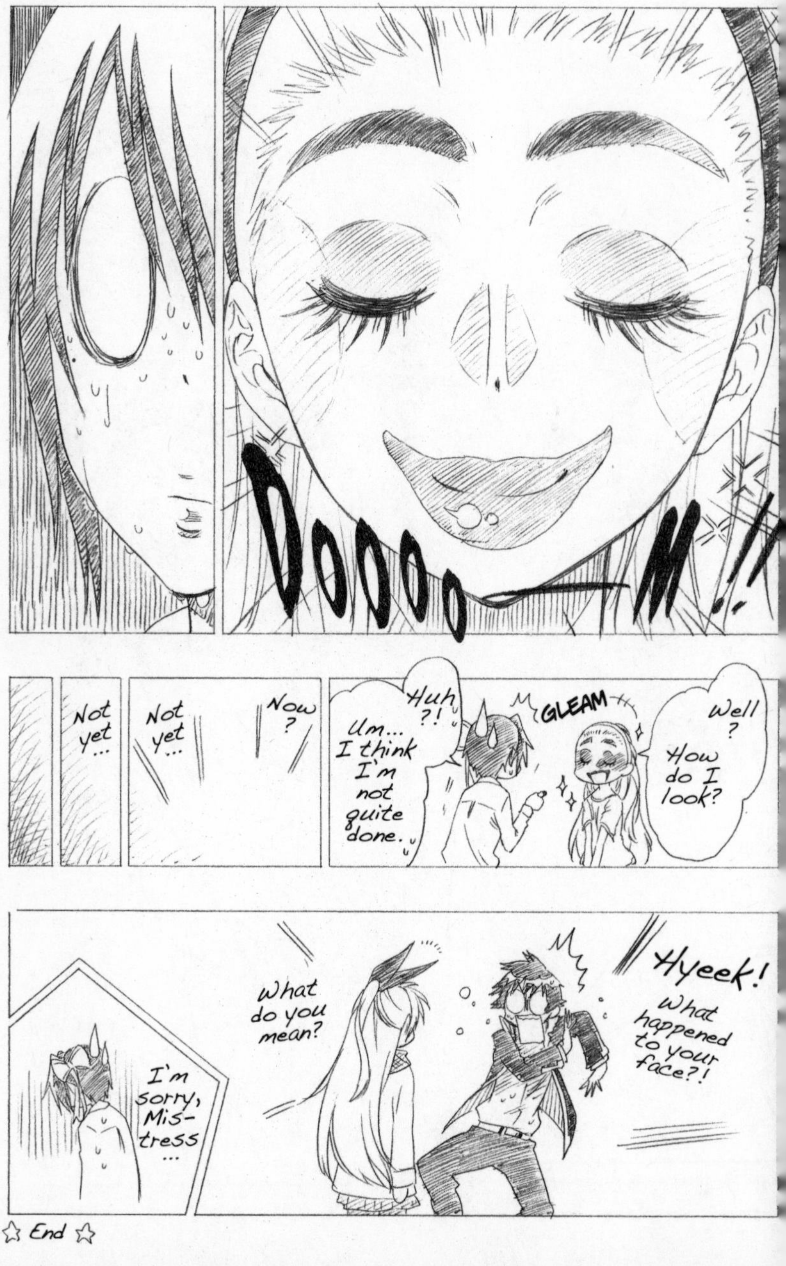
DOOOO—M!!
Well? How do I look?
GLEAM
Huh?!
Um... I think I'm not quite done.
Now?
Not yet...
Not yet...
Hyeek! What happened to your face?!
What do you mean?
I'm sorry, Mistress...

☆ End ☆

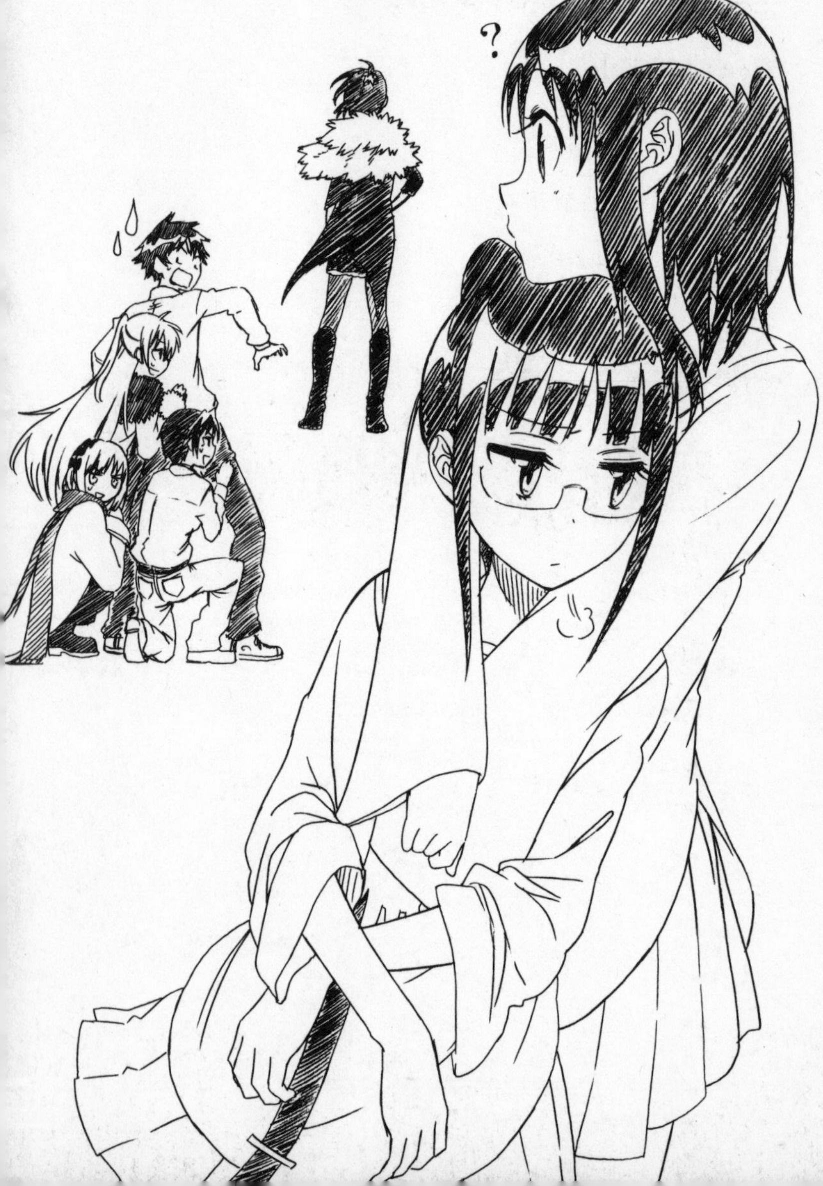